MASTERING GLOBAL HISTORY

Third Edition

JAMES KILLORAN

STUART ZIMMER

MARK JARRETT

JARRETT PUBLISHING COMPANY

EAST COAST OFFICE
P.O. Box 1460
Ronkonkoma, NY 11779
631-981-4248

WEST COAST OFFICE
10 Folin Lane
Lafayette, CA 94549
925-906-9742

1-800-859-7679 ❖ Fax: 631-588-4722
www.jarrettpub.com

Jarrett Publishing Company
Post Office Box 1460
Ronkonkoma, New York 11779

ISBN # 1-882422-44-9

Printed in the United States of America
Third Edition
10 9 8 7 6 5 4 3 2   08 07 06

ACKNOWLEDGMENTS

The authors would like to thank the following educators who reviewed the manuscript. Their comments, suggestions, and recommendations proved invaluable in preparing this book.

Steve Goldberg, Supervisor
New Rochelle High School, New Rochelle, New York

Virginia Gray, Peer Intervenor
Board of Education/U.F.T. Peer Intervention Program, New York, New York

Joe Nardi, Supervisor
Bay Shore High School, Bay Shore, New York

Ann-Jean Paci, Assistant Principal, Supervision
Bushwick High School, Brooklyn, New York

We would also like to thank **Julie Fleck** for her suggestions and comments on the manuscript.

Cover design by Maple Hill Press, Huntington, N.Y.

Artistic illustrations by Ronald Zimmer.

Maps and graphics by C.F. Enterprises, Huntington, New York.

Layout, graphics and typesetting by Burmar Technical Corporation, Albertson, N.Y.

This book is dedicated

to my wife Donna and my children Christian, Carrie, and Jesse — *James Killoran*
       and my grandchildren Aiden and Christian
to my wife Joan and my children Todd and Ronald — *Stuart Zimmer*
       and my grandchildren Katie Rose and Jared Samuel
to my wife Goska and my children Alexander and Julia — *Mark Jarrett*

ABOUT THE AUTHORS

James Killoran is a retired New York Assistant Principal. He has written *Government and You,* and *Economics and You.* Mr. Killoran has extensive experience in test writing for the New York State Board of Regents in Social Studies and has served on the Committee for Testing of the National Council of Social Studies. His article on social studies testing has been published in Social Education, the country's leading social studies journal. In addition, Mr. Killoran has won a number of awards for outstanding teaching and curriculum development, including, "Outstanding Social Studies Teacher" and "Outstanding Social Studies Supervisor" in New York City. In 1993, he was awarded an Advanced Certificate for Teachers of Social Studies by the N.C.S.S. In 1997, he became Chairman of the N.C.S.S. Committee on Awarding Advanced Certificates for Teachers of Social Studies.

Stuart Zimmer is a retired New York Social Studies teacher. He has written *Government and You,* and *Economics and You.* He served as a test writer for the New York State Board of Regents in Social Studies and has written for the National Merit Scholarship Examination. In addition, he has published numerous articles on teaching and testing in Social Studies journals. He has presented many demonstrations and educational workshops at state and national teachers' conferences. In 1989, Mr. Zimmer's achievements were recognized by the New York State Legislature with a Special Legislative Resolution in his honor.

Mark Jarrett is a former Social Studies teacher and a former attorney at the San Francisco office of Baker and McKenzie. Mr. Jarrett has served as a test writer for the New York State Board of Regents, and has taught at Hofstra University. He was educated at Columbia University, the London School of Economics, the Law School of the University of California at Berkeley, and Stanford University, where he is a doctoral candidate in history. Mr. Jarrett has received several academic awards including the Order of the Coif at Berkeley and the David and Christina Phelps Harris Fellowship at Stanford.

ALSO BY KILLORAN, ZIMMER AND JARRETT:

The Key To Understanding Global History
The Key To Understanding U.S. History and Government
Mastering U.S. History and Government
A Quick Review of U.S. History and Government
A Quick Review of Global History
Learning About New York State
Claves para la comprension de historia universal
Mastering the GHSGT in Social Studies
Los Estados Unidos: Su historia, su gobierno
Ohio: The Buckeye State

Ohio: Its Neighbors, Near and Far
Principios de economía
Mastering Ohio's Graduation Test in Social Studies
North Carolina: The Tar Heel State
Michigan: Its Land and Its People
Mastering the Grade 8 TAKS Social Studies Assessment
Mastering the Grade 10 TAKS Social Studies Assessment
Mastering The Grade 11 Social Studies Assessment

TABLE OF CONTENTS

PHOTO CREDITS

COVER: The Ruins of Pompei, ©The Stock Market

CHAPTER 2 — Page 15: Library of Congress.

CHAPTER 4 — Page 31: (t) Jarrett Archives, (m) Library of Congress, (b) Cincinnati Museum; **32:** Library of Congress; **34:** U.N.; **15:** © Michigan Bell Telephone Company, All Rights Reserved; **42:** Palphot Limited.

CHAPTER 5 — Page 53: (l) Jarrett Archives, (m) © Hillel Pitlik, (r) Jarrett Archives; **54:** Asian Art Museum of San Francisco; **56:** National Museum of African Art; **59:** Library of Congress; **61:** Library of Congress; **62:** Jarrett Archives; 66: © Hillel Pitlik; **67:** Asian Art Museum of San Francisco; **69:** Library of Congress; **71:** (t) Chinese Information and Culture Center, (b) Jarrett Archives; **79:** Library of Congress.

CHAPTER 6 — Page 81: (l&c) Jarrett Archives, (r) Shanghai Museum; **82:** Jarrett Archives; **83:** Jarrett Archives; **84:** (t) Thyssen-Bornemisza Museum (b) Library of Congress; **91:** (t) Jarrett Archives, (b) Library of Congress; **95:** Freer Gallery of Art; **96:** Japanese National Tourist Office.

CHAPTER 7 — Page 107: (l) National Museum of African Art, (b) Japanese National Tourist Office, (r) Library of Congress; **108:** Jarrett Archives; **109:** (t&b) Jarrett Archives; **110:** (t) Louvre Museum, (m & b) Jarrett Archives; **111:** (t) Uffizi Museum, (m) Jarrett Archives, (b) National Museum of African Art; **112:** (t) National Gallery of Art, (b) India Department of Tourism; **113:** (t) Freer Gallery of Art, (b) Japanese National Tourist Office; **114:** Young Memorial Museum; **119:** Library of Congress; **120:** Japanese National Tourist Office; **122:** Uffizi Museum; **123:** (l) Jarrett Archives, (c & r) Library of Congress; **124:** Uffizi Museum; **125:** Library of Congress.

CHAPTER 8 — Page 137: (l) U.S. Capitol Historical Society, (m) Uffizi Museum (r) Shanghai Museum; **138:** Library of Congress; **139:** National Archives; **142:** Mexican Government Tourism Office; **143:** Jarrett Archives; **144:** Library of Congress; **145:** Library of Congress; **146:** Library of Congress; **147:** Mexican Government Tourism Office; **148:** Library of Congress; **151:** Library of Congress; **152:** (t) Russian Embassy, (m & b) Library of Congress; **153:** (t) Jarrett Archives, (b) Library of Congress; **154:** Library of Congress; **157:** Jarrett Archives; **158:** Library of Congress; **159:** Shanghai Museum; **160:** Arthur M. Sackler Gallery.

CHAPTER 9 — Page 173: (l, m, r) Library of Congress; **174:** Jarrett Archives; **177:** (t & b) Jarrett Archives; **178:** Jarrett Archives; **179:** Jarrett Archives; **180:** Jarrett Archives; **181:** Library of Congress; **182:** Bureau of Engraving and Printing; **184:** Library of Congress; **185:** Jarrett Archives; **189:** (t) Jarrett Archives, (b) Library of Congress; **190:** (t & b) Library of Congress; **191:** Jarrett Archives; **192:** Jarrett Archives; **195:** (t) Japanese National Tourist Office, (b) Jarrett Archives; **196:** (t) Shanghai Museum, (b) National Archives.

CHAPTER 10 — Page 209: (l, r) Library of Congress, (b) National Archives; **210:** Embassy of Poland; **211:** (t&b) Library of Congress; **213:** Library of Congress; **214:** Library of Congress; **215:** Library of Congress; **216:** National Archives; **217:** Library of Congress; **218:** Library of Congress; **219:** (t&b) Library of Congress; **221:** (t&b) Library of Congress; **222:** National Archives; **223:** (t) Library of Congress, (b) National Archives; **224:** National Archives; **225:** Library of Congress; **226:** National Archives; **228:** National Archives; **229:** National Archives; **230:** Library of Congress; **231:** National Archives; **232:** (t) National Archives, (b) Library of Congress; **233:** Embassy of Poland; **234:** © Stewart Milstein; **235:** Consul General of India; **237:** Jarrett Archives; **238:** (t) U.N., (b) United Republic of Tanzania.

CHAPTER 11 — Page 249: (t) Jarrett Archives, (m&b) U.N.; **250:** Jarrett Archives; **252:** U.N.; **254:** (t) F.D.R. Library, (b) Library of Congress; **256:** Library of Congress; **257:** (t&b) Jarrett Archives; **258:** (t) National Archives, (b) U.N.; **259:** Library of Congress; **260:** Jarrett Archives; **261:** National Archives; **263:** U.N.; **265:** U.N.; **266:** U.N.; **269:** National Archives; **272:** (t) U.N.; **273:** U.N.; **274:** Embassy of Poland; **275:** Amnesty International; **276:** U.N.; **278:** U.N.; **279:** Consulate of People's Republic of China; **286:** Jarrett Archives.

CHAPTER 12 — Page 295 (t,r,b) U.N.; **296:** U.N.; **298:** N.A.S.A.; **300:** (t&b) U.N.; **301:** Library of Congress; **303:** U.N.; **304:** Jarrett Archives; **307:** N.A.S.A; **315:** National Archives.

CHAPTER 13 — Page 317: Library of Congress.

CHAPTER 14 — Page 336: Louvre Museum; **342:** Library of Congress; **346:** Museum of the City of New York.

HOW TO REMEMBER IMPORTANT INFORMATION

Examination questions often test your knowledge of important terms, concepts, and people. This chapter discusses one way to make it easier for you to remember key information so that you can improve your performance on all your tests.

REMEMBERING IMPORTANT TERMS

There are many important terms in global history. Such terms can be of many different types:

- document — *U.N. Charter*
- time period — *Renaissance*
- religion — *Hinduism*
- group — *serfs*

- event — *independence of Ghana*
- policy — *Russification*
- organization — *OPEC*
- war — *World War II*

What all these **terms** have in common is that they refer to a specific thing that actually happened or existed. Questions about a term will generally ask about its main features:

what it is (or was)   *its purpose*   *its causes and effects*   *its significance*

It is easier to remember a term if you jot down the main information about it and draw a simple illustration. Every time you read about an important term you should therefore complete a 3" by 5" index card similar to the following example:

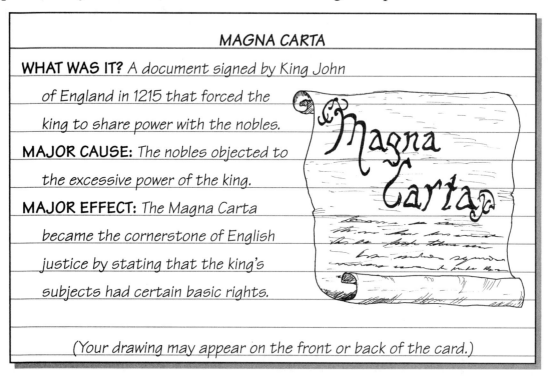

MAGNA CARTA

WHAT WAS IT? *A document signed by King John of England in 1215 that forced the king to share power with the nobles.*

MAJOR CAUSE: *The nobles objected to the excessive power of the king.*

MAJOR EFFECT: *The Magna Carta became the cornerstone of English justice by stating that the king's subjects had certain basic rights.*

(Your drawing may appear on the front or back of the card.)

If you have access to a computer, you might want to create a database of these cards.

REMEMBERING KEY CONCEPTS

Concepts are the building blocks of knowledge. They are words or phrases that refer to **categories of information.** Concepts allow us to organize vast amounts of information. For example, Italy, Nigeria, and China share common characteristics. The concept "country" acts as an umbrella, grouping these specific "examples" together by identifying what they have in common. Here, the concept "country" refers to an area that has a set of borders and a form of government that is not subject to any other government. The countries of Italy, Nigeria, and China all fit this description.

Questions about concepts usually ask for a definition or an example of the concept. Thus, when you study a concept, you should learn the following:

its definition   *an example*

Again, it would be easier to remember a concept if you jot down the definition and an example and draw a simple illustration on a 3" by 5" index card. Following is a sample card dealing with the concept *representative democracy.*

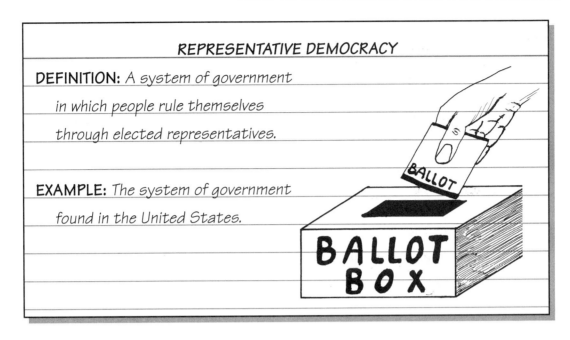

REMEMBERING FAMOUS PEOPLE

In global history you will also learn about many famous people. Test questions about these individuals will usually ask who they are and why they are famous. Therefore, when you study a famous person, it is important to learn:

- *the place and time period in which the person lived*
- *his or her background or position*
- *the person's accomplishments and impact*

It is easier to remember a famous individual if you jot down the main information and draw a simple illustration on a 3" by 5" index card, similar to the following example:

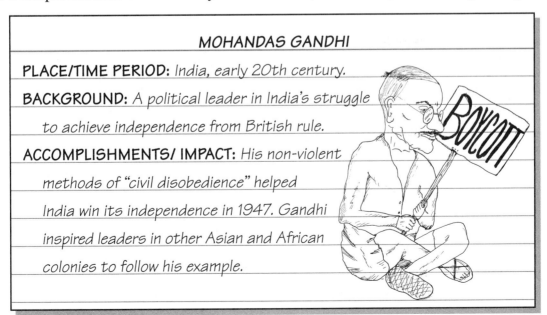

NOTE: In each chapter of this book, important terms, concepts and people will appear in **bold** type. At the end of each content section, you will be asked to complete two vocabulary cards about some important terms, concepts, or people in that section. You may want to make additional cards of other important terms, concepts, or people. This will greatly reinforce your learning and provide an invaluable tool for your year-end review.

INTERPRETING DIFFERENT TYPES OF DATA

Many examinations have questions based on interpreting information provided in the question itself. Such information is sometimes referred to as "data." The data in data-based questions may appear in various forms, such as a map, graph, or reading passage.

Knowing **how** to interpret different types of data is crucial to performing well on this form of test question. In this chapter, you will review the ten types of data bases most often found on global history tests:

- Maps
- Bar Graphs
- Line Graphs
- Pie Charts
- Tables

- Timelines
- Political Cartoons
- Outlines
- Speaker Questions
- Reading Passages

MAPS

WHAT IS A MAP?

A map is a diagram or representation of an area. Different kinds of information can be shown on a map:

◆ **Political maps** usually show the major boundaries between countries or states.
◆ **Physical maps** show the physical characteristics of a region, such as its rivers, mountains, vegetation, and elevation (*height above sea level*).
◆ **Theme maps** can provide information on almost any theme, such as natural resources, amount of rainfall, population density, languages spoken, or main points of interest.

KEYS TO UNDERSTANDING A MAP

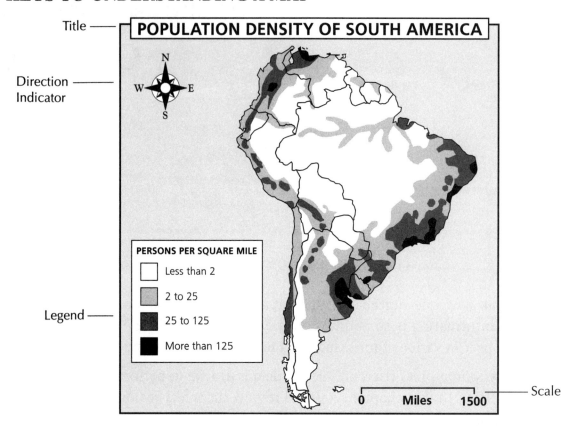

Title — **POPULATION DENSITY OF SOUTH AMERICA**

Direction Indicator

PERSONS PER SQUARE MILE

Less than 2

2 to 25

25 to 125

More than 125

Legend

0   Miles   1500 — **Scale**

Title. The title of the map usually identifies the area shown and any special information the map contains. For example, the title of the above map is *Population Density of South America*. The map shows the number of people living per square mile in South America.

Legend. The legend tells us about the information on the map. The legend shows the symbols used and identifies what each one represents. For example, in this map legend:

- the *white* box shows areas where the density is less than 2 people per square mile.
- the *light gray* box shows areas where the population density is from 2 to 25 people per square mile.
- the *dark gray* box shows areas where the density is from 25 to 125 people per square mile.
- the *black* box shows areas where the density is more than 125 people per square mile.

Direction. To find directions on a map, look at its **direction indicator** (*compass rose*). It is used to indicate the four basic directions: north, south, east, and west. If no indicator is shown, assume that north is at the top.

Scale. A map would be impossible to use if it were the same size as the area it represents. Mapmakers use a scale to show how much the distances have been reduced. A map scale is often a line marked in miles or kilometers. On this map, one inch equals 1,500 miles. The scale can be used to find the actual distance between any two points on the map.

✔ CHECKING YOUR UNDERSTANDING ✔

Use the map on page 6 to answer the following questions:

1. What areas of South America have the lowest population density?

2. What is the approximate length of South America from its northernmost to its southernmost point?

    1 1,500 miles   3 3,000 miles

    2 4,500 miles   4 6,000 miles

BAR GRAPHS

WHAT IS A BAR GRAPH?

A bar graph is a chart made up of parallel bars with different lengths. A bar graph is used to compare two or more things. It can also show how something has changed over time.

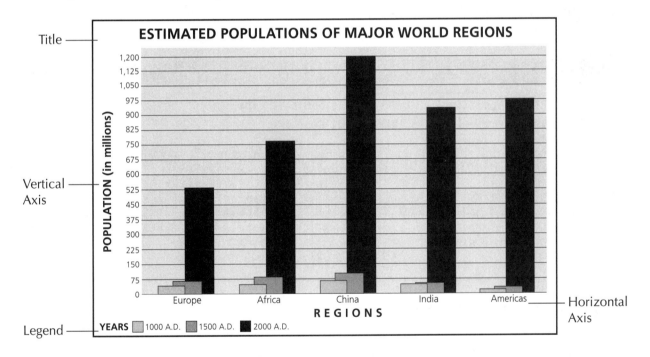

KEYS TO UNDERSTANDING A BAR GRAPH

Title. The title of the bar graph identifies the general topic of the graph. For example, the title of this bar graph is *Estimated Populations of Major World Regions*. The graph shows the estimated population of five world regions at three different time periods.

Legend. The legend shows what each bar represents:

- the *light gray* bars represent estimated populations in 1000 A.D.
- the *dark gray* bars represent estimated populations in 1500 A.D.
- the *black* bars represent estimated populations in 2000 A.D.

Vertical and Horizontal Axis. Every bar graph has a vertical and horizontal axis.

◆ The **vertical axis** runs from bottom to top. It allows the reader to measure the length of the bars. Here, the vertical axis measures the estimated population in millions. Thus, the first light gray bar for Europe (*1000 A.D.*) represents a population of about 40 million (*slightly more than halfway between 0 and 75*).

◆ The **horizontal axis** runs from left to right. It identifies what each individual bar represents. Here, the horizontal axis lists five world regions: Europe, Africa, China, India, and the Americas.

Trends. Sometimes a bar graph will reveal a **trend** — a general direction in which events are moving. We can often identify a trend from the height of the bars. For example, one trend shown in this graph is that the pace of population growth has increased dramatically in the past 500 years.

✔ CHECKING YOUR UNDERSTANDING ✔

Use the bar graph on page 7 to answer the following questions:
1. What was the population of Africa in 1500?

2. In which region will the population increase the most by the year 2000?
   1 Europe   3 Africa
   2 India   4 China

LINE GRAPHS

WHAT IS A LINE GRAPH?
A line graph is a chart composed of points connected in a line. It is often used to show how something has changed over a period of time. Some graphs have more than one line.

KEYS TO UNDERSTANDING A LINE GRAPH
Title. The title identifies the topic. For example, the title of the line graph on page 9 is *Estimated Native American Population of Mexico, 1518–1593*. Thus, the line graph shows changes in Mexico's Native American population for 75 years, from 1518 to 1593.

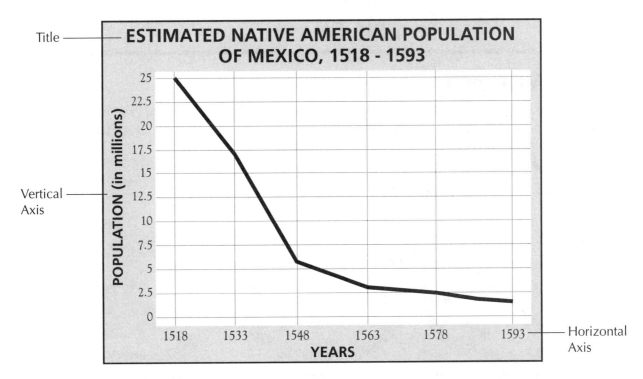

Title

Vertical Axis

Horizontal Axis

Vertical and Horizontal Axis. Each line graph has a vertical and horizontal axis.

- **Vertical Axis.** The vertical axis runs from bottom to top. It usually measures the size of items. Notice how, as you move up the vertical axis, the numbers increase. Since the population is shown in millions, the number "25" actually represents 25 *million* Native Americans.
- **Horizontal Axis.** The horizontal axis runs from left to right. Often, it measures the passage of time. In this line graph, the horizontal axis shows years. The first year is 1518, and the dates continue in fifteen-year intervals until 1593.

Legend. If the graph has many lines, a legend explains what each line represents. If it has only one or two lines, as in this graph, the information is often shown directly on the lines.

Trends. Often a line graph will reveal a trend. One trend shown in the graph above is that a sharp decrease in Mexico's Native American population occurred after 1518.

✔ CHECKING YOUR UNDERSTANDING ✔

Use the line graph on this page to answer the following questions:

1. What was Mexico's Native American population in 1533?

2. What does the vertical axis measure?

3. What factor might explain the decline in Mexico's Native American population after 1518?

PIE CHARTS

WHAT IS A PIE CHART?

A pie chart (or *circle graph*) consists of a circle divided into sections (*pieces*) of different sizes. A pie chart is often used to show the relationship between a whole and its parts. Sometimes several circles are used for comparisons.

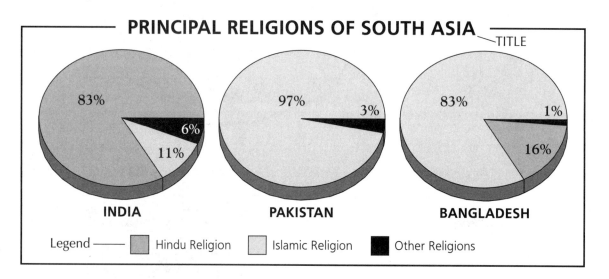

KEYS TO UNDERSTANDING A PIE CHART

Title. The title identifies the overall topic of the chart. For example, the title of the chart above is *Principal Religions of South Asia*. The three "pies" show the major religious groups of the three main South Asian countries: India, Pakistan, and Bangladesh.

Slices of the Pie. Each of the pies in the chart above has three slices. The first two slices represent Hinduism and Islam. The third slice represents all other religions. Each slice of the pie shows us the size of one of the parts compared to the whole pie. Think of the pie as representing 100% of something. If you add all the slices together, they must total 100%.

Size of Each Slice. The size of each slice tells you the relative size of that religious group in one of the three countries. For example, the largest religious group in India is Hindu, while Pakistan and Bangladesh are predominantly Muslim (*followers of Islam*). But you cannot tell which group in South Asia is largest just from this chart. You would also need to know the total population in each country to see which is the largest religious group in the region.

Legend. A pie chart may include a legend, as this one does. In some pie charts a separate legend is unnecessary because the individual pie slices are labeled.

✔ CHECKING YOUR UNDERSTANDING ✔

Use the pie chart on page 10 to answer the following questions:
1. What percentage of Bangladesh's population is Hindu?

2. Which of the three countries has the largest percentage of Muslims?

TABLES

WHAT IS A TABLE?
A table is an arrangement of information in columns and rows. A table is used to organize data so that particular facts can be easily located and compared.

Title —

ECONOMIC CONDITIONS IN LATIN AMERICA, 1997				
Nation	Population (in millions)	Infant Mortality (per 1,000)	Literacy (percent)	Life Expectancy (in years)
Bolivia	7.1	68	80	60
Brazil	162.6	55	83	62
Costa Rica	3.4	14	95	76
Haiti	6.7	104	45	49
Mexico	95.7	25	90	74
Venezuela	21.9	30	91	72

KEYS TO UNDERSTANDING A TABLE
Title. The title identifies the topic of the table. The title of the table above is *Economic Conditions in Latin America, 1997*. The table provides economic data for six Latin American nations for the year 1997.

Categories. A table contains various categories of information. In this table, there are five different categories: *nation, population, infant mortality, literacy,* and *life expectancy.* Each column represents one category, named in the heading at the top of the column. For example, "Infant Mortality" refers to the number of children that die in infancy. This figure gives us an idea of the extent and quality of maternity and child care in a country. Each row represents a different nation in Latin America. To find a particular piece of information, choose a category and look down that column until you reach the row of the country that is of interest.

Drawing Conclusions from the Data. By examining a table, it is often possible to identify trends or draw conclusions. For example, Haiti's high infant mortality and low life expectancy seem to indicate public health problems.

✔ CHECKING YOUR UNDERSTANDING ✔

Use the table on page 12 to answer the following questions:
1. Which country in the table has the largest population?
2. Which country is poorest? Explain how you reached this conclusion.

TIMELINES

WHAT IS A TIMELINE?

A timeline presents a series of events arranged along a line in chronological order. **Chronological order** is the sequence in which the events actually happened. Thus, the event that occurred earliest is the first event on the timeline. The distances between events on a timeline are usually in proportion to the actual time that passed between the events they represent. A timeline can span anything from a short period of time to thousands of years. The purpose of a timeline is to show how events relate to one another.

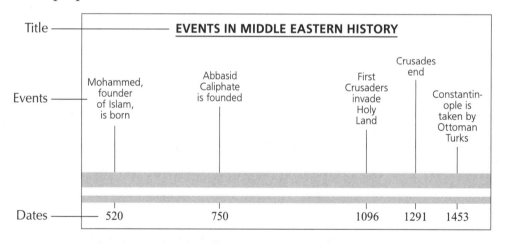

KEYS TO UNDERSTANDING A TIMELINE

Title. The title identifies the general topic. For example, the title of this timeline is *Events in Middle Eastern History.* The timeline lists important milestones in the history of the Middle East from 520 to 1453.

Events. All of the events on the timeline are related in some way to its title.

Dates. This timeline starts with the birth of Mohammed in 520 A.D. and continues until 1453, when Constantinople was captured by the Ottoman Turks. If you wanted to add another event, such as the Arab reconquest of Jerusalem by Saladin in 1187, where on the timeline would it go?

ANSWER: Since 1187 is closer to 1096 (*91 years*) than to 1291 (*104 years*), you would place it a bit closer to 1096 than to 1291.

Division Between B.C. and A.D. Dates in many parts of the world are based on when it is believed Jesus Christ was born. These dates are divided into two groups: B.C. and A.D. The dividing point is the birth of Christ.

- **B.C.** (Before Christ) refers to the time period before Christ was born. This term is also known as **B.C.E.** (*Before the Common Era*)
- **A.D.** (from the Latin words *Anno Domini* — meaning "in the year of our Lord") refers to the years from the birth of Christ onwards. Instead of A.D., some writers use **C.E.** (*Common Era.*)

Writers always add B.C. (or B.C.E.) to a date before the birth of Christ. However, they usually do not bother to write A.D. (or C.E.) if the date is *after* the birth of Christ. For example, if the present year is 2000 A.D., it is simply written as 2000.

Special Terms. To understand questions about timelines or time periods, you should be familiar with some special terms:

- A **decade** refers to a 10-year period.
- A **century** represents 100 years.
- A **millennium** spans 1,000 years.

NOTE: Identifying centuries may seem confusing at first. For example, the 20th century actually refers to the 1900s — the 100 years from 1901 to 2000. This is because the first century spanned the years 1–100. The second century went from 101–200; the third century was from 201 to 300, and so on. The 21st century — the third millennium — will actually begin on January 1, 2001. However, most people will choose to celebrate it on January 1, 2000, because of the dramatic change in dates from 1999 to 2000.

✔ CHECKING YOUR UNDERSTANDING ✔

Use the timeline on page 12 to answer the following questions:
1. How many years are covered by the timeline?
2. Which event happened first: the fall of Constantinople or the invasion of the Holy Land during the First Crusade?
3. Between which two events on the timeline would you place the destruction of Baghdad by the Mongols in 1258?

POLITICAL CARTOONS

WHAT IS A POLITICAL CARTOON?

A political cartoon is a drawing that expresses an opinion about a topic or issue. Many political cartoons are humorous, but they often make a serious point.

KEYS TO UNDERSTANDING A POLITICAL CARTOON

Title or Caption. Most political cartoons have a title or caption that helps explain the message the cartoonist is trying to get across.

Medium. Cartoonists want to persuade readers to adopt their point of view. They will use the size of objects, facial expressions, exaggerations, or words spoken by characters to satirize (*poke fun at*) some positions and to support others.

Symbols. Cartoonists often use symbols. A symbol can be any object that represents or stands for something else.

People. A cartoonist may want to draw attention to a particular issue by portraying a famous person closely associated with it.

The Future of World Oil Prices? —— Caption

A **caricature** is a drawing in which a person's features are exaggerated for comic effect. It is important to be able to recognize caricatures of important historical figures, who are often depicted in political cartoons.

| Adolf Hitler | Joseph Stalin | Fidel Castro | Mao Zedong |

OTHER VISUALS

Photographs, Drawings and Paintings. Photographs, drawings, and paintings are especially useful for understanding the past. They show how people once looked, dressed, and lived. A photograph lets us get a feeling for an earlier time or a different place. Since photography was only invented in the mid-1800s, we often rely on drawings and paintings to see what life was like before that time.

Russian women harvesting hay

Examine this photograph of Russian women working in a field in the late 19th century. What do the details in the photo tell you about what life was like for Russian peasants at that time?

Diagrams. A diagram is a symbolic drawing that shows how something is organized or how a process works. For example, the diagram to the right shows how the parliamentary form of government is structured. Although the United States is a democracy in which voters elect both the legislature and the chief executive, most democratic countries in the world have parliamentary systems of government.

This diagram shows the various branches of a parliamentary government and what each branch is called. It also indicates which officials are directly elected by citizens under the parliamentary system of government.

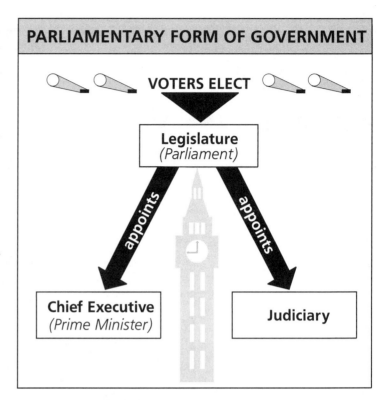

PARLIAMENTARY FORM OF GOVERNMENT

VOTERS ELECT

Legislature
(Parliament)

appoints

appoints

Chief Executive
(Prime Minister)

Judiciary

✔ CHECKING YOUR UNDERSTANDING ✔

Use the illustration above to answer the following questions:
1. Who elects the members of Parliament?

2. Who chooses the chief executive (*Prime Minister*)?

3. Who selects the judiciary in a parliamentary system of government?

OUTLINES

WHAT IS AN OUTLINE?

An outline is a brief plan or summary breaking up a topic into smaller units. The purpose of an outline is to reveal the logical relationships between the *main topic* and its *smaller units*. This breakdown helps us to grasp and remember what is important in a body of knowledge.

KEYS TO UNDERSTANDING AN OUTLINE

Title.   The title identifies the general theme of the outline.

Format. Most outlines follow a common format that allows you to understand easily how the main theme is divided into topics and sub-topics (*sections that are parts of a larger topic*).

◆ **Roman Numerals.** The first major divisions of the theme or major topic are given in Roman numerals (I, II, III, etc.).

◆ **Capital Letters.** If the topic covered by a Roman numeral needs to be further divided, its sub-topics are listed by capital letters (A, B, C, etc.).

◆ **Arabic Numerals.** If these sub-topics are divided still further, they are given Arabic numerals (1, 2, 3). To illustrate this process, assume you want to write about wars in the 20th century. You might outline what you plan to write as follows:

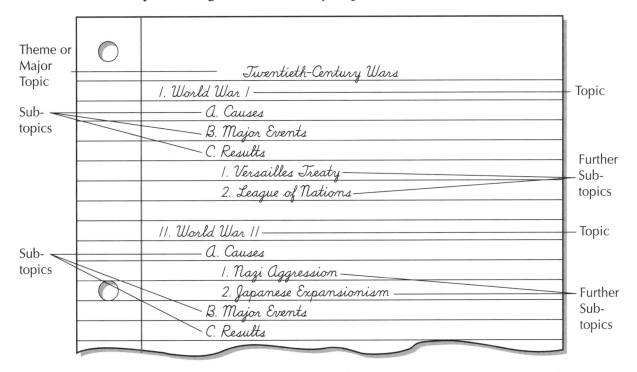

✔ CHECKING YOUR UNDERSTANDING ✔

Use the outline above to answer the following questions:

1. What are the main units that make up the theme *Twentieth-Century Wars*?

2. What parts make up the topic *World War II*?

3. If you were to add details about the *Results of World War II*, which would you use: Roman numerals, letters, or Arabic numerals?

SPEAKER QUESTIONS

WHAT IS A SPEAKER QUESTION?

A speaker question presents a series of statements by different speakers. There will usually be four speakers identified by the letters A, B, C, and D. The main function of this type of question is to present a discussion in which different viewpoints are expressed.

> **Speaker A:** We have given this backward colony a bright future. These people have benefited greatly from the introduction of our system of government and our laws. All we ask in return is the right to sell our finished goods to these people.
>
> **Speaker B:** The problems we find today in the homeland of our ancestors are not of our own doing. We lived in peace for centuries. Foreigners have enslaved our people, taken our land, and destroyed our heritage.
>
> **Speaker C:** Our people must unite. Our rights have been abused. We are not allowed to vote or to speak freely in our own land. Europeans treat us as second-class citizens. We must conduct acts of civil disobedience to persuade these foreigners to leave our homeland.
>
> **Speaker D:** We must think ahead to the day when we have our independence. We will be in desperate need of foreign investment and technology. We must maintain friendly ties with all nations, including our present rulers.

THE KEY TO UNDERSTANDING A SPEAKER QUESTION

To better understand speaker questions, remember that each speaker's statement usually expresses an opinion about a social studies term, concept, or situation.

Interpreting a Speaker Question. Start by asking yourself the following questions about each speaker:

◆ What idea, situation, or point of view is being discussed by **each** speaker? For example, Speaker A is describing the system of imperialism — the control of one country by another country. What does Speaker A say about imperialism?

◆ Check to see whether any of the speakers have similar or contrasting viewpoints.

◆ Do the opinions of the speakers remind you of the views of any individuals or groups you are already familiar with?

✔ CHECKING YOUR UNDERSTANDING ✔

Use the speakers' comments on page 18 to answer the following questions:

1. What concept is discussed by Speaker C?

2. Identify a basic disagreement among the speakers.

READING PASSAGES

WHAT IS A READING PASSAGE?

A reading passage is a written text about a topic. In a passage, the writer presents a series of related statements that tell facts or express ideas about the topic. The passage states a main idea, which is supported with facts, examples, and details. Questions based on passages require you to read and understand a quotation or paragraph. Often these passages present someone's particular point of view.

> No one in France ... doubts the benefits of colonization and the advantages it offers both to the mother country and to those who are colonized. Everyone agrees that colonies offer raw materials and products that the mother-country lacks, and that they open markets to the commerce and industries of the old country by the wants and needs of the people of the colony ...
>
> Paul Leroy Beaulieu, *The Ideology of French Imperialism*, 1871–1881

KEYS TO UNDERSTANDING A READING PASSAGE

Ask yourself the following questions about each reading selection:

When was the passage written? Who was its author?	What term, concept, or situation is discussed by the writer?	What is the **main idea** of the passage? What point is the writer trying to make?

WHAT TO ASK YOURSELF ABOUT EACH READING

What facts and details does the writer present to support the main idea?	What is the writer's point of view?	What do you know about the writer? Is there anything in the writer's background that explains the point of view?

To find the main idea of a passage, first think about its topic or subject. Then think about what the author is trying to say about that topic.

✔ CHECKING YOUR UNDERSTANDING ✔

Use the passage on page 19 to answer the following questions:

1. Who wrote the passage? _____

2. When was it written? _____

3. What concept is discussed by the writer? _____

4. What is the main idea of the passage? _____

5. What facts, examples, and details dos the write use to support the main idea in the passage? _____

6. What is the author's point of view? How does he feel about the concept he is discussing? _____

7. What do you know about the writer's background? For example, what country does he come from? How might this influence his views? _____

_____

FURTHER PRACTICE WITH DATA-BASED QUESTIONS

Two types of questions on global history examinations may involve the interpretation of data contained in the question. These are multiple-choice and document-based questions. To help you answer each of these types of questions:

◆ every content chapter in this book will include a special section that discusses one type of question in some detail.

◆ at the end of every content chapter there will also be a series of sample questions, some of which will be based on interpreting data.

◆ later in this book, you will learn more about interpreting historical documents.

By the end of this book, you will have had experience answering multiple-choice and document-based questions with every kind of data-base.

CHAPTER 3

DEVELOPING A SENSE OF TIME AND PLACE

Historians are people who are concerned with understanding and explaining past events. The study of history helps a society remember what it is and where it is going. Just as your own life would become meaningless if you had no memory of who you were or what you had done, each society looks to its history for a sense of identity. By recalling the deeds of times past, we help ensure that future generations will remember our own lives when we are gone.

SOURCES OF HISTORY

In a sense, a historian acts like a detective gathering clues. To find information about the past, historians rely on two kinds of sources:

◆ **Primary sources** are the original records of an event. They include documents left by eyewitnesses, records created at the time of the event, the texts of speeches and reports, letters by people involved in the event, and photographs or paintings from that time.

◆ **Secondary sources** are the later writings and interpretations of historians and other writers. Often secondary sources, like textbooks, provide convenient summaries of the information found in primary sources.

All our knowledge about the past can actually be traced back to primary sources and to interpretations of these primary sources.

HAVING A SENSE OF TIME AND PLACE

It is very important to have a good grasp of **time** and **place** when studying global history. The range of global history covers a vast period of time — from the beginning of humankind to the present, touching all areas of the world. In order to understand this vast sweep, you must do the following:

- **First,** you must have a strong general sense of the basic time periods of global history, including the major beliefs, ideas, technologies, and events of each time period.
- **Second,** you must know the main geographical features of the world — the stage where these events unfolded.

DEVELOPING A SENSE OF TIME

Let's begin by examining how history is divided into time periods. Historians divide history into **time periods** or **eras** — spans of time unified by common characteristics. There is no exact agreement on historical periods and their dates. Different periods often begin and end in different places at different times. Traditionally, historical periods have been tied to a particular region or culture. For example, the Middle Ages is a historical period closely tied to Europe, while the Ming Dynasty refers to a period in the history of China. However, it is possible to stretch the concept of a historical period to tie together events all over the world at one period of time.

This book divides the history of the world into eight such eras, each with its own distinctive features:

ERAS OF WORLD HISTORY

1. The Dawn of Civilization, 3500 B.C. to 500 B.C.
2. The Classical Civilizations, 500 B.C. to 500 A.D.
3. New Centers of Culture in an Age of Turmoil, 500 A.D. to 1200 A.D.
4. Warriors on Horseback and the Revival of Europe, 1200 to 1500
5. The Birth of the Modern World, 1450 to 1770
6. New Currents: Revolution, Industry, and Nationalism, 1770 to 1900
7. The World at War, 1914 to 1945
8. From Cold War to Global Interdependence, 1945 to the present

---

DEVELOPING A SENSE OF PLACE

Now, let's look at the different regions of the world and some of their physical characteristics.

CONTINENTS AND OCEANS

Geographers have divided the land masses of the world into separate areas called **continents.** They have identified seven continents — in order of size, they are: Asia, Africa, North America, South America, Antarctica, Europe, and Australia.

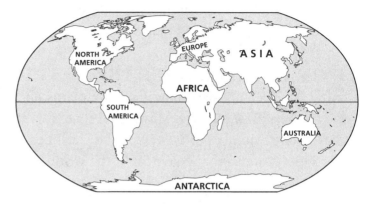

EASTERN/WESTERN HEMISPHERES

The continents of North America, South America, and part of Antarctica make up the **Western Hemisphere.** Asia, Africa, Europe, Australia, and part of Antarctica are the continents of the **Eastern Hemisphere.**

Most of the Earth's surface is covered by water. An **ocean** is an extremely large body of salt water. There are four oceans: (1) the **Atlantic,** (2) the **Pacific,** (3) the **Indian,** and (4) the **Arctic.**

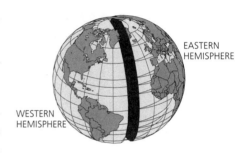

NORTH AND CENTRAL AMERICA

NORTH AMERICA

North America is the world's third largest continent in area. It is bordered by three oceans: the Atlantic, Pacific, and Arctic. South of Mexico, the land narrows into Central America, a strip of land that connects to South America.

The Impact of Geography. For much of its history, North America's location separated it from the civilizations of Africa, Asia, and Europe. Because of its large size, North America has a wide range of climates. To the north, it is extremely cold in winter, while to the south, the climate is generally hot. In Mexico, most people live on a high plateau in the center of the country because the weather is cooler there. North America's

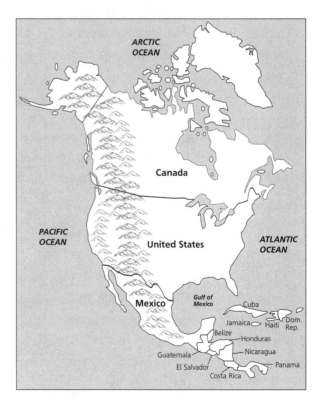

mountain ranges mainly extend along its western side from Canada into Mexico. To the east of these mountain ranges are plains with fertile farmland. Fertile plains and the protection of the ocean helped the United States to develop a prosperous democracy in the past 200 years.

CENTRAL AMERICA AND THE WEST INDIES

Central America consists mainly of mountains and rain forests. One of the earliest Native American civilizations, the Maya, arose there. Northeast of Central America are the West Indies, a large number of islands in the Caribbean that include Cuba and Jamaica. At one time, these islands produced most of the world's sugar.

The name *Latin America* is often applied to the Americas south of the United States: Mexico, Central America, the West Indies, and South America. The region is known as Latin America because the people mainly speak Spanish and Portuguese, languages derived from Latin.

SOUTH AMERICA

South America is surrounded by the Pacific and Atlantic Oceans and connected to Central America by Panama.

The Impact of Geography. Much of South America is warm because it is located near the **equator.** The most important river in the region is the **Amazon,** the second longest river in the world. The world's largest rain forest, the **Amazon rain forest,** occupies most of northeastern South America. The **Andes Mountains** run along the western side of South America and are among the highest mountains in the world. They were once home to the great Inca empire.

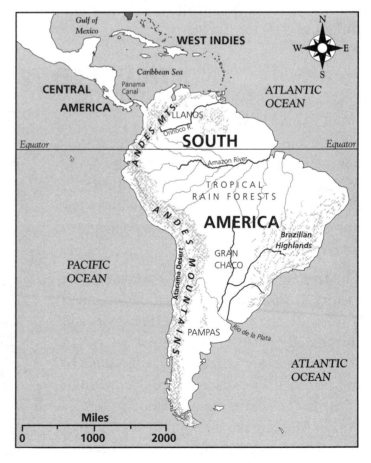

Mountains, rain forests, and poor soils make much of South America's land unproductive. Two important exceptions are the **pampas** and **llaños,** large grassy, treeless plains found in the southeast and northeast. Most South Americans live along the coast or on these fertile plains.

AFRICA

Africa is the second largest continent in area — almost three times the size of the United States. Most of Africa is a plateau (*level land raised above adjoining land*) with a narrow coastline. Today, this continent is home to more than 50 countries. Geographers often divide Africa into two separate regions: North Africa and sub-Saharan Africa.

◆ **North Africa,** whose people are mainly of Arab descent and followers of Islam, is often considered to be more closely tied to the countries of the Middle East than to the rest of Africa.

◆ **Sub-Saharan Africa,** the area south of the Sahara Desert, has a very different climate and topography from North Africa. With its non-Arab population, it is sometimes viewed as a separate and distinct region.

The Impact of Geography. North Africa has a warm and dry climate. On its northern border is the Mediterranean Sea. The **Sahara,** the world's largest desert, takes up most of North Africa. For centuries the Sahara has acted as a barrier separating the peoples north and south of it. The **Nile,** the world's longest river, also flows through North Africa. It made possible the rise of Egypt in ancient times.

A large part of sub-Saharan Africa is **savanna** (*land where tall, wild grasses grow*). The savanna provides the best land in Africa for growing crops and raising livestock.

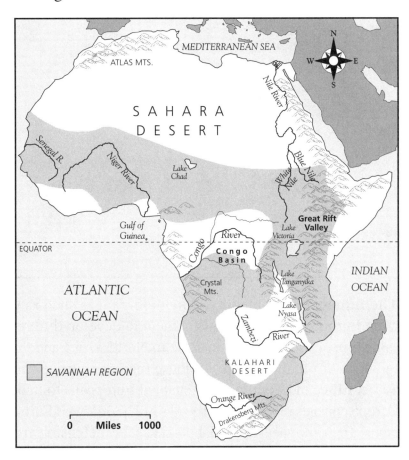

In East Africa, the **Great Rift Valley** runs through the highlands of Ethiopia and Kenya. The southern end of West Africa and much of Central Africa is tropical rain forest. These areas get from 60 to 100 inches of rainfall a year. Africa's mountains, deserts, lakes, and rivers have kept different groups apart, causing them to develop separate cultures, languages, and traditions. Africa's nearness to the Middle East and Europe led to the spread of Islam and Christianity in Africa, as well as the slave trade and imperialism.

EUROPE

Europe and Asia share the same land mass, which is so large that geographers have divided it into two continents. The dividing line between Europe and Asia runs through the center of Russia, along the Ural Mountains and Ural River into the Caspian Sea and southwest to the Black Sea. Europe is further bordered by the Baltic, North Sea, and Arctic Ocean to the north, the Atlantic Ocean to the west, and the Mediterranean Sea to the south.

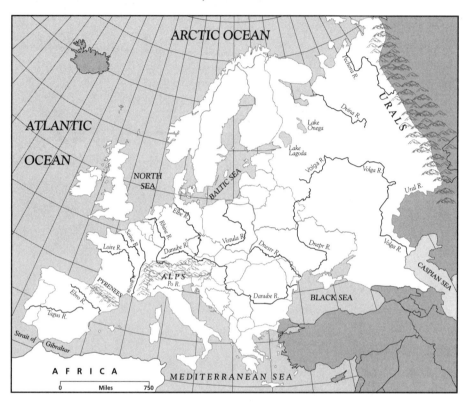

The Impact of Geography. Mountain ranges such as the **Pyrenees** and the **Alps** separated European peoples, causing them to develop different languages and cultures. At the same time, Europe's location close to North Africa and the Middle East enabled Europeans to borrow from the cultures of these regions. Europe's major rivers, the **Rhine, Danube, Seine, Elbe,** and **Vistula,** have enabled Europeans to trade with each other easily. Much of Europe consists of a broad fertile plain. This allowed Europeans to develop prosperous farmlands. To the northeast, this flat plain has few defensible frontiers. Thus, throughout their history, the borders of Russia, Poland, and Germany have constantly shifted. Because of Europe's dense population and many cultures, many different ethnic groups live close to one another. As a result, Europe has been the stage for frequent warfare throughout its history.

ASIA

Asia is the world's largest continent. Today, it is home to two-thirds of the world's population. Because of its immense size and the diversity of its cultures, geographers usually think of Asia as consisting of several distinct cultural regions.

THE MIDDLE EAST

The Middle East, located in southwest Asia, serves as the "crossroads of three continents." It connects Africa, Asia, and Europe. Some geographers consider North Africa as part of the Middle East.

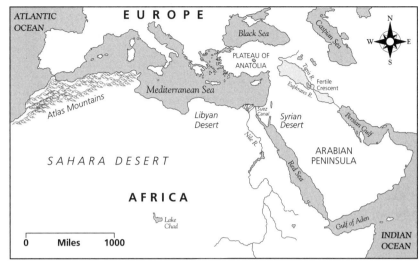

The Impact of Geography. The climate of this region is very hot. Much of this region is desert and lacks plentiful water. The greatest population density is found near the coasts and along major rivers, where water supplies are plentiful and crops can be grown more easily. In ancient times, the land in these river valleys was extraordinarily fertile. Two major rivers in the Middle East are the **Tigris** and the **Euphrates.** Today, the Middle East also provides about half of the world's oil supply.

NORTHERN ASIA

Northern Asia is occupied by the country of Russia, which stretches from Eastern Europe all the way east to the Pacific Ocean. It is the world's largest country in terms of area. Although three-quarters of its population, farmland, and industry are located in Europe, most of Russia's land area lies in Asia. Siberia, in northeastern Russia, is a cold region with forests, oil and gas deposits, diamonds, gold, and other precious metals.

The Impact of Geography. Most of Russia has long, cold winters and short mild summers. Northernmost Russia is **tundra,** where the ground is frozen much of the year. The Arctic Ocean, north of Russia, is also frozen most of the time. To the south, Russia is landlocked (*access to the sea is blocked by other countries*). The need for a ice-free port has been a major problem in Russian history, causing Russian rulers to expand their country southward and westward. Because of Russia's great distance from Western Europe, its culture developed independently.

CENTRAL ASIA

Central Asia consists of a vast corridor south of Russia and north of Iran, India, and China. It is mainly an area of deserts and treeless grasslands known as **steppes.**

The Impact of Geography. Central Asia has long been a crossroads for overland trade routes between China, India, the Middle East, and Europe. Because the **steppes** of Central Asia provided excellent grazing land, its people became herders and excelled at horsemanship. Throughout much of history, warriors on horseback from the Central Asian steppes periodically emerged to conquer peoples in neighboring lands.

EAST ASIA

East Asia includes three important countries: (1) China, (2) Korea, and (3) Japan.

China, one of the world's most ancient civilizations, is the world's third largest country in terms of area: only Russia and Canada are larger. At present and for most of its history, China has been the world's most populous nation. **Korea,** a peninsula extending from the northeastern coast of China, has been greatly influenced by Chinese culture. Situated between China and Japan, it has been invaded by both.

The Impact of Geography. China's southern and western borders are ringed by some of the world's highest and most rugged mountains: the Himalayan, Kunlun, and Tianjin Mountains. These mountains have protected and isolated China from the outside world. The **Gobi Desert** to the north and the Pacific Ocean to the east have further separated China. Eastern China consists of a vast plain with fertile river valleys. As a result, most of China's population has settled in this area.

The mountains, deserts, and seas surrounding China permitted it to develop a uniform culture in isolation from other centers of civilization. This isolation encouraged a centralization of power and concentration of resources that made China one of the world's most advanced civilizations for thousands of years.

Japan lies east of the Asian mainland, separated by the Sea of Japan. Japan consists of four main islands and thousands of smaller ones, extending 1,500 miles from its northern tip to its southern end.

Impact of Geography. Japan is a small country with 85% of its land covered by mountains. Nevertheless, Japan has a relatively large population — almost half that of the United States. Japan's high population density has led to a social closeness and promoted the ability of its people to work together. Japan lacks many important natural resources necessary for modern industry. This has caused the Japanese to seek raw materials from other nations, either through peaceful trade or aggressive military conquest

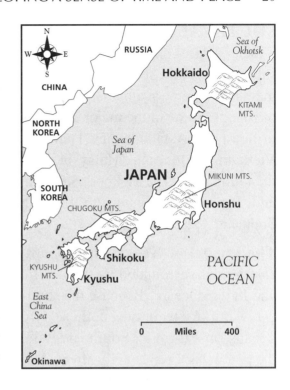

SOUTH ASIA

South Asia consists of a **subcontinent** (*a large piece of land smaller than a continent*). The Indian subcontinent forms a triangle about half the size of the United States, which juts out into the Indian Ocean. It contains India, Pakistan, Bangladesh, and several smaller nations. India has the world's second largest population, almost equal to that of China.

The Impact of Geography. The **Himalayan Mountains** are the highest mountains in the world. They separate the Indian subcontinent from the rest of Asia. South of the Himalayas are fertile river valleys and coastal plains, with a warm and humid climate. The main rivers of the Indian subcontinent, the **Indus** and **Ganges,** gave rise to some of the world's earliest civilizations. The subcontinent's location close to the Middle East led to the later spread of Islam throughout much of the area.

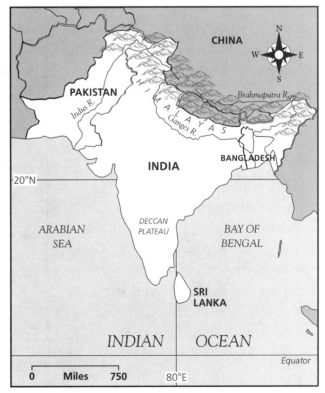

SOUTHEAST ASIA

Southeast Asia consists of a large peninsula on the southeast corner of the Asian mainland together with a large number of islands. Some of the major countries of Southeast Asia today are Thailand, Vietnam, Indonesia, Malaysia, and the Philippines. The Mekong, Salween, and Irrawaddy Rivers run through Southeast Asia.

The Impact of Geography. Southeast Asia is surrounded by the Pacific and Indian Oceans. Because the shortest water route between these two oceans runs through Southeast Asia, the region has been heavily affected by a large mix of peoples coming into this area, including Chinese, Indians, Arabs, and Europeans.

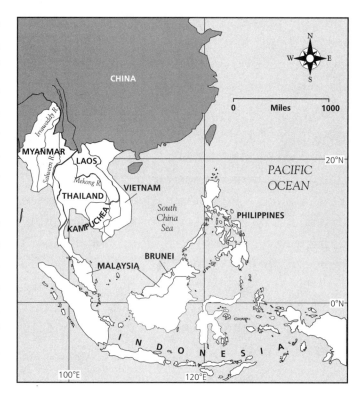

The islands of Southeast Asia, once known as the East Indies, export important spices such as pepper, cinnamon, and nutmeg, used in cooking all over the world. In earlier times, these spices were highly prized in Europe and the Middle East because they provided a way of preserving food that was more flavorful than using just salt.

The **monsoons** are the most important feature of the climate of South and Southeast Asia. These winds bring heavy summer rains. Rain waters the crops and supports life, but if the monsoons bring too much rain, they can cause flooding, destruction, and death. Because of the warm climate and humidity, much of the region is rain forest.

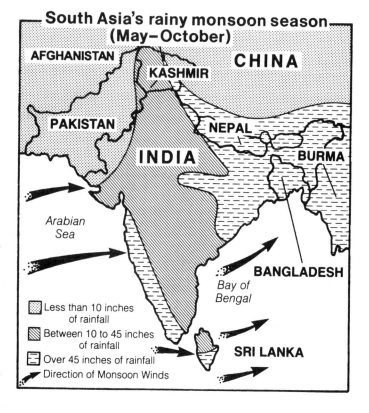

CHAPTER 4

THE DAWN OF CIVILIZATION
3500 B.C. – 500 B.C.

SECTION 1: THE FIRST HUMAN BEINGS
1. The Importance of Culture
2. The Neolithic Revolution

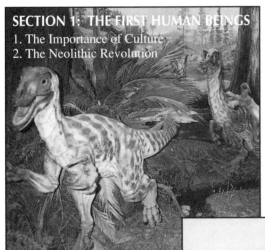

About 100 million years ago, dinosaurs stalked the earth.

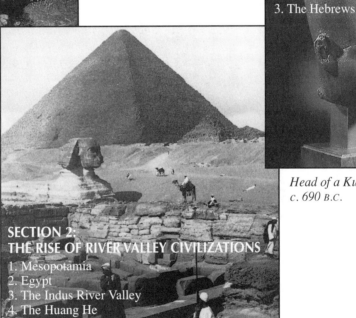

SECTION 3: OTHER EARLY CIVILIZATIONS
1. Kush
2. Phoenicia
3. The Hebrews

Head of a Kushite king, c. 690 B.C.

SECTION 2: THE RISE OF RIVER VALLEY CIVILIZATIONS
1. Mesopotamia
2. Egypt
3. The Indus River Valley
4. The Huang He

The Sphinx and Great Pyramid at Giza, Egypt

	3500 B.C.	3000 B.C.	2500 B.C.	2000 B.C.	1500 B.C.	1000 B.C.	500 B.C.
MIDDLE EAST	MESOPOTAMIAN CIVILIZATIONS:						
	SUMER			BABYLON	HITTITE		ASSYRIAN
				HEBREW CIVILIZATION			
INDIA			INDUS RIVER CIVILIZATION				
CHINA				HUANG HE CIVILIZATION			
NORTH AFRICA	EGYPTIAN CIVILIZATION						
							KUSH

WHAT YOU SHOULD FOCUS ON

In this chapter, you will learn how human beings first emerged many thousands of years ago. Gradually, the first humans spread around the world. Some groups developed farming and built permanent settlements. Eventually, settlements in the river valleys of Africa and Asia developed the world's first civilizations.

Studying this era enables you to appreciate the common past we all share. The study of human origins and ancient civilizations helps us to understand the basic problems that all societies face — how to organize to meet human needs.

Iron tools have been in use in Africa since ancient times.

By studying the civilizations of the past, we also develop a greater awareness of the tremendous debt we owe to those who came before us. You may even be surprised by how much of modern society is patterned after what was introduced in ancient times.

Writing. The ancient invention of writing allowed vast amounts of human knowledge to be recorded and passed down from one generation to the next.

Food and Clothing. Even today, many of our foods and clothing styles are affected by the legacy of ancient cultures.

OUR DEBT TO THE FIRST CIVILIZATIONS

Forms of Expression. Much of modern language, literature, and art closely follows what was done in ancient times.

Math and Science. Our knowledge of science and mathematics is built upon the foundations laid by ancient discoveries and inventions.

Knowing more about ancient civilizations can help us to uncover the factors that promote prosperity, stability, and innovation in our own day much as they did in the past. In studying this era, you should focus on the following questions:

➤ What were the consequences of the Neolithic Revolution?
➤ What factors led to the rise of the first civilizations?
➤ What were the most important contributions of early civilizations?

LOOKING AT GEOGRAPHY

In this chapter, you will learn how human beings first developed agriculture and how the first great civilizations arose. Geographical factors played a central role in these events. This introductory section takes a special look at the subject of geography so that you will better understand the connection between the geographic features of a place and its historical development.

THE FIVE THEMES OF GEOGRAPHY

Modern geographers have identified five major themes in the study of geography.

LOCATION

Location deals with where something is located in relation to other things. For example, where was Mesopotamia in relation to Egypt? To allow us to find the absolute location of any fixed point on the Earth's surface, geographers use the concepts of longitude and latitude.

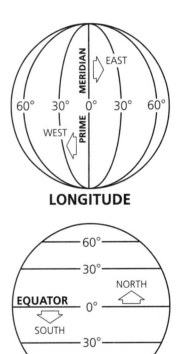

LONGITUDE

LATITUDE

- ◆ **Longitudes** are imaginary lines running up and down the Earth from the North to the South Pole. The middle longitude line is at zero degrees (0°) and is called the **Prime Meridian.** This line divides the world into the Western and Eastern Hemispheres. Every other longitude line is assigned a number in degrees to measure its distance east or west of the Prime Meridian.

- ◆ **Latitudes** are imaginary lines running horizontally across the Earth. The middle latitude line, known as the **equator,** is at zero degrees (0°). This line divides the world into the Northern and Southern Hemispheres. Every other latitude line is assigned a number in degrees to measure its distance north or south of the equator.

PLACE

"Place" refers to the special features of a location, distinguishing it from other locations. For example, what was Egypt like in ancient times? Was it hot or cool? Mountainous or flat? Geographers use special terms to describe the physical characteristics of a place. They look at its **topography** (*land surface features*) and **climate** (*weather conditions over a long period*). They also examine its **natural resources** (*such as minerals, fertile soil, or fresh water*).

REGIONS

A region is an area that shares common features and whose people have more contacts with others within the area than outside it. The concept of region in geography, like that of a time period in history, is flexible. Different regions, like that of ancient Egypt, may expand and contract over time. In studying any new region in global history, ask yourself: What makes this area a region? What are its common features?

HUMAN-ENVIRONMENT INTERACTIONS

This theme describes the ways in which the physical setting of a place interacts with the people who live there. Since ancient times, people have affected their environment in many ways: planting fields, irrigating the land, and building cities. You should also think how the environment helps shape what people do. How is the kind of society that develops in a desert different from a culture that emerges in a tropical rain forest?

Bedouin women herd goats in Jordan. The environment often influences how people live.

MOVEMENT

Throughout history, some areas have had surpluses of certain goods, while other areas have experienced shortages of the same goods. These differences have stimulated trade and other contacts among peoples. Understanding the movement of goods, services, ideas, and peoples from one place to another is a final important theme of geography.

ANSWERING TEST QUESTIONS ON GEOGRAPHY

Test questions on geography often focus on how the physical setting of an area affects the development of its people. To help answer these types of questions, keep in mind that location is often crucial in determining interactions with peoples of other areas. The kind of place an area is — its topography, climate, and resources — is usually crucial to the number of people who live in the area, where they live, and how they make their livelihoods. Population density is usually greatest along coasts, in river valleys, and on fertile plains. A culture is often shaped by the resources available to its people and how they make their living. Culture, in turn, affects the development of technologies that allow people to alter their environment.

MAJOR HISTORICAL DEVELOPMENTS

SECTION 1: THE FIRST HUMAN BEINGS

In this section you will read about the earliest human societies and how some humans began to change from hunter-gatherers to farmers who could grow their own food.

THINK ABOUT IT •

The dictionary defines a *revolution* as a rapid change. What was the radical change that occurred during the "Neolithic Revolution"?

Most social scientists believe that human beings first appeared in East Africa sometime between 200,000 and 400,000 years ago.

THE IMPORTANCE OF CULTURE

Early human beings had several important advantages over other animals: superior intellect, the use of hands to make tools, and the ability to communicate through speech. As a result, human beings were able to pass on their way of doing things to others. In this way, the first human cultures developed.

Culture **refers to a people's way of a life. It includes such things as their language, clothes, shelter, family organization, system of government, and methods of obtaining food.**

The primary activity of early humans was food gathering. They relied on hunting, fishing, and gathering wild plants for food. The search for food led the first humans to migrate from Africa to other parts of the world — Asia, Europe, the Americas, and Australia.

Herds of mammoths were an important source of food for early human hunters.

NEOLITHIC REVOLUTION

Wherever people went, they showed great ingenuity in adapting to local conditions. About 10,000 years ago, people in some areas first began to change from hunters and gatherers to producers of food. Most social scientists believe this change first occurred in the Middle East, where wild wheat and barley were plentiful. People noticed they could spread the seeds of these grains to grow crops. They also learned how to herd farm animals such as goats, sheep, and cattle. These advances are now referred to as the **Neolithic Revolution.**

With the introduction of agriculture, people no longer had to wander in search of food. They could now build permanent homes and villages and establish a fixed way of life. Populations grew. The Neolithic Revolution allowed people to grow more food than they had been able to gather or hunt; however, they were also more vulnerable to attack by other groups because they were settled in one location. The introduction of agriculture and villages led to the emergence of two new social classes: warriors and priests. Warriors defended the village, while priests conducted religious rituals to protect the village from danger.

ANSWERING THE FOCUS QUESTION •

The main change that occurred during the "Neolithic Revolution" was

_____ .

Writing

Directions: Complete each of the following vocabulary cards. Then answer the multiple-choice questions that follow.

CULTURE
What is culture?
Provide an example:

NEOLITHIC REVOLUTION
Define Neolithic Revolution:
What changes occurred because of
the Neolithic Revolution?

1   In its broadest sense, the term "culture" refers to
   1   art museums and symphony orchestras
   2   the complex languages found in developing societies
   3   a centralized form of government
   4   the way of living of the members of a society

2   Most social scientists believe that
   1   the earliest humans first evolved in East Africa
   2   farming societies developed before hunting and gathering societies
   3   all the continents were settled at the same time
   4   the wheel was used by all ancient societies

3   The Neolithic Revolution marked a radical change because humans
   1   started to inhabit the continents of Europe and Asia
   3   developed the ability to speak
   2   learned to herd animals and grow crops
   4   formed large economic associations

4 The beginning of the Neolithic Revolution was about

1 1 million years ago

2 100,000 years ago

3 10,000 years ago

4 1,000 years ago

SECTION 2: THE RISE OF RIVER VALLEY CIVILIZATIONS

In this section you will read about two of the world's first civilizations: Mesopotamia and Egypt.

THINK ABOUT IT •

Why did the first civilizations develop in river valleys?

Around 3500 B.C., the world's first **civilizations** began to emerge. The first civilizations developed in **river valleys.** Each year, rivers in these valleys overflowed, depositing fertile soil along their banks. People were able to grow abundant crops that could support large populations and more advanced cultures. Each of these river valleys also offered a mild climate, protection from foreign invasion, and a water route to other places.

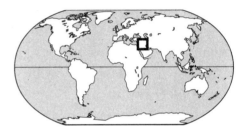

A *civilization* is an advanced form of human culture in which some people live in cities, have a form of writing, and are skilled at science and technology.

MESOPOTAMIA
(3500 B.C. – 1700 B.C.)

Social scientists believe the first civilization probably developed in Mesopotamia, the region located between the **Tigris** and **Euphrates Rivers** (*in present-day Iraq*).

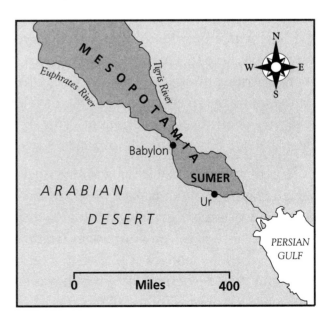

People in this area learned how to divert water from the Tigris and Euphrates Rivers to irrigate the extremely fertile soil. Irrigation allowed farming settlements to flourish and food supplies to increase. Increased food supplies allowed some people to specialize in activities other than farming and led to the rise of several city-states.

Some of the most important inventions in history were developed by the people of Mesopotamia, known as the **Sumerians.** They invented the wheel and sail boat, and developed the first tools and weapons of copper and bronze (*a mixture of tin and copper*). The Sumerians devised a calendar, dividing the year into 12 months. They also invented the earliest known writing system, **cuneiform,** a form of symbol-writing on clay tablets.

The Sumerians were also the world's first city-builders. They built walled cities, and stepped-pyramids known as **ziggurats.** The ziggurats were made of a series of square levels, with each higher level smaller that the one below it. The people of Mesopotamia also developed an elaborate system of laws. Hammurabi, a later ruler who conquered all of Mesopotamia, was responsible for the earliest known written law code — the **Code of Hammurabi.** Some of the

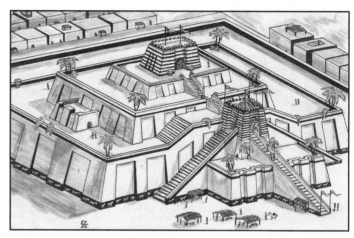

A Sumerian ziggurat

code's provisions punished criminals quite harshly, stressing the idea of "an eye for an eye, and a tooth for a tooth." This meant that whenever one person did wrong to another, the same harm should be done to that person as punishment.

EGYPT (3200 B.C. – 500 B.C.)

Egypt is located in North Africa. Although most of Egypt is occupied by desert, the world's longest river, the **Nile,** runs through it. Egyptian farmers were able to grow large numbers of crops on the fertile banks of the Nile where the river overflowed each year. These crops were able to support a large number of craftsmen, warriors, priests, and nobles. Ease of communication along the river encouraged the development of a highly centralized government. The surrounding deserts made Egypt difficult to invade.

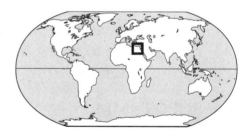

Egypt was governed by an absolute ruler known as the **pharaoh,** who commanded the army and controlled the supply of grain. Egyptians considered the pharaoh a god. They also believed in life after death. When the pharaoh died, his body was placed in a tomb called a **pyramid.** In the pyramid, the pharaoh was surrounded with precious objects for use in the afterlife.

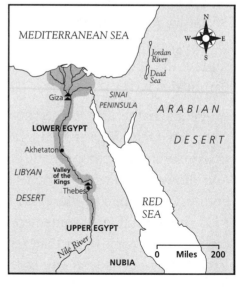

Building. Egyptian architects and engineers built magnificent pyramids, palaces, temples, and statues of stone. They were built so well that many examples of their work still survive today.

Hieroglyphics. Egyptians developed one of the earliest kinds of writing, based on picture symbols. Hieroglyphics appeared on temples, pyramids, and scrolls of paper known as papyrus.

ACCOMPLISHMENTS OF THE ANCIENT EGYPTIANS

Geometry and Astronomy. Egyptians used geometry to build the pyramids and other structures. By observing the stars, they developed a calendar based on 365 days.

Biology. Egyptians developed knowledge of the human body through embalming methods. They performed surgical operations, such as setting fractures.

THE INDUS RIVER VALLEY (2500 B.C. – 1500 B.C.)

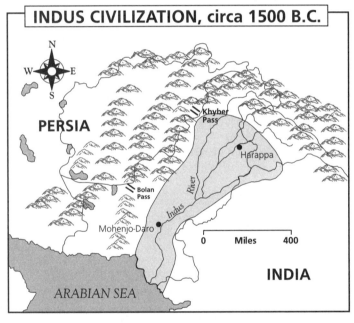

INDUS CIVILIZATION, circa 1500 B.C.

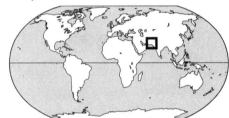

The Indus River Valley was another location of one of the first centers of civilization. As in Egypt and Mesopotamia, when the Indus River flooded, it deposited rich soil along its banks. Food surpluses allowed people to build large cities like Harappa and Mohenjo-Daro. The people of this civilization, sometimes called the **Harappans,** made the first cotton cloth and developed their own form of writing. They also made pottery and built sewage systems in their cities.

THE HUANG HE (2000 B.C. – 1027 B.C.)

China's first civilization emerged along the Huang He (*or Yellow River*). Around 1500 B.C., some people from the Huang He migrated southward to the Yangtze River, where they learned to grow rice and irrigate the land. Rice cultivation soon became common along the Huang He. The farming of soybeans and the raising of pigs, chickens, and dogs was also introduced.

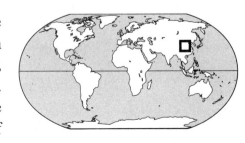

Around 1760 B.C., a ruling family (*dynasty*) known as the **Shang** took control of the region. Shang warriors used bronze weapons and horse-drawn chariots. The Shang built the first known Chinese cities. Each city had several large public buildings at its center, where the nobles lived. Potters, bronzesmiths, and other artisans lived just outside the city. The ancient Chinese became skilled in many crafts, such as making objects out of bronze. They also developed the ability to make silk from a silkworm's cocoon. The Chinese system of writing was based on pictographs, like that of ancient Egypt. Each *character* represented a different word.

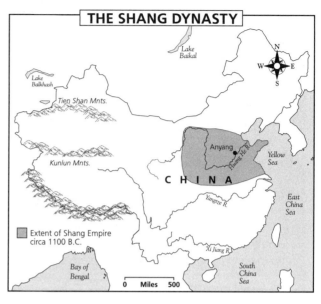

THE SHANG DYNASTY

Extent of Shang Empire circa 1100 B.C.

0   Miles   500

ANSWERING THE FOCUS QUESTION •

The first civilizations developed in river valleys because _____

_____ .

Writing

Directions: Complete each of the following vocabulary cards. Then answer the multiple-choice questions that follow.

CIVILIZATION
What is a civilization?
Provide an example:

RIVER VALLEY CIVILIZATIONS
What is a river valley civilization?
Name three ancient river valley
civilizations:

Base your answer to question 1 on the box below and your knowledge of global history.

> • living in cities
> • having a form of writing
> • being skilled at science and technology

1 The above examples are the essential characteristics of a
  1 civilization   3 time period
  2 culture   4 place

2 Which of the following was an important achievement of the early Sumerians?

  1 the development of hieroglyphics   3 the invention of the wheel

  2 the first cotton cloth   4 the first silk cloth

3 Cuneiform and hieroglyphics are similar in that they were both

  1 religious temples   3 holy books of ancient Egypt

  2 inventions of the Chinese   4 written forms of communication

4 The river valleys of the Tigris and Euphrates, the Nile, and the Indus became early centers of civilization because

  1 they had rich deposits of iron ore and coal

  2 they were isolated from other cultural influences

  3 their rivers provided a means of transportation and irrigation

  4 their borders were easy to defend from invasion

SECTION 3: OTHER EARLY CIVILIZATIONS

In this section you will read about how civilization spread to other areas, leading to the rise of the Kushite, Phoenician, and Hebrew civilizations.

THINK ABOUT IT •

What were the achievements of the Kushites, Phoenicians, and Hebrews?

The civilizations of ancient Egypt and Mesopotamia gradually influenced nearby areas. For example, different aspects of Egyptian life spread southward to the Kingdom of Kush. Phoenicians and Hebrews were influenced by both Mesopotamia and Egypt.

KUSH (750 B.C. – 350 A.D.)

Kush was an African kingdom located upstream on the Nile River, south of Egypt. The Kushites were nomadic cattle herders who frequently traded with the Egyptians. Egypt greatly influenced Kushite culture. The Kushites adopted Egyptian art forms, religious beliefs, and even the building of pyramids. Kush became well known for its

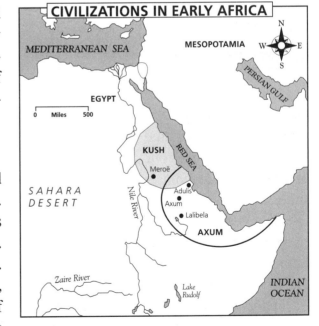

iron wares. Caravans traveled to Kush to obtain iron spears and iron plows to till the soil. Kush also grew rich from its trade of ivory, ebony, wood, animal skins, and slaves.

PHOENICIA

Phoenicia was located on the Mediterranean coast by present-day Lebanon. The Phoenicians became famous as sea-faring traders. They eventually established trading posts in Italy, Spain, and North Africa. They invented a new way of writing using just twenty-two symbols. Each symbol represented a different sound. Soon the Phoenician alphabet was being used all around the Mediterranean world. Our word *alphabet* comes directly from the first two letters of the Phoenician alphabet, *alpha* and *beta*.

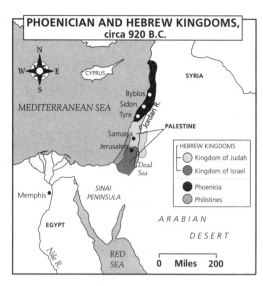

THE HEBREWS

The Hebrew (*or Jewish*) civilization developed in the area along the Mediterranean occupied by present-day Israel, Lebanon, and Jordan. **Judaism,** the religion of the ancient Hebrews, has had a great influence on many later civilizations.

KEY FEATURES OF JUDAISM

Monotheism. Other ancient peoples were **animists** (*believing each object had its own spirit*), or **polytheists** (*believing in many gods*). In contrast, the Hebrews were **monotheists** (*believing in only one God*).

Ten Commandments. These ten simple laws forbade stealing, murder, adultery, and other forms of immoral behavior.

Old Testament. The history of the ancient Hebrews and their relationship with God is told in the first books of the **Bible**, known as the **Old Testament**. Jews refer to the first five books of the Old Testament as the **Torah**.

According to Jewish tradition, the ancient Hebrews migrated from Israel to Egypt to escape food shortages from drought. They remained in Egypt for hundreds of years, where they eventually became enslaved. **Moses** later led the Hebrews out of Egypt and slavery. Their flight from Egypt is referred to as the **Exodus.** According to the Bible, after the Hebrews left Egypt, Moses presented his people with the Ten Commandments, which he said came directly from God. The Hebrews returned to Israel and defeated its occupants in a series of wars. By 1000 B.C., they established their capital at Jerusalem and erected a temple.

The Western (or "Wailing") Wall, one of Judaism's holiest sites, was once part of ancient Jerusalem's temple wall.

ANSWERING THE FOCUS QUESTION •

The most important achievements of some early civilizations were:

_____ (Kushites)

_____ (Phoenicians)

_____ (Hebrews)

Directions: Complete each of the following vocabulary cards. Then answer the multiple-choice questions that follow.

KUSH
Where was Kush located?
In what ways did Egypt influence the
Kushites?

JUDAISM
What are the key beliefs of Judaism?
How did Judaism differ from other
ancient religions?

1 The modern English alphabet is based in large part on the alphabet of the ancient

   1 Phoenicians   3 Egyptians

   2 Chinese   4 Sumerians

2 A student's report contains the following topics: *Old Testament*, *Moses*, and *Exodus*. The report is most likely about the

   1 Kushites   3 Phoenicians

   2 Hebrews   4 Sumerians

3 An important characteristic of Judaism is its belief in

   1 many gods   3 reincarnation

   2 monotheism   4 the New Testament

4 Which heading would be most appropriate in the space below?

> **I.** _____
>   A. Code of Hammurabi - Mesopotamia
>   B. alphabet - Phoenicia
>   C. wheel - Sumer

   1 Economic changes in the ancient world

   2 Buildings of ancient civilizations

   3 Contributions of ancient civilizations

   4 Religions of ancient civilizations

KEY TERMS, CONCEPTS, AND PEOPLE

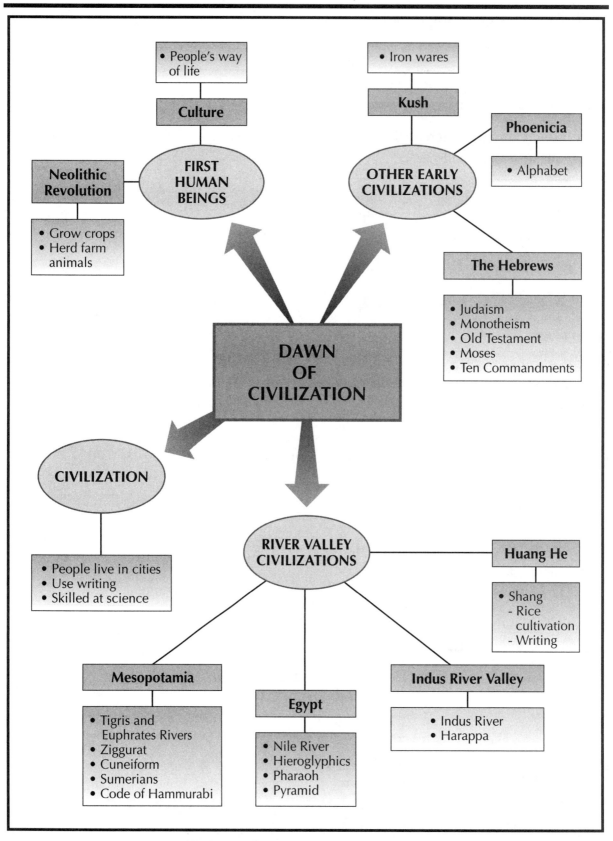

- People's way of life

Culture

FIRST HUMAN BEINGS

Neolithic Revolution

- Grow crops
- Herd farm animals

- Iron wares

Kush

OTHER EARLY CIVILIZATIONS

Phoenicia

- Alphabet

The Hebrews

- Judaism
- Monotheism
- Old Testament
- Moses
- Ten Commandments

DAWN OF CIVILIZATION

CIVILIZATION

- People live in cities
- Use writing
- Skilled at science

RIVER VALLEY CIVILIZATIONS

Huang He

- Shang
  - Rice cultivation
  - Writing

Mesopotamia

- Tigris and Euphrates Rivers
- Ziggurat
- Cuneiform
- Sumerians
- Code of Hammurabi

Egypt

- Nile River
- Hieroglyphics
- Pharaoh
- Pyramid

Indus River Valley

- Indus River
- Harappa

SUMMARIZING YOUR UNDERSTANDING

COMPLETING AN OUTLINE

Directions: Use these headings to complete the outline below. The first four items in the outline have been completed for you.

Mesopotamia
Egypt
Phoenicia
First Human Beings ✓
The Huang He
Other Early Civilizations
Rise of River Valley Civilizations

DAWN OF CIVILIZATION ✓
The Hebrews
The Importance of Culture ✓
Kush
The Neolithic Revolution ✓
The Indus River Valley

TITLE: _Dawn of Civilization_

I. MAJOR DIVISION: _First Human Beings_

   A. Sub-topic: _The Importance of Culture_

   B. Sub-topic: _The Neolithic Revolution_

II. MAJOR DIVISION: _____

   A. Sub-topic: _____

   B. Sub-topic: _____

   C. Sub-topic: _____

   D. Sub-topic: _____

III. MAJOR DIVISION: _____

   A. Sub-topic: _____

   B. Sub-topic: _____

   C. Sub-topic: _____

COMPLETING A GRAPHIC ORGANIZER

Select **one** ancient civilization that you have read about in this chapter and complete the following graphic organizer for it.

NAME OF ANCIENT CIVILIZATION: _____

Description of its Location: _____

Geographic Features:

Achievements:

COMPLETING A PARAGRAPH FRAME

The earliest civilizations made many important contributions to humankind. Select **one** ancient civilization from this chapter and **show how** two of its achievements helped future generations. To help you write this essay, a paragraph frame has been provided.

NOTE: Since this is the first "show how" paragraph frame, it has been started for you. Complete the remainder of the paragraph frame.

The **Selection** identifies what choice you have made, based on the question.

In this **Example** section, you give an example to support the general statement in the question.

For the **Show How Link,** you show how the example you gave actually supports the general statement.

The **Closing** summarizes what you have shown.

Selection: [*Ancient Egyptian civilization*] made many important and lasting contributions to humankind.

Example(s): Among the major contributions of the Egyptians was [*its system of writing*]. The Egyptians developed [*hieroglyphics, one of the earliest kinds of writing. Hieroglyphics used pictures to stand for ideas, words and sounds*].

Show How Link: [*The development of writing helped cultures to pass down their history and values from one generation to the next*].

Another Example: A second contribution of ancient Egyptian civilization was [_____].
Show How Link: [_____].

Closing: From these examples, we can see that the [*ancient Egyptians*] made many important and lasting contributions to humankind.

SHARPENING YOUR TEST-TAKING SKILLS

Test-taking, like most activities, requires certain skills to do well. At the end of each content chapter of this book, you will find a special section like this one for sharpening your test-taking skills. The purpose of these sections is to show you how to answer each type of question that may appear on a global history examination.

The types of questions you will learn about include multiple-choice questions, thematic essay questions, and document-based essay questions. Each of these assessment sections will begin with an explanation of one of these types of questions, followed by sample test questions on the chapter.

ANSWERING MULTIPLE-CHOICE QUESTIONS

The object of this first test-taking section is to familiarize you with multiple-choice questions. The majority of multiple-choice questions in global history can be grouped into a few basic types. They test your knowledge of the following information:

RECOGNITION OF IMPORTANT TERMS, CONCEPTS, AND PEOPLE

Many multiple-choice questions test your knowledge of important terms, concepts, and people. The examples below illustrate some of the ways these questions may be phrased:

- The concept of [*civilization*] is best illustrated by ...
- Which statement about the [*Neolithic Revolution*] is most accurate?

> To help you recognize major terms, concepts, and people, these will be in **bold type** in each content chapter. Key terms, concepts, and people are also listed as vocabulary cards and are found in questions at the end of each content section.

COMPREHENSION OF DATA

Comprehension questions test whether you understand data presented as part of a data-based question. Such a comprehension question may take any of the following forms:

- Which civilization is represented by the [*photo of a pyramid*]?
- According to the table, in which time period was [*rice production*] the greatest?

The crucial factor in answering comprehension questions is your ability to understand the different types of data-bases (*see Chapter 2*). Data-based questions appear frequently throughout this book, providing you with many opportunities to practice this skill.

CONCLUSION OR GENERALIZATION

Some questions will test your ability to make or understand a generalization. The following are typical examples of a generalization question:

- Which is the most accurate statement about [*ancient Egyptian*] customs, religion, and family structure?
- In an outline, one of these is a main topic, and the other three are sub-topics. Which is the main topic?

Generalizations summarize the main theme found in each section. To help you answer this type of question, generalizations are used throughout this book. In addition, generalization questions are found in each content chapter.

COMPARE AND CONTRAST

The act of comparing and contrasting allows us to highlight and separate particular events, ideas, and concepts, placing them in sharper focus. Compare-and-contrast questions might appear as follows:

- [*Moses*] and [*Hammurabi*] were similar in that both ...
- A major difference between [*ancient Egypt*] and [*Mesopotamia*] was that ...

As you read through each content chapter, test yourself by comparing and contrasting **new** terms, concepts, and people with those you already know. It is important to understand both how these things are **similar** and how they **differ.**

CAUSE AND EFFECT

History consists of a series of events leading to still other events. Causal explanations give history much of its meaning. Cause-and-effect questions test your understanding of the relationship between an action or event and its effects. In answering these questions, be careful to understand what answer is being asked for — the *cause* or the *effect*. Such questions might appear as follows:

- Which was a significant cause of [*the emergence of civilization*]? (*asks for a cause*)
- Which was a direct result of the [*Neolithic Revolution*]? (*asks for an effect*)

> To help you answer these types of questions, important cause-and-effect relationships are identified in each content chapter. In addition, many cause-and-effect relationships are found in graphic organizers you will be asked to complete at the end of each content chapter.

CHRONOLOGY

A list of events in chronological order starts from the earliest event and progresses to the latest one. This arrangement allows us to see patterns and sequences in a series of events. Chronological questions might appear as follows:

- Which sequence of events best describes the historical development of ancient Israel?
- Which group of events is in correct chronological order?

> To help you answer these types of questions, timelines are presented at the beginning of each chapter and at the back of this book.

FACT AND OPINION

Certain questions will ask you to distinguish between facts and opinions.

◆ A **fact** is a statement that can be verified. For example, the following is a factual statement: "Rulers of Egypt were known as pharaohs." We frequently check the accuracy of factual statements by looking at several sources.

◆ An **opinion** is an expression of someone's belief and cannot be verified. An example of an opinion would be: "Moses was the wisest man of the ancient world."

Questions asking you to distinguish fact from opinion could be phrased as follows:

- Which statement about the [*Code of Hammurabi*] expresses an opinion rather than a fact?
- Which statement about [*Shang rulers*] would be the most difficult to prove? (*An opinion statement would be the answer*)

The crucial factor is that the question asks you to know the difference between a fact and an opinion. To help you answer this type of question, each content chapter will have at least one multiple-choice question asking you to distinguish facts from opinions.

USE OF REFERENCE BOOKS

Historians and social scientists consult a wide variety of reference books to help them learn about the past. One standard reference book is an atlas. An **atlas** contains a collection of maps. It may also have information about topography, natural resources, population, cities, and other topics. Other standard reference books are **encyclopedias** and **almanacs.** Some questions may ask you to identify one of these specialized books of information.

- To find information about the topography of the [*the Middle East*], which source would you most likely consult?

The crucial factor is to know how these various types of reference books are used. To help you answer these types of questions, multiple-choice questions dealing with sources of information are found throughout this book.

TESTING YOUR UNDERSTANDING

1 Culture is sometimes referred to as a "blueprint for living" because it
   1 flourishes best in traditional societies
   2 includes all the things that contribute to a society's operation
   3 is determined by genetics
   4 requires people to be able to read and write

2 One result of the Neolithic Revolution was
   1 an increase in the number of nomadic tribes
   2 a greater reliance on hunting and gathering for food
   3 the establishment of permanent villages
   4 a decrease in trade between different cultural groups

3 Which characteristic did the early civilizations along the Nile, the Tigris and Euphrates, and the Huang He have in common?
   1 Each society held monotheistic beliefs.
   2 They used iron and steel tools.
   3 Slavery was forbidden.
   4 They developed in areas that had fertile soil and natural waterways.

4 Which statement about ancient Egyptian civilization expresses an *opinion* rather than a *fact*?
   1 The Egyptians used a form of picture-writing known as hieroglyphics.
   2 The Nile River deposited fertile soil along its banks.
   3 Egyptians made the greatest contributions of the ancient world to humanity.
   4 The pyramids were tombs for the pharaohs.

5 Judaism differed from other ancient religions in that its followers
   1 worshipped many gods
   2 were monotheists
   3 followed the Code of Hammurabi
   4 buried their rulers in pyramids

6 Which group of dates is arranged in chronological order?
   1 567 B.C., 214 B.C., 567 A.D., 1865 A.D.
   2 123 B.C., 124 A.D., 1785 A.D., 108 A.D.
   3 37 B.C., 38 B.C., 98 A.D., 1995 A.D.
   4 557 A.D., 56 A.D., 22 B.C., 234 B.C.

7 A team of scientists discovered the following items at an archeological site:

> • hieroglyphics written on stone walls
> • a well-preserved mummy
> • a gold mask, gold jewelry, and a gold crown

The site was most probably the location of
1   an Egyptian pharaoh's tomb   3   ancient Hebrew ruins
2   an early Kushite temple   4   the tomb of a Shang ruler

8 "If a nobleman has knocked out the tooth of a nobleman of his own rank, they shall knock out his tooth. But if he has knocked out a commoner's tooth, he shall pay one-third mina of silver."   —*Code of Hammurabi*

Which idea does this portion of the Code of Hammurabi reflect?
1   All men are equal under the law.
2   Fines are preferable to corporal punishment.
3   Divisions exist between social classes.
4   Violence should always be punished with violence.

Base your answer to questions 9 and 10 on the following map and your knowledge of global history.

9 According to the map, in which direction would you be traveling if you wanted to go from ancient Egypt to Mesopotamia?
1   northeast
2   southwest
3   northwest
4   southeast

10 The ancient civilization of Sumer developed along which river system?
1   A
2   B
3   C
4   D

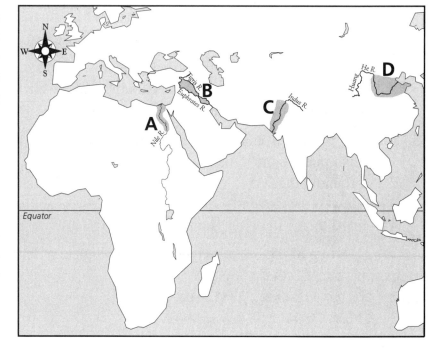

CHAPTER 5

THE CLASSICAL CIVILIZATIONS
500 B.C. – 500 A.D.

SECTION 1:
CLASSICAL CIVILIZATIONS OF THE WEST
1. The Persians
2. The Greeks
3. The Romans

Roman Forum — the center of political and commercial life in ancient Rome.

SECTION 3: MAJOR WORLD RELIGIONS EMERGE
1. Hinduism
2. Buddhism
3. Confucianism
4. Christianity

St. Peter's Basilica in the Vatican — the very heart of the Catholic religion today.

SECTION 2:
CLASSICAL CIVILIZATIONS OF THE EAST
1. India
2. China

Some of the 7,000 life-sized clay soldiers found in Shih Huang-ti's tomb.

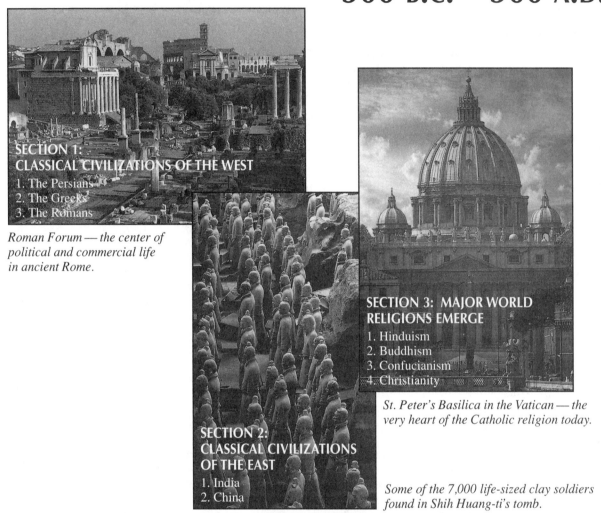

	500 B.C.	300 B.C.	100 B.C.	100 A.D.	300 A.D.	500 A.D.
GREECE	CITY-STATES	HELLENISTIC PERIOD				
ROME	ROMAN REPUBLIC			ROMAN EMPIRE		
ASIA	PERSIAN EMPIRE					
	ZHOU DYNASTY	QIN	HAN DYNASTY			
	ARYAN KINGDOMS	MAURYAN EMPIRE				GUPTA EMPIRE
RELIGIONS AND BELIEF SYSTEMS				CHRISTIANITY		
	CONFUCIANISM					
	HINDUISM					
	BUDDHISM					

| 500 B.C. | 300 B.C. | 100 B.C. | 100 A.D. | 300 A.D. | 500 A.D. |

WHAT YOU SHOULD FOCUS ON

In this chapter, you will learn about the world's classical civilizations. During this era, civilizations spread beyond river valleys. Some societies achieved the military power needed to conquer their neighbors and create giant empires. As civilizations matured, their members began to reflect more on morality and the purpose of life. As a result, some of the world's major religions emerged in this era.

These same civilizations developed new institutions, systems of thought, and cultural styles that still influence us today. Their arts and literature set the standards against which later works have often been judged. For these reasons, we refer to these societies as *classical* civilizations, meaning of the highest class or rank.

A bronze statue from China shows the influence of the Buddhist religion on China.

The **Persian** empire was the first to unite many civilizations, establishing a pattern for future empires.

The **Greeks** used human reason to inquire about nature and the human condition, laying the foundation for much of Western culture.

OVERVIEW OF CLASSICAL CIVILIZATIONS

The **Romans** spread Greek culture throughout Western Europe and left a legacy of language, laws, engineering, and Christianity.

India witnessed a flowering of Hindu and Buddhist culture, which spread throughout much of South and Southeast Asia.

China saw the emergence of great philosophers, who set the tone for much of East Asian thought and tradition.

In studying this era, focus on the following questions:
➤ What was the importance of military power, technology, law, and transportation in the development of large empires like Persia, China and Rome?
➤ What were the major cultural accomplishments of these civilizations?
➤ How were classical civilizations affected by their religions and belief systems?

LOOKING AT THE WORLD'S RELIGIONS

n this chapter, you will learn about the development of some of the world's major religions. Your focus should be on the way each religion relates to its society.

WHAT IS RELIGION?

All societies have some forms of religious belief. Because these beliefs touch on what people think about life itself, religion has had a great impact on the way people behave. Religion has been one of the most powerful influences on human history.

You may be surprised to learn that there is no precise definition of "religion." Nonetheless, most definitions of religion list three common elements:

CHARACTERISTICS OF A RELIGION

A set of **beliefs** about the nature of the universe, the existence of one God or several gods, the meaning of life, and what happens after death.

A set of **customs and practices** that relate to the worship of one God or several gods, and a set of rules for proper conduct.

An **organization**, such as a church or synagogue, that oversees the conduct of religious practices.

CLASSIFYING THE WORLD'S MAJOR RELIGIONS

One way to look at the world's major religions is to organize them according to their historical development. For example, Christianity and Islam both developed out of Judaism. Christianity later divided into Eastern Orthodox Christianity and Roman Catholicism. Finally, during the Protestant Reformation of the 16th century, Western Europe divided into Roman Catholicism and Protestantism. If we were to chart these relationships, they would appear as:

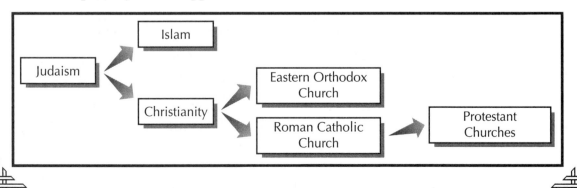

Another family of religions developed in India. Buddhism grew out of Hinduism. Sikhism brought together the beliefs of Hindus and Muslims. Zen Buddhism is a form of Buddhism that developed in Japan:

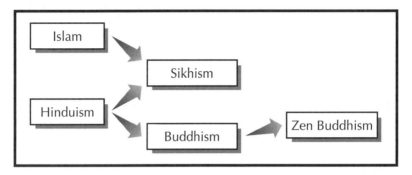

This way of grouping religions is useful because new religions often borrow ideas and practices from the religions they grow out of.

RELIGION AND THE ARTS

A knowledge of religion is necessary to understand many of the world's greatest cultural achievements. Because religion is tied to people's deepest feelings, much of the world's art, music, and literature has been religious in nature. Early cave paintings were related to a belief in spirits. The masks and dance rituals of traditional tribal groups in Africa, the Pacific islands, and the Americas

Dance and masks are used by this African tribe in conjunction with a young man's initiation rites.

were attempts to appease the spirits. The temples of ancient Greece and Rome were built to honor their gods. Medieval cathedrals were meant to represent God's kingdom on Earth. Much of the art of the Renaissance was inspired by religion.

ANSWERING QUESTIONS ABOUT RELIGION

Many test questions on global history examinations will focus on religious concerns. Usually such questions will focus on two aspects about religion:

◆ major beliefs of a religion and how they influenced history or culture; and
◆ the social conflicts that often arise out of religious differences. These social conflicts will be explored in later chapters of this book.

MAJOR HISTORICAL DEVELOPMENTS

SECTION 1: CLASSICAL CIVILIZATIONS OF THE WEST

In this section you will read about three classical civilizations that developed in the West — Persia, Greece, and Rome.

A note about the terms "East" and "West:" **Historians frequently refer to the civilizations that grew out of ancient Mediterranean cultures and flourished in Europe as Western Civilization. The civilizations of Asia are frequently referred to as the East, because they are east of Europe.**

THINK ABOUT IT •

What were the most important achievements of the classical civilizations of the West?

THE PERSIAN EMPIRE

Ancient Persia was a bridge between Asia and Europe. The Persians lived in the region between the Caspian Sea and the Persian Gulf. Beginning around 550 B.C., a succession of able rulers extended the territory of the Persia empire.

An *empire* is a state that rules over several different peoples.

At its height, the Persian empire stretched more than 3,000 miles from the Nile to the Indus River. Persians controlled their vast empire by dividing it into provinces and building a system of connecting roads. Each province was ruled by local officials loyal to the Persian king. Local customs were preserved, but each province was forced to pay tribute (*taxes*) to the Persian ruler.

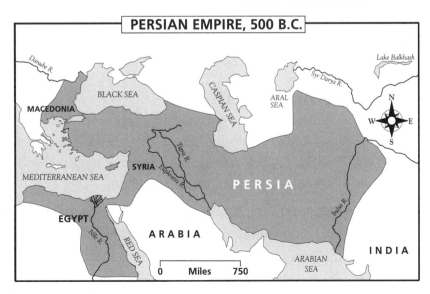

PERSIAN EMPIRE, 500 B.C.

At first, the Persians worshiped many gods. In 570 B.C., a new religion was introduced into the empire by Zoroaster. Known as **Zoroastrianism,** this religion taught that there were only two gods: the god of light and goodness and the god of darkness and evil. Persians believed the whole universe was the battleground between these two forces. Those who led good lives would eventually go to Heaven, while others would be doomed to Hell.

THE GREEKS

The ancient Greeks have had an enduring impact on Western civilization. They developed the first known system of democratic government. Their belief in human reason and their spirit of free inquiry led to important advances in mathematics, science, art, literature, and philosophy.

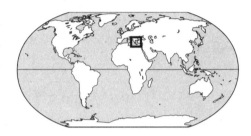

THE IMPACT OF GEOGRAPHY

Ancient Greece consisted of a large mountainous peninsula, the islands of the Aegean Sea, and the coast of present-day Turkey. Because of its hilly terrain, parts of Greece, like Athens, came to depend on trade. Greeks produced wine, olive oil, and pottery which they traded with other peoples of the Mediterranean. Through these contacts the Greeks became exposed to important ideas such as the Phoenician alphabet and Egyptian geometry. The Greeks benefited from the achievements of the ancient civilizations of the Middle East.

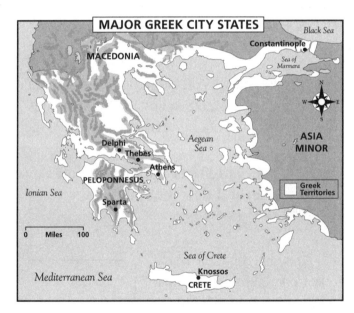

THE RISE OF CITY-STATES

Mountains caused Greek centers of population to be cut off from one another. As a result, separate **city-states** developed. Each city acted as a separate country. Although divided, Greeks shared a common culture based on language, religious beliefs, and customs. Two of the most important city-states were Sparta and Athens.

◆ **Totalitarian Sparta.** Spartans were a war-like people. They forced those they defeated to work as slaves on their farms. These people were called **helots.** The Spartans constantly had to use force to keep control over the helots, who outnumbered them. Because of this threat to Sparta, life was organized around military needs. Individualism and new ideas were discouraged. Strict obedience and self-discipline were emphasized.

◆ **Democratic Athens.** Athens developed a unique system of government. Every citizen could participate in government directly by voting on issues to be decided by the city-state. This type of government is called a **democracy.** Although Athens was a democracy, only a minority of Athenians were actually citizens. Women, foreigners, and slaves were not considered citizens and could not participate in government.

In the 5th century B.C., the Greek city-states cooperated in a war against the Persians, who had set out to conquer them. After defeating the Persians, the Greeks enjoyed a **"Golden Age"**

A *Golden Age* refers to a period in the history of a culture when people enjoy prosperity and make significant achievements in the arts and other fields.

Art, literature, and philosophy especially flourished in Athens during these years. The popular statesman, **Pericles,** championed democracy. Pericles used revenues collected from other city-states to help rebuild Athens. The Parthenon and other magnificent marble temples were constructed. But a rivalry soon developed between Athens and Sparta, which led to the **Peloponnesian War.** After thirty years, Sparta finally emerged as the victor.

ALEXANDER THE GREAT

In 338 B.C., the king of Macedonia (*an area north of Greece*) brought all the Greek city-states under his control. His son, Alexander the Great, went on to conquer most of the Mediterranean world — including Persia and Egypt. He founded new cities, some of which were named after him. Alexander even extended his conquests to the Indus River valley. Although his empire collapsed shortly after his early death, his conquests helped to spread Greek culture throughout the ancient world.

Alexander the Great

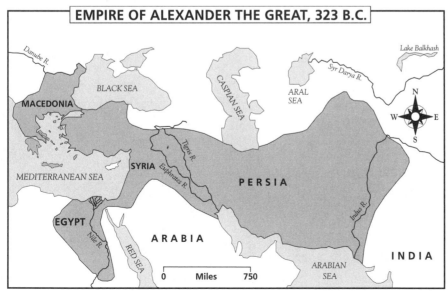

EMPIRE OF ALEXANDER THE GREAT, 323 B.C.

Danube R. · BLACK SEA · MACEDONIA · CASPIAN SEA · ARAL SEA · Syr Darya R. · Lake Balkhash · MEDITERRANEAN SEA · SYRIA · Tigris R. · Euphrates R. · PERSIA · Indus R. · EGYPT · Nile R. · RED SEA · ARABIA · INDIA · ARABIAN SEA · 0 Miles 750

His followers created separate kingdoms in Egypt, Persia, and the other areas Alexander had conquered. Greek immigrants, traditions, and use of the Greek language spread. An important new culture emerged. Known as **Hellenistic Culture,** it was a blend of Greek, Persian, Egyptian, and Indian influences.

THE LEGACY OF CLASSICAL GREECE

The roots of Western civilization can be traced in part to the contributions of the Greeks. Greek culture was characterized by a questioning spirit and a focus on human achievement.

Democracy. Athens developed the first known democratic government — a system in which citizens take part in governing.

Science and Mathematics. Key advances were made by Pythagoras, Euclid, and Archimedes — mathematicians who are still studied today.

Literature and History. The Greeks developed the first known dramas and historical writings.

ANCIENT GREEK ACHIEVEMENTS

Art and Architecture. The Greek ideal of beauty was based on harmony and proportion. In architecture, the Greeks built temples with beautiful columns, such as the Parthenon in Athens.

Philosophy. Greeks believed in the dignity of the individual. Through the use of reason, they believed humans could understand how the world worked. The greatest Greek philosophers were Socrates, Plato, and Aristotle.

THE ROMAN EMPIRE

One of the greatest civilizations to emerge in Europe was that of Rome. The Roman empire became a dominant force in the Western world for over 400 years.

THE IMPACT OF GEOGRAPHY

Italy is a long, narrow, boot-shaped peninsula extending into the Mediterranean. Rome was a city-state located on a fertile plain in the middle of Italy near the west coast. To the north, the Alps Mountains protected Rome and the rest of Italy from most invaders. The sea provided further protection against invaders, while serving as a route for Roman trade and expansion.

THE ROMAN REPUBLIC

The early Roman city-state contained two main social classes: **patricians** (*wealthy landowning families*) and **plebeians** (*small farmers, craftsmen, and merchants*). In early times, the Romans overthrew their king and made Rome into a **republic.** Rome was then governed by a patrician assembly known as the **Senate,** and elected officials, known as **Consuls.**

Definition

A republic refers to a state in which political power rests with its citizens and not a monarch. For example, the United States has a republican form of government.

During this period, the **Twelve Tables of Roman Law** were issued, mainly to protect the plebeians. The Twelve Tables covered civil, criminal, and religious law, and provided a foundation for later Roman law codes. Under Roman law, all citizens were equal under the law and innocent until proven guilty. Roman law played a major role in shaping later Western legal systems.

ROME EXPANDS TO AN EMPIRE

After conquering the rest of Italy, Rome defeated Carthage, its main rival in the Mediterranean. Carthage, a former Phoenician colony in North Africa, was completely destroyed. By 146 B.C., Rome dominated all of the Mediterranean world. The expansion of Rome changed its basic character. The Roman army became a professional force instead of a citizens' army. **Julius Caesar,** a general, conquered part of Gaul (*present-day France*) and Spain. He then marched his armies back to Rome itself. Caesar threatened to seize absolute power, but was assassinated in 44 B.C. Caesar introduced a new calendar which forms the basis for the calendar still in use today. Our month of July is named after him.

Roman General Julius Caesar leading an invasion of Britain.

THE PAX ROMANA

Caesar's nephew, who adopted the name **Augustus,** became the first Roman Emperor. Augustus began a long period of peace, known as the **Pax Romana** (*Roman peace*), which extended throughout Western Europe and the Mediterranean world. Rome's centralized political authority, trained officials, and traditions of law allowed it to govern its vast empire. The Romans built new public baths, aqueducts, stadiums, and other public buildings as centers of Roman culture. Romans generally respected local customs, promoted trade, and offered Roman citizenship throughout the empire.

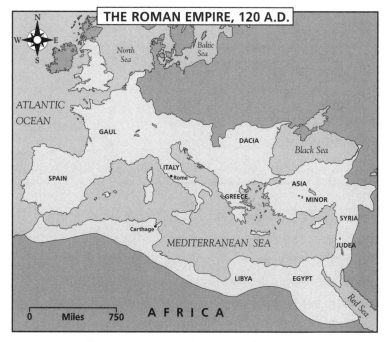

THE ROMAN EMPIRE, 120 A.D.

North Sea

Baltic Sea

ATLANTIC OCEAN

GAUL

DACIA

Black Sea

ITALY
Rome

SPAIN

ASIA

GREECE

MINOR

SYRIA

Carthage

MEDITERRANEAN SEA

JUDEA

LIBYA

EGYPT

Red Sea

0   Miles   750   A F R I C A

THE RISE OF CHRISTIANITY

The Romans permitted the existence of many religions throughout their empire. However, they expected conquered peoples to worship their emperor as divine (*godlike*). Jews and Christians refused, despite facing persecution and death. The Romans destroyed the Jewish temple in Jerusalem and drove many Jews out of Palestine (*Israel*). Many Jews fled to Europe, Persia, and North Africa. Despite attempts by the Roman government to eliminate Christianity, this new religion

The Colosseum, the largest amphitheater of the ancient world, where the slaughter of early Christians provided entertainment for the Roman masses.

slowly began to spread. In the 4th century, Emperor **Constantine** became a Christian. Not long afterwards, Christianity became the official religion of the Roman empire.

THE DECLINE OF THE ROMAN EMPIRE

Starting in the third century, the Roman empire began to weaken. Historians offer several explanations for this decline.

Political Weakness. Roman government depended on the abilities of the emperor, but many later emperors were corrupt and ineffective leaders.

Economic Problems. The costs of defending and administering the empire led to high taxes. Inflation and unemployment led to economic difficulties.

REASONS FOR THE DECLINE OF THE ROMAN EMPIRE

Military Decline. Later Roman armies relied on paid soldiers. These soldiers were often recruited from non-Roman peoples, who were less loyal than Roman citizens.

Invasions. Rome was under continual attack by fierce tribes from Northern Europe and Central Asia, such as the Goths and Huns. The Romans considered these tribes **barbarians**. Eventually, these tribes successfully invaded Rome.

THE COLLAPSE OF THE WESTERN EMPIRE

In 284 A.D., an attempt was made to reverse the empire's decline. To allow it to be governed more efficiently, the empire was divided into two parts: east and west. The Eastern empire was governed from Constantinople (*present-day Istanbul*). In the late 300s, the **Huns** from Central Asia began invading the Western empire. Germanic tribes, in turn, pushed towards Rome. A period of great turmoil followed, as invaders burned estates and seized Roman lands. In 476 A.D., the last Roman emperor was overthrown in the West. However, the Eastern empire, later known as the **Byzantine empire,** survived for another thousand years.

THE ENDURING LEGACY OF ROME

The Romans made many important and lasting contributions to world civilization.

Law. Roman concepts of justice, equality before the law, and natural law based on reason shaped later legal systems.

Language. Latin was the language of Rome. Several European languages evolved from it, including Spanish, French, Portuguese, Italian, and Romanian.

ACHIEVEMENTS OF THE ROMAN EMPIRE

Engineering. The Romans built thousands of miles of roads to connect distant parts of the empire with Rome. They built bridges and aqueducts to supply water to their cities. They developed concrete and the use of arches and domes.

Christianity. The adoption of the Christian religion by the Roman empire was a major turning point in the spread of Christianity.

ANSWERING THE FOCUS QUESTION •

Writing

Some of the achievements of the classical civilizations of the West were:

_____ (Persians)

_____ (Greeks)

_____ (Romans)

Directions: Complete each of the following vocabulary cards. Then answer the multiple-choice questions that follow.

CITY-STATE
Define the term:
Identify two city-states of Greece:

PAX ROMANA
Define the term:
What were its advantages?

1 Which ancient city-state had a democratic form of government?
1 Sparta
2 Athens
3 Sumer
4 Harappa

2 In both ancient Mesopotamia and the Roman republic, an important feature of life was the development of
1 a codified set of laws
2 aqueducts to provide water
3 social and political equality for all
4 a willingness to accept Christianity

3 The ancient Egyptian, Greek, and Roman civilizations were similar in that each
1 failed to develop a system of writing
2 established industrial societies
3 extended control over nearby peoples
4 adopted democratic political systems

4 The major reason for the *Pax Romana* was that the Romans
1 conquered the Mediterranean world
2 reached an agreement with Carthage
3 followed the Code of Hammurabi
4 allowed complete religious freedom

SECTION 2: CLASSICAL CIVILIZATIONS OF THE EAST

In this section you will read about the classical civilizations of India and China, which developed in the East.

THINK ABOUT IT •

What were the most important achievements of the classical civilizations of the East?

INDIA'S CLASSICAL AGE

About 1500 B.C., a people from Central Asia known as the **Aryans** arrived in India. The Aryans with their iron weapons and horse-drawn chariots, were excellent warriors. After conquering the peoples of the Indus River Valley, the Aryans moved into the Ganges River Valley, pushing the people living there further south.

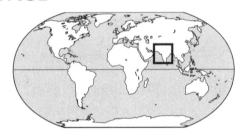

The Aryans brought their own religion to India, known as **Hinduism.** The Aryan conquest of India also led to the creation of a new social system, known as the **caste system.** Under this system, people were divided into five main social classes. Caste lines were rigid and based on birth. People were not permitted to marry outside their caste.

One group of people were labeled **Untouchables.** Untouchables were considered to be beneath all other social groups. They performed the lowliest tasks in society, such as sweeping the streets and cleaning up animal droppings. Hindus believed that people's souls were continually reborn. One's birth in a particular caste was therefore a punishment or reward for deeds in a past life.

THE MAURYAN EMPIRE

Around 500 B.C., a new religion emerged in India known as **Buddhism.** Buddhists believed in renouncing worldly desires to find inner peace. Missionaries carried Buddhist ideas throughout Southeast and East Asia. During this same period, a great empire emerged in northern India — the Mauryan empire. Its ruler, **King Asoka** (269 B.C. – 232 B.C.), converted from Hinduism to Buddhism. Asoka was a tolerant ruler who decreed that people of all religions should live peacefully with one another. He improved roads, built hospitals, and sent teachers throughout the empire to encourage education and spread the ideas of Buddhism. After Asoka's death, the Mauryan empire began to fall apart.

THE GUPTA EMPIRE, 320 A.D. – 535 A.D.

In 320 A.D., a new ruling family, the **Gupta,** emerged in northeastern India and united the territory around the Ganges. The Guptas encouraged peace, prosperity, and trade. Gupta emperors built universities and supported learning, the arts, and literature. Hindu scholars excelled at the sciences. Hindu mathematicians developed the concept of zero, the idea of infinity, and a decimal system. Artists painted colorful murals, while writers composed poems and plays in Sanskrit (*the literary and religious written language of*

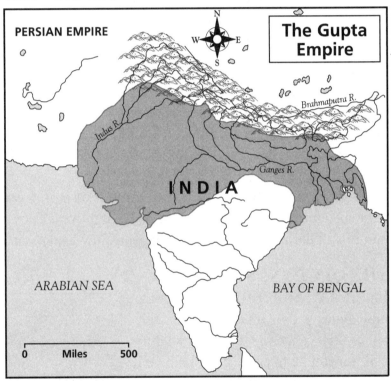

India). Because the Guptas were Hindus, the two centuries of Gupta rule are sometimes referred to as the **Golden Age of Hindu Culture.**

CHINA'S CLASSICAL AGE

Like the flowering of Greek and Roman culture in the West, China witnessed some of its greatest cultural achievements in this era. Chinese history is generally divided into periods based upon the **dynasty,** or ruling family, that governed China during that time. During the 1,200 years from 1027 B.C. to 220 A.D., China was ruled by three important dynasties: the Zhou, Qin, and Han.

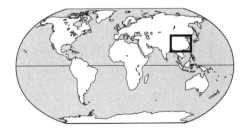

ZHOU DYNASTY, 1027 B.C. – 221 B.C.

The Shang had united the peoples living around the Huang He and the Yangtze River Valleys. In 1027 B.C., the Shang were conquered, marking the beginning of the Zhou Dynasty. Most ancient Chinese believed that their ruler was chosen to rule by Heaven, and that Heaven would also overthrow a bad ruler. The new Zhou ruler therefore justified his rule as the **Mandate of Heaven.** Later Chinese rulers continued to use this mandate as the basis of their authority.

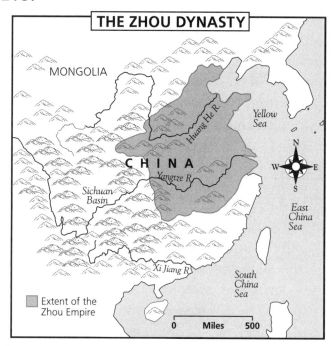

The greatest legacy of the Zhou Dynasty was the work of two philosophers, **Confucius** and **Lao-zi.** Both were deeply affected by the turmoil at the end of the Zhou dynasty. For Confucius, preserving the social order became the most important human value. He believed society depended on both good family relationships and good government. Lao-zi was the founder of a philosophy known as **Daoism.** Daoists believe nature has a *dao*, or way, in which it moves. They believe that people should respect nature and harmony, and accept things as they are — rather than trying to change them.

THE QIN DYNASTY (221 B.C. – 206 B.C.)

In 221 B.C., **Shih Huang-ti** began a new dynasty, the Qin (or *Ch'in*). Shih Huang-ti was the first Chinese ruler to call himself "emperor." Shih believed that people were not always good and required a strong ruler to keep control. Shih Huang-ti established a strong central government, built roads, and introduced a uniform system of writing and measurement throughout the empire. He also joined together several existing walls to form the **Great Wall of China.** The Great Wall pro-

The Great Wall of China

tected China from nomadic peoples to the northwest. Stretching over 1,500 miles, it stood 22 feet high and 15 feet thick and took thousands of laborers many years to complete. Shih Huang-ti's rule was so harsh that his dynasty came to an end just after his death.

HAN DYNASTY (206 B.C. – 220 A.D.)

The next dynasty, the Han, kept China unified for over four hundred years. Han emperors established examinations to select candidates for government service. Candidates were tested on Chinese history and Confucian philosophy. Examinations were open to all and viewed as a way for a few talented commoners to improve their social position. During the Han Dynasty, merchants established overland

A foreign merchant brings goods into China along the Silk Road.

trade routes to other centers of civilization. The **Silk Road** went through Central Asia, connecting China to the Middle East and Rome. Over these routes, China exported silk, iron, and bronze in exchange for gold, linen cloth, glass, ivory, animal hides, horses, and cattle. Contacts with India led to the introduction of Buddhism to China, which became popular during the Han Dynasty.

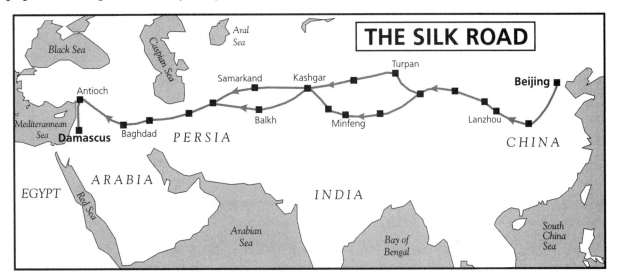

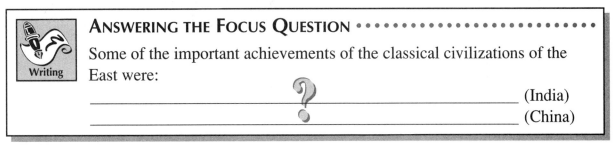

ANSWERING THE FOCUS QUESTION

Some of the important achievements of the classical civilizations of the East were:

_____ (India)

_____ (China)

Directions: Complete each of the following vocabulary cards. Then answer the multiple-choice questions that follow.

CASTE SYSTEM
Define the term.
What changes did it bring to India ?

DYNASTY
Define the term.
Name one Chinese Dynasty and
describe its achievements.

1   The caste system influenced traditional rural Indian society by
   1   creating fixed social classes   3   reducing the powers of landowners
   2   promoting political instability   4   contributing to greater social mobility

2   Confucianism in traditional China served to
   1   maintain social order
   2   encourage the desire for material wealth
   3   create ethnic unrest
   4   support democratic government

3   Early Chinese rulers based their authority to rule on the
   1   Code of Hammurabi   3   caste system
   2   Pax Romana   4   Mandate of Heaven

4   An important achievement of the Han Dynasty was the
   1   conquest of Japan
   2   introduction of the caste system into China
   3   birth of a democratic China
   4   establishment of examinations for government service

SECTION 3: MAJOR WORLD RELIGIONS EMERGE

In this section you will learn about one of the most important aspects of the classical era: the emergence of major new religions. These religions have had a tremendous influence over the lives of people in much of the world.

THINK ABOUT IT •

Thinking

What were the chief beliefs of the major religions that emerged during the classical era?

HINDUISM

Hinduism is largely based on the beliefs of the **Aryans,** invaders who came to the Indus River Valley from the Caucasus region. Like many religions, Hinduism serves as a guide, explaining everything a person should do from birth to death. Hinduism has no single holy book, but Hindu writings like the **Upanishads** and the **Bhagavad-Gita** provide guidance and inspiration. Hinduism remains the most popular religion of modern India. There are more than 700 million Hindus in the world today.

Gods. Hindus believe that there are many gods and goddesses. Each of these gods, however, is a manifestation (*form*) of one Supreme Being.

Reincarnation. Hindus believe that at death, a person's soul is reborn as another living thing. This creates an endless cycle of rebirth for each soul.

MAJOR BELIEFS OF HINDUISM

Karma. Karma refers to a person's behavior in life which Hindus believe determines that person's form in the next life. People who live a good life will be reborn in a higher caste. Those who do not are reborn in a lower caste.

Sacred Objects. Hindus believe the Ganges River is sacred and has the power to wash away sin and evil. The cow is also considered sacred, and religious Hindus do not eat beef.

BUDDHISM

The Buddhist religion began in India around 500 B.C. Prince **Siddhartha Gautama** (563–487 B.C.) lived a life of comfort and luxury. One day, he looked beyond the palace walls and was shocked by all the human suffering he saw. This prompted him to leave his wealth and family behind and to set out in search of truth. After six years, he concluded that all human suffering was caused by excessive desire. To end suffering, a person must come to accept the world as it is and block out selfish desires. Gautama became known as the **Buddha** or "Enlightened One." Missionaries carried his ideas throughout India and then on to China, Korea, and Japan.

A bronze statue of Buddha in Japan

Basic Philosophy. Buddhism is based on a philosophy of self-denial and meditation. Buddhists also believe in reincarnation.

Gods and Holy Books. Buddhists do not believe in a single Supreme Being (*God*). They also do not have a primary holy book. Their basic beliefs are found in books called **Sutras**.

MAJOR BELIEFS OF BUDDHISM

Four Noble Truths. These truths explain life's meaning. They explain that pain and suffering is caused by human desires such as for material wealth or selfish pleasures. Only by giving up these desires can a person find peace and harmony.

Eightfold Path. To give up human desires, Buddhists believe one should follow this path: give up wealth, act in a worthy manner, speak truthfully, live righteously, respect all living things, and meditate.

Nirvana. By following the Eightfold Path, an individual can escape the soul's endless reincarnations and achieve **nirvana** — a state of eternal bliss.

CONFUCIANISM

You have already learned that Confucianism is named after its founder, **Confucius** (551 – 479 B.C.). Confucius established a philosophy based on what he saw as the basic order of the universe. He urged people to follow traditional ways, which had worked well in the past. He believed these traditions could help maintain social peace and harmony. He further believed that the ruler must set an example for his subjects. Although Confucius did not write any books, his followers collected his sayings and later published them in the **Analects**.

Natural Order. There is a natural order to the universe and to human relationships. Each person has a role in society, which reflects his or her position in the universe.

Role of Each Person. Each person's social role brings a number of obligations. If everyone fulfills these roles by meeting their obligations, people and society will be in harmony.

MAJOR BELIEFS OF CONFUCIANISM

Relationships. In each relationship, there is a superior and an inferior. The superior must show love and responsibility, while the inferior must show loyalty and obedience.

Mandate of Heaven. If the ruler benefits his people and provides them with food and protection, then the people will obey their ruler, who will continue to hold the Mandate of Heaven (*the right to rule*).

For thousands of years, Confucianism was the official philosophy of the Chinese empire. Its emphasis on traditional values helped preserve Chinese civilization. Hopeful government candidates had to pass a demanding test based on the ideas of Confucius in order to be appointed to the emperor's service. Confucian ideals thus united all government officials and the Chinese upper classes as a whole. Confucianism also increased the importance of the family in Chinese life. The family served as a model for society, emphasizing performance of one's duties and good deeds.

One of many ceremonies held in China each year on September 28th in honor of Confucius.

CHRISTIANITY

Christianity began about 2,000 years ago in the Middle East. It is based on the beliefs and life of **Jesus Christ.** Jesus was born in Bethlehem, near Jerusalem. He preached forgiveness, mercy, and sympathy for the poor and helpless. However, the Romans regarded him as a troublemaker. Jesus was crucified by the Romans for claiming he was the Messiah or savior. After the death of Jesus, a band of his followers, known as the **Apostles,** helped to spread the new Christian religion. Many were attracted to the belief in an afterlife in which the poor and humble would be rewarded. Eventually, Christianity became the dominant religion of the Roman Empire. Today, it is the religion with the most followers in Europe, North America and Latin America.

The crucifixion of Jesus

MAJOR BELIEFS OF CHRISTIANITY

Role of Jesus. Christians believe Jesus was the son of God, and sacrificed himself to save humankind from punishment for their sins. Christians also believe that after his death, Jesus was resurrected and rose to Heaven.

Christian Conduct. Christians believe they will be saved and will go to Heaven after death if they have faith in Christ as their savior and treat others with love and respect.

The Christian Bible. The sacred book of Christianity consists of the **Old Testament** (*the Jewish Bible*), and the **New Testament**, which describes the life of Christ and the works of the Apostles.

ANSWERING THE FOCUS QUESTION •

The key beliefs of some major religions are

_____ (Hinduism)

_____ (Buddhism)

_____ (Confucianism)

_____ (Christianity)

Directions: Complete each of the following vocabulary cards. Then answer the multiple-choice questions that follow.

CONFUCIUS
Who was he?
What were some of his ideas?

SIDDHARTHA GAUTAMA
Who was he?
What were some of his ideas?

1 Which sacred book and religion are correctly paired?

1 Hinduism — Bhagavad-Gita
2 Judaism — New Testament
3 Christianity — Sutras
4 Buddhism — Old Testament

2 With which statement would Confucius most likely have agreed?

1 People should believe in only one God.
2 One should follow a life of self-denial and quiet meditation.
3 People who live a good life will go to Heaven after death.
4 People must fulfill their family and social responsibilities.

3 The religions of Judaism and Christianity share a common belief in

1 nirvana
2 monotheism
3 reincarnation
4 the role of Jesus

4 Buddhism teaches that salvation is earned by

1 following the Ten Commandments
2 worshipping only one God
3 learning to give up selfish desires
4 being baptized and confirmed

KEY TERMS, CONCEPTS, AND PEOPLE

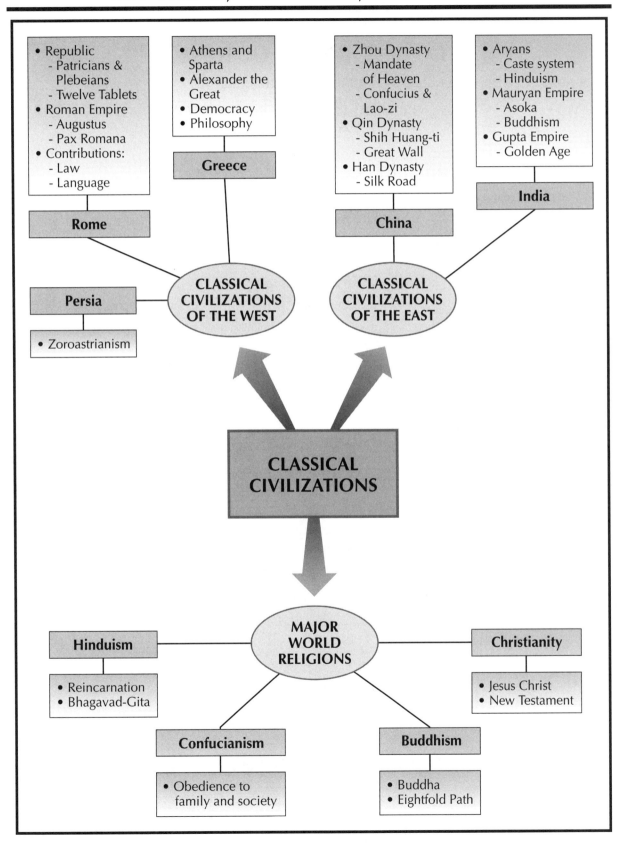

- Republic
  - Patricians & Plebeians
  - Twelve Tablets
- Roman Empire
  - Augustus
  - Pax Romana
- Contributions:
  - Law
  - Language

Rome

- Athens and Sparta
- Alexander the Great
- Democracy
- Philosophy

Greece

- Zhou Dynasty
  - Mandate of Heaven
  - Confucius & Lao-zi
- Qin Dynasty
  - Shih Huang-ti
  - Great Wall
- Han Dynasty
  - Silk Road

China

- Aryans
  - Caste system
  - Hinduism
- Mauryan Empire
  - Asoka
  - Buddhism
- Gupta Empire
  - Golden Age

India

CLASSICAL CIVILIZATIONS OF THE WEST

CLASSICAL CIVILIZATIONS OF THE EAST

Persia

- Zoroastrianism

CLASSICAL CIVILIZATIONS

MAJOR WORLD RELIGIONS

Hinduism

- Reincarnation
- Bhagavad-Gita

Confucianism

- Obedience to family and society

Buddhism

- Buddha
- Eightfold Path

Christianity

- Jesus Christ
- New Testament

SUMMARIZING YOUR UNDERSTANDING

COMPLETING AN OUTLINE

Directions: Use these headings to complete the outline below.

MAJOR WORLD RELIGIONS EMERGE
Buddhism
India
THE CLASSICAL CIVILIZATIONS
CLASSICAL CIVILIZATIONS OF THE WEST
The Roman Empire
Hinduism
The Greeks
The Persian Empire
Confucianism
China
Christianity
CLASSICAL CIVILIZATIONS OF THE EAST

TITLE: _____

I.   MAJOR DIVISION: _____

    A.   Sub-topic: _____

    B.   Sub-topic: _____

    C.   Sub-topic: _____

II. MAJOR DIVISION: _____

    A.   Sub-topic: _____

    B.   Sub-topic: _____

III. MAJOR DIVISION: _____

    A.   Sub-topic: _____

    B.   Sub-topic: _____

    C.   Sub-topic: _____

    D.   Sub-topic: _____

COMPLETING A GRAPHIC ORGANIZER

Select **one** major religion you have read about in this chapter and complete the following graphic organizer.

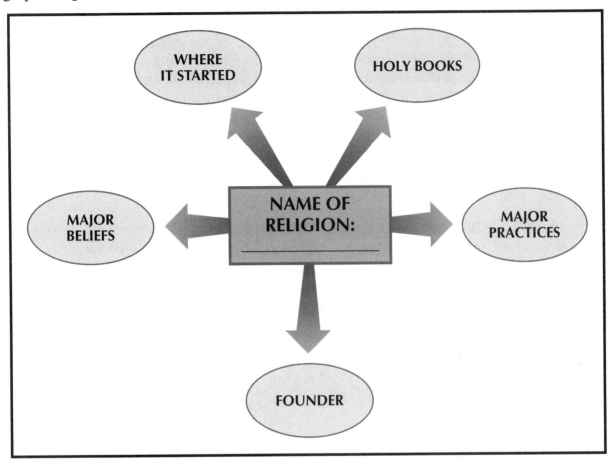

COMPLETING A TABLE

Test questions about civilizations often focus on their accomplishments. To answer these questions, keep in mind the accomplishments of each civilization. Use the following table to help you organize this information.

Name of Civilization	Time Period	Location	Major Accomplishments
Greek City-States			
Roman Empire			
Gupta Empire			
Zhou Dynasty			

SHARPENING YOUR TEST-TAKING SKILLS

INTERPRETING DIFFERENT TYPES OF DATA

Unlike multiple-choice questions, which ask you to choose an answer from a list, some examination questions require you to write out your answers. These more open-ended questions often begin with data that form part of the question. This data, in the form of a map, graph, chart, or written text, is followed by a question or a series of questions. Many of these questions will ask you to identify or to explain something.

◆ **"Identify" Questions.** In these questions, you are asked *to identify* one or more causes, features, or changes of something shown in the data.

◆ **"Explain" Questions.** This type of question calls for more than just identifying something. In this type of question, you are asked to *explain,* or *give reasons for something* by writing one or two sentences.

Look through the data carefully *before* answering these types of questions. If the data is a text, it may help to underline key terms. Look at the question and then review the data, or reread the document to find the information needed. Most often the question will focus on the main idea or most important aspect in the data.

I. THE WORLD'S FIRST CIVILIZATIONS

1   Based on the map, identify what geographical characteristic the world's earliest civilizations had in common.

_____

_____

_____

_____

_____

_____

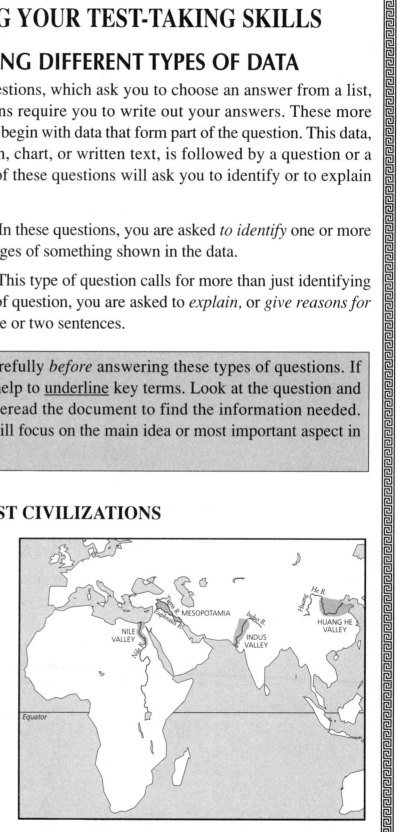

Notice that this question is just like the multiple-choice question in the previous chapter on page 47. The only difference is that here you do not have a list of possible answers to choose from.

"Our form of government does not enter into rivalry with the institutions of others. We do not copy them. It is time that we are called a democracy, for our government is in the hands of the many and not the few. While the law secures equal justice to all alike in their private disputes, excellence is also recognized. When a citizen is distinguished in any way, he is preferred in the public service — not as a matter of privilege, but as the reward of merit …. An Athenian citizen does not neglect the state because he takes care of his own household …. To sum up, I say that Athens is the school of Hellas [*Greece*]."

Speech by Pericles to the Athenians, 429 B.C.

1 According to this document, what was unusual about the government of Athens? _____

_____

_____

_____

To answer this kind of question, first read the document carefully. It is a speech by Pericles to the citizens of ancient Athens. From the first sentence, you can determine that he is talking about his city-state's form of government. The question asks you to identify how this form of government was unusual. The second sentence of the passage tells us that Athens does "not copy other states;" instead Athens sets an example for them. Then Pericles says that Athens' form of government is a democracy — rule by "the hands of the many and not of the few." This sentence holds the key to what was most unusual about Athenian government. Your task is to find this information and write it down as your answer in a simple sentence of two.

TESTING YOUR UNDERSTANDING

Test your understanding of this chapter by answering the following questions:

MULTIPLE-CHOICE QUESTIONS

1 The geography of Greece led to
   1 the development of transportation through the Alps Mountains
   2 a search for warm-water ports
   3 a dependence on trade with other peoples of the Mediterranean
   4 the establishment of trade barriers against other empires

2 A major reason for the decline of the Roman empire was that
   1 Europe came under Muslim control
   2 Rome was absorbed by the Byzantine empire
   3 invading barbarian tribes could no longer be stopped
   4 Carthage defeated the Roman navy

3 Which concept did Chinese emperors use to justify their right to rule?
   1 Pax Romana   3 Daoism
   2 karma   4 Mandate of Heaven

4 Ancient Egyptian, Greek, and Roman civilizations were all similar in that each
   1 failed to develop a system of writing   3 extended control over nearby peoples
   2 established industrial economies   4 adopted democratic political systems

5 Which person is correctly paired with the civilization to which he belonged?
   1 Asoka — Mesopotamia   3 Julius Caesar — Classical Greece
   2 Confucius — Zhou Dynasty   4 Socrates — Roman empire

6 Which event occurred last?
   1 Moses received the Ten Commandments
   2 Asoka established a powerful empire
   3 Rome was sacked by invaders
   4 The Neolithic Revolution began in Mesopotamia

7 "There are two ends not to be sought by a seeker of truth. They are the pursuit of desires, which is base, common, and unprofitable; and the pursuit of hardship, which is grievous and unprofitable. The Middle Way avoids both of these."

   The ideas contained in the above statement most clearly reflect the beliefs of which religion?
   1 Buddhism   3 Judaism
   2 Christianity   4 Confucianism

Base your answer to question 8 on the information in the box and your knowledge of global history.

> • the major agricultural products of India
> • the present population of China
> • the elevation of Mount Everest

8   This information can most likely be found in
1   an atlas
2   an almanac
3   a newspaper
4   a magazine

Base your answer to question 9 on the photograph to the right and your knowledge of global history.

9   Which statement best explains why this structure was built?
1   China sought to protect itself from outside invaders.
2   Rome needed to keep out Germanic tribes.
3   Persia sought a highway to other civilizations.
4   Chinese rulers needed to prevent peasants from escaping their harsh rule.

Base your answer to question 10 on the pie chart to the right and your knowledge of global history.

10   Which is a valid conclusion based on the information in the chart?
1   The city-state of Athens was a military dictatorship.
2   Life in Athens was based on the ideal of social equality.
3   Only some residents of Athens had the right to vote.
4   The majority of people in Athens had the right to vote.

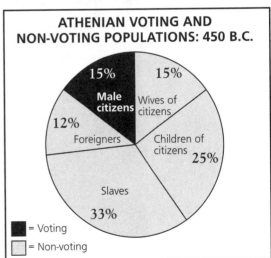

ATHENIAN VOTING AND NON-VOTING POPULATIONS: 450 B.C.

15% Male citizens
15% Wives of citizens
12% Foreigners
25% Children of citizens
33% Slaves

■ = Voting
□ = Non-voting

INTERPRETING DOCUMENTS

1. INTERPRETING A READING

> "First, they will not under any circumstances accept terms that would mean slavery for Greece. Secondly, they will fight you even if the rest of Greece submits. There is no use in asking if their numbers are adequate to enable them to do this. Suppose a thousand take the field, then that thousand will fight you."
>
> *— Demaratus advising Xerxes of Persia*
>
> "Our form of government does not copy the institutions of others. We do not imitate our neighbors, but are an example to them. We are called a democracy because the administration of our government is in the hands of the many and not of the few. Our laws afford equal justice to all alike in their private disputes, while advancement in public life is based on reputation and ability.
>
> *— Pericles*

1   Which speaker is discussing Sparta? _____

2   Citing specific historical examples, show how the ancient Greek city-states of Sparta and Athens were different. _____

2. INTERPRETING A MAP

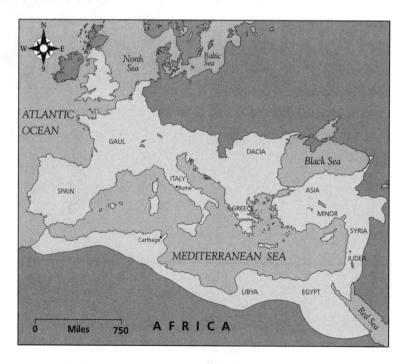

1   Which empire is shown on the map? _____

2   List **two** reasons for the decline of this empire.

    A. _____   B. _____

CHAPTER 6

NEW CENTERS OF CULTURE IN AN AGE OF TURMOIL, 500 TO 1200 A.D.

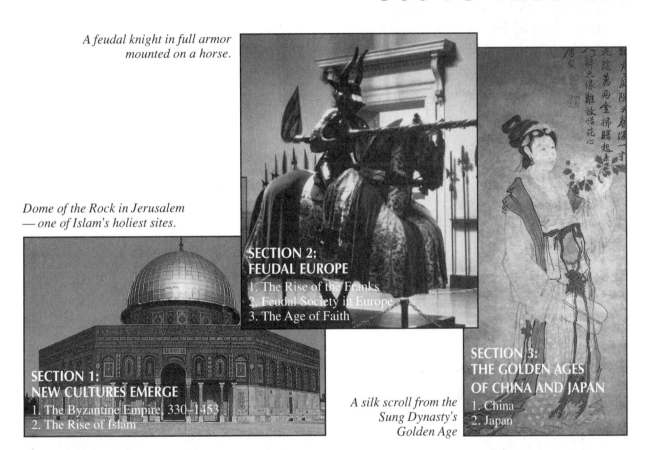

A feudal knight in full armor mounted on a horse.

Dome of the Rock in Jerusalem — one of Islam's holiest sites.

SECTION 2:
FEUDAL EUROPE
1. The Rise of the Franks
2. Feudal Society in Europe
3. The Age of Faith

SECTION 1:
NEW CULTURES EMERGE
1. The Byzantine Empire, 330–1453
2. The Rise of Islam

SECTION 3:
THE GOLDEN AGES
OF CHINA AND JAPAN
1. China
2. Japan

A silk scroll from the Sung Dynasty's Golden Age

	500	620	740	860	980	1100	1220
BYZANTIUM				BYZANTINE EMPIRE			
RUSSIA				EMERGENCE OF KIEVAN RUSSIA			
EUROPE			MIDDLE AGES:				
	BARBARIAN INVASIONS	RISE OF FRANKS		VIKING INVASIONS		CHRISTIAN CRUSADES	
MIDDLE EAST		ISLAMIC EXPANSION				ISLAMIC WORLD	
						SELJUK TURKS INVADE	
CHINA		T'ANG DYNASTY			SUNG DYNASTY		
JAPAN			HEIAN PERIOD				

WHAT YOU SHOULD FOCUS ON

In the late 400s, much of the world entered a period of great turmoil. In the West, the Roman empire collapsed. In the East, civil war followed the fall of the Han Dynasty in China. The following centuries were spent re-establishing law and order and preserving the cultural heritage of the ancient world in the face of constant warfare and invasion. The following four regions of the world experienced great changes:

Byzantium. The eastern part of the Roman empire continued for another 1,000 years under the name of the Byzantine empire. It preserved much of Roman and Greek culture, while it developed its own form of Christianity.

Middle East. A new religion, Islam, appeared in the 7th century. Arab nomads swept across Southwest Asia and North Africa, establishing a new Islamic empire.

CHANGES AFTER THE FALL OF ROME AND THE COLLAPSE OF THE HAN DYNASTY

Western Europe. Much of the Greek and Roman heritage was lost. Christianity became the main binding force. A new method of social and political organization emerged, known as feudalism.

China. Basic patterns of Chinese culture re-emerged after a period of civil war. China was also affected by the introduction of Buddhism from India. Meanwhile, Chinese culture spread to Japan.

In contrast to Western Europe, the civilizations of Byzantium, the Islamic world, and China each experienced a "Golden Age" in which arts and technology flourished. By the end of this era, the Crusades brought Europeans into greater contact with these other cultures. In studying this era, focus on the following questions:

Crusaders pray in a cathedral before leaving to battle Muslims in the Holy land.

➤ What were the main cultural achievements of this era?
➤ What role did the major religions — Christianity, Islam, Confucianism and Buddhism — play in the events of this period?
➤ What was feudalism, and how did it operate?

LOOKING AT GOVERNMENT

he Greek philosopher Aristotle once wrote that people are social beings who cannot live in isolation. People depend on one another and must live in groups or communities to survive, resulting in the need for government.

WHAT IS GOVERNMENT?

Our need to be with others has important consequences. All communities need to make rules to decide disputes among members and to protect themselves from others who may be hostile. The body given the authority to carry out these functions is known as the **government.** The word "govern" comes from the ancient Greek word for steering a ship. Just as a pilot guides a ship, a government guides the conduct and behavior of the members of a community in their dealings with themselves and outsiders.

WHAT FORMS DOES GOVERNMENT TAKE?

Throughout global history, governments have taken many forms. The following presents a chronological survey of some of the more important ones.

TRIBAL GOVERNMENTS

In primitive societies, people were often governed by a chief or tribal elders. Most often the chief or tribal elders were respected members of the tribe who had skills in warfare or were considered to have great wisdom. Because there were no written laws, people relied on oral traditions, customs, and the decisions of their leaders.

ANCIENT MONARCHIES

In the ancient civilizations of Mesopotamia, Egypt, India, China, and the Americas, one leader eventually emerged as an all-powerful king. Usually, the king claimed to act as a god, combining political and religious powers. The king extended his power over others when his armies conquered neighboring states.

DEMOCRACY

The ancient Athenians were the first to develop **democracy** — rule by the people. Citizens elected their leaders and made decisions directly by voting in a large assembly. For a democracy to work, citizens must have basic rights such as freedom of speech, freedom from unjustified imprisonment, and the right to a fair trial.

Egyptian Pharaoh and his queen (2520 B.C.)

FEUDALISM

Feudalism was a social and political system that often emerged in areas where central government was weak, such as in medieval Europe. The king relied on the services of his nobles, who were given nearly absolute power over their own local areas.

DIVINE RIGHT MONARCHY OR ABSOLUTISM

Louis XIV, absolute ruler of France, once remarked, "I am the state."

Under divine right monarchy, also known as **absolutism,** European rulers controlled their subjects by claiming to derive their authority from God. Writers like **Niccolo Machiavelli** and **Thomas Hobbes** believed human nature was essentially bad. A strong ruler was therefore needed to maintain order in society. In East Asia, similar traditions developed. Chinese emperors claimed to rule with the Mandate of Heaven. Emperor Shih-Huang-ti argued that because people were naturally bad, they needed a strong, absolute ruler to control them.

THE SOCIAL CONTRACT
AND CONSTITUTIONAL MONARCHY

John Locke's ideas greatly influenced America's ideas on government.

In the late 17th Century, **John Locke** proposed the **social contract** theory of government. According to Locke, a king ruled with the consent of his subjects. The subjects entered into a contract with the king, promising to obey him as long as he protected their rights. This system, in which the king governs according to a constitution, is known as a **constitutional monarchy.** If the king violated his subjects' rights, Locke argued, the people had a right to overthrow him.

TOTALITARIANISM

Totalitarianism is a 20th century system similar in some ways to earlier absolutism. A single dictator claims to rule in the name of the people. Individual citizens have no real rights. The government controls all aspects of public and private life. Modern technology has made totalitarianism far more ruthless than royal absolutism ever was. Hitler's Germany, Stalin's Soviet Union, and Mao's China were examples of totalitarian states.

MAJOR HISTORICAL DEVELOPMENTS

SECTION 1: NEW CULTURES EMERGE

In this section you will read about two new centers of culture that emerged during this period — the Byzantine and Arab empires.

THINK ABOUT IT •

What were the achievements of the Byzantine and Islamic cultures?

THE BYZANTINE EMPIRE, 330–1453

Because of the threats faced by Rome, in 330 A.D. Emperor Constantine moved the capital of the Roman empire from Rome to Byzantium — a Greek city in the eastern part of the empire. Constantine renamed the city **Constantinople** after himself.

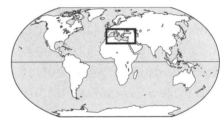

THE EMERGENCE OF THE BYZANTINE EMPIRE

Although the western half of the Roman empire collapsed in the 5th century, the eastern half of the empire, which became known as the **Byzantine empire,** survived for a thousand years beyond the fall of Rome. At the crossroads of Europe and Asia, the empire was a natural center for trade. Silk and spices from the east, furs from Russia, and grains, olives, and wines from the empire itself brought great wealth. The emperor held absolute power.

The Byzantines developed their own form of Christianity. They were greatly influenced by Greek culture, and spoke mainly Greek. The Bishop of Constantinople, known as the **Patriarch,** did not accept the Pope in Rome as his superior. The break between the two churches, became official in 1054 when each leader excommunicated the

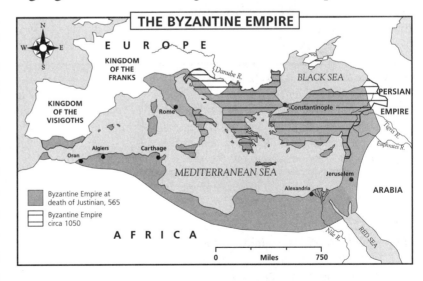

other. The eastern branch of the Christian church became known as the **Eastern Orthodox Church,** while the western church continued to be known as the **Roman Catholic Church.**

DECLINE OF THE BYZANTINE EMPIRE

In its early centuries, the Byzantine empire ruled over all of the Balkan Peninsula, the Middle East, and parts of Italy. The emperor ruled with a centralized army and bureaucracy (*government officials*). But the Byzantines were almost continuously at war with the Slavs, the Persians, and the Muslims. The empire eventually began to unravel from continuous attack. The final decline of the Byzantine empire began when city-states in northern Italy began to compete with Constantinople for Mediterranean trade. By the 1440s, the great Byzantine empire was reduced to a small area around the capital city itself. In 1453, the city of Constantinople was conquered by the Ottoman Turks.

THE BYZANTINE INFLUENCE ON RUSSIA

Russia began as an organized state in the 800s. A people known as the Slavs, from the forests north of the Black Sea, organized a kingdom centered in Kiev. Other Russian city-states, such as Moscow, developed to the north. Russian culture grew out of a blending of Slavic and Byzantine traditions. Byzantine trade with early Russian cities influenced Russia in significant ways. Byzantine culture, such as Orthodox Christianity and the Cyrillic alphabet, were introduced into Russia. In addition, the absolute power held by Byzantine emperors became a model for future Russian rulers. The roots of Eastern European culture can be traced to the contributions of the Byzantines.

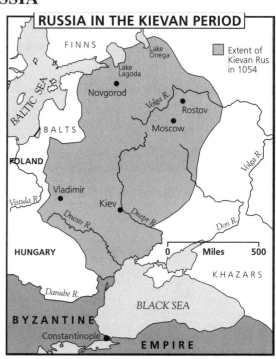

RUSSIA IN THE KIEVAN PERIOD

Extent of Kievan Rus in 1054

Preserved Ancient Cultures. The Byzantines preserved the rich cultural heritage of classical civilization: copies of ancient Greek and Roman texts were saved despite destruction in the West.

Code of Justinian. Emperor Justinian consolidated Roman laws into a single legal code which served as a guide on most legal questions. It greatly influenced later Western legal systems.

THE BYZANTINE LEGACY

New Form of Christianity. Eastern Orthodox Christianity was led by the Patriarch and the emperor in Constantinople, rather than the Pope in Rome.

The Arts. The Byzantines were renowned for their mosaics, painted icons, gold jewelry, and silks. Constantinople's cathedral, **Hagia Sophia**, is considered one of the world's most beautiful buildings.

THE RISE OF ISLAM

Warfare between the Byzantine and Persian empires interrupted overland trade routes from East Asia. Trade in spices, Chinese silks, and Indian cottons shifted to sea routes connecting India with Arabia and the Red Sea. Overland caravans carried goods up the western coast of the Arabian peninsula. Towns developed at oases along these caravan routes. **Mecca** emerged as one of the most important of these towns. In the 600s, a new religion — Islam — made its appearance on the Arabian Peninsula.

MOHAMMED: THE PROPHET OF ISLAM

The Islamic religion was founded by an Arab merchant named **Mohammed.** He had a vision that commanded him to convert the Arab tribes to believe in a single God, known in Arabic as **"Allah."** This was the same God worshiped by Jews and Christians. Mohammed started to preach his beliefs, and soon developed a large following.

Merchants in Mecca were jealous of Mohammed's growing influence. Fearing for his life, Mohammed fled from Mecca to the city of Medina in 622. This event, known as the **Hegira,** is the starting point of the Muslim calendar. In Medina, Mohammed became a popular religious leader. He gathered an army to retake Mecca in a **jihad** or "holy war." In 632, two years after recapturing Mecca, Mohammed died. His teachings were recorded by his followers in the **Qu'ran** (*Koran*), Islam's holiest book.

THE FIVE PILLARS OF FAITH

The Five Pillars of Faith are the basic religious duties that all followers of Islam, (*called Muslims*), must fulfill:

Confession of Faith
Muslims must affirm: "There is no God but Allah and Mohammed is his prophet."

Prayer
Muslims must pray five times a day, while facing the city of Mecca.

Charity
Muslims must give money to the poor and pay taxes to the mosque.

Fasting
During the month of Ramadan, Muslims cannot eat or drink during daylight hours.

Pilgrimage
If physically able, a Muslim must make a pilgrimage (*religious trip*) to Mecca.

THE ISLAMIC RELIGION SPREADS

Islam united the various Arab tribes with a common religion and language (*Arabic*). Arabs then set out on a "holy war" against non-believers. The Arabs were desert fighters who fought with enthusiasm to gain entry into Heaven. In contrast, the Byzantines and Persians were weak from centuries of fighting one another. Over the next century, the Arabs created a vast empire — an area even larger than the Roman empire at its height.

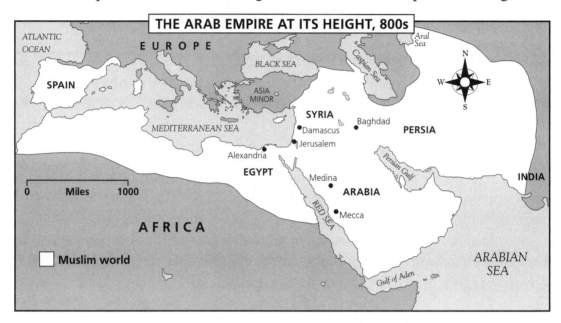

THE GOLDEN AGE OF ISLAMIC CULTURE

The Arabs were influenced by the great civilizations of the ancient Middle East, as well as by the achievements of Greece and Rome. Arab rulers were known as **caliphs.** The capital of the caliphate moved first to Damascus in Syria and then to Baghdad in Iraq. During these centuries, while learning was in decline in Western Europe, a **Golden Age** flourished in the Islamic world. Arabs tolerated Christians and Jews, who contributed to Arab scholarship and culture.

Mathematics. Arab scholars borrowed the concept of zero from India and developed Arabic numerals, which were eventually adopted by other cultures. These developments led to great advances in algebra and geometry.

Arts and Crafts. Mohammed forbade making images of God or people. Islamic art is largely made up of geometric designs, flowers, and stars. Their textiles, leather works, and rugs are highly prized.

ARAB CULTURAL ACHIEVEMENTS

Medicine. Arab doctors discovered that blood moves to and from the heart. They learned to diagnose many diseases, including measles and smallpox.

Architecture. Muslim rulers built beautiful palaces and mosques, richly decorated with mosaics, calligraphy, and geometrical designs.

ANSWERING THE FOCUS QUESTION •

Writing

Some achievements of the Byzantine and Islamic cultures were:

_____ (Byzantines)

_____ (Muslims)

Directions: Complete each of the following vocabulary cards. Then answer the multiple-choice questions that follow.

CODE OF JUSTINIAN
What was it?
What other code in ancient times was
similar to it?

ISLAM
Who was the founder of Islam?
List two beliefs or practices of the
Islamic religion.

1 One reason the Byzantine empire survived a thousand years beyond the fall of Rome was that it

   1 was the center of the Islamic world   3 was a natural center for trade

   2 had a democratic form of government   4 had the military protection of Russia

2 In the Byzantine and Roman empires, a key feature of life was

   1 a set of codified laws   3 social and political equality

   2 the Islamic religion   4 a civil service examination

Base your answers to questions 3 and 4 on the passage below and your knowledge of global history.

> **IN THE NAME OF ALLAH**
> **THE COMPASSIONATE, THE MERCIFUL**
> Praise be to Allah, Lord of the Creation,
> The Compassionate, the Merciful,
> King of the last Judgment!
> You alone we worship,
> and to You we pray for help

3 People who accept the beliefs stated in this passage practice

   1 polytheism   3 ancestor worship

   2 monotheism   4 animism

4 In which book can this passage be found?

   1 New Testament   3 Talmud

   2 Bhagavad-Gita   4 Qu'ran

SECTION 2: FEUDAL EUROPE

In this section you will read about what historians often call the **Middle Ages** or **Medieval Period.** This is a period of European history which lasted from the fall of Rome in 476 A.D. to the 1400s. During this period, many important changes took place in Western Europe.

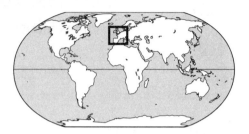

THINK ABOUT IT •

What do you know about the social, economic, and political characteristics of European feudalism?

BARBARIAN INVASIONS

Even in the days when the Roman empire was at its height, Germanic tribes like the Goths, Vandals, and Franks lived beyond Rome's frontiers. The Romans considered these peoples "barbarians." In the 4th century, a war-like tribe known as the **Huns** moved from Central Asia to Europe, pushing the Germanic tribes westward into the Roman empire. Eventually, these tribes defeated the Romans, causing the empire's collapse. The barbarian tribes then established new kingdoms in

many parts of Western Europe. They mixed their own customs and beliefs with what they learned from the Romans, and gradually adopted Christianity.

The constant migrations and warfare of this period disrupted trade and made travel unsafe. Bridges and roads fell into disrepair. Cities, towns, and villages were abandoned. Shortages of food and other goods grew. People gave up their interest in learning. Churches and monasteries became the only places with people who could read and write.

CHARLEMAGNE AND THE FRANKS

The Franks established the largest of the new Germanic king-doms. **Charlemagne** became king of the Franks in 768. He expanded the Frankish practice of giving land to his nobles in exchange for their promises of loyalty and service. At the same time, the nobles gave land to those below them in exchange for similar promises. Peasants put themselves in service to their local lords for security. Charlemagne expanded the Frankish kingdom to include present-day France, Germany, Holland, Belgium, and northern Italy. He resisted the further expansion of the Muslims who had conquered Spain. In 800, he was crowned Holy Roman Emperor by the Pope. Although his empire did not last, Charle-magne established the social, cultural, and political foundations for much of Western Europe for the next several centuries.

Charlemagne

FEUDAL SOCIETY IN EUROPE

To protect themselves from violence and provide for basic economic needs, people throughout Western Europe adopted the system used by the Franks. This new arrangement became known as **feudalism.** Feudalism in Europe was characterized by a number of key social, economic, and political relationships.

A SOCIAL SYSTEM

A major characteristic of feudal soci-ety was the development of a strict class structure based on the control of land and military power. Local nobles (*lords*) were given land by their rulers in exchange for military service. The lords had small armies of their own made up of **knights** (*armed warriors on horseback*). People were born as serfs or lords and could not change their social position.

Each feudal knight was a skilled warrior.

AN ECONOMIC SYSTEM

During the Middle Ages, most people lived on manors. A **manor** consisted of the lord's house and the peasants living around it. Each manor produced its own food, clothing, and shelter. **Serfs** (*peasants*) gave their lord part of their harvest in return for the use of land and other services they needed. In exchange, the lord protected the serfs from attacks by out-siders. Each lord had almost complete power over the serfs who lived on his manor. Serfs were bound to the land and had no voice in most matters.

A POLITICAL SYSTEM

Under the feudal system, the leading nobles controlled political life. The king relied on them for his armies, and they often fought among themselves or challenged the king's authority. Through warfare, feudal lords defended their estates, seized new territories, and increased their wealth. Civil wars were frequent, and powerful nobles often grabbed the throne for themselves.

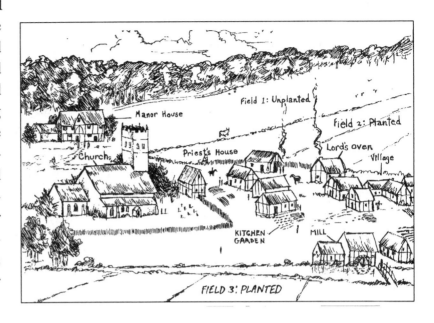

THE AGE OF FAITH

ROLE OF THE ROMAN CATHOLIC CHURCH

During the Middle Ages, the Roman Catholic Church was the single most powerful organization in Western Europe. There were many reasons for this.

REASONS FOR THE CHURCH'S POWER

The Role of Faith. People were very religious. They believed the Church represented God and held the power to send a person to Heaven or Hell. Most felt united by their common faith.

Power and Wealth. Many nobles left land to the Church when they died, hoping to gain entry into heaven. The Church became Europe's largest landowner. Church wealth also increased through **tithes** (*church taxes*).

Center of Learning. The Church was the main center of learning. Church officials were usually the only people who could read and write. Rulers often relied on Church officials, since they were the most educated people.

THE CRUSADES

The power of the Church can be seen in its ability to organize the Crusades — a series of wars to recapture the Holy Land from Muslim rulers. For hundreds of years, Christian pilgrims had visited Jerusalem, where the sacred events depicted in the Bible were believed to have occurred. However, early in the 11th century, the Seljuk Turks took control of the "Holy Land," and drove out Christian pilgrims. Shocked and angered, the Pope called on all Christians in Europe to unite and fight a holy **Crusade.**

Seven Crusades, fought over the next two centuries, were the result. The Crusades brought rulers and nobles from different parts of Europe together in a common cause. Although the Crusades never achieved more than temporary control of Jerusalem, the Crusades had many important effects:

THE EFFECTS OF THE CRUSADES

New Ideas and Products. Europeans had greater exposure to new ideas, such as the use of zero in mathematics, and to foreign products, such as silk, rice, spices, coffee, perfumes, cotton cloth, raisins, and glass mirrors.

Increased Trade. The European demand for foreign products, like spices, sugar, lemons and rugs eventually led to increased trade with other parts of the world.

Growth of Intolerance. The Crusades led to the Christian persecution of Jews and Muslims, as well as to the Muslim persecution of Christians.

ANSWERING THE FOCUS QUESTION •

Writing

The major characteristics of European feudalism were:

_____ (Social characteristics)

_____ (Economic characteristics)

_____ (Political characteristics)

Directions: Complete each of the following vocabulary cards. Then answer the multiple-choice questions that follow.

CHARLEMAGNE
Who was Charlemagne?
What was his importance ?

CRUSADES
What were the Crusades?
Identify one of their effects.

1   "Western Europe went into a long, deep sleep. Learning was found only among the religious orders. Fear and chaos reigned." This quotation best describes the

1   rise of Christianity   3   the Crusades
2   the collapse of the Roman empire   4   the Black Death

2 Feudal societies are generally characterized by
   1   an exchange of land for services
   2   a representative government
   3   widespread economic opportunity
   4   the protection of individual rights

3 The manor system and feudal ties are characteristics of the
   1   Middle Ages in Europe
   2   Neolithic Revolution
   3   Roman empire
   4   Byzantine empire

4 Which is the most valid generalization about the Crusades?
   1   They led to permanent Christian control of the Holy Land.
   2   They eventually led to increased trade between Europe and Asia.
   3   They brought European influence to Africa.
   4   They promoted religious freedom.

SECTION 3: THE GOLDEN AGES OF CHINA AND JAPAN

In this section you will learn about the flourishing of two important cultures in East Asia — China and Japan. The same centuries as the Middle Ages in Western Europe witnessed Golden Ages in these two advanced civilizations.

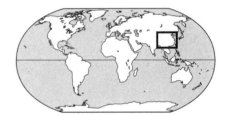

THINK ABOUT IT •

What accomplishments did China and Japan achieve during their Golden Ages?

Thinking

CHINA

THE WARRING KINGDOMS

Like Western Europe after the decline of the Roman empire, China entered a long period of unrest after the collapse of the Han Dynasty. As in the West, the advance of the Huns helped to hasten the collapse. Several warring kingdoms arose, leading to a decline in science, the arts, and learning in general.

T'ANG DYNASTY, 618–907

By the early 600s, this period of civil unrest came to an end with the rise of the T'ang Dynasty. During the T'ang period, China experienced a **Golden Age.** T'ang rulers re-united China and brought peace and prosperity. They ruled over an immense empire of more than 50 million people. During this period, China expanded into Korea, Manchuria and parts of Central Asia.

The examination system was re-established and Confucianism provided the empire with a guiding philosophy. Architecture, sculpture, painting, and porcelain all made great advances. The Chinese developed a unique method of gardening designed

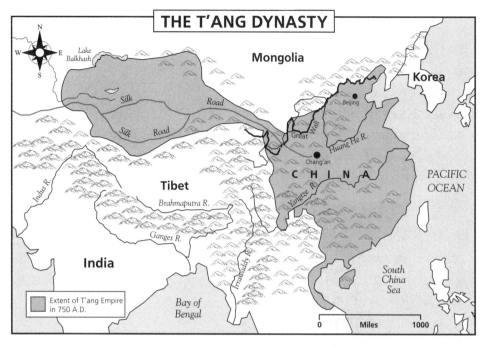

THE T'ANG DYNASTY

Mongolia

Korea

Beijing

Silk Road

Great Wall

Huang He R.

Chang'an

C H I N A

PACIFIC OCEAN

Lake Balkhash

Silk Road

Tibet

Brahmaputra R.

Indus R.

Ganges R.

Yangtze R.

Irrawaddy R.

India

South China Sea

Extent of T'ang Empire in 750 A.D.

Bay of Bengal

0   Miles   1000

for peaceful contemplation — making use of streams, rocks, and trees. T'ang China also developed block printing, so that copies of Confucian texts could be printed.

SUNG DYNASTY, 960–1279

The T'ang dynasty ended in 907. The Sung Dynasty arose soon afterwards to take its place. Sung China remained the most populous and advanced civilization of its time. Merchants, craftspeople, and scholars lived in large towns and cities. The capital of China housed more than a million people. The Chinese engaged in trade with many other parts of the world. Caravans carried Chinese silks across Central Asia. Large ships brought Chinese goods to Korea, Japan, Southeast Asia, and India. Sung China also continued to build upon the cultural achievements of the T'ang and introduced many inventions that later influenced the rest of the world.

T'ang artists often painted with black ink on silk paper.

ACHIEVEMENTS OF THE T'ANG AND SUNG DYNASTIES

Technology. Block printing, the crossbow, gunpowder, and the abacus (*a machine that counts beads for arithmetic*) were first developed in China during the T'ang and Sung dynasties.

Compass. The Chinese discovered that a magnetized needle floating in a water bowl always points north-south. Traders at sea used the compass to determine their direction when sailing.

The Arts. Chinese artists perfected the art of making porcelains and painting with black ink on silk paper. Chinese poets and historians wrote important works.

JAPAN

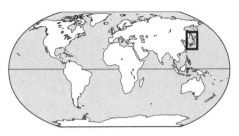

Like China, Japan also experienced a flourishing of arts and culture in these centuries. Society in earliest Japan revolved around **clans** — groups of families who worshiped the same gods, had common ancestors, and followed the same chief. By the 5th century, the leader of one clan unified the country and established himself as the emperor. The emperor claimed to be descended directly from the Sun Goddess.

CHINA'S INFLUENCE ON JAPAN

The Imperial Court, with officials bowing to the Emperor.

Because of Japan's nearness to China, it was greatly influenced by Chinese ideas, culture, and technology. Scholars and merchants brought Chinese culture to Japan, including their method of writing, Confucianism, and Buddhism, which had spread from India to China. Chinese culture influenced Japanese styles and tastes, including such fields as music, art, pottery, and cooking.

The Japanese emperor claimed absolute power, like the emperor of China, and built a capital city. However, Japanese society was never an exact copy of China. The Japanese rejected several Chinese practices. For example, the Japanese never adopted the Chinese idea that a ruler could be overthrown by the Mandate from Heaven. This was because the Japanese believed their emperor was directly descended from the Sun Goddess. The Japanese also had unique religious traditions, like **Shinto,** the worship of spirits found in nature.

JAPAN'S GOLDEN AGE: THE HEIAN PERIOD, 794–1185

During the **Heian period,** Japan's "Golden Age," members of leading noble families spent much of their time at the imperial court with the emperor. Art and literature flourished. One of the earliest novels ever written and a classic of Japanese literature, the *Tale of Genji,* was completed in 1008 by **Lady Murasaki,** a member of the court. The novel tells the story of Genji, the emperor's son, and his many romances and adventures at the imperial court. As time passed, the emperors of Japan gradually freed some nobles from their tax burdens, allowing them to establish large private estates. By the end of the Heian period, noble landowners began to raise their own private armies of warriors, known as **samurai.** The imperial government, collecting less taxes, grew weaker and was unable to prevent the nobles from fighting one another for power and control.

ANSWERING THE FOCUS QUESTION •

Writing

Some major accomplishments of China and Japan during their Golden
Ages were:

_____ (China)

_____ (Japan)

Directions: Complete each of the following vocabulary cards. Then answer the multiple-choice questions that follow.

T'ANG DYNASTY
When was it?
List two of its accomplishments.

SAMURAI
Who were the samurai?
Which social class in feudal Europe was similar to the samurai?

1   Which aspect of Chinese culture was never adopted by the Japanese?
  1   the Mandate of Heaven   3   ceramics
  2   eating rice   4   Buddhist beliefs

Base your answer to question 2 on the information below and your knowledge of global history.

> • Block printing
> • Development of the abacus
> • Invention of the compass

2   The above achievements were accomplishments of the
  1   T'ang and Sung Dynasties   3   Byzantine empire
  2   Heian period in Japan   4   Gupta empire

3   The traditional Japanese concept of the role of the emperor and the Chinese belief in
    the Mandate of Heaven were both based on
  1   the democratic election of rulers
  2   a division of power between the nobility and the emperor
  3   the belief that political power comes from a divine source
  4   a constitution that defines individual rights

4   The samurai of Japan were similar to which social class in Western Europe?
  1   knights   3   lords
  2   serfs   4   townspeople

KEY TERMS, CONCEPTS, AND PEOPLE

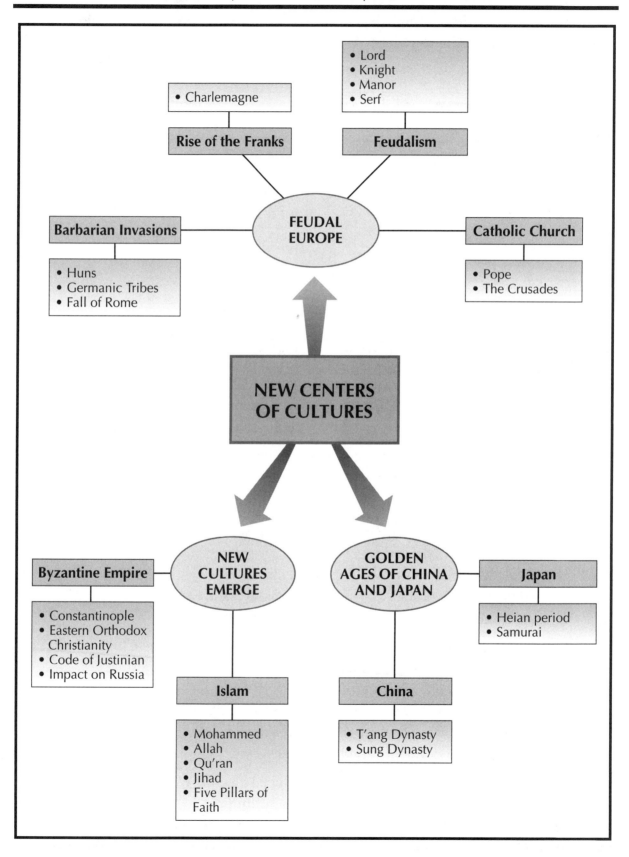

- Lord
- Knight
- Manor
- Serf

- Charlemagne

Rise of the Franks

Feudalism

Barbarian Invasions

FEUDAL EUROPE

Catholic Church

- Huns
- Germanic Tribes
- Fall of Rome

- Pope
- The Crusades

NEW CENTERS OF CULTURES

Byzantine Empire

NEW CULTURES EMERGE

GOLDEN AGES OF CHINA AND JAPAN

Japan

- Constantinople
- Eastern Orthodox Christianity
- Code of Justinian
- Impact on Russia

- Heian period
- Samurai

Islam

China

- Mohammed
- Allah
- Qu'ran
- Jihad
- Five Pillars of Faith

- T'ang Dynasty
- Sung Dynasty

SUMMARIZING YOUR UNDERSTANDING

COMPLETING AN OUTLINE

Directions: Use these headings to complete the outline below.

NEW CULTURES EMERGE
The Rise of Islam
Feudal Society in Europe
The Rise of the Franks
China
NEW CENTERS OF CULTURE
FEUDAL EUROPE
Japan
The Age of Faith
GOLDEN AGES IN CHINA AND JAPAN
The Byzantine Empire
Barbarian Invasions

TITLE: _____

I. MAJOR DIVISION: _____

    A. Sub-topic: _____

    B. Sub-topic: _____

    C. Sub-topic: _____

    D. Sub-topic: _____

II. MAJOR DIVISION: _____

    A. Sub-topic: _____

    B. Sub-topic: _____

III. MAJOR DIVISION: _____

    A. Sub-topic: _____

    B. Sub-topic: _____

COMPLETING A GRAPHIC ORGANIZER

The collapse of the Roman empire was followed by a period of chaos and disorder. Complete the following graphic organizer describing the new social system that arose in Western Europe as a result of the fall of the Roman empire.

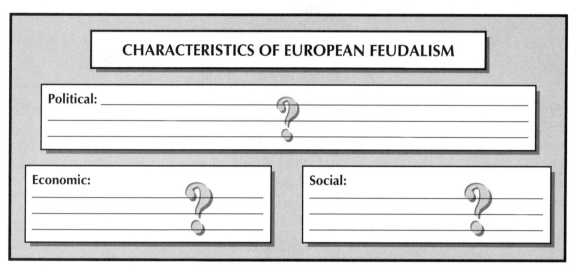

CHARACTERISTICS OF EUROPEAN FEUDALISM

Political: _____

Economic: _____

Social: _____

COMPLETING A PARAGRAPH FRAME

The T'ang and Sung Dynasties of China, the Byzantine empire, and the Arab Islamic empire made many important contributions. Select **one** of these cultures and **show how** it made a lasting contribution.

Selection: An important contribution of the _____ was _____ _____.

Fact(s)/Example(s): _____ _____ _____.

Link: _____ _____ _____.

Closing: _____ _____ _____.

LEARNING TO WRITE GOOD PARAGRAPHS

On some global history examinations, you may be asked to write an essay. Because of the importance of good writing in answering essay questions, this section looks a little more closely at the process of writing.

After you have developed a plan for your essay, you must put it into written form. Each major heading of your outline will become one or more paragraphs. As you know, a **paragraph** is a group of related sentences that deal with the same topic or theme. A good paragraph displays three important characteristics:

UNITY   COMPLETENESS   ORDER

Let's examine each of these characteristics in greater detail.

UNITY

Every paragraph should be unified — all of the sentences in the paragraph should deal with a single topic, even though they might deal with different aspects of that topic. Sentences that are not directly related to the topic of the paragraph should be moved to other paragraphs. Writers use several techniques to give a paragraph unity. They often use a topic sentence to identify — *in a single sentence* — what the main idea of the paragraph is. Through proper planning, all sentences in a paragraph should be clearly related to its topic sentence. Good writers may also repeat key terms throughout the paragraph. Notice how many times *slavery* or *slaves* is used to unify the paragraph below:

Slavery played an important role in ancient times. Slaves, for example, built the Egyptian pyramids and other wonders. The Bible says the ancient Hebrews were enslaved in Egypt. Later civilizations also depended on slavery. Ancient Athens, for example, was a democracy, but only free citizens could participate in government. Most work was performed by slaves. Slavery also affected ancient Rome. As Rome grew, wealthy landowners bought large numbers of slaves. These slaves were captured foreigners or Romans sold into slavery to pay off debts. Slaves grew most of Rome's food, performed household tasks, and even made goods. Some historians believe this over-reliance on slavery weakened Rome and helped lead to its collapse.

COMPLETENESS

A second characteristic of a good paragraph is **completeness**. Each paragraph should thoroughly develop the idea expressed in its **topic sentence**. How much explanation is needed will depend upon the subject. In general, you should provide enough details and supporting facts for your reader:

(1) to understand the main idea of your topic sentence, and

(2) to have enough details to conclude that your main idea could be correct.

To see if your idea is complete, pretend you are the reader and re-read your own paragraph. Does it meet the criteria for completeness, or do you need to add more information to make your point clear to your reader?

How long should a paragraph be? The answer really depends. If there is not enough relevant information presented in the paragraph to completely support the main idea, then the paragraph is probably too short. If the paragraph is very long, it may deal with too many aspects of the same topic and should probably be broken up. Following is a paragraph with a topic sentence and details that support it:

> Modern civilization owes a large debt to the ancient Greeks. Athenians developed the world's first democracy, or system of self-government. The United States and other countries around the world now enjoy this system of government. The ancient Greeks also laid the foundations for modern scholarship and art. Their philosophers asked questions about how the world worked and how humans should behave. Two of their philosophers, Plato and Aristotle, are still studied today. The Greeks wrote the first histories, dramas and comedies. They built beautiful buildings with columns and pleasing proportions, which are still widely copied.

• Do you think this paragraph is complete?

• Do the details show that modern civilization owes a large debt to the ancient Greeks?

ORDER

All the sentences of the paragraph should be presented in a **logical order**. In other words, the paragraph should move in a consistent direction. This is one of the most essential aspects of the task of writing. The direction in which the paragraph will move will depend upon the purpose of the paragraph.

Below are some the most common ways for logically presenting information in a paragraph.

★ **Sequential (*Chronology*).** This type of paragraph presents a series of events or steps in a process in the order in which they have occurred or should occur.

★ **From General to Specific.** This kind of paragraph opens with a general topic sentence and then provides examples or details to explain it. Examples are organized from the most important to the least, or from the least important to the most. Sometimes the topic sentence is restated in different words as a conclusion at the end.

★ **From Specific to General.** A paragraph may also start with a series of examples or details that lead to a more general conclusion. The conclusion at the end of the paragraph can serve as the topic sentence.

★ **Parts to a Whole.** Here, the purpose of the paragraph is to identify or describe a number of "parts" to something. The parts should be described in any order that will make sense to the reader. Often, we start with the least important so we can end the paragraph with the item having the most importance.

★ **Cause-and-Effect.** Another way to organize a paragraph is to begin with an effect, stated in the topic sentence, followed by its causes. The topic sentence could be stated as a question, such as "Why did the Roman Empire decline?" or as a statement: "There were many reasons why the Roman Empire declined." The rest of the paragraph would then explain causes of the decline of the Roman Empire.

Besides organizing sentences into the most logical order, good writers rely on **transition words** to help make this order more obvious. Transition words serve as signposts, letting readers know what to expect.

Function	Transitional Phrase
To explain a new point about the same idea or topic	*Moreover in addition, also, furthermore, then, similarly, again, next, secondly, finally*
To introduce an example	*For example, thus, to illustrate, in this case*
To introduce a conclusion or effect	*Therefore, in conclusion, thus, to sum up, as a result, in consequence*
To mention a contrast or qualification	*Nevertheless, on the other hand, nonetheless, however, despite*

TESTING YOUR UNDERSTANDING

Test your understanding of this chapter by answering the following questions:

MULTIPLE-CHOICE QUESTIONS

1 An important achievement of the Golden Age of Islamic culture was the
  1   spread of democratic government
  2   increased participation of women in government
  3   invention of the compass
  4   development of Arabic numerals

2 In Western Europe, which development was a cause of the other three?
  1   warfare disrupted trade
  2   travel became unsafe because of violence
  3   cities, towns, and villages were abandoned
  4   the Roman empire fell to barbarians

3 After the fall of Rome, the eastern portion of the Roman empire became known as the
  1   Persian empire   3   Mongol empire
  2   Byzantine empire   4   Gupta empire

4 In European feudal society, an individual's social status was generally determined by
  1   birth   3   individual abilities
  2   education and training   4   physical characteristics

5 Which statement best describes the role of the Roman Catholic Church in Western Europe during the Middle Ages?
  1   The Church encouraged individuals to question authority.
  2   Church leaders were involved solely in spiritual activities.
  3   The Church gave away most of its wealth to the poor.
  4   The Church provided a sense of stability, unity, and order.

6 What did both the caste system in India and the feudal system in Europe have in common?
  1   belief in monotheism   3   hereditary social classes
  2   belief in social equality   4   democratic government

7 One similarity between the cultures of traditional China and Japan was that
  1   their emperors claimed to have divine authority
  2   religion played a minor role
  3   social mobility was encouraged
  4   all citizens helped elect their political leaders

8 Which pair of events is arranged in correct chronological order?

1   Fall of the Roman empire
    T'ang Dynasty in China

3   Buddhist religion begins in India
    Neolithic Revolution

2   Japan's Heian period
    The start of the Roman empire

4   Mauryan empire begins in India
    Rise of the Phoenicians

Base your answer to question 9 on the map and your knowledge of global history.

9 According to the map, when did Christianity first reach Africa?

1   by 400 A.D.

3   by 1100 A.D.

2   by 800 A.D.

4   following 1100 A.D.

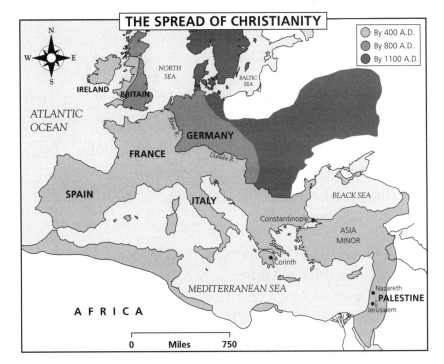

THE SPREAD OF CHRISTIANITY

○ By 400 A.D.
● By 800 A.D.
● By 1100 A.D.

Base your answer to question 10 on the timeline below and your knowledge of global history.

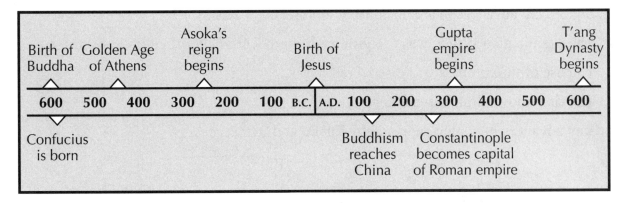

10 According to the timeline, which event occurred during the 2nd century A.D.?

1   Confucius was born

2   Asoka's reign began

3   Buddhism reached China

4   Constantinople became the capital of the Roman empire

INTERPRETING DOCUMENTS

I. INTERPRETING A TIMELINE

570	622	632	700s
Mohammed is born in Mecca	Fearing for his life, Mohammed flees to Medina	Mohammed dies, and his followers select a new leader.	The Arabs invade North Africa and Europe, and spread Muslim culture

1 Circle the theme of global history represented by the timeline:

Rise of the   Rise of Islam   Birth of
Roman empire   Christianity

2 Using specific evidence, identify and describe **one** effect of the developments shown on the timeline. _____

II. CATEGORIZING INFORMATION

Identify similarities and differences between the Golden Age of the Classical Greek Period and the T'ang and Sung Dynasties by writing the numbers of the listed characteristics in the appropriate places on the circles below.

1 Democracy developed as a form of a government

2 A time of general peace and prosperity

3 Significant advances in architecture, sculpture, and painting

4 The examination system was used for selecting government officials

5 The use of the compass was discovered

6 The first known dramas were developed

7 Key advances in math were made by Euclid and Pythagoras

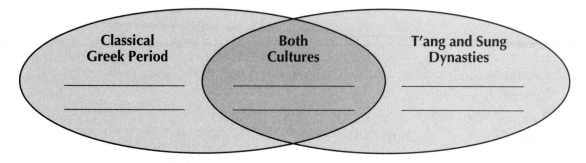

CHAPTER 7

WARRIORS ON HORSEBACK AND THE REVIVAL OF EUROPE, 1200 TO 1500

SECTION 1:
THE KINGDOMS OF AFRICA

1. Geographical Setting
2. The West African Kingdoms
3. Other African States

A gold pendant from the Kingdom of Mali.

SECTION 3:
THE RESURGENCE OF EUROPE

1. The Decline of Feudalism
2. The Renaissance
3. The Protestant Reformation

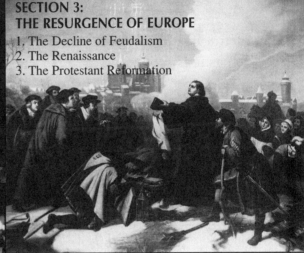

Martin Luther burns a decree of the Pope.

SECTION 2:
THE WARRIOR STATES OF ASIA

1. The Mongol Empire
2. Japan's Feudal Period, 1200 to 1600

Modern-day warriors dressed as samurai.

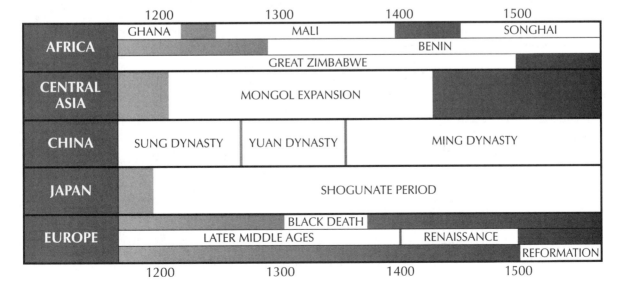

	1200	1300	1400	1500
AFRICA	GHANA	MALI		SONGHAI
			BENIN	
		GREAT ZIMBABWE		
CENTRAL ASIA		MONGOL EXPANSION		
CHINA	SUNG DYNASTY	YUAN DYNASTY	MING DYNASTY	
JAPAN		SHOGUNATE PERIOD		
EUROPE			BLACK DEATH	
	LATER MIDDLE AGES		RENAISSANCE	
				REFORMATION

WHAT YOU SHOULD FOCUS ON

This chapter explores the period from 1200 to 1500. During this era, different civilizations continued to follow separate paths of development but began to influence each other more than in previous eras. As trade increased and ideas spread, the cultures of Eurasia and Africa became more connected.

Nomads from Central Asia were feared warriors.

These were times of great stress. Nomadic invaders from Central Asia were greatly feared by neighboring civilizations. The Bubonic Plague, a deadly disease from Central Asia, brought equal devastation in the 1300s.

West Africa. Important empires prospered on the basis of the gold and salt trades.

Asia. Mongol warriors swept across the Asian mainland, uniting much of Asia under their rule.

OVERVIEW OF THE PERIOD, 1200 TO 1500

Japan. Japan developed a political and social system similar to the system of feudalism in Europe.

Europe. Western Europe experienced a rebirth of trade and learning, contributing to the decline of feudalism and the achievements of the Renaissance.

During these same centuries, Islamic civilization continued to grow and began to penetrate India. The remaining territories of the Byzantine empire fell to Turkish invaders. New civilizations arose in Southeast Asia. Important empires flourished in the Western Hemisphere, which are discussed in the next chapter.

In learning about this era, you should focus on the following:

➤ What led to the rise of the West African kingdoms?
➤ What were the effects of the Mongol conquests?
➤ What factors contributed to the decline of feudalism in Western Europe?
➤ What were the achievements of the European Renaissance?

LOOKING AT THE ARTS

 ll cultures have the need both to create works of beauty and to express their deepest beliefs and feelings through the arts — painting, sculpture, architecture, literature, music, and dance. Works of art can therefore reveal a great deal about the values of the society that produced them.

A CAPSULE SURVEY OF WORLD ART

The earliest examples of art date back to prehistoric times. Caves have been discovered in Spain and France decorated with prehistoric pictures of animals and hunting scenes.

MIDDLE EASTERN ART

◆ **Ancient Egypt.** Much of Egyptian art focused on the pharaoh, who was seen as a god. Huge monuments and buildings celebrated the pharaoh's power. Pyramids were built to house the pharaoh after his death. Objects inside the pyramid provided the pharaoh with everything he would need in the afterlife. Wall paintings inside the pyramids often paid tribute to the greatness of the pharaoh.

Gold mask from Pharaoh Tutankamen's tomb.

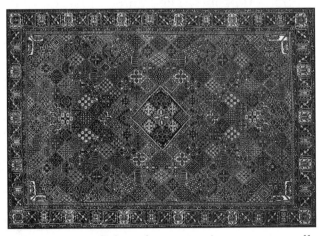

◆ **Islamic Art.** Islamic artists generally did not depict people in their artworks, since the Qu'ran forbids it. Instead, these artists excelled at the decorative arts, using highly complex floral designs and geometric patterns in their architecture, metalwork, glasswork, and textiles. Carpets provided a particularly good way to display their highly developed sense of color, proportion, and intricate

A Persian rug dislays the geometric patterns usually identified with Islamic art.

design. Carpet designers aimed at achieving a perfect balance and harmony.

EUROPEAN ART

◆ **Ancient Greece.** Greek art emphasized a sense of proportion and realism. The Parthenon was built to honor Athena — the goddess of wisdom and protector of Athens. With its perfect proportions, it is considered by many to be the finest example of Greek architecture, craftsmanship, and design. The Greeks were also renowned for their superb marble sculptures of the human figure, which they painted and decorated for greater realism. Greek sculptures mixed idealism of the human body with realism. The Winged Victory of Samothrace, carved by an unknown sculptor, was created to mark a victorious Greek naval battle. It captures the grace and beauty of the ideal human body in motion.

Winged Victory of Samothrace

◆ **Ancient Rome.** Roman artistry was most evident in architecture. The arch, the dome, and concrete were combined by Roman artisans to build impressive structures. One of the most famous buildings of the Romans was the Colosseum, an arena built for contests among gladiators. Made of stone and concrete, it held 55,000 people. The Pantheon is said to be the most perfect of all classical monuments in Rome. Built at the time of Augustus, its most notable feature is its perfect dome.

The Pantheon in Rome

◆ **Middle Ages.** Medieval paintings and sculpture were largely used for religious purposes. Medieval painters were less concerned with realism than with religious symbolism. The greatest achievements of medieval architecture were Gothic cathedrals. These were huge stone structures with pointed arches, flying buttresses, spires, and high vaulted ceilings, built by entire communities as monuments to God.

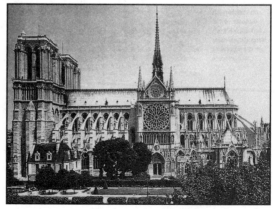

Notre-Dame's stained glass-windows, statuary, and paintings retell the stories of the Bible.

◆ **Renaissance.** The Renaissance marked a sharp departure from Medieval art. Some Renaissance art even dealt with non-religious themes. Renaissance art borrowed heavily from classical Greece and Rome and strove for simplicity and proportion. Renaissance painters like Leonardo Da Vinci, Michaelangelo, and Raphael reached

A detail of Botticelli's painting "Primavera" (Spring).

new levels of realism, developing new techniques such as perspective.

◆ **Modern European Art.** European art has gone through many different styles since the Renaissance including Baroque, Romanticism, Impressionism, Cubism, and Surrealism. These styles have fluctuated between increased realism, formal beauty, and the depiction of inner emotions. The abstract styles of 20th century art reflect the excitement and confusion of contemporary life. In Cubism, Spanish artist Pablo Picasso broke three-dimensional objects into small fragments, which he brought together again to form complex patterns.

Cubist painting by Picasso

AFRICAN ART

Traditional African art often expressed religious beliefs. Tribal art was a way of communicating with the spirit world and protecting individuals against evil forces. Among traditional African art forms were masks worn during ceremonial dances and tribal rites. Many tribes also made statues of humans or animals, often exaggerated in size for symbolic or religious purposes. African music and dance were characterized by great vitality with a strong emphasis on rhythm.

Even today in parts of Africa masks play an important role in ceremonial dances and in tribal rites.

ART IN THE AMERICAS

Two Pre-Columbian civilizations to leave behind significant works of art were the Maya and the Aztec. The **Maya** developed one of the most advanced civilizations in the Americas. They constructed pyramids which first served as tombs. Later Maya pyramids were built as vast temples, approaching the size of the Egyptian pyramids. These pyramids were decorated with flattened sculptures depicting Maya gods.

The **Aztecs** developed free-standing stone sculptures that excelled at portraying human emotions. Their artists and artisans produced beautiful gold and silver jewelry, carved jade, and lacquered objects. Since the exploration and colonization of the Americans by Europeans, American art styles have been strongly influenced by Europe.

An Aztec statue made of basalt (approximately 1450–1521).

ASIAN ART

◆ **South and Southeast Asia.** Dancing is an important element of the culture of South and Southeast Asia. Dance first developed in connection with religious ceremonies. Dancers told the stories of Hindu gods and goddesses, often portraying the struggle between good and evil. Through the movement of hands and feet, and facial expressions, dancers communicated emotions and feelings to their audience in the course of telling their stories. Classical Hindu sculpture similarly depicted the human body in various postures, representing both gods and goddesses. Later Indian art and architecture were influenced by both Persian and Islamic styles.

Indian dancers use all parts of their body to communicate a story to their audience.

◆ **China.** Chinese paintings, pottery, and porcelain emphasize the harmony, symmetry, and balance found in nature. Chinese painters often illustrated poems written in calligraphy on paper scrolls. China's earliest pottery met religious as well as practical needs. Wealthy people were buried with earthenware, dishes, models of animals, and other objects. Later, Chinese craftsmen perfected the art of making porcelain. Unlike other pottery, porcelain is shiny, smooth, white, and translucent.

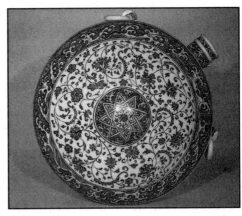

A fine Chinese porcelain canteen, early Ming dynasty, 1400–1430.

◆ **Japan.** Like Chinese art, Japanese art emphasizes simplicity, harmony, order, and the beauty of nature. For example, the tea ceremony is performed slowly and quietly to promote meditation. Flower arranging emphasizes the symbolism of natural beauty. Origami is the art of folding paper into animal forms and

Origami, the Japanese craft of making paper items.

other shapes. Haiku are simple, graceful poems reflecting the harmony of nature.

QUESTIONS ABOUT THE ARTS

Art questions on global history examinations frequently ask how a work of art reflects the spirit of its culture or times. You must be able (1) to interpret the artwork, and (2) to show how the artwork reflects the time or culture in which it was produced. When faced with this type of question, ask yourself the following:

◆ What is being portrayed in the artwork?
◆ What is the theme or major point of the artwork?
◆ In which time period and place was the artwork probably created?
◆ What does it tell us about the culture of the people who produced it?

MAJOR HISTORICAL DEVELOPMENTS

SECTION 1: THE KINGDOMS OF AFRICA

In the last chapter, you learned about the spread of Islam from Arabia to North Africa, Asia, and Europe. The peoples of sub-Saharan Africa lived south of the Islamic empire, separated from it by a vast desert.

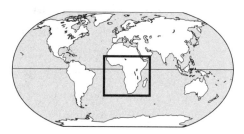

THINK ABOUT IT •

What role did geography play in the rise of the West African kingdoms?

THE GEOGRAPHICAL SETTING

Much of North Africa is occupied by the **Sahara Desert.** Just below this desert is a wide band of grassland known as the **savanna.** The savanna stretches across the entire width of Africa, from the Atlantic to the Indian Ocean. South of the savanna lies the tropical rain forests of equatorial Africa.

African mask showing merchants in the gold-salt trade.

The Sahara acted as a barrier that separated the peoples of sub-Saharan Africa from the Mediterranean world and the rest of Eurasia. African tribes developed their own customs and beliefs, such as **animism** — the belief that objects in nature, such as trees, have their own sprits. Despite this separation, trade across the desert was never cut off completely. Merchants, traveling on camels able to go several days without water, crossed the Sahara. They were motivated by the gold and other riches they could obtain from trade with West African societies. At the same time, West Africans lacked salt, which is vital to human survival. Merchants, moving in caravans across the desert, picked up large blocks of salt on their journey to exchange for gold. A thriving trade developed, based on this gold-salt trade.

THE WEST AFRICAN KINGDOMS

Around the eighth century, West Africa saw the rise of a series of powerful kingdoms. For the next thousand years, their civilizations dominated West Africa — leading to an increased exchange of ideas, the rise of cities, and greater wealth.

KINGDOM OF GHANA (750–1200)

The kingdom of Ghana was founded around 750. The people of Ghana used their ability to make iron swords, spears, and lances to defeat their neighbors and gain control over West Africa's major trade routes. Caravans would bring salt south to Ghana, and return north with gold from areas southwest of Ghana.

The power of the kings of Ghana rested on their ability to tax all trade passing through the region, especially the salt and gold trade. The rulers of Ghana built a capital city, developed a large cavalry, and governed a wide area. However, in 1076, they were invaded by Muslims from North Africa. Ghana never fully recovered and eventually dissolved into many smaller states.

KINGDOM OF MALI (1240–1400)

In 1240, Mali conquered Ghana. Mali's rulers established a new empire and brought gold and salt mines under their control. Mali's rulers converted to Islam, although most of their people did not adopt that faith.

Mali's most famous ruler, **Mansa Musa,** expanded his kingdom greatly. In the 1330s, he made a religious pilgrimage to Mecca. Mansa Musa turned his capital city of **Timbuktu** into a flourishing center of trade and learning. Because of the importance of studying the Qu'ran, more West Africans learned to read and write. Later rulers of Mali proved less capable than Mansa Musa, and the empire collapsed in the 1400s.

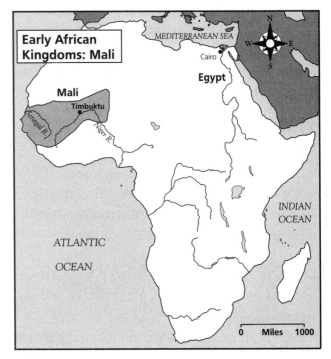

THE KINGDOM OF SONGHAI (1464–1600)

In 1464, the Songhai people captured Timbuktu and brought the middle of the Upper Niger region under their control.

The kingdom of Songhai emerged as the largest of Africa's three trading empires. The people of Songhai were skilled at farming, fishing, and trading. Like Ghana and Mali, Songhai grew rich from trade across the Sahara Desert. Songhai expanded its trading network as far as Europe and Asia. Like Mali, it was also Muslim. Despite its riches and power, the kingdom of Songhai lasted only about 100 years. In 1591, Songhai fell to the invading armies of Morocco. The fall of Songhai marked the end of the great West African kingdoms. West Africa again split into a large number of independent areas.

OTHER AFRICAN STATES

The growth of kingdoms in the West African savanna like Ghana, Mali, and Songhai was matched by the rise of other trading centers in Africa.

BENIN

Benin developed in the rain forests of West Africa. Benin was famous for its bronze sculptures, among the finest in all of African art. By the 16th century, Benin became involved in the slave trade. Benin traded captives from other tribes and exchanged them with Europeans for guns and iron goods.

ZIMBABWE

Farther to the south, Zimbabwe became one of Africa's best known trading kingdoms. The existence of gold deposits was crucial to its rise. Zimbabwe traded gold, copper, and ivory to traders who appeared along Africa's east coast.

COASTAL CITIES OF EAST AFRICA

Around the 10th century, a number of independent city-states arose along the east coast of Africa. Gold from the African interior was sent down the Zambezi and other rivers to these cities, where it was sold to merchants from Arabia and India.

ETHIOPIA

Ethiopia, a continuation of the ancient kingdom of Axum, became a Christian state in the 4th century. It remained Christian despite the rise of Islam, which cut Ethiopia off from the rest of the Christian world until the 1400s.

ANSWERING THE FOCUS QUESTION •

Writing

One of the ways that the West African kingdoms were influenced by geography was _____

_____

Directions: Complete each of the following vocabulary cards. Then answer the multiple-choice questions that follow.

WEST AFRICAN KINGDOMS

Name two West African kingdoms:

(1)

(2)

What factors explain the rise of these

kingdoms?

MANSA MUSA

Who was Mansa Musa?

What changes did he bring to his

kingdom?

---

1 One reason the kingdoms of the West African savanna prospered was that they
   1 were located along the Tigris and Euphrates Rivers
   2 had no contact with the rest of the world
   3 followed the Hindu beliefs of their rulers
   4 controlled an extensive trade in gold and salt

2 Mansa Musa's journey to Mecca in the 1300s demonstrated that
   1 the Crusades had a great influence on West Africa
   2 most African leaders were educated in the Middle East
   3 European culture was superior to the cultures of West Africa
   4 Islam had a major influence on the Mali empire

3 Which of the following African kingdoms became a Christian state?
   1 Songhai   3 Mali
   2 Benin   4 Ethiopia

4 Which city is correctly paired with its civilization?
   1 Athens — Roman empire   3 Constantinople — Persian empire
   2 Mecca — T'ang Dynasty   4 Timbuktu — kingdom of Mali

SECTION 2: THE WARRIOR STATES OF ASIA

In this section you will learn about the Mongols, nomadic peoples who lived in Central Asia. During the 1200s, they established the greatest empire the world had ever seen. At about the same time, in another part of Asia, Japan witnessed the rise of a feudal system similar to that of Europe.

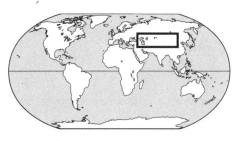

THINK ABOUT IT •

What changes did Mongol warriors and Japanese samurai bring to Asia?

THE MONGOL EMPIRE

Stretching across Eurasia is an almost unbroken band of dry, treeless grasslands, known as **steppes.** The steppes provided a unique environment in which nomadic peoples could excel at horsemanship and develop fierce fighting skills. Throughout much of history, various nomadic peoples have pushed out of this region

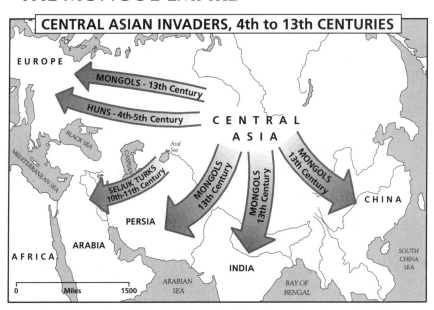

to conquer their neighbors, sometimes with devastating effects. For example, the **Huns,** repelled by the Chinese emperors, invaded Europe in the 4th century and contributed to the collapse of the Roman empire. Later, the **Turks** and the **Mongols** also came out of Central Asia.

CHINGGIS KHAN CREATES THE MONGOL EMPIRE

Like other nomadic peoples, the Mongols were divided into several tribes. A Mongol leader named **Chinggis** (*or Ghengis*) **Khan** (1162–1227) united the Mongol tribes and began attacking neighboring peoples beyond Mongolia, including northern China. Chinggis Khan ran his army by imposing strict discipline and demanding complete loyalty. Skilled horsemen, his soldiers could travel for days on little more than a handful of grain and a cup of milk. In 1219, Chinggis turned westward and captured the Muslim states of Central

Asia. Under his successors, Mongol rule eventually extended over Persia, Russia, Iraq, and all of China. At their height, the Mongols held sway over one of the largest empires the world has ever seen — reaching from the Black Sea to the Pacific Ocean. The Mongol empire was so vast that it was divided into four separate khanates or kingdoms.

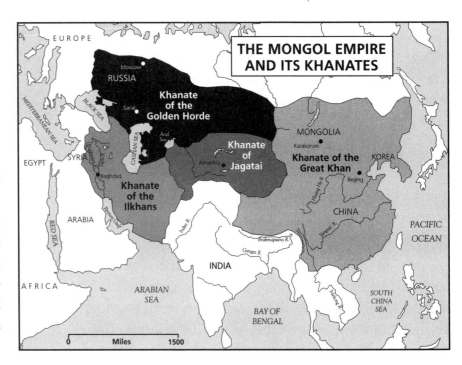

THE YUAN DYNASTY, 1279–1368

Chinggis' grandson, **Kublai Khan,** became emperor of northern China in 1260. In 1279, he reunited all of China under his rule. Kublai Khan encouraged the Mongols to adopt Chinese ways, and he even adopted the Chinese name of **Yuan** for his dynasty. **Marco Polo,** an Italian merchant, visited China in the 1270s. He was astounded at the magnificence of Kublai Khan's court and the technological superiority

Marco Polo was 17 when he left Venice with his father and uncle for China. This illustration shows their arrival in China.

of the Chinese. After returning to Italy, Polo published a book about his travels, which inspired great curiosity in Europe about China. Despite these achievements, Kublai Khan's successors proved unable to maintain control of China. The Yuan Dynasty was overthrown in 1368.

MONGOL RULE IN RUSSIA

In the 13th century, Mongol warriors also conquered most of Russia, which they controlled for the next 200 years. Russians were cut off from Western Europe. Many Mongol words, customs, and types of clothing found their way into the Russian language and culture. However, the Mongols established only loose control over the Russian states. The Muscovites, the people living around present-day Moscow, gradually began to resist Mongol rule. In 1480, **Ivan the Great** declared Muscovy's independence from the Mongols and proclaimed himself **Tsar** (*or emperor*). He soon increased Muscovy's size by conquering neighboring lands.

JAPAN'S FEUDAL PERIOD, 1200 TO 1600

One part of Asia the Mongols were never able to conquer was Japan. In the last chapter, you learned about the achievements of the early Japanese emperors. By the 1100s, the emperor's power was so weakened that Japan collapsed into civil war. A system of **feudalism,** similar to that found in Europe, eventually arose.

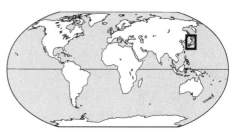

THE SHOGUN

In 1192, Japan's most powerful noble had the emperor appoint him as Japan's "Supreme Military Governor" or **Shogun.** For the next 600 years, the Shoguns were the real rulers of Japan, while the emperors acted as mere figureheads. The Shogun stood at the top of the Japanese feudal system. To provide military protection for their lands, the **daimyo** (*noble landowners*) recruited samurai warriors. Each samurai swore an oath of loyalty to the emperor and to his local daimyo. The samurai promised to follow a strict code of honor, known as **Bushido.** Bushido emphasized the

ORGANIZATION OF JAPAN'S FEUDAL SOCIETY

Shogun
|
Daimyo (lords)
|
Samurai (warriors)
|
Farmers/merchants/artisans

loyalty of the samurai to the daimyo. If a samurai warrior dishonored his daimyo, he was expected to take his own life. In return for their loyalty, the daimyo provided the samurai with social status and economic support.

ART FORMS FLOURISH AMID TURMOIL

In 1274, Kublai Khan sent an army to invade Japan, but his forces were defeated. The costs of preparing for the invasion weakened the power of the Shogun. Japan fell into a new period of chaos and civil war by the end of the 13th century.

For the next century, the daimyo controlled their own lands with little interference by the central government. Despite this chaos, this was a period of intense cultural activity in Japan. The art of flower arranging, the Japanese tea ceremony, landscape painting, and the art of garden-

This woman is partaking in sado — the ceremonial art of drinking tea.

ing all developed at this time. Each of these art forms represented a way to reflect on life and the beauty of nature. Japanese painting in this period stressed contemplation, meditation, and spiritual enlightenment.

ANSWERING THE FOCUS QUESTION •

Writing

Mongol warriors and Japanese samurai brought the following changes to Asia:

_____ (Mongol warriors)

_____ (Japanese samurai)

Directions: Complete each of the following vocabulary cards. Then answer the multiple-choice questions that follow.

CHINGGIS KHAN
Who was Chinggis Khan?
What significant events occurred during his rule?

SHOGUN
What role did the Shogun play in Japanese society?
What was the relationship between the daimyo and the Shogun?

1 Which person is correctly paired with his empire or dynasty?
   1 Marco Polo — Roman empire
   2 Ivan the Great — Byzantine empire
   3 Kublai Khan — Yuan Dynasty
   4 Chinggis Khan — T'ang Dynasty

2 What factor enabled the nomadic tribes of Central Asia to conquer many of their neighbors?
   1 A warm climate encouraged population growth.
   2 Diseases like the bubonic plague drove Central Asians into Europe.
   3 Vast grasslands supported large numbers of warriors on horseback.
   4 The Hindu faith encouraged them to fight.

3 Which was a characteristic of feudalism in both medieval Europe and Japan?
   1 Merchants acquired more power than any other class.
   2 Political power was held by a strong central government.
   3 The army encouraged strong national feelings among the people.
   4 People pledged absolute loyalty to their social superiors.

4 In an outline, one of these is the main topic and the others are sub-topics. Which is the main topic?
   1 Shogun
   2 Daimyo
   3 Samurai
   4 Japan's Feudal Period

SECTION 3: THE RESURGENCE OF EUROPE

In this section you will read about how life in Europe began to change from the 1200s onwards. These changes brought about a revival of learning and challenges to the Pope's supremacy.

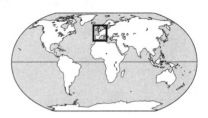

THINK ABOUT IT •

What were the major ideas of the Renaissance and Reformation?

THE DECLINE OF FEUDALISM

Beginning in the 1200s, increased trade led to the growth of towns, the development of a middle class, and the greater use of money in Europe. The use of gunpowder, introduced from China, gradually made knights on horseback less important. Kings with large armies gained new power over their nobles. In the mid-1300s, rats with fleas carrying a disease from Asia called the **Black Death** (*bubonic plague*) entered Europe on trading ships. Between 1347 and 1351, nearly 25 million people — about one-third of Europe's population — died in this epidemic. The epidemic created a labor shortage in Europe, allowing large numbers of peasants to escape from serfdom when landowners offered them freedom in exchange for work. The rise of cities, the emergence of powerful kings, the decline of knights, and the end of serfdom gradually spelled the end of the old feudal order.

THE RENAISSANCE

A new interest in learning about classical civilizations, especially those of ancient Greece and Rome, developed in the city-states of Italy in the 1400s. This period of great intellectual and artistic creativity became known as the **Renaissance.** It began in the Italian states in part because of their strategic location. Situated between Europe and Asia, the Italian city-states, like Florence and Venice, grew rich from East-West trade. Italy was also home to many classical ruins from ancient

Italian city-states like Venice grew rich as a result of their location on frequently used trade routes.

times. Wealthy Italian merchants and nobles acted as patrons supporting artists, writers, and scholars. Gradually, the Renaissance spirit of inquiry spread across the rest of Europe.

During the Renaissance, Europeans began to show a greater interest in the concerns of this world than in the life hereafter. There was a growth of **secularism** — looking at the world from a non-religious standpoint. Scholars used observation and experience to explain the world, rather than simply looking to Church teachings. Renaissance thinkers had confidence in the powers of human reason to explain the world. **Humanists** placed greater emphasis on the uniqueness and worth of each person.

HIGHLIGHTS OF THE RENAISSANCE

ART:
Leonardo Da Vinci represented the ideal "**Renaissance man**." He was a painter, sculptor, designer, and inventor. His paintings include *Mona Lisa* and *The Last Supper*.

Michelangelo. His paintings on the ceiling of the Sistine Chapel in Rome are considered among the greatest works of art of all time. His major sculpures include *David*, *Moses*, and the *Pieta*.

LITERATURE:
Niccolo Machiavelli wrote *The Prince*, advising rulers to do anything necessary to maintain and increase their power, including the use of deceit and force. He believed "the end justifies the means."

William Shakespeare wrote plays whose popularity has endured for centuries. His dramas *Hamlet*, *Macbeth*, and *Romeo and Juliet*, explore the full range of human activities and emotions.

SCIENCE AND TECHNOLOGY:
Nicholas Copernicus stated that the earth and other planets revolved around the sun. This idea contradicted Church teachings, which said the earth was the center of the universe.

Galileo Galilei and **Francis Bacon** rejected reliance on authorities and developed the **scientific method**, which emphasized direct observation, measurement, and experimentation.

Michelangelo's Pieta

William Shakespeare

Nicholas Copernicus

THE PROTESTANT REFORMATION

The spirit of inquiry of the Renaissance also led to a questioning of widespread abuses within the Catholic Church. These questions led to new challenges to the Pope's authority in the early 1500s.

THE IMPACT OF LUTHER AND HIS IDEAS

In 1517, **Martin Luther** posted **ninety five theses** (*statements*) on a church door in Germany. Luther called for reforms within the Catholic Church. He especially challenged the Pope's right to sell **indulgences** — pardons from punishment for committing a sin, allowing a buyer to enter Heaven.

Martin Luther

Luther believed that neither priests nor the Pope had special powers to provide salvation to individuals. He taught that only through personal faith in God could a person be saved and go to Heaven. Luther also lectured against other Church practices he felt were corrupt. The Pope **excommunicated** (*expelled from the Catholic Church*) Luther for these beliefs. Luther found protection from several German princes and responded to the Pope's condemnation by establishing his own new church. Luther stressed salvation by faith alone — no amount of good works could win salvation without faith. Only trust in God could win salvation.

The invention of movable type in 1455 by another German, **Johann Gutenberg,** helped reformers like Luther to spread their ideas all over Europe. They printed thousands of pamphlets in native languages like German, French, and English — instead of in Latin — to win popular support. They also translated and printed copies of the Bible, since they believed people should interpret its text for themselves. Other reformers, like John Calvin, also started their own churches. These reformers were called **Protestants** because they protested against abuses of the Catholic Church.

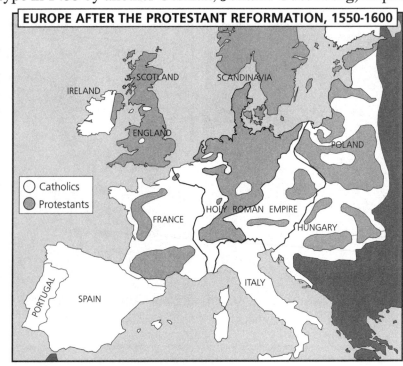

EUROPE AFTER THE PROTESTANT REFORMATION, 1550-1600

IRELAND
SCOTLAND
SCANDINAVIA
ENGLAND
POLAND
○ Catholics
● Protestants
FRANCE
HOLY ROMAN EMPIRE
HUNGARY
PORTUGAL
SPAIN
ITALY

EFFECTS OF THE REFORMATION

End of Religious Unity. The religious unity of Western Europe, which had lasted for a thousand years, was shattered forever. Europe's religious differences led to a century of warfare between Protestants and Catholics.

Growth of Royal Power. Without a powerful central Church, the power of European kings began to grow. In England, King Henry VIII broke with the Pope and became the head of the Church of England in 1534.

Persecution. Rulers tried to ensure that their subjects were all of one faith. This often led to the persecution of religious minorities.

THE CATHOLIC CHURCH FIGHTS BACK

The Protestant Reformation seriously weakened the power of the Catholic Church. As Protestantism swept across the European continent, the Church reacted by making limited reforms and halting its previous abuses. This movement is known as the **Catholic Counter Reformation.**

THE CATHOLIC COUNTER REFORMATION

The Council of Trent (1545– 1563) was held to redefine Catholic beliefs and to stop the spread of Protestantism. The Council ended the sale of indulgences.

The Inquisition was used by Church officials to end heresy by force. Trials were held to examine, often by torture, those who denied Church teachings.

The Jesuits, begun by Ignatius Loyola in 1534, were dedicated to defending and spreading the Catholic faith.

Under the leadership of the Pope and with the support of the Holy Roman Emperor, Catholics checked the further spread of Protestantism and even won some areas back to Catholicism. Germany and the Netherlands became involved in a series of bloody wars, ending in the **Thirty Years War** (1618–1648) in which one-third of Europe's population died.

Sometimes protesters against the Church were burned at the stake.

ANSWERING THE FOCUS QUESTION •

Writing

What were some of the major ideas of the Renaissance and Reformation?

_____ (Renaissance)

_____ (Reformation)

Directions: Complete each of the following vocabulary cards. Then answer the multiple-choice questions that follow.

RENAISSANCE

Where did the Renaissance begin?

What important changes did the

Renaissance bring about?

PROTESTANT REFORMATION

Why did the Reformation begin?

What important changes did the

Reformation bring about?

1 One reason Italian city-states were able to dominate trade routes at the start of the Renaissance was that they were
   1. strategically located between Europe and Asia
   2. situated north of the Alps
   3. located on the Baltic and North Sea
   4. unified under Mongol rule

2 Which statement best describes a change that occurred during the Renaissance?
   1. Feudalism became the dominant political system.
   2. The use of reason and logic was discouraged.
   3. Technology and science became less important.
   4. A new questioning spirit and attitude emerged.

3 The sale of indulgences and the worldly lives of the clergy were the subject matter of
   1. Lady Murasaki's *The Tale of Genji*
   2. Martin Luther's *Ninety-Five Theses*
   3. William Shakespeare's *Hamlet*
   4. Niccolo Machiavelli's *The Prince*

4 The Council of Trent and the founding of the Jesuits were
   1. actions taken by the Catholic Church to oppose the Reformation
   2. two early Protestant achievements
   3. actions taken by European Christians to regain the Holy Land
   4. events that stimulated overseas exploration

KEY TERMS, CONCEPTS, AND PEOPLE

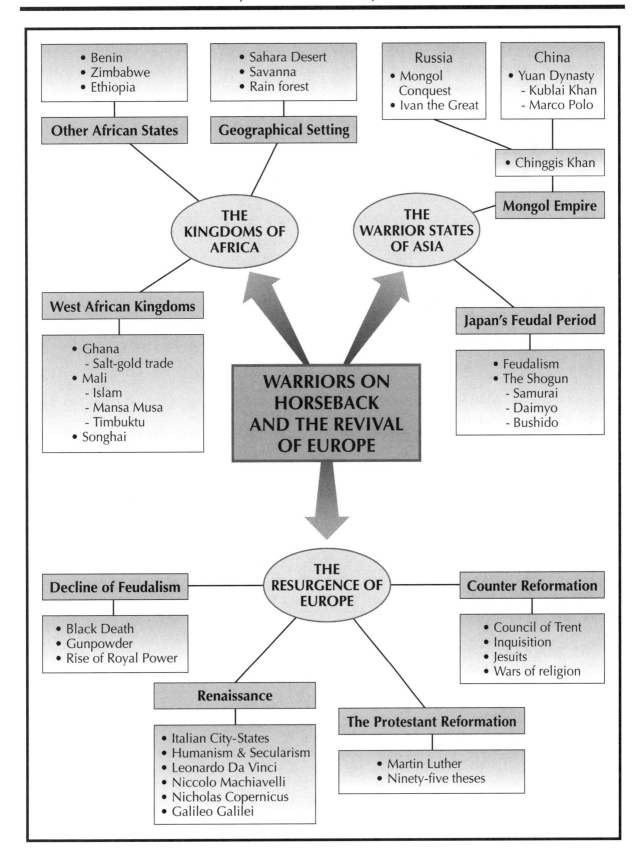

Other African States
- Benin
- Zimbabwe
- Ethiopia

Geographical Setting
- Sahara Desert
- Savanna
- Rain forest

Russia
- Mongol Conquest
- Ivan the Great

China
- Yuan Dynasty
  - Kublai Khan
  - Marco Polo

- Chinggis Khan

Mongol Empire

THE KINGDOMS OF AFRICA

THE WARRIOR STATES OF ASIA

West African Kingdoms
- Ghana
  - Salt-gold trade
- Mali
  - Islam
  - Mansa Musa
  - Timbuktu
- Songhai

Japan's Feudal Period
- Feudalism
- The Shogun
  - Samurai
  - Daimyo
  - Bushido

WARRIORS ON HORSEBACK AND THE REVIVAL OF EUROPE

THE RESURGENCE OF EUROPE

Decline of Feudalism
- Black Death
- Gunpowder
- Rise of Royal Power

Counter Reformation
- Council of Trent
- Inquisition
- Jesuits
- Wars of religion

Renaissance
- Italian City-States
- Humanism & Secularism
- Leonardo Da Vinci
- Niccolo Machiavelli
- Nicholas Copernicus
- Galileo Galilei

The Protestant Reformation
- Martin Luther
- Ninety-five theses

SUMMARIZING YOUR UNDERSTANDING

COMPLETING AN OUTLINE

Directions: Use these headings to complete the outline below.

THE KINGDOMS OF AFRICA
The Renaissance
Other African States
THE RESURGENCE OF EUROPE
The Mongol Empire
Japan's Feudal Period
The Protestant Reformation
WARRIOR STATES OF ASIA
West African Kingdoms
WARRIORS ON HORSEBACK & THE REVIVAL OF EUROPE
Decline of Feudalism

TITLE: _____

I. MAJOR DIVISION: _____

    A. Sub-topic: _____

    B. Sub-topic: _____

II. MAJOR DIVISION: _____

    A. Sub-topic: _____

    B. Sub-topic: _____

III. MAJOR DIVISION: _____

    A. Sub-topic: _____

    B. Sub-topic: _____

    C. Sub-topic: _____

COMPLETING A GRAPHIC ORGANIZER

Many consider the Renaissance to be one of the "Golden Ages" of Western civilization. Complete the following graphic organizer on the accomplishments of the Renaissance.

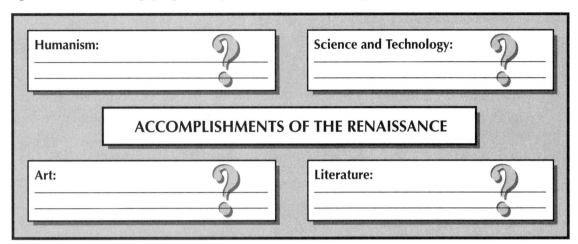

COMPLETING A PARAGRAPH FRAME

Between 1200 and 1500, great empires arose in Africa and Asia. These empires were greatly affected by the achievements of neighboring civilizations. Select either Mali, Songhai, or the Mongol empire and show how it was influenced by another culture.

Selection: One of the great empires to arise in the period from 1200 to 1500 was _____. This empire was greatly affected by _____.

Fact(s)/example(s) to support your selection: _____

_____

_____.

_____.

Link: _____

_____.

Closing: _____.

_____

_____.

SHARPENING YOUR TEST-TAKING SKILLS

THE "ACTION WORDS" OF ESSAY QUESTIONS

Global history examinations usually contain essay questions. In order to answer an essay question, you must understand what the question asks for. The exact instructions for what you are supposed to do in writing your answer are found in the question's "action words." The most common action words in essay questions include:

Describe or Discuss   Explain or Show How   Explain or Show Why

In this section we will examine each of these "action words" to see specifically what they require you to do when answering an essay question.

DESCRIBE OR DISCUSS

Describe or **discuss** means to "illustrate something in words or to tell about it." The words "describe" or "discuss" are used when you are asked for the **"who," "what," "when,"** and **"where"** of something. Not every "describe" or "discuss" question requires all four of these elements. However, your answer must go beyond just a word or a sentence. The following are examples of "describe" and "discuss" questions:

- *Describe* a scientific achievement that occurred during the Renaissance.
- *Discuss* the expansion of the Mongol empire.

Here is what a sample answer might look like to the "describe" question above:

Sample Answer: *One important achievement of the Renaissance was the realization that the earth moves around the sun. For hundreds of years the Catholic Church had taught Europeans that the earth was the center of the universe. During the Renaissance, an astronomer named Nicholas Copernicus studied the movements of the planets, stars, and moon. He concluded that the sun, not the earth, was the center of our solar system. His discovery was an important scientific achievement.*

Notice how the answer describes a particular scientific achievement. The description creates a verbal picture of **who** (*Nicholas Copernicus*), **what** (*his conclusion that the sun was the center of the solar system*), **when** (*the Renaissance period*), and **where** (*Europe*). A helpful hint: Go through your own mental checklist of *who, what, where,* and *when* whenever you are asked to *describe* or *discuss* something.

EXPLAIN AND SHOW

Explain and *show* are often linked with the additional word *how* or *why*. The key in approaching any question with these action words is to determine whether the question asks you to give an answer for *how* something happened or *why* it happened.

◆ **How Questions.** This type of question asks you to explain "how" something works or "how" it relates to something else. It usually focuses on events or effects, not causes. Let's look at two examples:
  * *Explain how* improvements in technology can affect a country's social and economic development.
  * *Show how* feudalism created a new system of government in Western Europe during the Middle Ages.

In each case you are expected to provide facts and examples that demonstrate how the statement is true. Let's look at an answer to the second question, which asks you to show how feudalism created a new system of government in Western Europe:

Sample Answer: *By the 8th century, the Franks developed the system of feudalism in which kings and nobles gave the use of land to their vassals in exchange for loyalty and service. Feudalism provided the basis for a new decentralized system of government in Western Europe, in which lords governed with the help of vassals and knights. People looked to their local lord for protection and justice.*

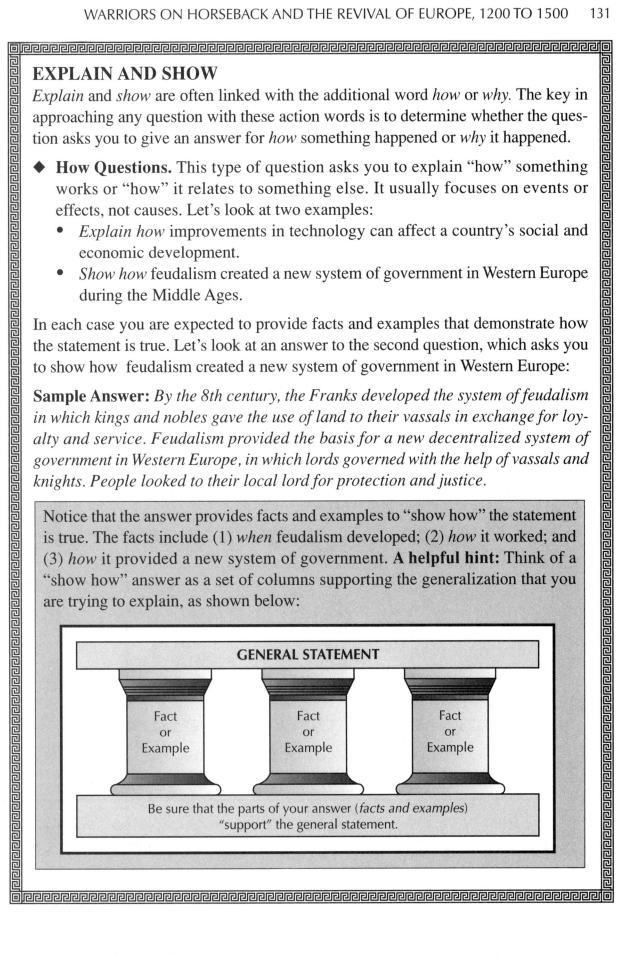

Notice that the answer provides facts and examples to "show how" the statement is true. The facts include (1) *when* feudalism developed; (2) *how* it worked; and (3) *how* it provided a new system of government. **A helpful hint:** Think of a "show how" answer as a set of columns supporting the generalization that you are trying to explain, as shown below:

GENERAL STATEMENT

Fact or Example

Fact or Example

Fact or Example

Be sure that the parts of your answer (*facts and examples*) "support" the general statement.

◆ **Why Questions.** To explain *why* means to give reasons why something took place. *Explain why* or *show why* questions focus on causes. Your answer should identify the reasons why something took place and briefly describe each reason. Two examples of such questions are:
  * *Explain why* the first civilizations emerged six thousand years ago.
  * *Show why* feudalism developed in Japan.

In each case, you must present reasons or causes that explain why the event occurred. Let's look at a sample answer to the first question above.

Sample Answer: The first civilizations emerged in the river valleys of Mesopotamia, Egypt, India, and China about 6,000 years ago. This important development occurred because people learned to plant crops and tame animals. In the fertile plains along the Tigris and Euphrates, the Nile, the Indus, and the Huang He farmers were able to produce surplus food. Having extra food allowed some people to pursue new occupations. As a result, those societies were able to build cities, develop writing systems, and acquire new technical skills.

Notice how the answer "explains" the reasons supporting the statement "why" the first civilizations emerged:

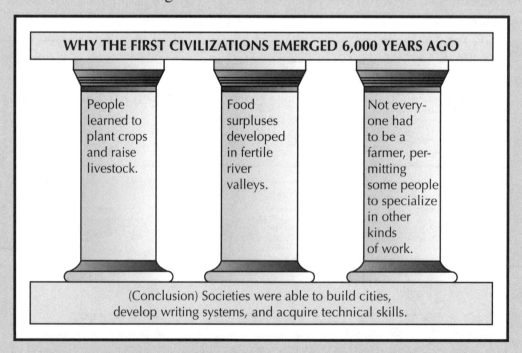

WHY THE FIRST CIVILIZATIONS EMERGED 6,000 YEARS AGO

| People learned to plant crops and raise livestock. | Food surpluses developed in fertile river valleys. | Not everyone had to be a farmer, permitting some people to specialize in other kinds of work. |

(Conclusion) Societies were able to build cities, develop writing systems, and acquire technical skills.

Helpful Hint: When asked to "explain why" something occurred, go through a checklist of reasons or causes to be sure they add up to a satisfactory explanation.

TESTING YOUR UNDERSTANDING

Test your understanding of this chapter by answering the following questions:

MULTIPLE-CHOICE QUESTIONS

1 Which leader is correctly paired with his empire?

1 Mansa Musa — Islamic empire

2 Chinggis Khan — Mongol empire

3 Kublai Khan — Roman empire

4 Julius Caesar — Persian empire

2 The fifth century B.C. in Greece, often called the Golden Age of Greece, and the Renaissance in Europe were both characterized by

1 submission to religious authority

2 economic decline

3 unity under foreign rule

4 artistic and literary achievements

3 Which characteristic was shared by the kingdom of Ghana and the Mongol empire?

1 They thrived on taxing the peasants.

2 They had large cavalries in grassland regions.

3 They adopted the cultural achievements of the Chinese.

4 Their rulers made pilgrimages to Mecca.

4 The Renaissance and Protestant Reformation were similar in that both were

1 stimulated by a spirit of inquiry

2 supported by the peasantry

3 limited to Italy and Germany

4 reactions to the spread of Islam

5 The growth of feudalism in Europe during the Middle Ages was primarily caused by the

1 rivalry between colonial empires

2 suppression of internationalism

3 decline of the Roman Catholic Church

4 collapse of strong central government

6 Which slogan for leaders would Niccolo Machiavelli most likely support?

1 The end justifies the means.

2 Leaders should forgive their enemies.

3 Leaders should follow the desires of their people.

4 It is more important for a leader to be loved than feared.

7 One way that the European Renaissance differed from the Middle Ages was that

1 the Church was no longer influential

2 human individuality was given greater emphasis

3 economic activity declined

4 the power of the townspeople decreased

8 Which leader declared independence from the Mongols and proclaimed himself as Tsar?

1 Mansa Musa   3 Julius Caesar
2 Chinggis Khan   4 Ivan the Great

Base your answer to question 9 on the following diagram and your knowledge of global history.

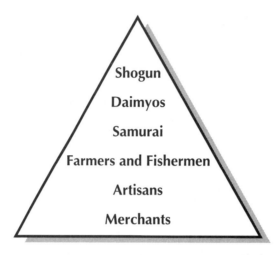

9 The Shogun is shown at the top of this social pyramid of feudal Japan because he

1 was the most powerful noble
2 passed a civil service examination
3 was able to read and write
4 held the highest religious post in Japan

Base your answer to question 10 on the timeline and your knowledge of global history.

1517	1521	1534	1536	1555
Luther nails 95 theses on church door	Luther is excom- municated	Henry VIII establishes the Church of England	Calvin publishes *Institutes of the Christian Religion*	Emperor Charles V lets German princes choose their subjects' religion

10 Which period of European history is represented by the events on this timeline?

1 Roman empire
2 Renaissance
3 Middle Ages
4 Protestant Reformation

INTERPRETING DOCUMENTS

I. INTERPRETING A MAP

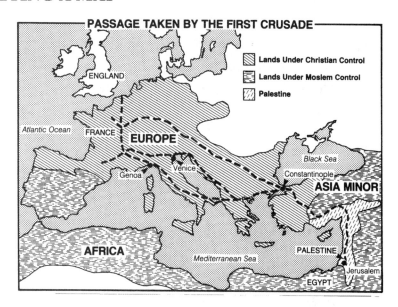

1   According to the map, most of Europe at the time was under (*circle one*):

Christian control   Muslim control   Palestinian control

2   The Crusades had many important effects. List **two** effects of the Crusades:

A. _____   B. _____

II. INTERPRETING A DIAGRAM

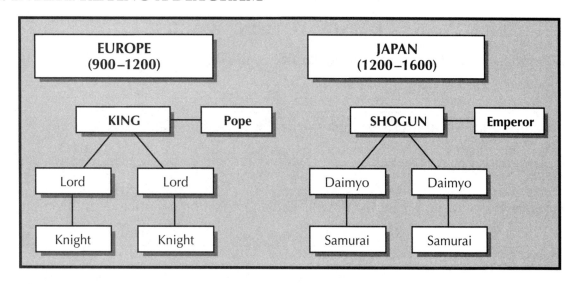

1   What is the name of the political system that is associated with the social structure in the above illustration? _____

2   Choose either Europe or Japan. Explain the relationship between any two members in the chart. _____

III. CREATING AN OUTLINE

The events listed below occurred between 1400 and 1600. In the space provided, use these events to construct an outline.

Michelangelo completes work on his "Pieta"
War breaks out between Protestants and Catholics
Ignatius Loyola begins the Jesuit Order
Leonardo Da Vinci paints *The Last Supper*
William Shakespeare writes *Julius Caesar*
Major events in Western Europe
Martin Luther nails 95 theses to the door of a church

TITLE: _____

The Renaissance	The Reformation
1. _____	1. _____
2. _____	2. _____
3. _____	3. _____

IV. PRACTICE IN ANSWERING "ACTION" WORDS

1 *Describe* a style of art from a particular time and place. _____

_____

Suggestion: You may use examples from the art of the Middle East, Europe, Africa, or Asia.

2 *Explain how* a geographical feature has had an impact on a particular civilization.

_____

_____

Suggestion: You may use examples from the early River Valley Civilizations, the Classical Civilizations, or the societies of Asia.

CHAPTER 8

THE BIRTH OF THE MODERN WORLD, 1500 TO 1770

Columbus plants the flag of Spain in the New World

SECTION 1:
THE ENCOUNTER BETWEEN EUROPE AND THE AMERICAS

1. The First Americans
2. The European Age of Discovery
3. European Conquest of the Americas
4. Effects of the Encounter

SECTION 2:
EUROPE IN THE AGE OF KINGS, 1600–1770

1. Commercial Revolution
2. Rise of Royal Power
3. Scientific Revolution
4. Enlightenment

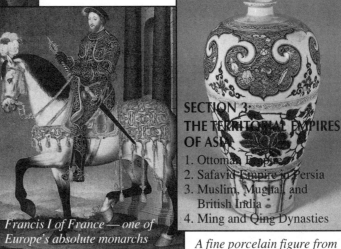

Francis I of France — one of Europe's absolute monarchs

SECTION 3:
THE TERRITORIAL EMPIRES OF ASIA

1. Ottoman Empire
2. Safavid Empire in Persia
3. Muslim, Mughal, and British India
4. Ming and Qing Dynasties

A fine porcelain figure from the Ming Dynasty

	1200	1300	1400	1500	1600	1700	1800
EUROPE			AGE OF DISCOVERY		COMMERCIAL REVOLUTION		
				AGE OF KINGS			
					ENLIGHTENMENT		
AMERICAS		MAYA CIVILIZATION					
		AZTEC CIVILIZATION					
		INCA CIVILIZATION					
				EUROPEAN COLONIZATION			
CHINA			MING DYNASTY			QING DYNASTY	
MIDEAST			OTTOMAN EMPIRE				
PERSIA			SAFAVID EMPIRE				
INDIA	DELHI SULTANATE			MUGHAL EMPIRE			

WHAT YOU SHOULD FOCUS ON

The centuries from 1500 to 1770 witnessed the birth of the "modern world," with the following important developments:

➤ a greater awareness of other cultures
➤ creation of a global economy
➤ the rise of powerful nation-states
➤ major technological advances
➤ a deepening reliance on science

In this chapter, you will read about the impact of these developments on three major areas of the world:

Europe in the 1500s was on the brink of the modern era, as explorers like Magellan linked Europe with the rest of the world.

The Encounter Between Europe and the Americas. This encounter brought together the major centers of civilization and created a truly global economy. By creating colonial empires in the Americas and transporting slaves from Africa, Europeans exerted a greater influence on the world than ever before.

Europe in the Age of Kings. European kings formed large armies and created absolute monarchies by taxing new wealth. New challenges to traditional thinking emerged with the Scientific Revolution and the Enlightenment.

The Territoral Empires of Asia. Great territorial empires flourished in the Middle East, Persia, India, and China. Nevertheless, the pace of technological change in this part of the world fell behind that of Europe.

In studying this era, you should focus on the following questions:

➤ What were the principal achievements of the pre-Columbian civilizations?
➤ What were the main causes and effects of the European encounter with the Native Americans?
➤ How did the Scientific Revolution and the Enlightenment affect European society and thought?
➤ What were the basic characteristics of the great territorial empires that dominated Asia from the 16th to the 18th centuries?

LOOKING AT THE IMPACT
OF HISTORICAL EVENTS

ave you ever seen the movie *Back to the Future*? In this film, the main character travels back in time and meets his mother while she is still a teenager. His sudden appearance in his mother's teenage life triggers effects that threaten to change events so that he will never be born.

Travel into the past may be wildly unrealistic, but part of the excitement of this film comes from the fact that it reveals an important truth: if we could alter even a single past event, we might change the entire course of history.

Why is this? It is because every event has effects, and these effects in turn have still further effects. Some events can affect the entire development and direction of a society. For example, the decisions a society takes may affect its social organization, political structure, or economic activities. Choices by leaders at critical turning points can be especially decisive.

For instance, a country's leader may decide to go to war, which can lead to the complete overhaul of a country's political, social, and economic system. These changes may, in turn, lead to other developments, both within that society and elsewhere in the world.

What impact did the arrival of Spanish Conquistadors have on the future development of Latin America?

In this chapter, for example, you will learn how wars of religion helped to increase the powers of some European kings.

CAUSE AND EFFECT

Historians are particularly interested in examining the chains of cause and effect that connect events.

◆ The **causes** of something are the conditions or factors that have led to it or brought it about. The event would not have happened except for this cause. For example, my turning the switch of a light is the *cause* of the light's going on.

◆ The **effects** of something are any of the things that happen because of it. They are the results of an action or event. For example, the light's going on was the *effect* of my turning the switch.

CAUSE
I turned the switch on.

EFFECT
The light went on.

ANSWERING QUESTIONS ABOUT HISTORICAL EVENTS

Very often, global history examinations will ask you questions about the causes and effects of historical events. The question will usually name a historical event, movement, or development. Then you will be asked to discuss the event or development and to explain either its causes or impact.

In answering this type of question, first think carefully about the event, movement, or development. Then:

FOR QUESTIONS ON CAUSES	**FOR QUESTIONS ON EFFECTS**
Begin by listing all the things you can think of that caused the event or helped make it happen. Consider all the possible political, social, economic, and religious causes. Then choose the causes you think were the most important.	Make a list of all the *effects* of the event, movement, or development. Did the event lead to positive or negative results? Be sure to explore the political, social, economic, and religious consequences of the event. Also, think about both the short-term and long-term effects.

MAJOR HISTORICAL DEVELOPMENTS

SECTION 1: THE ENCOUNTER BETWEEN EUROPE AND THE AMERICAS

While complex civilizations were flourishing in Asia, Africa, and Europe, equally striking developments had been occurring in the Americas. In this section you will learn about pre-Columbian cultures and what happened when the peoples of the Americas first encountered Europeans.

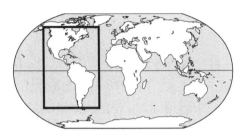

 THINK ABOUT IT •

What were the main causes and effects of the European encounter with the Native Americans?

THE FIRST AMERICANS

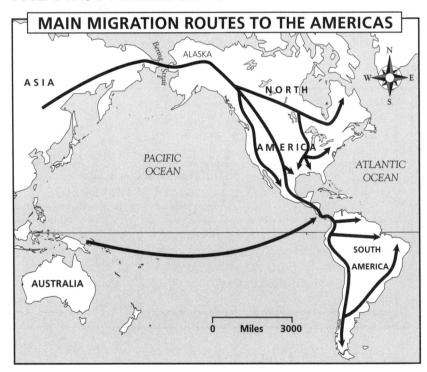

MAIN MIGRATION ROUTES TO THE AMERICAS

Scientists believe that during the Ice Age, Asia and Alaska were attached by a land bridge where the Bering Straits are found today. So much water froze into thick sheets of ice that the sea level dropped, exposing this land bridge. As long as 25,000 years ago, groups of Asian hunters crossed this land bridge following the migrations of herds of bison and mammoths. Over time, these nomadic hunter-gatherers followed the herds further southward.

These people eventually spread throughout North America, Central America, the islands of the Caribbean, and South America. Separated by vast mountains, dense jungles, grasslands, and deserts, these "Native Americans" developed their own languages and cultures.

The peoples of the Americas experienced their own Neolithic Revolution in which they learned to grow corn (*maize*) and other crops. Several complex civilizations emerged in **Mesoamerica** (*present-day Mexico and Central America*). Unlike the early civilizations of Africa and Eurasia, the first Native American civilizations did not emerge in river valleys. Historians refer to these civilizations as **pre-Columbian** because they existed in the Americas before the arrival of the explorer Columbus in 1492.

THE MAYA, 1500 B.C.–1546 A.D.

More than 3,000 years ago, the Maya developed a complex civilization in the rain forests of present-day Guatemala. Around the 9th century, the Maya migrated northward to the Yucatan peninsula in present-day Mexico, where they built a new series of city-states. One of these later Maya cities is still well-preserved at **Chichen Itza.** Its stone pyramids served as tombs for nobles and religious leaders. Some pyramids reached heights as tall as some

Chichen Itza

modern skyscrapers. Constant warfare from the 13th to the 16th centuries led to the decline and collapse of Maya civilization.

Builders. The Maya built huge cities in the jungle with large palaces, temples, and pyramids.

Writing System. The Maya developed their own hieroglyphics — a writing system using picture symbols.

MAYA ACHIEVEMENTS

Math and Science. The Maya developed a complex numbering system, with the use of zero. Their calendar consisted of 365 days and was used to keep track of the changing seasons.

Artistry. Maya artists painted colorful murals to decorate their pyramids, palaces, and temples. They developed a ball game, played in a rectangular court, that became popular throughout the Americas.

THE AZTECS, 1200–1521

The Aztecs were an alliance of several Native American groups living in central Mexico. Around 1300, the Aztecs settled in the Valley of Mexico. They learned to grow corn and acquired other skills from their neighbors. Over the next two centuries, they engaged in frequent warfare to conquer other peoples of the region.

Like other Native American cultures, the Aztecs worshipped many gods. The Aztecs believed the Sun God needed human blood to continue his journeys across the sky. For this reason, the Aztecs practiced human sacrifices on a massive scale. Captured warriors from other tribes were sacrificed, as well as Aztecs who volunteered for this honor, believing their sacrifice was necessary to keep the universe in motion.

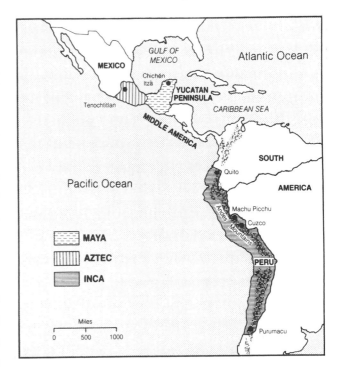

THE INCA EMPIRE, 1200–1535

The Inca empire developed along the Pacific coast and in the Andes mountains of South America. About 1400, the Inca began extending their rule across the Andes. Eventually they ruled an empire covering much of present-day Peru, Ecuador, Bolivia, and Chile. They built stone roads stretching over ten thousand miles to unite the distant corners of their empire. Unlike the Maya, the Inca never developed a form of writing. Instead, they used **quipu** — bundles of knotted and colored ropes to count, keep records, track crops, and send messages.

The Inca grew potatoes and other root crops that could resist cold nights. They kept llamas and alpacas for their meat and wool, and to carry goods. Superb engineering skills allowed the Inca to construct vast stone buildings high in the Andes. The ruins of **Machu Picchu,** an ancient fortress city high in the

Abandoned for 300 years, the ruins of Machu Picchu were re-discovered in 1911.

Andes Mountains, provides the best surviving example of Inca building skills. Its walls were made of blocks expertly cut and fitted together without the use of mortar.

THE EUROPEAN AGE OF DISCOVERY

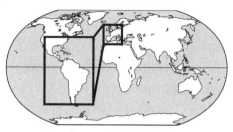

The spirit of inquiry of the Renaissance led Europeans to explore the oceans. The conquest of the Byzantine empire by the Ottoman Turks in 1453 cut Europe off from trade with East Asia. As a result, new incentives were created to find new all-water passages to the East. The European encounter with the peoples of the Americas brought the major civilizations of the world together for the first time and had a profound impact on all peoples.

Desire for Foreign Products. The Crusades, Marco Polo's reports, and other contacts had greatly stimulated European interest in East Asian goods like spices, perfumes, and silks.

Search for New Trade Routes. Renaissance Europeans desired to explore the oceans. European rulers correctly believed that control of trade with East Asia would bring them vast wealth.

MOTIVES FOR OVERSEAS EXPLORATION

Technology. Better navigation skills and instruments, like the compass and moveable rudder, allowed Europeans to sail farther than ever before.

Religion. Christian rulers in Europe wanted to spread their religion through overseas exploration.

SPAIN AND PORTUGAL LEAD THE WAY

Spain and Portugal led the way in looking for an all-water route to East Asia. Both countries were located on the Atlantic Ocean and had the resources needed to finance costly overseas exploration. Spain's rulers hoped to spread Catholicism and to glorify their country through overseas exploration. Starting in the late 1400s, European monarchs competed with one another in sending out explorers to find new trade routes and seek new lands.

◆ **Christopher Columbus** (1451–1506) was convinced that he could reach Asia by sailing westward. In 1492, he accidentally landed in the Americas instead of reaching the East Indies. His "discovery" of the Americas provided new sources of wealth and raw materials that would forever alter the economy of Europe.

Christopher Columbus at the court of Ferdinand and Isabella, rulers of Spain.

♦ **Vasco Da Gama** (1460–1524) discovered an all-water route from Europe to India by sailing around the southern tip of Africa in 1497. His discovery made it possible for Europeans to obtain Asian goods without relying on overland routes.

♦ **Ferdinand Magellan** (1480–1521). In 1519, Magellan led the first expedition of ships to **circumnavigate** (*circle*) the world. Sailing around South America and across the Pacific, Magellan confirmed that the world was round.

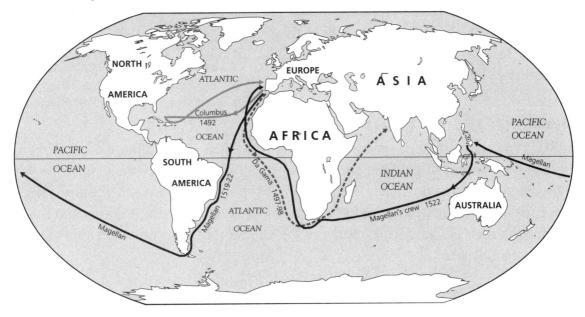

THE EUROPEAN CONQUEST OF THE AMERICAS

The arrival of Europeans had a profound impact on Native Americans. Spanish **conquistadors** (*conquerors*) and priests arrived soon after the first explorers. They conquered native peoples, seized their gold and silver, brought new diseases, and converted native peoples to Christianity. Small numbers of Spanish soldiers — using horses and firearms, and acting with local allies — quickly overcame large numbers of Native Americans and conquered the greatest Native American empires of that time: the Aztec and Inca.

THE CONQUEST OF MEXICO

In 1519, **Hernando Cortés** sailed to Mexico with a force of soldiers in search of gold and silver. Cortés met the Aztec Emperor **Montezuma.** The Aztecs at first believed that the Spaniards were gods and showered them with gifts. Later, Cortés allied with the enemies of the Aztecs. With a few hundred Spaniards and several thousand native allies, Cortés defeated the Aztecs in 1521.

Cortés and his army defeated the Aztecs.

Cortés triumphed in part because the Aztecs fought with clubs, spears, and bows while the Spaniards had guns, steel swords, dogs, horses and cannons. In addition, the Aztecs were worn down by an outbreak of smallpox, accidentally introduced by the Europeans. The Aztecs had no immunity against smallpox and other new diseases brought by the Europeans. Because of these factors, Cortés was quickly able to conquer the once powerful Aztec empire.

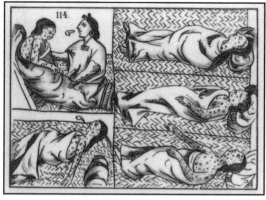

This illustration by an Aztec artist shows the impact of smallpox on the Native Americans.

THE CONQUEST OF PERU

In 1530, **Francisco Pizarro** set out to conquer the Inca. High in the Andes Mountains, Pizarro and a handful of soldiers defeated a much larger force of Inca warriors. Again, Native Americans were no match for the more technologically advanced Europeans. Pretending friendship, Pizarro invited the Inca emperor to visit him. Pizarro and his army ambushed the imperial party and murdered the emperor. Pizarro was then able to conquer the Inca capital by 1533.

THE EFFECTS OF THE ENCOUNTER

The European encounter with the Native Americans led to an exchange of ideas, customs, and technologies. Such exchanges between cultures are referred to as **cultural diffusion.**

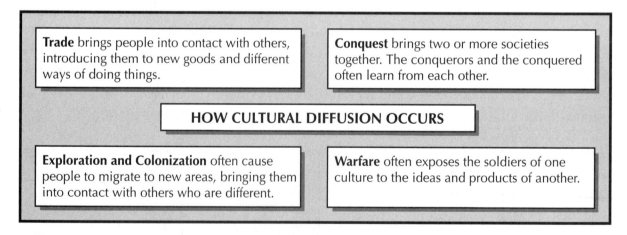

Trade brings people into contact with others, introducing them to new goods and different ways of doing things.

Conquest brings two or more societies together. The conquerors and the conquered often learn from each other.

HOW CULTURAL DIFFUSION OCCURS

Exploration and Colonization often cause people to migrate to new areas, bringing them into contact with others who are different.

Warfare often exposes the soldiers of one culture to the ideas and products of another.

NEW FOODS AND INCREASED TRADE

Because of the encounter, the European diet was greatly altered by the introduction of new foods like tomatoes, corn, potatoes, and chocolate. Western Europe became the center of a vast global trading network, with trade shifting away from the Mediterranean to the Atlantic coast. Raw materials obtained from the Americas hastened European economic development. Wealth from the "New World" enriched European merchants and their kings, especially in the states bordering the Atlantic — Portugal, Spain, England, France, and Holland.

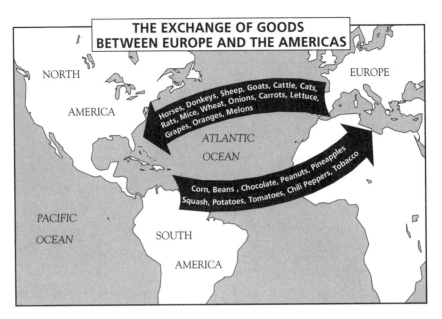

THE EXCHANGE OF GOODS
BETWEEN EUROPE AND THE AMERICAS

NORTH

AMERICA

EUROPE

Horses, Donkeys, Sheep, Goats, Cattle, Cats, Rats, Mice, Wheat, Onions, Carrots, Lettuce, Grapes, Oranges, Melons

ATLANTIC

OCEAN

Corn, Beans , Chocolate, Peanuts, Pineapples, Squash, Potatoes, Tomatoes, Chili Peppers, Tobacco

PACIFIC

OCEAN

SOUTH

AMERICA

THE COLONIAL EXPERIENCE IN LATIN AMERICA

The Spanish conquest of Latin America brought many important changes to Latin American society. Spain sent royal governors to rule these colonies in the king's name. Gold and silver from the Americas were shipped to Spain, making it the strongest power in Europe in the 16th century. Conquered lands in the Americas were often divided among the soldiers. The conquerors used Native Americans to farm the land and work the mines. This system of forced labor was called the **encomienda system.** At the same time, Native American populations declined rapidly because they had no immunity to diseases brought by the conquerors like measles and smallpox.

Catholic Churches in Mexico are a reminder of Spain's influence on Latin American culture.

Peninsulares were European-born nobles sent from Spain and Portugal to govern the colonies. They held the most power in the New World.

Creoles were people born in the Americas of European parents. Creoles consisted of wealthy landowners, lawyers, and priests.

SOCIAL CLASSES IN COLONIAL LATIN AMERICA

Mestizos and Mulattos were people of mixed European and Native American or African ancestry. Their status was slightly above Native Americans and Africans.

Native Americans and Africans worked in the fields and made up most of the population. Native Americans worked under serf-like conditions. Africans were enslaved. Both groups lacked social standing.

THE TRANSATLANTIC SLAVE TRADE

The death of many Native Americans from new diseases and the harsh working conditions created a need for a work force for the Spanish colonists. The solution to the problem was found in the Transatlantic slave trade. Slavery had existed in Africa long before European intervention. The Transatlantic slave trade expanded slavery on a massive scale.

Enslaved people were usually captured by warring African tribes and traded to European and American slave traders in exchange for guns and other goods. Slave traders removed millions of Africans over the next 300 years. Many of the captives died during the voyage, known as the "Middle Passage," because of the conditions on board the ships. Those that survived found themselves prisoners in a strange land.

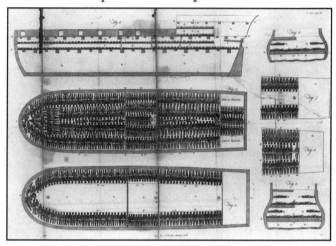

During the Middle Passage slaves were chained down.

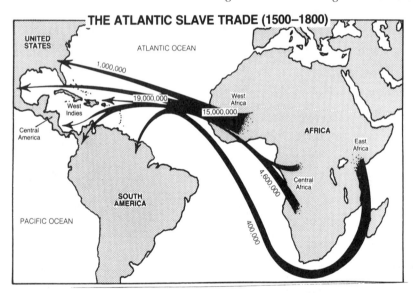

THE LEGACY OF THE TRANSATLANTIC SLAVE TRADE ON AFRICA

Encouraged African Warfare
The slave trade encouraged tribes to go to war with each other to obtain slaves to trade for European guns and other goods.

Disrupted African Culture
The slave trade destroyed much of Africa's rich heritage and disrupted its development. It create a legacy of violence, bitterness, and social upheaval.

Increased Cultural Diffusion
The exchange of ideas and goods increased. Slave traders brought new weapons and other goods to Africa, while slaves brought their beliefs, legends, and music to the Americas.

ANSWERING THE FOCUS QUESTION •

Writing

The major causes and effects of the European encounter with the Native Americans were the following:

_____ (Causes)

_____ (Effects)

Directions: Complete each of the following vocabulary cards. Then answer the multiple-choice questions that follow.

PRE-COLUMBIAN CIVILIZATIONS
Name two of these civilizations:
1.   2.
What was a major reason for their decline?

TRANSATLANTIC SLAVE TRADE
What was the Transatlantic slave trade?
What impact did the slave trade have on Africa?

1 One reason European monarchs sought an all-water route to Asia was that
   1 they sought a place to send their excess population
   2 they wanted a place to sell manufactured goods
   3 the fall of the Byzantine empire cut off Europe from trade with East Asia
   4 Muslims had gained control of the Holy Land

2 A major difference between the pre-Columbian civilizations and the ancient civilizations of Egypt and Mesopotamia is that the pre-Columbian civilizations
   1 believed in monotheism
   2 did not first develop in river valleys
   3 developed the idea of democratic government
   4 believed in the Mandate of Heaven

3 Which was an immediate effect of the European Age of Discovery?
   1 Islamic culture spread across Africa and Asia
   2 European influence spread to the Western Hemisphere
   3 Independence movements developed in Asia and Africa
   4 Europe was unified under a single ruler

4 During the colonial period in Latin America, a major reason for the importation of Africans as slaves was the
   1 scarcity of Native American labor
   2 need for skilled industrial workers
   3 development of advanced farming
   4 desire to promote Christianity

SECTION 2: EUROPE IN THE AGE OF KINGS, 1600–1770

In this section you will learn about important changes that took place in Europe between 1600 and 1770. The Commercial Revolution, the Scientific Revolution, and the Enlightenment all began in Europe in these years but had far-ranging impacts on the rest of the world.

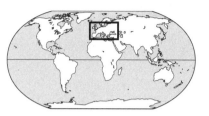

THINK ABOUT IT •

How did the Commercial Revolution, the Scientific Revolution, and the Enlightenment affect European society and thought?

THE COMMERCIAL REVOLUTION

During this period, the fastest growing part of the European economy was in the trade of goods, especially those from Asia and the Americas. The **Commercial Revolution** marked an important step in the transition of Europe from the local economies of the Middle Ages to leadership of a global economy. The Commercial Revolution had the following aspects:

MERCANTILISM

European kings hoped to increase their power through the system of **mercantilism.** Mercantilists taught that real wealth and power were based on ownership of gold and silver. For this purpose, France, England and Holland established overseas colonies in imitation of Spain and Portugal. Each so-called "mother country," besides mining for gold and silver, exported finished goods to the colonists in exchange for less costly raw materials. The competition for colonial empires spilled over into a series of wars between the European powers.

GLOBAL EMPIRES OF EUROPE, 1700

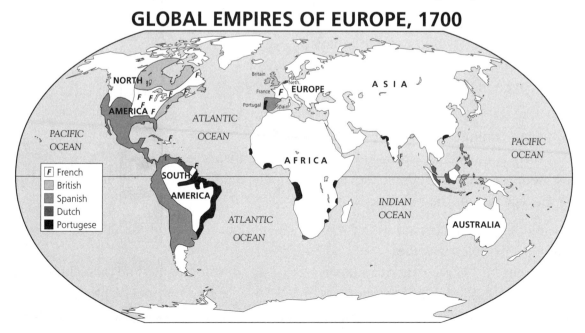

THE EMERGENCE OF CAPITALISM

Merchants and bankers laid the foundations for a system known as **capitalism.** Under this system, business owners risked their capital (*money*) in business in order to make profits. The growth of new businesses led to a demand for huge sums of money. To raise these sums, **joint stock companies** were sometimes formed. These ventures were privately-owned companies that sold stock to investors hoping to make a profit. Joint stock companies, merchants, and bankers also lent large sums of money to European rulers to help them raise armies.

THE RISE OF ROYAL POWER IN EUROPE

The spirit of the Renaissance, the effects of the Reformation, and the European encounter with the Americas all served to increase the power of European **monarchs** (*kings and queens*) and to enrich European society.

EFFECTS OF THE REFORMATION

The religious wars that followed the Reformation provided European rulers with an opportunity to build large standing armies and to increase their wealth through new taxes. The growing middle classes in the towns often allied with their king, who offered greater stability against the nobles. Kings also assumed control of religious affairs within their own borders.

DIVINE RIGHT THEORY

Monarchs began to justify their increased power on the basis of **divine right.** According to this theory, the king was God's deputy on Earth. Royal commands expressed God's wishes. The Englishman **Thomas Hobbes** wrote that kings were justified in assuming absolute power because only they could maintain order in a society.

LOUIS XIV, 1638–1715: A CASE STUDY IN ABSOLUTISM

Absolutism refers to a monarch's total control over his subjects. Louis XIV of France provided a model for other absolute monarchs. Under his rule, the king's command was law. Critics who challenged the king were punished. To subdue the nobles, Louis built a large palace at Versailles. Leading nobles were expected to spend most of the year at the royal court, under the watchful eye of the king. Louis also interfered in the economic and religious lives of his subjects. He demanded that Protestants convert to Catholicism or leave France. Finally, Louis involved his subjects in a series of wars to expand France's frontiers and to bring glory to his rule.

RUSSIA UNDER THE TSARS

Moscow during the time of Peter the Great

The rulers of Russia adopted the system of royal absolutism on a grand scale. By the end of the 15th century, the local rulers of the region around Moscow had declared their independence from the Mongols and set about conquering neighboring lands. The bulk of Russia's population were **serfs** — peasants required by law to stay on the land and work for noble landowners. Unlike Western Europe, serfdom continued in Russia and Eastern Europe in this period. Russian nobles exercised almost absolute power over their serfs. In return for their privileges, the nobility pledged absolute loyalty to the Tsar. Two of the most notable Russian rulers during this era were:

Peter the Great

◆ **Peter the Great** (1682–1725). Peter turned Russia from a backward nation into a modern power by introducing Western ideas, culture and technology. He often used brutal methods to force nobles to adopt Western customs. Peter moved the capital of Russia from Moscow to St. Petersburg, a city he built on the Baltic coast so that Russia would have a "window on the West." By the end of his reign, Peter had expanded Russian territory, gained ports on the Baltic Sea, and created a mighty Russian army.

◆ **Catherine the Great** (1762–1796). Catherine continued Peter's policies of expansion and Westernization. She promoted limited reforms during her reign by reorganizing the government, codifying the laws, and educating children at state expense. Despite these reforms, she refused to part with any of her absolute power. During her long reign, the conditions of the Russian serfs actually worsened.

Catherine the Great

ENGLAND BECOMES A LIMITED MONARCHY

Unlike France and Russia, England's monarchs were never able to secure absolute rule. In England, strong checks were already established on the king's power during the Middle Ages. Later events turned England into a limited **constitutional monarchy,** in which subjects enjoyed basic rights and political power was shared between the king and Parliament:

STEPS IN THE DEVELOPMENT OF CONSTITUTIONAL MONARCHY

Magna Carta. In 1215, English nobles forced King John to sign the Magna Carta. This guaranteed that Englishmen could not be fined or imprisoned except according to the laws of the land.

Rise of Parliament. Parliament was established as a legislative body made up of nobles in the House of Lords and elected representatives in the House of Commons. Parliament claimed the right to approve taxes.

The Puritan Revolution (1642–1660) and the Glorious Revolution (1688). During these two revolutions, Parliament established its supremacy over the king. The **Bill of Rights of 1689** confirmed that English monarchs could not collect new taxes or raise an army without Parliament's consent.

Parliament building

One of the most influential writers to emerge during this period was **John Locke.** Locke believed that governments obtain their power from the people they govern, not from God as divine right theory supposed. According to Locke, the main purpose of government was to protect a people's rights to life, liberty, and property. Locke defended people's right to rebel when the government abused its power. His ideas were influential beyond the times in which he wrote. A century later, Locke's writings greatly influenced the leaders of the American and French Revolutions.

NEW WAYS OF LOOKING AT THE WORLD

THE SCIENTIFIC REVOLUTION

The Scientific Revolution began during the Renaissance and continued through the 17th and 18th centuries. It rejected traditional authority and church teachings in favor of a new **scientific method,** in which scientists observed nature, made **hypotheses** (*educated guesses*) about relationships, and tested their hypotheses through experiments. Galileo, for example, tested the movements of falling objects. However, the most influential thinker of the Scientific Revolution was **Sir Isaac Newton.**

Sir Isaac Newton

In his book, *Principia Mathematica,* Newton developed a theory to explain both the movements of planets and how objects fall on earth. Newton reduced all these patterns to a single formula: the law of gravity. Newton's discovery raised hopes that all of the universe acted according to certain fixed and fundamental laws. It seemed that all scientists had to do was to apply observation, experimentation, and mathematics to understand and predict the natural world.

THE INFLUENCE OF THE ENLIGHTENMENT

The **Enlightenment** refers to an important movement in Europe during the 18th century. Leading Enlightenment thinkers believed that by applying reason and scientific laws, people could better understand both nature and society. They also hoped to apply these principles to improve society. Enlightenment thinkers questioned the divine right of kings and the power of the Catholic Church.

Adam Smith, one of the key thinkers of the Enlightenment

Voltaire (1694–1778) poked fun at traditional authority in society, government, and the church. His views on religious toleration and intellectual freedom influenced the leaders of the American and French Revolutions.

Jean-Jacques Rousseau (1712–1778) believed a government should express the "general will" of the people. His book, *The Social Contract,* helped to inspire the democratic ideals of the French Revolution.

KEY THINKERS OF THE ENLIGHTENMENT

Montesquieu (1689–1755) argued for separation of powers in government as a check against tyranny. His book, *The Spirit of Laws,* encouraged the development of a system of checks and balances later in the U.S. Constitution.

Adam Smith (1723–1790) described capitalism in his book, *The Wealth of Nations.* Smith explained how competition and the division of labor help to guide a free-market economic system based on self-interest.

Enlightenment ideas were adopted by American colonists in 1776 in their Declaration of Independence from England. The Declaration recognized the existence of "natural rights" such as the right to life, liberty, and the pursuit of happiness. The Declaration further stated, like Locke, that the purpose of government was to protect these rights. Enlightenment ideas also influenced absolute rulers such as Catherine the Great, who attempted to reform their societies from above. They attempted to use some of the ideas of the Enlightenment, such as encouraging education and trade, while at the same time maintaining their traditional royal powers. Such rulers were called **Enlightened Despots.**

THE BIRTH OF THE MODERN WORLD, 1500 TO 1770

ANSWERING THE FOCUS QUESTION •

Writing

The impact of the major movements and revolutions in Europe from 1600 to 1770 were:

_____ (Commercial Revolution)
_____ (Scientific Revolution)
_____ (Enlightenment)

Directions: Complete each of the following vocabulary cards. Then answer the multiple-choice questions that follow.

CAPITALISM
Define capitalism:
What impact did capitalism have on the world economy?

DIVINE RIGHT THEORY
What was the divine right theory?
Name two monarchs that justified their power by referring to divine right:

1 The concept of mercantilism is best illustrated by the
   1 political structure of China during the Zhou dynasty
   2 the social kinship system of the Kushite people
   3 military strategies of the Roman empire
   4 the economic relationship between Spain and its "New World" colonies

2 In an outline, one of these is a main topic, and the other three are sub-topics. Which is the main topic?
   1 Signing of the Magna Carta   3 The Glorious Revolution
   2 Growth of Constitutional Monarchy   4 The Puritan Revolution

3 "Kings are God's lieutenants on earth." Which type of government is best characterized by this quotation?
   1 direct democracy   3 constitutional monarchy
   2 limited monarchy   4 divine right absolutism

4 Which person is correctly paired with his ideas?
   1 "Only kings can maintain order in society" — Newton
   2 "The end justifies the means" — Hobbes
   3 "The laws of gravity control the movements of planets" — Machiavelli
   4 "Governments obtain their powers from the people they govern" — Locke

SECTION 3: THE TERRITORIAL EMPIRES OF ASIA

While Europeans were creating a new global order in Africa and the Americas, large traditional empires continued to flourish further east in Turkey, Persia, India, and China.

THINK ABOUT IT •

What were the basic characteristics of the territorial empires that dominated Asia from the 16th to the 18th centuries?

Like the absolute monarchs of Europe, the rulers of Asia used firearms and large armies to govern vast empires. These empires did not, however, advance as rapidly in science and technology as European states did, and would later feel the impact of European expansion.

THE OTTOMAN EMPIRE, 1453–1918

In Chapter 6, you learned how Arab Muslims created a vast Islamic civilization that once spread from Spain to the Indus River. The **Ottoman Turks,** a people from Central Asia, emerged as the rulers of the Islamic world in the 13th century. In 1453, they succeeded in capturing Constantinople, capital of what remained of the Byzantine empire, which they renamed Istanbul. The Ottomans also conquered Egypt and North Africa, re-uniting all of the Muslim world under their rule except Persia and Afghanistan. By the mid-1500s, under the leadership of **Suleiman the Magnificent,** the Ottoman empire was the largest in the world.

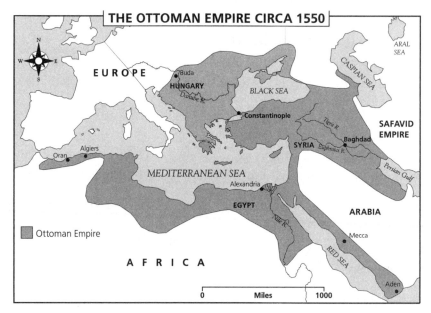

THE OTTOMAN EMPIRE CIRCA 1550

At the heart of the Ottoman system of government was the **Sultan** (*ruler*) and his lavish court in Istanbul. Under the Sultan's rule, the Ottoman empire was well-organized and efficiently governed. The Sultan controlled his entire empire as an all-powerful ruler.

At the same time, the Ottomans recognized cultural diversity by letting Christian and Jewish communities largely govern themselves. Ottoman control over the crossroads of trade promoted prosperity and stability for several centuries.

THE SAFAVID EMPIRE IN PERSIA

The Safavids (*present-day Iranians*) created an empire in Persia in the early 1500s, extending as far south as the Persian Gulf and east to the Indus River. The Safavids were Shi'ite Muslims. This made them hostile to the Ottomans, who followed the Sunni branch of Islam. Safavid rulers, known as **Shahs,** used their large armies to maintain control of their empire. They also did much to encourage trade. Miniature painting flourished in Safavid Persia, as well as the production of beautiful rugs. Literature, medicine, and the study of astronomy thrived. However, high taxes and continuous warfare with the Ottomans gradually weakened the Safavids. In 1722, the Safavid empire was conquered by neighboring Afghanistan.

MUSLIM, MUGHAL, AND BRITISH INDIA

THE MUSLIM INVASIONS

In the 11th and 12th centuries, another group of Turkish Muslims, different from the Ottomans, invaded India's northern plains. They destroyed Hindu temples and cities. The Muslim invaders established independent kingdoms in northern India, known as **Sultanates.** The most important Sultanate was established at Delhi. For 300 years, the Sultans of Delhi ruled much of northern and

central India. At the end of the 14th century, the city of Delhi was destroyed and its inhabitants were slaughtered by Tamerlane, a descendant of the Mongols. The Delhi Sultanate never recovered from this blow.

THE MUGHAL EMPIRE (1526–1837)

In 1526, the Mughal empire was founded. The Mughals were Muslims with close ties to Safavid Persia. The most famous Mughal was **Akbar the Great** (1542–1605). Akbar conquered neighboring states, uniting northern India under his rule. To govern his empire efficiently, Akbar divided it into twelve provinces. His policy of toleration for Hindus successfully promoted peace and prosperity.

Europeans bring gifts to Shah-Jahan, grandson of Akbar the Great.

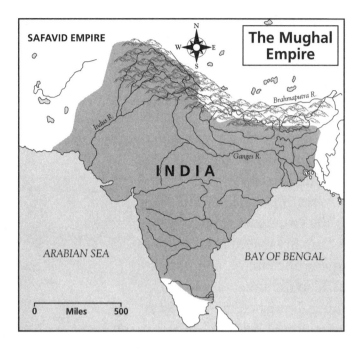

Akbar's grandson **Shah Jahan** (1628–1658), in contrast, showed little sympathy for the Hindus and ordered the destruction of many Hindu temples. Many Indian Hindus converted to Islam during Jahan's reign. Some people changed their religion to avoid special taxes, while others converted because they were from lower castes and hoped to escape the prejudices of the caste system. Jahan built many palaces, fortresses, and mosques to glorify his reign. The most famous and beautiful of his buildings was the **Taj Mahal.** Shortly after Jahan's reign began, his wife died giving birth to their fourteenth child. Overcome with grief, Jahan built the world's greatest tomb for his wife. Soon after Jahan's death, the Mughal empire began to weaken.

The Taj Mahal

INDIA UNDER BRITISH RULE

While the Mughals had been extending their territories to the north, the **British East India Company** had laid the foundation for future British control of India in the south. The East India Company carried on trade between India and Britain at ports along the Indian coastline. In the 1750s, a local ruler attacked the British at their trading post at Calcutta. The East India Company recaptured the town, and soon became the largest military power in India. Over time, the company expanded its territories to protect its trading interests. Gradually, India came under British influence. By the early 19th century, the East India Company had gained control over almost the entire Indian subcontinent, turning India largely into a British possession. You will learn more about British rule in India in the next chapter.

THE MING AND QING DYNASTIES IN CHINA

You learned how China was re-unified under Mongol rule in the 13th century. Despite this achievement, Mongol rule remained unpopular among the Chinese. In 1368, the Mongols were overthrown by a Chinese monk, who became the founder of the Ming Dynasty.

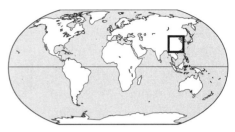

MING DYNASTY, 1368–1644

During the **Ming Dynasty,** China enjoyed nearly three hundred years of stability and prosperity. Ming emperors expanded the Chinese empire to include Korea, Burma, and Vietnam. The Ming constructed a magnificent Imperial Palace in Beijing, known as the **Forbidden City,** which became home to all later Chinese emperors.

Under the Ming, Chinese literature and art also flourished. Craftsmen excelled at printing and in producing silks and porcelains. Trade prospered as China exported silk, porcelain, and other luxury goods. Early Ming rulers even sponsored great naval expeditions, such as the voyages of **Zheng He** to India, Arabia, and Africa in the early 1400s. These were stopped when the imperial government changed its policies.

Chinese craftsmen excelled at producing porcelain.

Direct European contact with China was established in the 16th century. Silver from the Americas was used by Spanish and Portuguese traders to buy goods from China. Although some Catholic missionaries attempted to convert the Chinese to Christianity, Christianity had only limited appeal. Like many other peoples, the Chinese believed that their own culture was superior to others. The Chinese elite looked upon the Europeans as barbarians, lacking the civilized ways of the "Middle Kingdom" — China. Such a belief in one's own cultural superiority is known as **ethnocentrism.** China's growing isolation from other cultures helped encourage the belief that the Chinese way of life was superior to all others.

QING (MANCHU) DYNASTY, 1644–1912

Towards the end of the Ming Dynasty, corruption among public officials weakened the government. Population pressure led to a series of peasant uprisings. In 1644, the Manchus, from the northeast, invaded and conquered China. The Manchu conquerors founded the **Qing** or **Manchu Dynasty.** Like the Mongols centuries earlier, the Manchus adopted Chinese ways to rule their new empire. They continued the traditional civil service examinations and governed

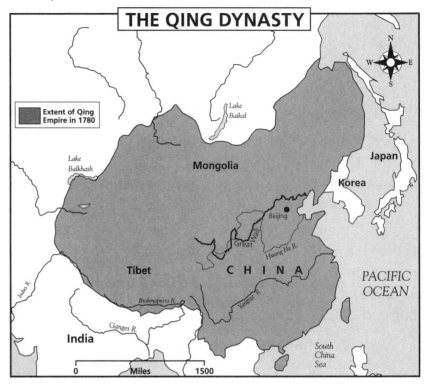

through local officials. They also became strong patrons of Chinese literature, art, and music. Nevertheless, the Manchus did introduce changes to China. They forced Chinese men to wear their hair in pigtails as a symbol that they had submitted to Manchu rule. *The Dream of Red Chamber,* considered China's greatest novel, was written in this period.

Qing rulers brought a period of peace and prosperity to China for the first 150 years of the dynasty. They built new roads and canals, cleared additional land for agriculture, and built store-houses for grain. During the 1700s, Qing emperors such as Kang XI and Qian Long promoted scholarship and education while reducing taxes. By 1750, the population of China was more than 150 million. Large urban centers housed merchants, scholars, and craftspeople.

During these same years, however, European technology gradually surpassed China. China's isolation from the West and the imperial government's resistance to change prevented China from keeping pace with

A Qing noble and his wife

Western advances in industry and science. In later chapters, you will see how China faced new challenges from Europe in the early 19th century.

ANSWERING THE FOCUS QUESTION •

Writing

The basic characteristics of the Asian territorial empires of this era were

_____ (Ottoman Empire)

_____ (Safavid Empire)

_____ (Mughal Empire)

_____ (Ming and Manchu Dynasties)

Directions: Complete each of the following vocabulary cards. Then answer the multiple-choice questions that follow.

AKBAR THE GREAT
Who was he?
What impact did he have?

BRITISH EAST INDIA COMPANY
What was it doing in India?
What role did it play in Indian history?

1 The Ottoman, Safavid, and Mughal empires were similar in that they all
   1 were Islamic
   2 established overseas colonies
   3 invaded Europe
   4 had very large navies

2 Which statement about the Ottoman empire is most accurate?
   1 It followed Roman Catholicism.
   2 Its capital was at Istanbul.
   3 It was ruled by the Shah.
   4 It was located in Central Asia.

3 Which head of state is correctly paired with his empire?
   1 Mansa Musa — Aztec empire
   2 Montezuma — Mughal empire
   3 Akbar the Great — Mali empire
   4 Suleiman the Magnificent — Ottoman empire

4 In China, ethnocentric beliefs were encouraged by
   1 a historic reliance on foreign nations
   2 a long history of democratic government
   3 a strong belief in Christianity
   4 geographic isolation

KEY TERMS, CONCEPTS, AND PEOPLE

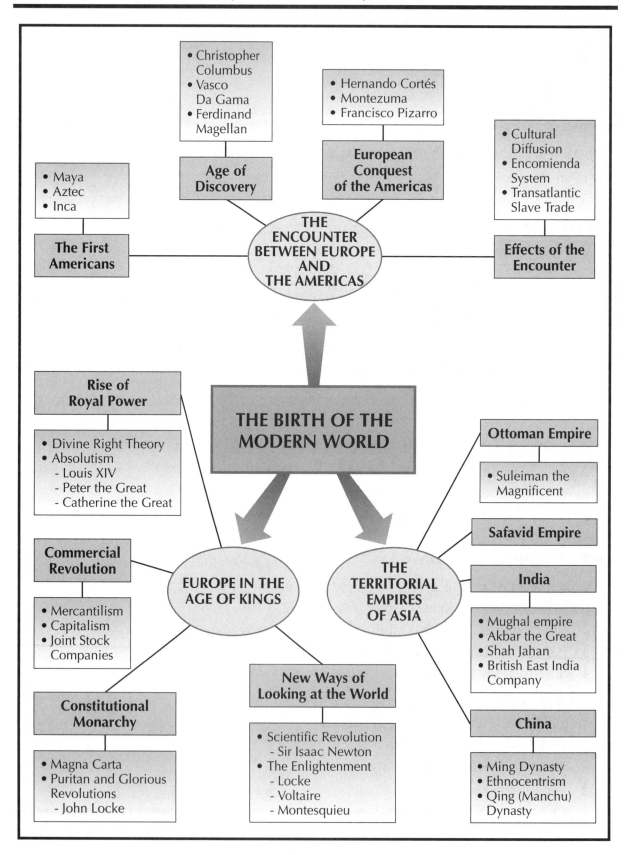

- Christopher Columbus
- Vasco Da Gama
- Ferdinand Magellan

Age of Discovery

- Hernando Cortés
- Montezuma
- Francisco Pizarro

European Conquest of the Americas

- Cultural Diffusion
- Encomienda System
- Transatlantic Slave Trade

Effects of the Encounter

- Maya
- Aztec
- Inca

The First Americans

THE ENCOUNTER BETWEEN EUROPE AND THE AMERICAS

THE BIRTH OF THE MODERN WORLD

Rise of Royal Power

- Divine Right Theory
- Absolutism
  - Louis XIV
  - Peter the Great
  - Catherine the Great

Commercial Revolution

- Mercantilism
- Capitalism
- Joint Stock Companies

Constitutional Monarchy

- Magna Carta
- Puritan and Glorious Revolutions
  - John Locke

EUROPE IN THE AGE OF KINGS

New Ways of Looking at the World

- Scientific Revolution
  - Sir Isaac Newton
- The Enlightenment
  - Locke
  - Voltaire
  - Montesquieu

THE TERRITORIAL EMPIRES OF ASIA

Ottoman Empire

- Suleiman the Magnificent

Safavid Empire

India

- Mughal empire
- Akbar the Great
- Shah Jahan
- British East India Company

China

- Ming Dynasty
- Ethnocentrism
- Qing (Manchu) Dynasty

SUMMARIZING YOUR UNDERSTANDING

COMPLETING AN OUTLINE

Directions: Use these headings to complete the outline below.

THE TERRITORIAL EMPIRES OF ASIA
The Ottoman Empire
The First Americans
The Rise of Royal Power
Commercial Revolution
New Ways of Looking at the World
The Safavid Empire
The European Age of Discovery
The European Conquest of the Americas
EUROPE IN THE AGE OF KINGS
Muslim, Mughal, and British India
THE ENCOUNTER BETWEEN EUROPE AND THE AMERICAS
THE BIRTH OF THE MODERN WORLD
Effects of the Encounter
The Ming and Qing Dynasties

TITLE: _____

I.   MAJOR DIVISION: _____
   A. Sub-topic: _____
   B. Sub-topic: _____
   C. Sub-topic: _____
   D. Sub-topic: _____

II. MAJOR DIVISION: _____
   A. Sub-topic: _____
   B. Sub-topic: _____
   C. Sub-topic: _____

III. MAJOR DIVISION: _____
   A. Sub-topic: _____
   B. Sub-topic: _____
   C. Sub-topic: _____
   D. Sub-topic: _____

COMPLETING A GRAPHIC ORGANIZER

Complete the following graphic organizer by describing some of the major events in Europe.

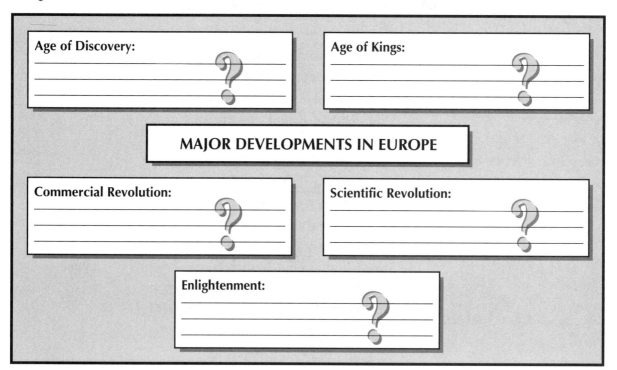

COMPLETING A TABLE

Use the table below to organize the information that you have read about some of the major empires of this era.

Name	Time Period	Location	Major Achievements
Maya			
Aztec			
Inca			
Ottoman			
Safavid			
Mughal			
Ming			
Qing			

SHARPENING YOUR TEST-TAKING SKILLS

EXAMINING THEMATIC ESSAYS

At the end of the last chapter, you learned about essay questions and the major "action words" used in most essay questions. This section focuses in more detail on one type of essay question found on many global history tests — **thematic essay questions.** Let's begin by looking at a typical thematic essay question:

Directions: Write a well-organized essay that includes an introduction with a topic statement, several paragraphs as explained in the Task, and a conclusion.

Theme: Geography

> The geographical features of an area often affect
> historical developments taking place there.

Task:

> Choose *two* past civilizations from your study of global history and geography.
>
> For *each* civilization:
> - Describe a geographical feature that affected it.
> - Explain how that feature had an impact on that civilization.

You may use any example from your study of global history and geography. Some suggestions you might wish to consider include: ancient Egypt, the ancient Greeks, the Roman Empire, the Byzantine Empire, and the Mongol Empire.

You are *not* limited to these suggestions.

Notice that a thematic essay question opens with directions. The directions tell you the form in which your answer must be written. Next, you are provided with a generalization. Here the generalization is about geography. The question then gives you a task to complete. Some suggestions provide helpful examples you might use in your essay to support the generalization, but are not limited to those examples. Thus, what you are essentially asked to do is:

(1) to show your understanding of a *generalization* by giving specific facts to support it; and

(2) to write a well-organized essay with a thesis statement based on the generalization, several paragraphs as explained in the task, and a conclusion.

WHAT IS A GENERALIZATION?

To answer a thematic essay question, you must understand what a generalization is and how to support it. **Generalizations** are powerful organizing tools used to summarize large amounts of information in simpler form. To understand how a generalization works, read the following list of facts:

◆ Ancient Egyptian civilization arose along the banks of the Nile River.
◆ Mesopotamian civilizations emerged in the area between the Tigris and Euphrates Rivers.
◆ Chinese civilization first started along the banks of the Huang He.
◆ The Harappan civilization originated in the Indus River Valley.

These are four facts about ancient civilizations. However, they all have something in common: each of these ancient civilizations began in river valleys. When a general statement identifies a common pattern, it is called a **generalization.** It shows what several facts have in common.

Let's see how this generalization might look in diagram form:

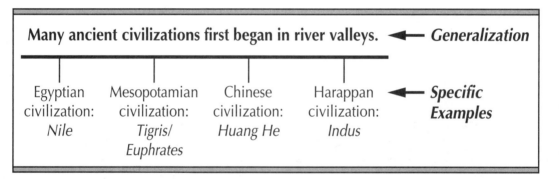

The specific examples support the generalization that many ancient civilizations first began in river valleys. Thus, the key is to use specific examples to support a general statement. Thematic essay questions are always based on a generalization, identified as the "theme." Your job will be to provide the supporting details and examples.

WRITING A WELL-ORGANIZED ESSAY

The "task" part of the question tells you what specific things you need to include in your essay about the theme. Start by reading the "Task" on page 165. The task may have several parts. To better focus on what you need to do, <u>underline</u> each "action word" in the task, and ⬭circle⬭ the *number of examples* the question requires you to provide for each part.

NOTES FOR YOUR ESSAY

Taking notes first can help you to organize your essay. Use this sample as a possible guide for taking notes:

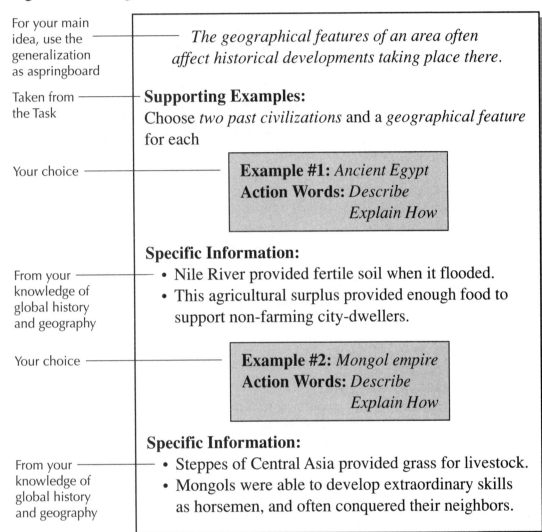

For your main idea, use the generalization as a springboard

The geographical features of an area often affect historical developments taking place there.

Taken from the Task

Supporting Examples:
Choose *two past civilizations* and a *geographical feature* for each

Your choice

Example #1: *Ancient Egypt*
Action Words: *Describe*
                          Explain How

From your knowledge of global history and geography

Specific Information:
- Nile River provided fertile soil when it flooded.
- This agricultural surplus provided enough food to support non-farming city-dwellers.

Your choice

Example #2: *Mongol empire*
Action Words: *Describe*
                          Explain How

From your knowledge of global history and geography

Specific Information:
- Steppes of Central Asia provided grass for livestock.
- Mongols were able to develop extraordinary skills as horsemen, and often conquered their neighbors.

USING THE "CHEESEBURGER" METHOD

Now let's use the information from your notes to write an essay. Imagine your answer resembles a cheeseburger with a top bun, a slice of cheese, patties of meat, and a bottom bun. The top bun states your **main idea.** The cheese slice is your **transition sentence.** These two parts make up your first paragraph. You may include additional background or ideas in your introduction. The patties of meat are the **body of your essay** with your supporting statements. The bottom bun is your **conclusion.** In writing your essay, be sure to include all these parts.

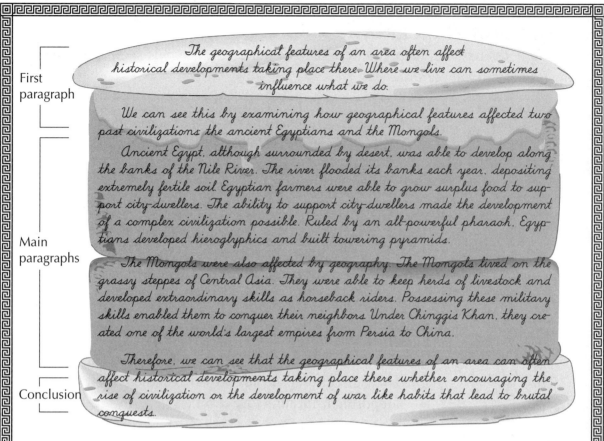

First paragraph

The geographical features of an area often affect historical developments taking place there. Where we live can sometimes influence what we do.

We can see this by examining how geographical features affected two past civilizations: the ancient Egyptians and the Mongols.

Ancient Egypt, although surrounded by desert, was able to develop along the banks of the Nile River. The river flooded its banks each year, depositing extremely fertile soil. Egyptian farmers were able to grow surplus food to support city-dwellers. The ability to support city-dwellers made the development of a complex civilization possible. Ruled by an all-powerful pharaoh, Egyptians developed hieroglyphics and built towering pyramids.

Main paragraphs

The Mongols were also affected by geography. The Mongols lived on the grassy steppes of Central Asia. They were able to keep herds of livestock and developed extraordinary skills as horseback riders. Possessing these military skills enabled them to conquer their neighbors. Under Chinggis Khan, they created one of the world's largest empires from Persia to China.

Conclusion

Therefore, we can see that the geographical features of an area can often affect historical developments taking place there whether encouraging the rise of civilization or the development of war like habits that lead to brutal conquests.

Top Bun (Topic Sentence). In the first sentence, you provide a main idea or thesis statement. To write the thesis statement, you can often use the generalization in the *Theme* part of the question and express it in a different form. To get a higher score, you need to provide added background or ideas to introduce your thesis.

Cheese Slice (Transition Sentence). The "cheese" sentence connects the thesis statement to the more specific information you are about to give.

Patties of Meat (Main Paragraphs). Here you give specific examples, facts and details to support your thesis statement. This is the main part of your essay. It is where you "show off" your ability to *describe*, *explain*, *analyze*, *evaluate*, and *compare* issues or events. In this example, notice how the two main paragraphs in the "cheeseburger" correspond to the examples in your notes on page 167.

Bottom Bun (Conclusion). The last part of your essay should be similar to your thesis statement, except that it is now expressed as a conclusion. Summarize the main points supporting your thesis. There are several ways to introduce your conclusion: *"Therefore, we can see that ..."* or *"Thus, it is clear that ...."* The closing sentence informs the reader that the essay has come to an end.

TESTING YOUR UNDERSTANDING

Test your understanding of this chapter by answering the following questions:

MULTIPLE-CHOICE QUESTIONS

1 The Maya, Aztec, and Inca were all examples of
1 pre-Columbian societies
2 Native American tribes in Mexico
3 cultural diffusion
4 encomienda system

2 The economic relationship between European countries and their "New World" colonies was known as
1 Code of Justinian
2 Pax Romana
3 mercantilism
4 Mandate of Heaven

3 The Magna Carta was important to the development of English democracy because it
1 limited the power of the monarch
2 took away land from the nobles
3 created a bicameral legislature
4 extended voting rights to peasants

4 Which activity provides the best example of cultural diffusion?
1 the use of masks in traditional West African ceremonies
2 the construction of the pyramids in Egypt
3 the adoption of Islam by Mali's rulers
4 the cultivation of silk by the Chinese

5 A major result of the European Age of Discovery was the
1 conversion of a majority of Europeans to Protestantism
2 growth of trade between Europe and Latin America
3 development of feudalism in Japan
4 weakening of the power of the middle class in China

6 Which situation most contributed to the Age of Exploration?
1 strong rulers censored new ideas
2 scientific advances in navigation
3 a wealthy middle class supported the arts
4 rulers sought to recapture the Holy Land

7 The Ming and Qing Dynasties were similar in that both
1 were founded by a Chinese monk
2 enjoyed periods of peace and prosperity
3 were popular among the Chinese people
4 were ruled by Roman Catholics

8 The belief that the purpose of government is to protect the natural rights of individuals developed during the
1   Middle Ages
2   Renaissance
3   Reformation
4   Enlightenment

Base your answer to question 9 on the pie chart to the right and your knowledge of global history.

9 Which is a valid conclusion based on the information in the pie chart?
1   Most slaves were destined for the cotton fields of North America.
2   Europe and Asia did not participate in importing African slaves.
3   The largest number of slaves were sent to various Caribbean islands.
4   Most slaves were sent to Brazil.

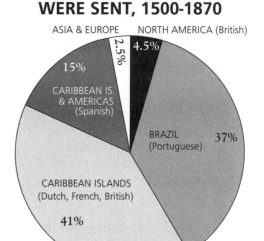

WHERE AFRICAN SLAVES WERE SENT, 1500-1870

ASIA & EUROPE 15%
NORTH AMERICA (British) 4.5%
2.5%
CARIBBEAN IS. & AMERICAS (Spanish)
BRAZIL (Portuguese) 37%
CARIBBEAN ISLANDS (Dutch, French, British) 41%

Base your answer to question 10 on the graph and on your knowledge of global history.

10 Which statement can best be supported by the information in the line graph?
1   Mexico's Native American population steadily increased between 1518 and 1548.
2   The effects of the Spanish conquest on the Native American population of Mexico were most severe between 1518 and 1548.

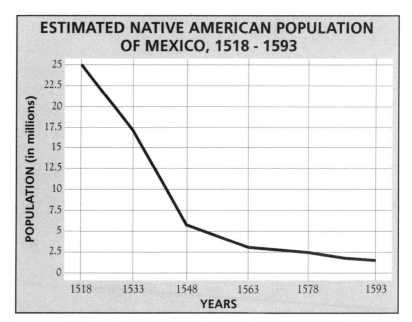

ESTIMATED NATIVE AMERICAN POPULATION OF MEXICO, 1518 - 1593

POPULATION (in millions)

YEARS

3   The Spanish conquest of Mexico improved standards of living for the Native American population of Mexico from 1518 to 1548.
4   Spanish influence in Mexico ended by 1593.

INTERPRETING DOCUMENTS

I. FINDING MAIN IDEAS AND SUPPORTING DETAILS

Read the passage below to find its main idea and its supporting details.

> The world owes a tremendous debt to China. For centuries, China introduced many important technological and cultural advances. The Chinese were the first to discover that the cocoons of silk worms could be use to make thread for silk cloth, and that special clay could be use to make fine porcelain. The Chinese also invented the compass, an instrument used to navigate at sea. They were the first to make gunpowder, although they did not fully realize its military potential at first. The Chinese were also the first to make paper. This led to the development of block printing, which allowed the Chinese to produce books.
>
> The Chinese also made major contributions to philosophy, art, and literature. They applied the Confucian, Buddhist, and Daoist schools of thought to improve education and government. In art, they created beautiful landscape paintings, using the beauty of nature as their theme. In literature, the Chinese excelled at poetry and wrote some of the world's first novels.

1. Main Idea: _____

2. Supporting Details: A _____ B _____ C _____

II. INTERPRETING A DIAGRAM

The diagram below illustrates colonial society in Latin America.

Peninsulares

Creoles

Mestizos and Mulattos

Native Americans

Slaves

1 Circle the characteristic of colonial Latin American society best illustrated by the diagram on page 171.

| Social | Rigid | Cultural |
| mobility | class system | diffusion |

2 Circle the era of Latin American history represented by the diagram:

| 500 B.C. to 100 A.D. | 900 to 1200 | 1500 to 1800 |

3 Choose **one** of the social classes in the diagram. Describe its role in colonial Latin American society. _____

_____

_____

THEMATIC ESSAY QUESTION

Directions: Write a well-organized essay that includes an introduction, several paragraphs explaining your position, and a conclusion.

Theme: Movement of Goods and People

> Throughout history, cultural diffusion has taken place when one society establishes contact with or conquers another society.

Task:

> Choose *two* examples from your study of global history and geography in which one society established contact with or conquered another society.
>
> For *each* example:
> • Explain how cultural diffusion occurred.
> • Describe one way in which either society changed as a result.

You may use any example from your study of global history and geography. Some suggestions you may wish to consider include: ancient Greece, ancient Rome, the Islamic Empire, the Crusades, the Mongols, and the Age of Discovery.

You are *not* limited to these suggestions.

CHAPTER 9

NEW CURRENTS: REVOLUTION, INDUSTRY, AND NATIONALISM 1770 TO 1900

SECTION 1: THE FRENCH REVOLUTION AND ITS IMPACT

1. The French Revolution
2. Napoleon
3. Restoring Europe's Old Order
4. The Independence of Latin America

Storming of the Bastille — July 14, 1789

Count Cavour — a leader for Italian independence

SECTION 3: NATIONALISM AND IMPERIALISM

1. Unification of Italy and Germany
2. Nationalism in Russia and Turkey
3. Imperialism in India and Africa
4. Opening of China and Japan

During the Industrial Revolution, many children worked in factories.

SECTION 2: THE INDUSTRIAL REVOLUTION

1. Start of the Industrial Revolution
2. Industrial Revolution Brings Change
3. Marx and Communism

	1750	1770	1790	1810	1830	1850	1880	1910
JAPAN	TOKUGAWA SHOGUNATE					JAPAN OPENED TO TRADE	MEIJI RESTORATION	
EUROPE	OLD REGIME IN FRANCE		FRENCH REVOLU-TION/NAPOLEON	METTERNICH ERA		REVO-LU-TIONS / GERMAN, ITALIAN UNIFIC.	SCRAMBLE FOR COLONIES	
	INDUSTRIAL REVOLUTION							
MIDEAST	OTTOMAN EMPIRE							
LATIN AMERICA	COLONIAL RULE			INDEPENDENCE MOVEMENTS	AGE OF CAUDILLOS			
AFRICA			END OF SLAVE TRADE				EUROPEAN IMPERIALISM	
INDIA	MUGHAL RULE WEAKENS		EXPANSION OF EAST INDIA COMPANY		BRITISH EMPIRE			
CHINA	QING (MANCHU) DYNASTY							

1750	1770	1790	1810	1830	1850	1880	1910

WHAT YOU SHOULD FOCUS ON

The period you are about to study is one in which large-scale changes began to take place with increasing speed. A person born in France during the Middle Ages would probably not have felt too out of place 300 years later during the Renaissance. But someone born in France before the French Revolution who returned a century later would have found the dramatic changes that had taken place in those one hundred years almost incomprehensible.

Napoleon poses in his coronation robes, 1804.

It is easiest to group the changes that occurred during this era into four main areas:

The French Revolution was a political event that challenged the way people thought about traditional political authority and social divisions.

The Industrial Revolution used new sources of power to replace human and animal power, bringing about the greatest changes in lifestyles and technology since the dawn of civilization.

NEW CURRENTS EMERGING IN THE WORLD, 1770–1900

Nationalism caused problems for rulers with several nationalities under their control, when each national group attempted to acquire its own unified national state.

Imperialism changed the map of the world. The changes brought by the Industrial Revolution and nationalism caused the leading European powers to seek to acquire areas in Asia, Africa, and the Pacific.

In studying this era, you should focus on the following questions:

➤ What were the causes and effects of the French Revolution?
➤ What were the causes and effects of the Industrial Revolution?
➤ How did nationalism affect Europe?
➤ What were the benefits and drawbacks of imperialism in Africa and Asia?

LOOKING AT THE FORCES OF SOCIAL CHANGE

Just as we experience change throughout our lives, societies also undergo change. Historians are especially interested in understanding why and how societies change, and what forces influence the pace and direction of change. The following have been identified as some important causes of historical change:

Conflict among Groups in a Society. Many societies are composed of people of different religious and ethnic groups, of different social classes, and of different backgrounds. Often these groups have conflicting interests that must be resolved by reform, or sometimes even by violence and revolution.

New Ideas. New ideas can transform a society. These ideas may be theories about government and society, like democracy or Communism. They may be new religious beliefs like Islam or Protestantism, or even new ideas about nature, such as those introduced by the Scientific Revolution of the 1500s–1600s.

MAJOR FORCES OF SOCIAL CHANGE

Contacts with other Societies. Contacts with other societies often lead to the introduction of new ideas and products through cultural diffusion. For example, the Native American encounter with Europeans in the Americas led to the introduction of new foods to Europe, as well as to the introduction of horses and cattle to the Americas.

Technological Innovation. New inventions can often be powerful ingredients of historical change. For example, the invention of the printing press played an important role in spreading the Reformation by allowing Church critics to communicate their ideas widely.

THE PACE OF CHANGE

Social change can be gradual or extremely rapid. In some historical periods, change has been so slow that it goes almost unnoticed. These societies are usually agricultural and tied to existing traditions. Gradual change, known as **evolutionary change**, allows different groups and institutions time to adapt to change and to evolve with it. **Revolutionary change** is much more rapid and abrupt. New ideas, methods of production, or political and social institutions replace old ones almost overnight.

Political **revolutions** frequently occur when intellectual, economic, and social changes create tensions within a society. New groups challenge the existing order. In a moment of weakness, the existing government collapses and new groups take charge — introducing far-ranging changes in government and society.

MAJOR HISTORICAL DEVELOPMENTS

SECTION 1: THE FRENCH REVOLUTION AND ITS IMPACT

Since the days of Louis XIV, France had been the most populous, richest and most powerful country in Western Europe. France set European trends in literature, fashion, the arts, and politics. In this section, you will learn how conditions made France ripe for revolution by 1789.

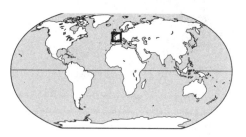

THINK ABOUT IT ••

What were the causes and long-term effects of the French Revolution?

THE FRENCH REVOLUTION

PRECONDITIONS TO REVOLUTION

Prior to 1789, French society (*known as the Old Regime*) was divided into three classes or **estates.** The first estate was made up of the clergy (*priests*); the second were the nobles. The third and largest estate were the commoners. The most influential group in the third estate were the **bourgeoisie,** or middle class, composed of merchants, professionals, and shopkeepers.

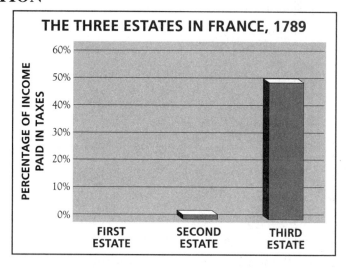

Based on age-old traditions, there were many inequalities in Old Regime France that we would find hard to accept today. The clergy and nobles held many special privileges, such as being exempt from most taxes. Only nobles could fill certain posts in the army or the King's court. As the bourgeoisie grew wealthier, they came to resent the special privileges of the nobles.

THE REVOLUTION BEGINS

During the 1700s, French kings almost bankrupted the state through expensive wars and excessive borrowing. In 1789, Louis XVI's ministers came to believe the only way to solve the government's financial problems was to tax the nobles.

The nobles refused to agree to pay taxes unless the king first summoned an **Estates General** — a national assembly in which each of the three social classes would be represented. **King Louis XVI** reluctantly gave in to this demand, and the Estates General met in May, 1789.

THE RULE OF THE MODERATES

Although the crisis began as a contest for power between the king and the nobles, once the Estates General met, the focus turned towards the bourgeoisie. The delegates from the Third Estate declared themselves to be a **National Assembly.** When the king threatened to break up the Assembly, Parisians seized a royal prison known as the **Bastille.** Rather than start a civil war, Louis XVI let the National Assembly continue its sessions.

Louis XIV nearly bankrupted France by building the Palace of Versailles and engaging in decades of war.

With its new-found power, in August, 1789 the National Assembly issued a **Declaration of the Rights of Man,** proclaiming that government rested on the consent of the people, not on the divine right of the king. The National Assembly then abolished the privileges of the nobles and the clergy. The slogan of the Revolution became "Liberty, Equality, and Fraternity (*brotherhood*)." The Assembly adopted a written constitution, created a National Legislature, and turned France into a constitutional monarchy.

THE REVOLUTION TAKES A RADICAL TURN

These events in France posed a threat to other European rulers, who governed by divine right. As a result, France found itself at war with other European states. Once war began, radicals gained control of the government. They feared attempts to restore the King's absolute power, and executed Louis XVI — turning France into a republic.

A Parisian crowd looks on expectantly as the queen is about to be beheaded.

The new French government formed a special executive committee, the **Committee of Public Safety,** which took over the Revolution. Led by **Maximilien Robespierre,** the Committee launched a **Reign of Terror** in 1793 to save the Revolution from foreign invasion and domestic protesters.

Violence erupted and suspected traitors, including nobles and priests, were executed. Many aspects of the Old Regime, from the calendar to clothing styles, were rejected by the new government. They also armed ordinary citizens to defend France against foreign invaders. Their policies were extremely successful, but power shifted back to more moderate leaders when the threat of foreign invasion passed and France tired of internal violence.

The Revolution challenged the idea of the divine right of kings and the privileges of the nobility in Europe.	The Revolution stood for democratic government and social equality. Political power in France shifted from the king and his nobles to the bourgeois class.

SIGNIFICANCE OF THE FRENCH REVOLUTION

The Revolution removed feudal restrictions from France, clearing the way for the creation of a modern capitalist economy.	Both the American and French Revolutions served as models for citizens in other countries seeking political change.

NAPOLEON

Napoleon Bonaparte (1769–1821) came from a family of lower nobility but was sympathetic to the ideals of the Revolution. He proved to be one of the most gifted generals of all time.

MILITARISM AND EMPIRE BUILDING

Napoleon came to power at the end of the Revolution, when France was still at war with most of Europe. Under Napoleon's command, French armies invaded Italy and defeated the Austrians and Russians, who were at war with France. In 1799, Napoleon seized power in France itself, becoming a dictator. Napoleon attempted to combine the social reforms

Napoleon on the battlefield

of the French Revolution with his own absolute power. Five years later, he crowned himself emperor. By 1805, he had defeated all of the other European powers except England, and had created a French empire covering much of Europe.

THE DOWNFALL OF NAPOLEON

Napoleon's ambition united Europe against him. In 1812, Napoleon invaded Russia with an army of half a million men. The Russians burned their own crops and buildings as they retreated, depriving the invaders of food and shelter. By the time Napoleon reached the city of Moscow, he found the city in ruins, set on fire by the Russians. In bitter winter weather, Napoleon's army retreated. Less than one in ten men survived the homeward march.

After Napoleon's defeat in Russia, the other European powers combined to overthrow him. After invading France, the foreign powers brought the old French royal family back to power in 1814. An attempt by Napoleon to recapture the French throne in 1815 failed when he was defeated at **Waterloo.** Although Napoleon had ruled France for only fifteen years, he had an enormous impact on France, Europe and the rest of the world:

Napoleon bids farewell to his troops.

NAPOLEON'S IMPACT ON FRANCE, EUROPE AND THE WORLD

France. Napoleon created stability by establishing the **Code Napoleon**, a law code that consolidated such achievements of the Revolution as social equality, religious toleration, and trial by jury.

Europe. Napoleon seized a large portion of Europe, introducing the ideas of the French Revolution and ending feudal restrictions and serfdom wherever he conquered.

The World. French rule stimulated the growth of nationalism. Napoleon weakened Spain, causing it to lose its colonial empire in Latin America. He sold the Louisiana Territory to the United States in 1803.

RESTORING EUROPE'S OLD ORDER

THE CONGRESS OF VIENNA (1814–1815)

After the defeat of Napoleon, European ministers and rulers met at the Congress of Vienna to redraw the boundaries of Europe. The great powers of Europe — Great Britain, Prussia, Russia, and Austria dominated the Congress. They restored many former rulers and borders. In some places, like Belgium and Poland, this meant ignoring popular feelings. These changes helped to bring Europe back in some measure to the way it had been before the French Revolution.

A cartoon critical of the work being done at the Congress of Vienna.

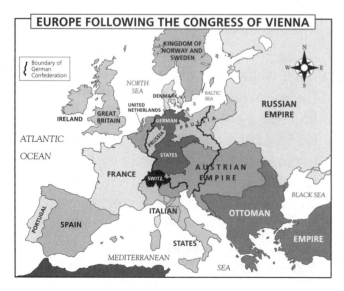

EUROPE FOLLOWING THE CONGRESS OF VIENNA

Under the leadership of Austria's **Prince Metternich,** the statesmen at Vienna also sought to establish a **balance of power.** This term, introduced in the 18th century, referred to a system in which the chief powers of Europe were roughly equal in military strength, so that no single power like France could dominate the others. To further prevent future French domination or the spread of democratic revolutions in Europe, the four major powers also formed a new alliance.

THE SPIRIT OF NATIONALISM

Nationalism is the belief that each **nationality** (*ethnic group*) is entitled to its own government and homeland. The French Revolution ignited the spirit of nationalism in Europe by spreading the view that government should be based on the will of the people. At the same time, the statesmen at Vienna were intent on ignoring or crushing nationalist feelings.

The thirty years following the Congress of Vienna witnessed a series of unsuccessful revolutions in Italy, Germany, and Poland. However, both Greece and Belgium achieved independence by 1830. French citizens established a constitutional monarchy that same year. In 1848, the revolutionary fever again gripped Europe. The constitutional monarchy of France was overthrown and France became a republic. Revolutions occurred in Italy, Germany, Austria, and Hungary. However, the revolutions outside of France were put down within the year by the armies of Austria, Russia, and Prussia.

THE INDEPENDENCE OF LATIN AMERICA

By the late 18th century, the Spanish and Portuguese colonial system was creating unrest in Latin America. Colonists resented restrictions that forbid them to trade with countries other than Spain or to manufacture their own goods. In addition, the American and French Revolutions had spread the idea to Latin America that people were entitled to a government that protected their interests. When Napoleon conquered Spain, Latin Americans were able to govern themselves. When Napoleon was defeated in 1814, many Latin American colonies refused to return to Spanish rule, and demanded independence.

A statue of the Great Liberator — Simon Bolivar — in a plaza in Venezuela.

Toussaint L'Ouverture led an uprising of African slaves in 1791, forcing the French out of Haiti — making Haiti the first Latin American colony to achieve independence.

José de San Martín worked to liberate Argentina and Chile from Spanish rule in the years 1816 to 1818.

LEADERS IN THE WARS FOR INDEPENDENCE

Simón Bolívar defeated Spanish forces between 1819 and 1825, liberating Venezuela, Colombia, Ecuador, Peru, and Bolivia.

Miguel Hidalgo, a priest, began a rebellion against Spanish rule in Mexico in 1810, but the uprising failed. Mexico later achieved its independence in 1821.

The Monroe Doctrine (1823)

The United States recognized the independence of these new Latin American nations, but feared that Spain might try to re-conquer them. As a result, President Monroe issued the **Monroe Doctrine.** It stated that the United States would oppose any attempt by European powers to establish new colonies in the Western Hemisphere or to re-conquer former colonies that had achieved independence. At the same time, Monroe agreed not to interfere with those European colonies still in existence. The Monroe Doctrine made it clear to the world that the United States had special interests in the Western Hemisphere.

President James Monroe

LATIN AMERICA IN THE 19TH CENTURY

After independence, very few democratic governments were in fact established in Latin America. Dictatorships and unstable governments flourished throughout the 19th and early 20th century. Land and wealth still remained in the hands of a small elite. Several Latin American countries came under the rule of powerful military leaders or political bosses, known as **caudillos.** The caudillo often came to power by force.

ANSWERING THE FOCUS QUESTION •

The main causes of the French Revolution were _____
Some of the most important effects of the French Revolution were ____
_____

Directions: Complete each of the following vocabulary cards. Then answer the multiple-choice questions that follow.

ESTATES GENERAL
What was the Estates General?
What role did the calling of the Estates General play in the French Revolution?

NAPOLEON BONAPARTE
Who was Napoleon Bonaparte?
What role did he play in world history?

1 Which phrase best expresses the ideals of the French Revolution?

    1 "blood and iron"   3 "liberty, equality, fraternity"

    2 "white man's burden"   4 "peace, bread and land"

2 What did Justinian of the Byzantine empire and Napoleon of France have in common?

    1 defeated Islamic forces in Spain

    2 believed in the Mandate of Heaven

    3 attacked the idea of the divine rights of kings

    4 established law codes

3 One result of the French Revolution was that

    1 France enjoyed a lengthy period of peace and prosperity

    2 the Church was restored to its former role and power in France

    3 political power shifted to the bourgeoisie

    4 most European nations became republics

4 One of the main goals of the statesmen at the Congress of Vienna (1814–1815) was to

    1 establish a balance of power in Europe

    2 create a European Court of Justice

    3 promote the ideas of the French Revolution

    4 rebuild the French economy

SECTION 2: THE INDUSTRIAL REVOLUTION

While the revolution in France had encouraged political change, a second revolution in Great Britain encouraged rapid economic and social change. In this section, you will learn about this second revolution, which had effects even more far-reaching and significant than those of the French Revolution.

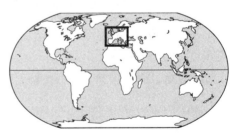

THINK ABOUT IT •

What were the causes and effects of the Industrial Revolution?

The **Industrial Revolution** brought about an important change in the nature of society by introducing **mass production** (*the large-scale production of goods*) and the use of new sources of energy to meet human needs. Science became more closely tied to technology, resulting in a stream of constant innovation.

THE START OF THE INDUSTRIAL REVOLUTION

The Industrial Revolution began in Great Britain in the 1750s. It quickly spread to other parts of Europe, the United States, and later to the rest of the world. Several factors help explain why the Industrial Revolution first began in Great Britain:

Geographical Advantages. Great Britain had many harbors and rivers, and plentiful coal. As an island, it was well protected from invasion. It was close to European markets and well-located for trade with other parts of the world.

Transportation and Communications. Great Britain had a well-developed coastal trade, canals, port towns, an excellent postal service, daily newspapers, and the most powerful navy in the world.

PRE-CONDITIONS FOR INDUSTRIALIZATION

Large Colonial Empire. Britain's far-flung colonial empire brought valuable raw materials to her ports. The experience of running a colonial empire contributed to the development of sophisticated financial and commercial skills.

Powerful Middle Class. A large and powerful middle class participated in government and promoted free enterprise and economic improvement. They were able to bring together capital, labor, and new industrial inventions.

Agricultural Improvements. British farmers introduced scientific methods to agriculture to boost productivity, such as rotating crops and careful animal breeding. Fewer people were needed to work on farms and more were available to work in industry.

THE INDUSTRIAL REVOLUTION BRINGS CHANGE

Before the Industrial Revolution, weavers and craftsmen worked at home, spinning cotton and linen by hand into finished cloth. This was known as the **domestic system.**

Two important British inventions helped trigger the Industrial Revolution. The **spinning jenny** (1764) allowed one person to spin six or seven threads at once. Later, refinements in the spinning jenny increased this number to over eighty. This permitted weavers to make fabric quickly and inexpensively. As the factory system spread, a need arose for more power than horses or water could provide. **James Watt's** improved **steam engine** (1769) made steam power available for mechanical pur-

James Watt

poses. Steam power could be used to drive many machines at once. The steam engine led in turn to the construction of large factories, the invention of the steamboat, and the development of railroad trains.

THE SHIFT FROM HOME TO FACTORY

Cracow, Poland in 1900 — typical of many European cities during industrialization.

With the Industrial Revolution, workers were placed together in factories. In factories, workers could be supervised and could use machines driven by water or steam power, resulting in increased production. As a result, the price of textiles decreased. Because of lower prices, the demand for textiles rose. Ordinary people could now afford factory-made clothes. As demand grew, more and more factories were built, employing ever greater numbers of workers.

◆ **Working Conditions.** As factory owners grew richer and more powerful, the conditions of the new working class worsened. Early factories were often unsafe places to work. Working hours were long, and workers received barely enough to live on. Women and children were forced to work for their families to survive, but received even lower wages than men.

◆ **Urbanization.** With the shift of work to factories, large numbers of workers moved from the countryside to cities. This shift from rural communities to cities, known as **urbanization,** marked one of the greatest population shifts in history. As a result, many cities became crowded and unsanitary. This shift in population can be seen in the following table of British cities:

POPULATION OF SELECT BRITISH CITIES, 1685–1881			
City	1685	1760	1881
Birmingham	4,000	30,000	400,000
Bristol	29,000	100,000	206,000
Liverpool	4,000	35,000	555,000
Manchester	6,000	45,000	394,000
Nottingham	8,000	17,000	112,000

◆ **Growth of Railroads.** Steam engines powered locomotives, creating the first railroads in the early 1830s. Railroads unified the economy of a region by linking cities, factories, towns, and the countryside together. At the same time, railroad construction required vast amounts of coal, iron, and steel, greatly stimulating the growth of heavy industry.

THE EMERGENCE OF INDUSTRIAL CAPITALISM

A new middle class of capitalists, composed of merchants, factory-owners, and bankers, emerged. They demanded and received greater political power in leading industrial countries like Britain and France. These capitalists helped to develop the economic system now known as **laissez-faire capitalism.**

CHARACTERISTICS OF 19TH-CENTURY CAPITALISM

Role of the Entrepreneur
The means of production (factories) were owned by people known as entrepreneurs. Entrepreneurs organize, manage and assume responsibility for a business in hopes of making a profit.

Role of the Worker
Former farm workers left their homes in the countryside for jobs in more populated and industrialized areas. These workers provided their labor, for which they received wages.

Role of the Government
Nineteenth-century governments followed a policy of **laissez-faire**. This meant that the government did not interfere in relations between workers and business owners.

REFORM MOVEMENT

The problems created by the Industrial Revolution led to a call for social and political reform. By the late 19th century, the misery of the working classes and the injustices of capitalism disturbed the consciences of many of the new middle class. There was also a fear of working-class violence. Workers organized into **unions** and threatened to strike if they did not obtain better conditions. Eventually, laws limiting child and female labor, shorter working hours, and safer working conditions were introduced in Britain and other European countries.

MARX AND COMMUNISM

Two leading critics of the capitalist system were **Karl Marx** (1818–1883) and **Friedrich Engels.** Their ideas were published in *The Communist Manifesto* (1848). Marx later wrote *Das Kapital* (1867). Marx's ideas became the basis of **Communism** (also known as *Marxism*):

Class Struggle. Every society is divided into conflicting social classes. Modern industrial society is divided into two such classes: the *bourgeoisie* (*who own the means of production like factories*) and the *proletariat* (*workers*).

Exploitation of the Workers. The wealthy bourgeoisie live off the labor of their workers. Owners cheat their workers by taking most of the wealth they produce, leaving them with only the bare minimum needed for survival.

THE MAIN IDEAS OF COMMUNISM

Communist Revolution. Communists believed the bourgeoisie would never give up their wealth and power peacefully. As capitalists pushed their workers to produce even more, the plight of workers would become so desperate that they would unite in a violent revolution.

Dictatorship of the Proletariat. After overthrowing the bourgeoisie, workers would establish a society in which they jointly owned the means of production. All citizens would be equal, sharing the fruits of their labor. Class struggles would end. Government would become unnecessary and "wither away."

ANSWERING THE FOCUS QUESTION •

The main causes of the Industrial Revolution were _____

The most important effects of the Industrial Revolution were _____

_____

Directions: Complete each of the following vocabulary cards. Then answer the multiple-choice questions that follow.

CAPITALISM
What is capitalism?
What are the main characteristics of capitalism?

COMMUNISM
What is Communism?
In what book was Communist theory first explained?

1   The Neolithic and Industrial Revolutions are often compared because both
   1   encouraged families to work together in the home
   2   resulted in the movement of population into large, crowded cities
   3   led to major changes in the way goods were produced
   4   first occurred in Great Britain

2   "Government should not interfere in relations between workers and business owners. Let the free market determine their relations."

   The ideas in this quotation would most likely be expressed by a
   1   Renaissance humanist   3   mercantilist
   2   laissez-faire capitalist   4   Communist

3   The most basic difference between capitalism and Communism is in their approach to
   1   ownership of the means of production
   2   the establishment of labor unions
   3   military strength
   4   social security

4   One response of workers to the unsafe working conditions of the late 1800s was to
   1   form labor unions   3   become mercantilists
   2   create joint stock companies   4   return to the domestic system

SECTION 3: NATIONALISM AND IMPERIALISM

The Industrial Revolution helped strengthen the influence of the middle classes throughout Europe. In this section, you will learn how the Industrial Revolution helped stimulate nationalism in Europe and led to a rebirth of European imperialism in Africa and Asia.

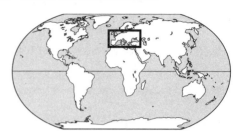

THINK ABOUT IT •

What effect did nationalism and imperialism have on the countries of Europe?

THE UNIFICATION OF ITALY AND GERMANY

You have already learned that nationalism is the belief that each ethnic group should have its own national state and government. Following the failure of the revolutions of 1848 in Italy and Germany, statesmen like Cavour and Bismarck managed to unify the Italians and Germans through skillful diplomacy and force.

ITALY (1859–1860)

For centuries, Italy had consisted of a number of separate, smaller states. Middle-class nationalists called for unification of Italy into a single country. In 1852, **Count Cavour** became Prime Minister of the Kingdom of Piedmont (also known as *Sardinia.*) With French help, Cavour drove the Austrians out of northern Italy after a war in 1859. Cavour then annexed (*took over*) most of the other states of northern and central Italy. To the south, the nationalist leader **Giuseppe Garibaldi** overthrew the king of Naples. He then joined Naples (*also known as the Kingdom of the Two Sicilies*) to Cavour's enlarged Piedmont. By 1860, Italy had become a united kingdom.

Many problems faced the new Italian kingdom. National unification failed to end the cultural and economic divisions that separated the north and south. The south was poor and agricultural, but the north had begun to industrialize.

Monument in Rome to King Victor Emmanuel II, to celebrate Italian independence

GERMANY (1863–1871)

Like Italy, Germany consisted of a number of smaller states. German liberals, like Italian liberals, had failed to unite their nation in the revolutions of 1848. Now **Prussia,** one of the largest German states, took the lead in uniting Germany. Its Prime Minister, **Otto von Bismarck,** followed a policy of **"blood and iron,"** in which he combined skillful diplomacy and Prussian military power to achieve German unification.

Otto von Bismarck

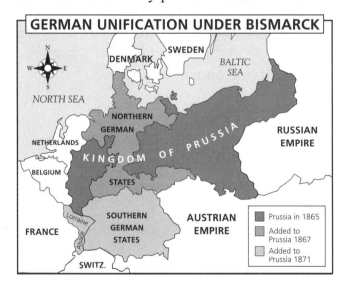

GERMAN UNIFICATION UNDER BISMARCK

SWEDEN
DENMARK
BALTIC SEA
NORTH SEA
NORTHERN GERMAN
NETHERLANDS
KINGDOM OF PRUSSIA
RUSSIAN EMPIRE
BELGIUM
STATES
Lorraine
SOUTHERN GERMAN STATES
AUSTRIAN EMPIRE
FRANCE
Alsace
SWITZ.

Prussia in 1865
Added to Prussia 1867
Added to Prussia 1871

After a rapid series of successful wars, Germany was finally unified in 1871. The Prussian king became the Kaiser (*emperor*) of all Germany. The newly united German nation drafted a constitution. Although there was a national assembly, it was controlled by conservative Prussian landowners. Real power lay in the hands of the Kaiser and his Chancellor.

NATIONALISM IN RUSSIA AND TURKEY

The French Revolution and the rise of nationalism in Europe made the Russian Tsars fearful of reform. Although the middle classes were gaining power in Western Europe, the Tsars of Russia continued to rule as **autocrats** (*absolute rulers*). Through the use of the secret police and censorship, they repressed new ideas and attempts at political or social reform. Most Russians remained illiterate serfs, living in poverty. These serfs remained bound to the land, long after serfdom had been abolished in Western Europe.

THE RISE OF RUSSIAN NATIONALISM

After Russia was defeated in the Crimean War (1854–1856) by Britain and France, **Tsar Alexander II** listened to reformers and **emancipated** (*liberated*) the serfs in 1861. He was assassinated shortly afterwards, bringing hopes of further reforms to an end. Later Tsars opposed all change and used repression to maintain the existing social order.

*Tsar Alexander II
of Russia*

Russia contained many nationalities. Under Russification, all these nationalities were forced to adopt Russian customs.

The new spirit of nationalism did have some effect on Russian rulers. The government acted as the protector of new Slav states in the Balkans (*countries north of Greece*). The Russian Government also adopted the policy of **Russification.** Under this policy, non-Russian peoples in the Russian empire, such as the Finns, Poles, and the peoples of Central Asia — were forced to adopt the Russian language, Russian culture, and the Russian Orthodox Church. Jews in Russia faced state organized riots known as **pogroms.**

OTTOMAN TURKEY, THE "SICK MAN OF EUROPE"

The forces of nationalism also accelerated the decline of the Ottoman empire, which began to weaken in the 1700s. Historians cite a number of reasons for the Ottoman decline.

Disunity. Because of its vast size, the empire was never highly centralized. The Sultan relied on provincial officials to control his vast empire.

Failure to modernize. The Ottoman Turks failed to keep pace with Western technology and science. Muslim religious leaders often opposed change.

REASONS FOR THE DECLINE OF THE OTTOMAN EMPIRE

Warfare. The Ottomans lost important territories to Austria and Russia in the 1700s. Russia, as the protector of Orthodox Christians, waged a series of wars against the Ottoman Turks in the 1800s.

Nationalism. As nationalism became more widespread, the difficulties of governing different nationalities grew. Serbs, Greeks, and Romanians gained independence from the Ottomans in the early 19th century. In the 1870s, rebellions in the Balkans led to the independence of several other Slavic groups.

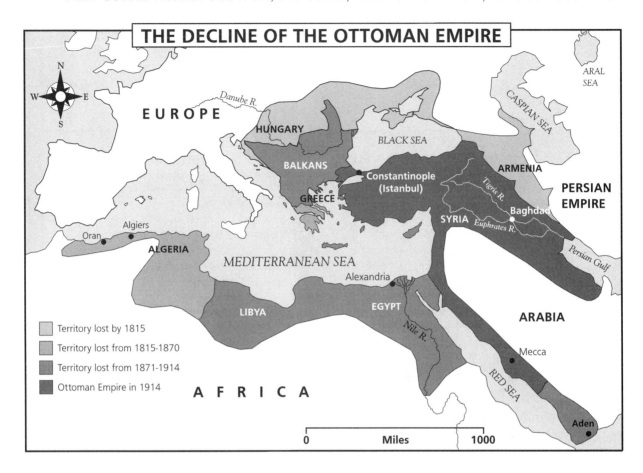

THE DECLINE OF THE OTTOMAN EMPIRE

EUROPE

Danube R.

HUNGARY

BLACK SEA

BALKANS

Constantinople
(Istanbul)

GREECE

ARMENIA

CASPIAN SEA

ARAL SEA

PERSIAN EMPIRE

Tigris R.

Baghdad

SYRIA   Euphrates R.

Persian Gulf

Oran   Algiers

ALGERIA

MEDITERRANEAN SEA

Alexandria

LIBYA

EGYPT

ARABIA

Nile R.

Mecca

☐ Territory lost by 1815
☐ Territory lost from 1815-1870
☐ Territory lost from 1871-1914
☐ Ottoman Empire in 1914

A F R I C A

RED SEA

Aden

0   Miles   1000

IMPERIALISM IN ASIA AND AFRICA

Imperialism refers to the political and economic control of one area or country by another. The triumph of nationalism in Europe led to a renewed expansion of European imperialism in Asia and Africa between 1870 and 1900.

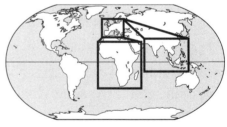

You have already learned how, beginning in the late 1400s, European nations had developed vast overseas empires. Despite the independence of the United States and Latin America, European imperialism never fully died out. European rule continued in India, South Africa, the East Indies, and other places. In the 1880s, interest in imperialism renewed when new European countries like Belgium, Germany, and Italy sought colonial empires of their own. Even the older colonial powers like Britain and France joined in the mad scramble for new colonies.

A political cartoon from 1875, critical of European imperialism in Africa.

THE NEW AFRICAN MISSION.

Technology. New technology — such as steamships, rifles, telegraphs, and better medicines — made it possible to penetrate deeply into Africa, Asia, and the Pacific nations for the first time.

Economic Motives. European industries needed raw materials to keep their factories busy. Industrialists sought new markets in which to sell their manufactured goods.

REASONS FOR RENEWED INTEREST IN IMPERIALISM

Nationalism and the Balance of Power. Europeans wished to acquire colonies to demonstrate their power. European countries also sought to preserve the balance of power among themselves. When one country obtained a new colony, other powers felt it was necessary to do the same.

Other Motives. Many Europeans believed in **Social Darwinism** — the theory that some societies were more successful because their cultures were superior. Other Europeans wanted to spread Christianity.

THE BRITISH EMPIRE IN INDIA

In the 1830s, the East India Company came under the control of the British government. British rule in India brought many changes. The British built railways, schools, and colleges. English became the language of the government. Despite these improvements, many Indians resented British rule.

In 1857, a large number of British-trained Indian soldiers, known as **sepoys,** rebelled against their British officers. The mutiny began when the sepoys had to bite off bullet cartridges which they thought were greased with pork or beef fat. Muslim and Hindu soldiers believed they were being forced to violate their religion.

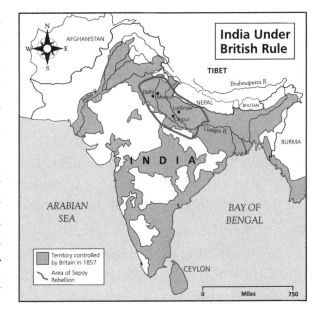

Fighting during the Sepoy Mutiny

The angry sepoys rose up against their British officers. The Sepoy rebellion quickly spread to cities across northern and central India. One effect of the mutiny was that the British government took over formal rule of India and abolished the East India Company. As a result, the mutiny was put down and India now became a British possession.

THE BRITISH RULE OF INDIA

During two centuries of British rule, many aspects of Indian life changed:

Government. The British provided a single system of law and government, unifying India. They provided jobs, increased educational opportunities, and introduced English as a unifying language.

Economic. The British built roads, bridges, and railroads and set up telegraph wires. However, India's **cottage industries,** in which products were made by people in their homes, were hurt by competition with British manufactured goods.

IMPACT OF BRITISH RULE IN INDIA

Health. The British built hospitals, introduced new medicines, and provided famine relief. At the same time, health care improvements led to a population explosion without a similar increase in economic opportunities.

Social. Indians were looked down upon by the British and their culture was treated as inferior to European culture. Indian workers provided the British with inexpensive labor — for long hours, often under terrible working conditions.

EUROPEAN IMPERIALISM IN AFRICA, 1870–1898

As late as 1870, Europeans controlled very little actual territory in Africa except along the coasts. But in the following twenty years, due to the renewed interest in imperialism, this picture changed dramatically. European powers engaged in a **"Scramble for Africa,"** during which most of Africa came under their direct control. By 1890, only Ethiopia and Liberia remained independent. The discovery of resources like gold and diamonds sharpened European interests in Africa.

The major European powers to acquire African territories were Great Britain, France, Germany, Belgium, Portugal, and Italy. The French acquired much of northwestern Africa above the Sahara, as well as Central Africa. The king of Belgium ruled the Congo like a private estate. The British established colonies in West Africa and along the length of most of East Africa from Egypt to South Africa. Germany acquired territories in East and West Africa. Disputes among the imperial powers were worked out at the **Berlin Conference of 1884–1885,** where the remainder of Africa was divided up.

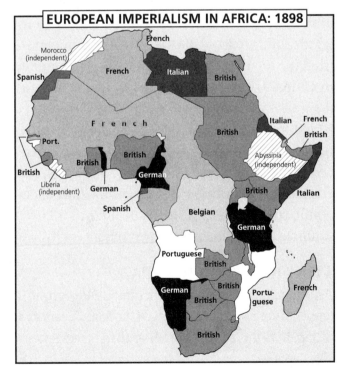

EUROPEAN IMPERIALISM IN AFRICA: 1898

THE BALANCE SHEET OF EUROPEAN IMPERIALISM IN AFRICA

European colonization had both positive and negative effects on Africa:

POSITIVE EFFECTS	NEGATIVE EFFECTS
European medicine and improved nutrition increased the life-span of Africans. This led to an expansion of population.	European domination led to an erosion of traditional African values and destroyed many existing social relationships.
Europeans introduced modern transportation and communications, such as telegraphs, railroads, and telephones.	African peoples were treated as inferior to Europeans. Native peoples were forced to work long hours for low pay.
A small minority of Africans received improved education and greater economic opportunities. Some served as administrators or in the army.	Europeans divided Africa artificially, ignoring tribal, ethnic, and cultural boundaries. This has led to continuing tribal conflicts in many African nations.

THE OPENING OF CHINA AND JAPAN

EUROPEAN IMPERIALISM IN CHINA

Western nations were interested in China because its huge population offered a giant market for European manufactured goods. In the early 1800s, the Chinese imperial government tried to stop the British practice of selling opium from India in China. By this time, however, China lacked the military technology to defy the British. The British easily defeated China in the **Opium War (1839–1842)**. British leaders then forced China to open several "treaty ports," giving the British new trading privileges. In this way, the British established several **spheres of influence** — areas of China under British economic control. Other European countries followed the British example and obtained their own spheres of influence in China.

THE OPENING OF JAPAN

Another Asian country to encounter Western influence in the late 19th century was Japan. Two hundred years earlier, the rulers of Japan — the **Tokugawa Shoguns** — had almost completely cut off Japan from European trade. The Japanese were forbidden to travel to other countries and foreigners were banned from Japan.

Although Japan was isolated from the West, the Tokugawa Shogunate was a period of peace and economic growth. Agricultural production doubled between 1600 and 1850. Merchants and craftspeople crowded into large cities like Tokyo. Although the samurai remained powerful, warfare was infrequent.

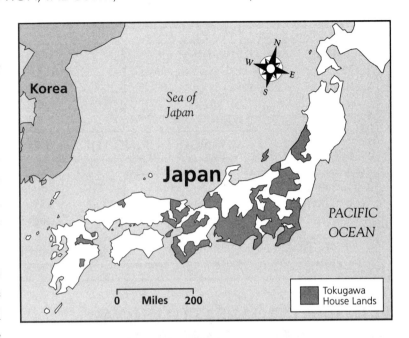

In 1853, the United States government sent Commodore **Matthew Perry** with a naval squadron to Japan to halt the mistreatment of shipwrecked American sailors. The United States also sought to develop new markets and to establish a port where American ships could obtain supplies on their way to China. Fearing what had happened to China, Japanese leaders opened their ports to American trade. Within a few years, the British, Russians, and Dutch negotiated similarly favorable trade treaties.

Commodore Perry lands in Japan.

THE MEIJI RESTORATION, 1868–1912

Mutsuhito — the Meiji Emperor

The Shogun was severely criticized for opening Japan to the West. A group of lower samurai overthrew him and suddenly "restored" to power the young emperor, whose ancestors had been mere puppets for over a thousand years.

Emperor Meiji, the new ruler, became convinced that Japan had to adopt Western ways if it was to escape future domination by Western powers. Foreigners were invited to Japan to modernize its military, establish factories, build railroads, and reform schools. Under Emperor Meiji, Japan successfully imitated and adapted to Western ways.

Feudalism Abandoned. Feudalism and serfdom were abolished. The samurai lost their special social status.	**Western Technology Adopted.** Industrial development based on Western technology, such as the building of railroads and factories, was encouraged.

CHANGES DURING THE MEIJI RESTORATION

Government Changes. Japan was given a written constitution, although the emperor kept his full powers. A Western-style army and navy were created.	**Education Changes.** Universal compulsory education was introduced. Many students went abroad to study European and American economic policies and technological innovations.

FURTHER INROADS INTO CHINA

China's army was ill-prepared to defend China from violations to its sovereignty.

As a result of the reforms of the Meiji Restoration, Japan developed a powerful army and navy. In 1894, Japan went to war with China and defeated it. Japan then annexed Korea and created its own sphere of influence in China.

By 1899, American leaders feared they might be shut out of China's profitable trade. To prevent this, the United States proposed that all nations should have equal trading rights in China. America's **Open Door Policy** discouraged European powers from further dividing up China, and helped keep China "open" to trade.

Many Chinese resented the growing foreign influence in their homeland. Their anger against foreigners finally exploded in 1899. A Chinese group, known as the **"Boxers,"** arose in rebellion in an attempt to drive out all foreigners from China. Hundreds of foreigners were killed by angry mobs. The Boxers were secretly supported by the Chinese government. An international police force, composed of troops from imperialist powers, finally crushed the **Boxer Rebellion.** Although the rebellion failed, it served to fan the flames of Chinese nationalism.

Chinese "Boxers" hoped to drive out foreigners who appeared to be taking over their country.

ANSWERING THE FOCUS QUESTION •

The benefits and drawbacks of Imperialism in Africa and Asia were:

	Benefits	Drawbacks
Africa	?	?
Asia	?	?

Writing

Directions: Complete each of the following vocabulary cards. Then answer the multiple-choice questions that follow.

IMPERIALISM

Define it.

Give two examples.

(1)

(2)

MEIJI RESTORATION

What was the Meiji Restoration?

How did the Meiji emperor hope to avoid European domination?

---

1 "All great nations ... desire to set their mark upon barbarian lands, and those who fail to participate in this great rivalry will play a pitiful role in times to come."

This quotation supports the concept of
1 socialism
2 human rights
3 revolution
4 imperialism

2 Both the Sepoy Mutiny in India and the Boxer Rebellion in China attempted to
1 end foreign domination
2 halt the trading of illegal drugs
3 promote imperialism
4 resist Mongol control

3 During the late 19th century, the African continent was affected most by
1 the Commercial Revolution
2 the introduction of socialism
3 the Crusades
4 European imperialism

4 Peter the Great of Russia and the Meiji Emperor of 19th-century Japan were similar in that both
1 established democratic government
2 introduced Western ideas to their nations
3 converted to Christianity
4 expanded political and human rights

KEY, TERMS, CONCEPTS, AND PEOPLE

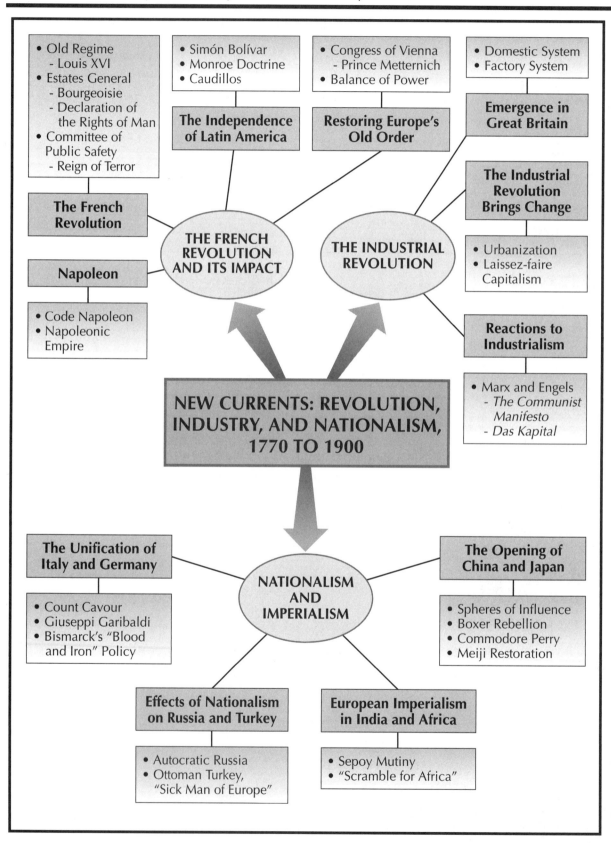

- Old Regime
  - Louis XVI
- Estates General
  - Bourgeoisie
  - Declaration of the Rights of Man
- Committee of Public Safety
  - Reign of Terror

The French Revolution

Napoleon

- Code Napoleon
- Napoleonic Empire

- Simón Bolívar
- Monroe Doctrine
- Caudillos

The Independence of Latin America

THE FRENCH REVOLUTION AND ITS IMPACT

- Congress of Vienna
  - Prince Metternich
- Balance of Power

Restoring Europe's Old Order

- Domestic System
- Factory System

Emergence in Great Britain

The Industrial Revolution Brings Change

- Urbanization
- Laissez-faire Capitalism

THE INDUSTRIAL REVOLUTION

Reactions to Industrialism

- Marx and Engels
  - *The Communist Manifesto*
  - *Das Kapital*

NEW CURRENTS: REVOLUTION, INDUSTRY, AND NATIONALISM, 1770 TO 1900

The Unification of Italy and Germany

- Count Cavour
- Giuseppi Garibaldi
- Bismarck's "Blood and Iron" Policy

NATIONALISM AND IMPERIALISM

The Opening of China and Japan

- Spheres of Influence
- Boxer Rebellion
- Commodore Perry
- Meiji Restoration

Effects of Nationalism on Russia and Turkey

- Autocratic Russia
- Ottoman Turkey, "Sick Man of Europe"

European Imperialism in India and Africa

- Sepoy Mutiny
- "Scramble for Africa"

SUMMARIZING YOUR UNDERSTANDING

Directions: Use these headings to complete the outline below.

COMPLETING AN OUTLINE

THE FRENCH REVOLUTION AND ITS IMPACT
Restoring Europe's Old Order
The Effects of Nationalism on Russia and Turkey
The Start of the Industrial Revolution in Great Britain
THE INDUSTRIAL REVOLUTION
The Opening of China and Japan
REVOLUTION, INDUSTRY, AND NATIONALISM
The Independence of Latin America
Napoleon
Marx and Communism
The Unification of Italy and Germany
NATIONALISM AND IMPERIALISM
Imperialism in India and Africa
The French Revolution
The Industrial Revolution Brings Change

TITLE: _____

I. MAJOR DIVISION: _____
   A. Sub-topic: _____
   B. Sub-topic: _____
   C. Sub-topic: _____
   D. Sub-topic: _____

II. MAJOR DIVISION: _____
   A. Sub-topic: _____
   B. Sub-topic: _____
   C. Sub-topic: _____

III. MAJOR DIVISION: _____
   A. Sub-topic: _____
   B. Sub-topic: _____
   C. Sub-topic: _____
   D. Sub-topic: _____

COMPLETING A GRAPHIC ORGANIZER

Complete the following graphic organizer by listing the major effects of the Industrial Revolution.

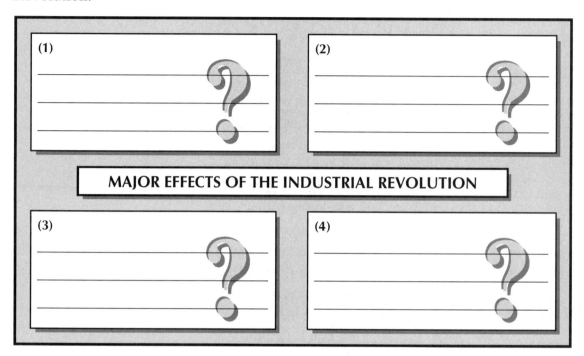

COMPLETING A TABLE

Use this table to organize information on the developments you just read about.

Event	When it Began	Where it Began	Brief Description
French Revolution			
Industrial Revolution			
Rise of Nationalism			
"New" Imperialism			

SHARPENING YOUR TEST-TAKING SKILLS

READING HISTORICAL DOCUMENTS

Questions on global history examinations sometimes require you to read and interpret actual historical documents. These historical documents can come in many forms — charts, graphs, timelines, and of course readings. Earlier in this book you learned how to interpret different types of data. This section looks at what is involved in reading short original sources.

THE SEARCH FOR MEANING

Have you ever stopped to think about what a complex process reading really is? Reading requires you to understand the meaning of a group of words. When reading a passage, a good reader begins by making mental guesses of what the passage is about. As the reader continues along, he or she modifies earlier guesses based on new information in the passage. Each word, each sentence — provides clues to the text's meaning. Reading can thus be defined as a search for meaning.

Most document-based questions on global history examinations will present short passages of two or three sentences. Such short passages are usually excerpts from longer speeches or writings.

Keep in mind that most historical documents were written from a particular viewpoint. You must be able to use your imagination to send yourself back in time in order to understand someone else's point of view. A writer in the past may have had very different attitudes from those we have today.

UNDERSTANDING DIFFERENT POINTS OF VIEW

In reading a historical document, you must therefore be a critical reader. It helps to know something about the writer's social position and background, so that you can see how these affect his or her ideas. Following are some of the main questions you should ask when reading any historical document or passage.

When and where was the document written?

What do you know about the author?

BEING A CRITICAL READER

What is the main idea of the passage?

What facts does the writer present to support his or her views?

What is the tone of the passage?

DETERMINING THE MEANING OF WORDS FROM CONTEXT CLUES

Sometimes you may come across words or phrases that are unfamiliar to you. At this stage, you should use **context clues** to help you figure out what they mean. Think of yourself as a detective. The surrounding words, phrases, and sentences provide clues that help you determine the meaning of the unfamiliar word.

Part of Speech. From the words in the sentence, can you guess what part of speech the unfamiliar word is — adjective, noun, verb, or adverb?

Substitute Words. Can you guess the meaning of the word from the tone or meaning of the rest of the passage? What other words might make sense if you substituted them in place of the unfamiliar word?

USING CONTEXT CLUES TO FIND THE MEANING

Related Familiar Words. Is the word similar to any other words you already know? Does that help you to figure out what the word means? Can you make out what the word is by breaking it up into parts — a prefix, word stem, or suffix?

Bypass the Word. Can you understand the main idea of the sentence without knowing the meaning of the unfamiliar word? If so, it may not be important to spend time trying to figure out its meaning.

PRACTICE WITH HISTORICAL DOCUMENTS

Let's practice interpreting documents by examining two passages about the Industrial Revolution in England:

DOCUMENT 1:

"Suddenly cotton mills have appeared everywhere in our town. They billow out endless smoke day and night. The poor souls working in these factories suffer the worst torments imaginable. Young children work from 6 in the morning to 8 at night. They have no schooling and no rest. Many die before the age of 13 by falling into those large, merciless machines driven by steam."

— *A Manchester citizen testifying before the British Parliament (1835)*

Suppose you did not understand the word *mills* in the first sentence. Following is a way of figuring out the meaning of this word.

What part of speech is the word?	The word is a noun that designates a person, place, or thing. *Mills* must be things since they refer to *something* appearing in the town.
Do you know any related words?	You may recall the word wind*mill*, a building with machinery used to process or grind grain.
Is the word referred to in the surrounding text?	The *mills* billow smoke all day. The following sentence refers to them as *factories*. Cotton *mills* must, therefore, be factories that produce cotton thread and cloth — just like windmills produce grain.

Now consider the background and viewpoint of the author:

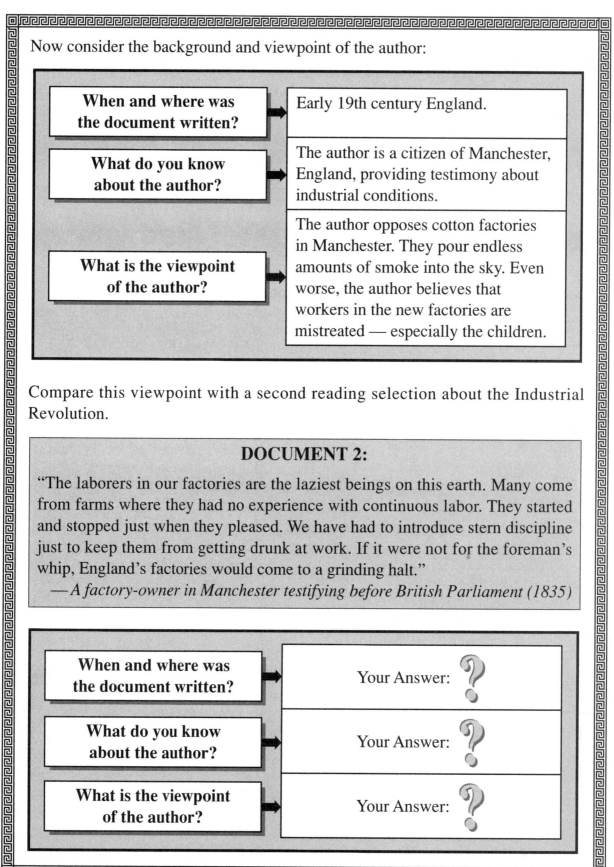

When and where was the document written?	→	Early 19th century England.
What do you know about the author?	→	The author is a citizen of Manchester, England, providing testimony about industrial conditions.
What is the viewpoint of the author?	→	The author opposes cotton factories in Manchester. They pour endless amounts of smoke into the sky. Even worse, the author believes that workers in the new factories are mistreated — especially the children.

Compare this viewpoint with a second reading selection about the Industrial Revolution.

DOCUMENT 2:

"The laborers in our factories are the laziest beings on this earth. Many come from farms where they had no experience with continuous labor. They started and stopped just when they pleased. We have had to introduce stern discipline just to keep them from getting drunk at work. If it were not for the foreman's whip, England's factories would come to a grinding halt."

— *A factory-owner in Manchester testifying before British Parliament (1835)*

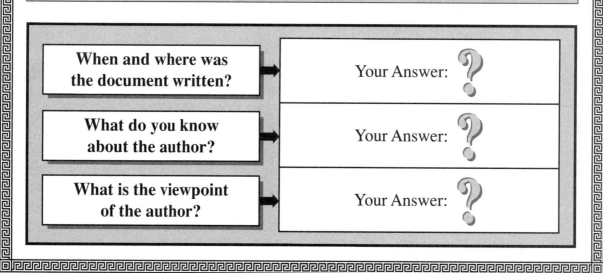

When and where was the document written?	→	Your Answer:
What do you know about the author?	→	Your Answer:
What is the viewpoint of the author?	→	Your Answer:

TESTING YOUR UNDERSTANDING

Test your understanding of this chapter by answering the following questions:

MULTIPLE-CHOICE QUESTIONS

1 • People are born free but everywhere they are in chains.
 • Everyone has a natural right to life, liberty, and property.
 • Slavery, torture, and religious persecution are wrong.

During which period of European history would the ideas in these statements have most likely been expressed?
 1 Pax Romana
 2 Age of Charlemagne
 3 Enlightenment
 4 Middle Ages

2 Which quotation best reflects the spirit of nationalism?
 1 "An eye for an eye and a tooth for a tooth."
 2 "Do unto others as you would have others do unto you."
 3 "For God, King, and Country."
 4 "Opposition to evil is as much a duty as cooperation with good."

3 Which term best describes the political system of Russia in the 19th century?
 1 constitutional monarchy
 2 parliamentary democracy
 3 imperial autocracy
 4 military dictatorship

Base your answer to question 4 on the pie charts below and your knowledge of global history.

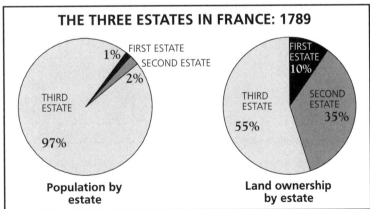

THE THREE ESTATES IN FRANCE: 1789

FIRST ESTATE
SECOND ESTATE
1%
2%
THIRD ESTATE
97%
Population by estate

FIRST ESTATE 10%
SECOND ESTATE 35%
THIRD ESTATE 55%
Land ownership by estate

4 Based on these charts, which statement is most accurate?
 1 The three estates in France owned land equally.
 2 The second estate was the most numerous of the three.
 3 The first two estates had landholdings out of proportion to their population size.
 4 The combined population of the first and second estates was larger than the third estate.

5 In Japan, the Meiji Restoration resulted in
1 a restoration of European power
2 the industrialization of the nation
3 abolition of the position of emperor
4 government control by samurai

6 "I will never allow my hands to be idle nor my soul to rest until I have broken the chains laid upon us by Spain." This statement was most likely made by a
1 Latin American nationalist
2 Portuguese explorer
3 Roman Catholic bishop
4 Spanish conquistador

Base your answer to question 7 on the illustration and your knowledge of global history.

7 Which aspect of the Industrial Revolution are workers reacting to in the illustration?
1 machines replacing workers
2 slum housing conditions
3 rise of labor unions
4 development of Communism

Base your answer to question 8 on the cartoon below and your knowledge of global history.

8 The main idea of the cartoon is that
1 tribal interests in Africa were harmful to African unity
2 Africa benefited from trade with European countries
3 African nations successfully resisted European imperialism
4 Africa was carved up into colonies by European imperial powers

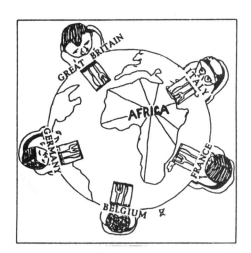

9 Four important events in global history are listed below.

A. Birth of Mohammed   C. Start of the Industrial Revolution in England
B. Fall of Constantinople   D. Unification of Germany

Which is the correct chronological order of these events?
1 **A → B → C → D**
2 **D → C → A → B**
3 **A → B → D → C**
4 **C → D → A → B**

Base your answer to question 10 on the graph below and your knowledge of global history.

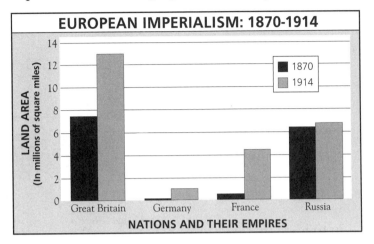

EUROPEAN IMPERIALISM: 1870-1914

10 Which statement is best supported by the data in the graph?
   1   Most European nations had colonial empires in 1870.
   2   An increase in Europe's birth rate led to overseas expansion.
   3   European colonial territories increased from 1870 to 1914.
   4   By 1914, Germany controlled the most land area.

INTERPRETING DOCUMENTS

I. INTERPRETING A GRAPH
The graph below shows a change in the world brought about by the Industrial Revolution.

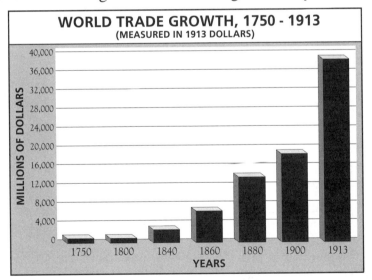

WORLD TRADE GROWTH, 1750 - 1913
(MEASURED IN 1913 DOLLARS)

1   What was the approximate value of world trade in 1900? _____

2   Define the term "Industrial Revolution:" _____

3   List two changes brought about by the Industrial Revolution:

   Change 1: _____   Change 2:_____

II. INTERPRETING A POLITICAL CARTOON

1   Which areas of the world are represented by the two people pulling the cart? _____

_____

2   Who is represented by the person sitting in the cart? _____

3   Describe the historical situation that led to the events shown in the cartoon. _____

_____

"Learning civilized ways is hard work."

THEMATIC ESSAY QUESTION

Directions: Write a well-organized essay that includes an introduction, several paragraphs explaining your position, and a conclusion.

Theme: Change

> Some events in global history are called "turning points" because they have had a significant political, social, or cultural impact.

Task:

> Choose *two* major events from your study of global history and geography.
>
> For *each* turning point:
> • Describe the event.
> • Explain its political, social, or cultural impact as a turning point in history

You may use any example from your study of global history and geography. Some suggestions you may wish to consider include: Neolithic Revolution, Arab conquest of the Middle East, Industrial Revolution, rise of kingdoms in West Africa, the encounter between Europe and the Americas, the French Revolution, and the Meiji Restoration.

You are *not* limited to these suggestions.

CHAPTER 10

THE WORLD AT WAR, 1900 TO 1945

During the Russian Revolution, as food shortages grew, fighting spilled out on to the streets.

SECTION 2: THE WORLD BETWEEN THE WARS

1. The Soviet Union
2. Prosperity and Depression
3. The Rise of Fascism
4. The Nazi Dictatorship

The effects of the depression — mother and child in front of their "home."

SECTION 1: THE CRISIS OF THE EARLY 20TH CENTURY

1. Reform through Revolution
2. World War I
3. The Russian Revolution of 1917

U.S. soldiers attack in the final assault on Germany.

SECTION 3: WORLD WAR II AND ITS AFTERMATH

1. World War II, 1939–1945
2. Global Impact of World War II
3. Decolonization of Asia and Africa

	1905	1915	1925	1935	1945	
EUROPE		WORLD WAR I	RISE OF FASCISM		WORLD WAR II	COLD WAR
RUSSIA	TSAR NICHOLAS II	REVOLUTION: LENIN	STALIN			
AFRICA	EUROPEAN CONTROL				INDEPENDENCE MOVEMENTS	
TURKEY	SULTANATE	YOUNG TURK GOVT.	MODERN TURKEY			
MIDEAST	OTTOMAN EMPIRE	EUROPEAN PROTECTORATES			INDEPENDENCE MOVEMENTS	
MEXICO	RULE OF DIAZ	REVOLUTION	REPUBLIC OF MEXICO			
CHINA	MANCHU DYNASTY	REPUBLIC OF CHINA				
JAPAN	JAPAN'S RISE TO POWER			WORLD WAR II	U.S. OCCUPATION	
INDIA	INDIAN NATIONALIST MOVEMENT DURING BRITISH RULE				INDEPENDENCE	
S.E. ASIA	EUROPEAN COLONIZATION				INDEPENDENCE MOVEMENTS	
	1905	1915	1925	1935	1945	

WHAT YOU SHOULD FOCUS ON

In this chapter, you will learn how the forces of industrialization and nationalism led to the rise of new political systems like Communism and Fascism. You will also see how humankind experienced two world wars, causing greater devastation than at any other time in human history. As a result, European rule over much of the world was shattered, and the United States and the Soviet Union emerged as super-powers. The developments of this era occurred in four main stages:

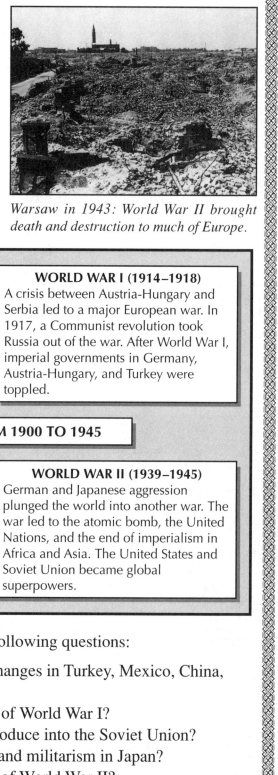

Warsaw in 1943: World War II brought death and destruction to much of Europe.

PRE-WAR YEARS (1900–1914)

Around the world, educated elites, frustrated by their nation's problems, often sought change through revolution. Meanwhile, European governments armed themselves for war. In Asia and Africa, European powers controlled vast colonial empires.

WORLD WAR I (1914–1918)

A crisis between Austria-Hungary and Serbia led to a major European war. In 1917, a Communist revolution took Russia out of the war. After World War I, imperial governments in Germany, Austria-Hungary, and Turkey were toppled.

FOUR KEY STAGES FROM 1900 TO 1945

THE INTER-WAR YEARS (1919–1939)

The mid-1920s saw general prosperity, followed by the world-wide Great Depression of the 1930s. Economic crisis gave rise to Fascist dictators like Hitler in Germany. Meanwhile, Stalin ruled the Soviet Union as a Communist dictator.

WORLD WAR II (1939–1945)

German and Japanese aggression plunged the world into another war. The war led to the atomic bomb, the United Nations, and the end of imperialism in Africa and Asia. The United States and Soviet Union became global superpowers.

In studying this era, you should focus on the following questions:

➤ What conditions led to revolutionary changes in Turkey, Mexico, China, and Russia in the early 20th century?

➤ What were the main causes and effects of World War I?

➤ What changes did Lenin and Stalin introduce into the Soviet Union?

➤ What factors led to Fascism in Europe and militarism in Japan?

➤ What were the main causes and effects of World War II?

LOOKING AT INFLUENTIAL PEOPLE IN HISTORY

Each of us touches the lives of those around us. However, a number of exceptional people have had an important effect on the lives of millions of people. In studying any of these unusual individuals, the key question to think about is: *How has the world been changed by the actions of this person?*

Two groups of people who have often had a significant impact on the lives of others have been leaders and thinkers.

◆ **Leaders** are people who rule a country, head a political party or religious movement, or lead an army. They affect history because they are able to persuade or force millions of other people to follow their commands.

◆ **Thinkers** are philosophers, religious thinkers, writers, inventors, explorers, scientists, or artists. They affect history because their ideas or actions stimulate others to act, or lead to technological or artistic breakthroughs.

ANSWERING TEST QUESTIONS ABOUT INDIVIDUALS

On global history tests, essay questions dealing with individuals will ask you to discuss their accomplishments. The content of your answer will depend in part on whether the individual was a *leader* or a *thinker*.

WHAT YOU SHOULD DISCUSS FOR A LEADER

For a leader, your answer should contain the following:

(1) What country or group did he or she lead?

(2) What problems did the country face?

(3) What policies did this leader favor?

(4) What were the effects of these policies? How was the world changed by the activities of this leader?

WHAT YOU SHOULD DISCUSS FOR A THINKER

Mao Zedong — Chinese Communist leader

For a thinker, your answer should contain the following:

(1) In what field of art or science, etc., did this person make a contribution?

(2) What did people think before this contribution?

(3) What did this person do that was new or unique? What factors helped this thinker make this contribution?

(5) How was the world changed by this person's activities?

Karl Marx, the Father of Communism

KEY LEADERS AND THINKERS
IN GLOBAL HISTORY

Asian Political Leaders

Asoka the Great (273–238 B.C.)   Mao Zedong (1893–1976)
Kublai Khan (1215–1294)   Mohandas Gandhi (1869–1948)
Akbar the Great (1542–1605)   Deng Xiaoping (1904–1996)
Sun Yat-sen (1866–1925)   Indira Gandhi (1917–1984)

African Political Leaders

Mansa Musa (1270–1332)   Kwame Nkrumah (1909–1972)
Jomo Kenyatta (1894–1978)   Nelson Mandela (1918–present)

European Political Leaders

Alexander the Great (356–323 B.C.)   Napoleon Bonaparte (1769–1821)
Charlemagne (742–814)   Otto von Bismarck (1815–1898)
Elizabeth I (1553–1603)   Vladimir Ilyich Lenin (1870–1924)
Peter the Great (1672–1725)   Joseph Stalin (1879–1953)
Catherine the Great (1729–1796)   Adolf Hitler (1889–1945)

Middle Eastern Political Leaders

Suleiman the Magnificent (1490–1566) Anwar el-Sadat (1918–1981)

Latin American Political Leaders

Simon Bolivar (1783–1830)   Fidel Castro (1927–present)

Religious Leaders

Siddharta Gautama (563–483 B.C.)   Mohammed (570-632)
Confucius (551–479 B.C.)   Martin Luther (1483–1546)
Mencius (372–289 B.C.)   Ignatius Loyola (1491–1556)
Jesus (1–30 A.D.)   Ayatollah Khomeini (1900–1996)

Thinkers and Writers

Socrates (469–399 B.C.)   Voltaire (1694–1778)
Plato (427–347 B.C.)   Adam Smith (1723–1790)
Niccolo Machiavelli (1469–1527)   Karl Marx (1818–1883)
John Locke (1632–1704)   Thomas Malthus (1766–1834)

Scientists and Inventors

Johann Gutenberg (1398–1468)   Isaac Newton (1642–1727)
Nicolas Copernicus (1473–1543)   James Watt (1736–1819)
Charles Darwin (1809–1882)   Albert Einstein (1879–1955)

MAJOR HISTORICAL DEVELOPMENTS

SECTION 1: THE CRISIS OF THE EARLY 20TH CENTURY

In 1900, most Europeans were enjoying peace and prosperity. Nevertheless, in some places the forces of discontent were stirring. This social unrest would soon contribute to a devastating military conflict among the world's great powers.

THINK ABOUT IT •

What were the causes and consequences of World War I?

REFORM THROUGH REVOLUTION, 1900–1914

Unable to achieve reform through moderate means, reformers in Turkey, Mexico, and China sought to overthrow their existing governments through revolution.

THE OTTOMAN EMPIRE AND THE YOUNG TURKS

In the late 19th century, the ruler of the Ottoman empire, Sultan **Abdulhamid II,** used secret police and brutality against potential opponents. He also ordered the brutal massacre of Armenians in eastern Turkey in 1894–1896. Young educated members of the Turkish elite, known as the **Young Turks,** demanded reform. In 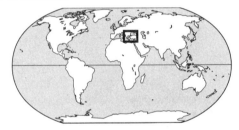 1908, part of the Ottoman army rebelled and the Sultan gave in to their demands. In the following year, Sultan Abdulhamid was overthrown. A new Young Turk government encouraged industrialization, public education, and an improved treatment of women. However, even the Young Turks could not prevent the further loss of Ottoman territories in Europe.

THE MEXICAN REVOLUTION OF 1910

Pancho Villa, rebel Mexican leader

From 1877 to 1910, Mexico was governed by Porfirio Diaz, a moderate dictator who encouraged foreign investment but limited popular liberties. The **Mexican Revolution of 1910** began as a reaction against Diaz's rule. A wealthy liberal, Francisco Madero, began the revolt and took over the government. Madero soon faced opposition from peasant leaders, including **Pancho Villa,** who led a private army in the north. Madero was assassinated and a civil war followed. After a period of confusion, the forces of reform were victorious.

As a result of the revolution, large estates were broken up, Church lands were seized, and millions of acres of land were transferred to peasants. Mexico also adopted a new constitution. The **Constitution of 1917,** still in effect in Mexico today, led to greater democracy in Mexico. It established public education, universal voting, and an 8-hour work day. The new constitution also gave workers the right to strike.

REVOLUTION ERUPTS IN CHINA

Young members of China's educated elite were deeply troubled by China's defeat by Japan in 1894, by the foreign intervention against the Boxer rebellion, and by the refusal of the Manchu government to allow changes. In 1911, an uprising began among soldiers. It quickly spread to cities throughout China. China's five-year-old emperor was forced to **abdicate** (*give up his throne*). After 2,500 years of rule by emperors, China became a republic in 1912.

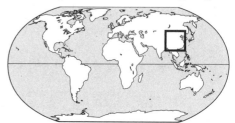

Dr. Sun Yat-Sen sought to make China a democracy.

Sun Yat-Sen, a revolutionary leader, gained control of China's government in 1916. Sun introduced policies based on three principles: "Democracy, Nationalism, and the People's Livelihood." The first principle meant that China should become a democracy with a representative government. The second principle referred to freeing China from foreign control. The last principle was directed towards strengthening China's economy. Unfortunately, Sun was never fully able to bring all of China under his control. In many parts of China, the power of local military commanders — known as **warlords** — remained too great. Rival armies battled for control of China — bringing economic hardship to millions of peasants.

WORLD WAR I, 1914–1918

THE CAUSES OF THE WAR

The forces of nationalism and reform not only affected places like Mexico and China, but also had an explosive impact on the multi-ethnic empire of Austria-Hungary. These forces eventually brought Europe into World War I. A complex event like the outbreak of World War I naturally had several underlying causes:

◆ **Nationalism.** Nationalism encouraged rivalries among Britain, France, Germany, Austria-Hungary, and Russia. Nationalism had also led to the creation of new independent nations in the Balkans: Greece, Serbia, Bulgaria, and Albania. Austria-Hungary, on the other hand, still consisted of many different ethnic groups, most of which wanted their own national states. These demands threatened to break the Austro-Hungarian empire apart.

In 1867, Austrians made a concession to nationalism by giving Hungary some degree of self-government within the empire. Afterwards, Serbia hoped to liberate Serbs still under Austrian rule, found in the southwest of Austria-Hungary. By annexing these regions, land-locked Serbia could also gain access to the Adriatic Sea.

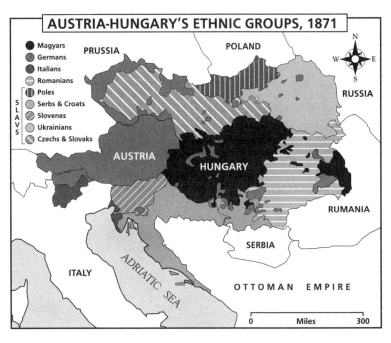

AUSTRIA-HUNGARY'S ETHNIC GROUPS, 1871

- Magyars
- Germans
- Italians
- Romanians
- Poles
- Serbs & Croats
- Slovenes
- Ukrainians
- Czechs & Slovaks

SLAVS

PRUSSIA   POLAND
RUSSIA
AUSTRIA
HUNGARY
RUMANIA
SERBIA
ITALY
ADRIATIC SEA
OTTOMAN EMPIRE

0   Miles   300

◆ **Economic Rivalries and Imperialism.** The European powers had competing economic and political interests. German industrialization seemed to challenge British economic supremacy. Russian interests in the Balkans threatened Austria-Hungary and Turkey. Competition for African and Asian colonies had created further tensions among the major powers.

◆ **The Alliance System.** By 1914, Europe came to be divided into two large alliances. On one side stood Germany and Austria-Hungary. On the other side was Russia, France, and Great Britain. Any dispute involving countries from different alliances threatened to bring in all the others.

Russia's large army made her an important partner in any alliance.

◆ **Militarism.** The late 1800s saw a rise in militarism — glorification of the military. Military planning and arms races played key roles in the outbreak of World War I. Germany and Britain competed to build the largest navy. Military leaders of the day thought it would be better to attack first rather than to wait until being attacked. Whenever a crisis occurred, they urged political leaders to jump into battle.

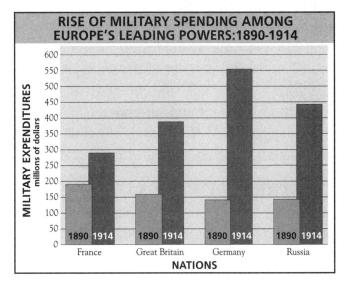

RISE OF MILITARY SPENDING AMONG EUROPE'S LEADING POWERS: 1890-1914

MILITARY EXPENDITURES
millions of dollars

France   Great Britain   Germany   Russia
1890 1914   1890 1914   1890 1914   1890 1914

NATIONS

THE FLASHPOINT THAT IGNITED THE WAR

In 1914, Austria's Archduke **Francis Ferdinand** was assassinated by Slav nationalists. Austrians believed Serb officials had helped the assassins, and decided to invade Serbia. This action set off a chain reaction that soon involved all of Europe's major powers. What began as a minor local crisis quickly escalated into a major world war. During the war, Germany, Austria-Hungary, and Turkey became known as the **Central Powers.** Britain, France, and Russia were known as the **Allies.**

A NEW FORM OF WARFARE

New weapons were used in the war, including the machine gun, poison gas, submarines, and airplanes. Soldiers dug themselves into trenches, protected by barbed wire and machine guns. Soon these trenches extended hundreds of miles. World War I brought a new type of warfare that no one had ever seen before.

AMERICA ENTERS THE WAR

Although officially neutral, Americans were sympathetic to Britain and France. When American ships were attacked by Germany in 1917, the United States entered the war. In the same year, Russia dropped out of the war. America's entry broke the deadlock in Europe. By the end of 1918, the Central Powers laid down their weapons and surrendered. The costs of World War I were staggering. Millions were killed or injured, and by the end of the war famine and malnutrition threatened much of Europe.

A U.S. Marine receives first aid while fighting in French trenches (1918).

THE TREATY OF VERSAILLES (1919)

In a speech to the United States Congress, President Wilson announced **Fourteen Points** that he felt should be the basis for the coming peace settlement. Wilson planned to redraw the map of Europe so that each nationality would have its own government. He also demanded freedom of the seas, an end to secret diplomacy, and the creation of a League of Nations.

Believing that Wilson's offer would be the basis of the peace, Germans agreed to end the war and overthrew their emperor, the Kaiser, in November 1918. Nevertheless, the final peace terms turned out to be extremely harsh towards Germany. Wilson could not restrain French and British leaders. Allied public opinion sought revenge. The **Treaty of Versailles** (1919) concluded the peace with Germany; related treaties dealt with Austria and Turkey.

President Wilson (right) meets with other Allied leaders in Paris while writing the Treaty of Versailles.

Germany's Territorial Losses. A new independent Poland was created. Germany lost territory to France and Poland, as well as all of its overseas colonies.

Austria-Hungary and Turkey. The Austro-Hungarian empire was divided into several smaller national states. Turkey lost its territories in the Middle East.

THE PEACE TERMS ENDING WORLD WAR I

Punishing Germany. Germany lost its navy, while its army was reduced to a small police force. Germany was forced to accept blame for starting the war and was required to pay huge **reparations** (*payments for damages*) to the Allies.

League of Nations. The Treaty created the League of Nations, an organization of nations pledged to defend each other against aggressors. The League was weakened when several major powers, such as the United States and Russia, failed to join it.

EUROPE FOLLOWING THE TREATY OF VERSAILLES

In the Middle East, most of Ottoman Turkey's former territories (*Arabia, Palestine, and Syria*) were placed under British and French rule. The Turkish leader, **Kemal Atatürk,** kept the rest of Turkey from being dismembered. He overthrew the system of government headed by a Sultan and created a new Turkish republic. Ataturk forced through a program of radical reforms. He made Turkey a modern nation along western lines. For example, he created a modern secular (*non-religious*) state in which religion was separated from government.

THE RUSSIAN REVOLUTION OF 1917

THE RUSSIAN REVOLUTION OF 1905

By the early twentieth century, the Russian empire stretched from Eastern Europe to the Pacific Ocean. Compared to Western Europe, Russia remained backward. Peasants and factory workers lived in poverty, while landowning nobles enjoyed wealth and leisure.

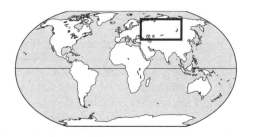

THE EXPANSION OF RUSSIA

- Russia in 1801
- By 1815
- By 1867
- By 1914

Sharp social divisions and an authoritarian government made Russia ripe for revolution. Some students and workers became professional revolutionaries. The crisis came to a head after Russia was defeated by Japan in the Russo-Japanese War of 1904. When troops fired on peaceful demonstrators in 1905, revolutions broke out across Russia. Tsar **Nicholas II,** to quell the unrest, granted limited reforms, including the creation of a new legislative assembly known as the **Duma.**

Tsar Nicholas II (right) and his cousin, the King of England

THE RUSSIAN REVOLUTION OF 1917

Russian soldiers march off to fight in World War I — often inadequately trained and poorly equipped.

In addition to establishing the Duma, Nicholas II introduced other reforms. Peasants were allowed to buy village lands. France lent money to help build railroads. The Russian economy showed some signs of improvement, but Russia was still unprepared for the strains of war. In 1914, Nicholas brought Russia into the conflict against Germany. More than one-third of all Russian men were forced into the army. Poorly trained and badly equipped, Russian soldiers suffered disastrous defeats. Military disasters led to widespread discontent and desertion in the army. Meanwhile, Russian industries proved incapable of producing enough weapons, food, or supplies.

Early in 1917, German forces cut Russian railroad lines, preventing food from reaching cities or soldiers. Strikes and food riots broke out across Russia. Millions of soldiers deserted. When soldiers refused to carry out orders to fire on striking workers, Nicholas II realized he was powerless to govern the nation. In March, 1917, Nicholas was forced by army leaders and spreading strikes to give up his throne. The leaders of the Duma declared a republic and centuries of Tsarist rule came to an end.

A provisional government was set up, but it lacked support when it refused to withdraw from the war. The **Bolsheviks,** a revolutionary group following the ideas of Karl Marx, promised "Peace, Bread, and Land" — peace for soldiers, bread for workers, and land for peasants. Led by **Vladimir Lenin,** the Bolsheviks seized power in November 1917.

Lenin speaks to a group of Russian workers.

Soon after taking power, the Bolsheviks changed their name to **"Communists".** They also changed the name of the Russian empire to the **Union of Soviet Socialist Republics** (*U.S.S.R.*) or **Soviet Union.** Russia had become the world's first Communist country. The new Soviet government signed a peace treaty with Germany, giving up Poland, the Ukraine, and other territories. A brutal civil war soon broke out across Russia, which was eventually won by the Communists.

ANSWERING THE FOCUS QUESTION •

The main causes of World War I were _____

Some important consequences of World War I were _____

_____

Writing

Directions: Complete each of the following vocabulary cards. Then answer the multiple-choice questions that follow.

TREATY OF VERSAILLES
What was it?
List two of its provisions:
(1)
(2)

RUSSIAN REVOLUTION OF 1917
What conditions led to the
Russian Revolution of 1917?
What changes did it bring to Russia?

1 What did Mexico, China, and Russia have in common at the start of the 20th century?

  1 A majority of their populations was prosperous.

  2 Their governments encouraged social mobility.

  3 Their citizens could participate in the political process.

  4 There were sharp social divisions in these countries.

2 The Russian Revolution and the French Revolution both resulted in

  1 new democracies   3 violent political changes

  2 restoring old monarchies   4 increasing the Church's power

3 Which provision of the Treaty of Versailles revealed the intent of the Allies to punish the Central Powers for their role in World War I?

  1 "All nations shall maintain open convenants (*agreements*)."

  2 "Germany will accept full responsibility for causing the war."

  3 "Territorial settlements shall be based on nationality."

  4 "Freedom of the seas will be protected."

4 Four important events in global history are listed in the box to the right. Which is the correct chronological order of these events?

  1 **B → D → A → C**

  2 **D → B → C → A**

  3 **C → B → A → D**

  4 **D → B → A → C**

> A. Tsar Nicholas II is forced from the Russian throne.
> B. The French Revolution begins.
> C. Bismarck unifies Germany.
> D. Suleiman the Magnificent expands the Ottoman empire.

SECTION 2: THE WORLD BETWEEN THE WARS — PROSPERITY AND DEPRESSION

In this section, you will learn about the period following World War I. These years witnessed a period of general prosperity, followed by a world-wide depression. This was also a time when dictatorial governments in Russia, Germany, and Italy came to power.

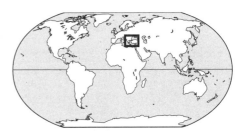

Thinking

THINK ABOUT IT •

What changes did Communists introduce to the Soviet Union and Nazis bring to Germany?

THE SOVIET UNION UNDER LENIN AND STALIN

LENIN INTRODUCES COMMUNISM

Once in power, Lenin and the Communists withdrew from World War I. They then introduced a series of domestic changes involving every aspect of Soviet life. Millions of acres of land were transferred to poorer peasants, while workers were organized to control and operate factories. All industries were **nationalized** (*taken over by the government*).

You have already read that a civil war followed between those who supported Lenin's program, known as the *"Reds,"* and those who opposed it, known as the *"Whites."* Although Communist methods were brutal, their opponents had little to offer workers and peasants. By 1921, the Red army defeated the Whites. Lenin then introduced the

Vladimir Ilyich Lenin

New Economic Policy, or N.E.P. Private ownership was permitted in small-scale manufacturing and agriculture, although the government continued to control major industries.

STALIN AND THE RISE OF THE MODERN TOTALITARIAN STATE

Lenin died in 1924 at the age of 54. Leon Trotsky and **Joseph Stalin** competed to succeed him as leader of the Soviet Union. Stalin quickly outmaneuvered Trotsky, who was expelled from the Soviet Union. Later, agents of Stalin murdered Trotsky in Mexico. Stalin eliminated other rivals by accusing them of disloyalty to Communist ideals. Once in power, Stalin immediately set about making changes in Soviet society — and established a **totalitarian** state.

Joseph Stalin

Totalitarianism is a political system in which a one-party government controls all aspects of individual life. Citizens are denied the rights of free speech and dissent. Secret police, censorship, and terror are used to enforce government control.

CHANGES UNDER STALIN

Reign of Terror. In so-called "purges," Stalin's secret police arrested and executed potential rival leaders. Stalin built enormous slave labor camps in Siberia, known as **gulags**. Tens of millions of people died, victims of his reign of terror.

Control of Cultural Life. Stalin used the government to control Soviet education, ideas, the economy, and even music and the arts. In movies, theatres, and schools, Soviet citizens heard only about Communist ideals and successes.

Collectivization. Private land was taken from the peasants, who were forced to work on farms owned by the government (*called collectives*). In the Ukraine, the peasants rejected collectivization. Stalin sealed off the entire region after seizing food supplies, so that millions of Ukrainians starved to death.

Five-Year Plans. Stalin sought to turn his country from an agricultural land into an industrialized nation. He introduced a series of **Five-Year Plans** in which national goals were set and all aspects of the economy were controlled. Heavy industry was developed, while consumer needs were ignored. These Five-Year Plans were considered great successes.

Glorification of Stalin. Stalin glorified his part in building the nation, portraying himself as Russia's greatest leader. Streets and cities were named after him; his picture appeared everywhere in public. Statues portrayed him as a gentle, fatherly ruler. Children memorized his sayings in school. Artists and writers boasted of Stalin's accomplishments.

THE WORLD IN PROSPERITY AND DEPRESSION

RECONSTRUCTION AND PROSPERITY IN THE 1920s

Life in 1919 differed in many significant ways from before the war. The former imperial governments of Germany, Russia, Austria-Hungary, and Ottoman Turkey were gone. New states like Poland, Czechoslovakia, Hungary, Yugoslavia, and the Baltic states had emerged.

In Europe, the first years after World War I were not easy ones. Central European peoples suffered from famine. Farms, cities, and railroad lines had been torn up in the fighting. Europeans spent the next five years rebuilding and recovering from the war.

German soldiers fighting in World War I. After the war many faced unemployment.

Meanwhile, the United States emerged from the war as the world's greatest economic power. American prosperity gradually spread to Europe and the rest of the world. The 1920s also saw the expression of new values. Women in the United States, Great Britain, and many other countries gained the right to vote and enjoyed greater freedom than ever before.

After fighting for democracy in World War I, it became exceedingly difficult in the United States to deny women the right to vote.

THE GREAT DEPRESSION (1929)

In 1929, the bubble burst. A stock market crash in New York started a chain reaction that sent the American economy into the **Great Depression.**

A *depression* is a severe economic downturn in which large numbers of businesses fail and many workers are unemployed over an extended period of time.

Because of the Depression, many American banks and investors decided to recall their loans from Europe. European production slowed down and unemployment increased. Europeans bought less goods from their colonies in Africa and Asia, causing the depression to spread worldwide. At the height of the depression, as many as 50 million people

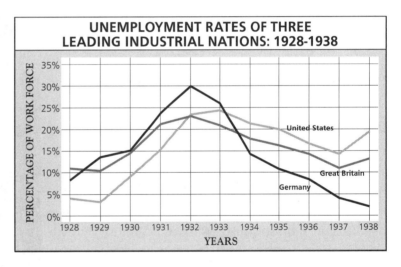

were unemployed in the United States, Germany, Japan, and other industrialized countries.

THE RISE OF FASCISM

Benito Mussolini was the first person to use the term Fascism. *Fascism* refers to a political system that appeared in Italy after World War I. The term is also used more generally to identify similar systems such as Nazism in Germany.

Two of Europe's best known fascist leaders — Benito Mussolini and Adolf Hitler

Most varieties of European Fascism shared the following basic characteristics:

Nationalism. Fascists were extreme nationalists, who believed that the highest value was the nation. They took this belief to extremes, claiming that their nation was superior to others. Fascists were also strongly opposed to communism.

Unity of All Social Classes. Fascists felt a single national party should unite all classes. They also believed that the strong had a natural right to dominate the weak. They opposed worker unions and strikes.

MAIN CHARACTERISTICS OF EUROPEAN FASCISM

All-Powerful Leaders. Fascists believed that a single all-powerful leader, like Mussolini or Hitler, could best represent the national will and lead the nation.

Extreme Militarism. Fascists used violence to defeat their political opponents and prepared to use war for national expansion. Fascists saw war as a glorious experience.

THE ROOTS OF FASCISM

Some long-held beliefs helped prepare the way for the rise of Fascism. **Anti-Semitism,** a hatred of Jews, was an established trend among many Europeans. Jews often faced persecution because their beliefs made them easy targets in times of social unrest and economic difficulty. **Racism** is a contempt for other races. This, too, was an established trend in European culture. European racism was strengthened by the experiences of overseas imperialism and by the spirit of nationalism. **Social Darwinism** made racism and anti-Semitism respectable. Social Darwinists, using the ideas of Charles Darwin about evolution in nature, believed that all human groups competed for survival. Social Darwinists claimed that stronger groups had the right to succeed and that weaker groups deserved to die out.

In Germany during the 1930s, scenes like this were common. The sign says, "Germans! Defend yourselves! Do not buy from Jews."

THE OLD ORDER COLLAPSES

Europe had been shaken to its core by World War I. In the aftermath of World War I, most people sought to return to life as it had been prior to 1914. However, important political changes had taken place. New countries had been created, and old ruling families had been overthrown.

◆ **Germany.** The Kaiser was forced to abdicate at the end of the war. A new democratic republic, known as the **Weimar Republic,** was created but remained very weak. Many landowners, industrialists, and military leaders opposed the new republic. They would have preferred to give all political power to a single, strong leader rather than to the common people.

◆ **Russia.** Russian Communists demonstrated how to build a totalitarian state. The middle classes in other European countries feared the spread of Communism, leading them to support extremists like Mussolini and Hitler.

◆ **Italy. Benito Mussolini** copied Bolshevik practices while denouncing their ideas. Like the Bolsheviks, he had a party newspaper, a party organization, and a private army of party members. He used violence against his opponents. In 1922, Mussolini seized power and turned Italy into the first Fascist state.

THE NAZI DICTATORSHIP IN GERMANY

RISE OF THE NAZI PARTY

In Germany, the leaders of the Weimar Republic were blamed for signing the Treaty of Versailles, which ended World War I. Under the treaty, Germany was forced to pay huge reparations to Britain and France. The reparation payments led to a soaring inflation rate in Germany in the early 1920s. In 1930, the Great Depression spread from the United States to Germany. More than one-third of the German work force lost their jobs. The Weimar government could not cope with this catastrophe. In elections, unemployed workers and mem-

Hitler receives the Nazi salute after delivering a speech to a meeting of Nazi Party officials.

bers of the middle class turned to the more radical solutions offered by **Adolf Hitler** (1889–1945), the leader of the **Nazi Party.** Hitler published his main ideas in his book, **Mein Kampf:**

HITLER'S VISION FOR GERMANY		
Condemnation of the Weimar Republic. Hitler blamed Germany's humiliation at Versailles on Weimar leaders. He urged Germans to abandon democracy and return Germany to glory under a strong leader.	**Aryan Race.** Hitler believed that Germans were a superior "Aryan" race that should rule the world. He planned to eventually wipe out Slavic peoples like the Poles to make room for German settlers in Eastern Europe.	**Anti-Semitism.** Hitler called the Jews an "evil race" that should be destroyed for causing Germany's defeat in the war. He saw Communism as a Jewish plot to control the world.

GERMANY UNDER NAZI CONTROL

When the Great Depression hit Germany, support for the Nazi party increased rapidly. Germany's President appointed Hitler as chief minister in 1933. Hitler acted quickly to secure complete control of Germany by secretly ordering the German Parliament building to be set on fire and blaming the Communists. The German Parliament then agreed to Hitler's request for emergency laws giving him absolute power.

Almost immediately, Hitler used his new powers to crush all opposition. All political parties, except the Nazis, were banned. All artistic and intellectual activity was brought under Nazi control. Hitler called his government the *Third Reich,* ("Third Empire") believing his system would last 1,000 years. Like Stalin, Hitler turned Germany into a totalitarian state:

Human Rights Violations. Human rights were suppressed. People were arrested and executed without trial. Rival political parties, unions, and independent newspapers were closed and replaced by pro-Nazi ones.

Economic Changes. Hitler made used of public works projects like building highways and military rearmament to secure full employment. Economic prosperity returned to Germany.

HITLER'S NAZI DICTATORSHIP

Persecution of Jews. Jews were thrown out of government jobs. Jews lost their citizenship, were forced to wear yellow stars on their clothes, and were barred from marrying other Germans. Jewish shops were vandalized and synagogues were burned down. Later, Jews would be forced into special **ghettoes** and concentration camps.

Secret Police. Newspapers, radios, and films blared out Nazi propaganda. No other sources of information were permitted except those under Nazi control. The **Gestapo** (*secret police*) arrested suspected opponents, who were thrown into **concentration camps** where they were mistreated, tortured, and killed.

Concentration camp victims

ANSWERING THE FOCUS QUESTION •

Some important changes introduced by Communism in the Soviet Union and Nazism in Germany were:

_____ (*Soviet Union*)

_____

_____ (*Germany*)

_____

Directions: Complete each of the following vocabulary cards. Then answer the multiple-choice questions that follow.

VLADIMIR LENIN
What were Lenin's main beliefs?
What changes did Lenin introduce to Russia?

ADOLF HITLER
What were Hitler's main beliefs?
What changes did Hitler introduce to Germany?

1 The harsh conditions imposed by the Treaty of Versailles after World War I helped lay the foundations for the
   1 rise of Nazism in Germany
   2 French Revolution
   3 downfall of Mexican dictator Diaz
   4 Bolshevik revolution in Russia

2 Fascism in Europe during the 1920s and 1930s can best be described as
   1 an example of laissez-faire capitalism that promoted free enterprise
   2 a political system that glorified the nation above the individual
   3 a type of economic system that stressed a classless society
   4 a program of humanistic ideals emphasizing individual worth and dignity

3 One similarity between Fascism and Communism in the 1930s was that both systems generally
   1 provided for hereditary rulers
   2 promoted ethnic diversity
   3 supported democratic elections
   4 suppressed opposition views

4 Which factor contributed most to the rise of totalitarian governments in Europe before World War II?
   1 improved educational systems
   2 an expanding League of Nations
   3 increased political stability
   4 worsening economic conditions

SECTION 3: WORLD WAR II AND ITS AFTERMATH

The war that began in 1939 was in part a renewal of the war that had ended in 1918. Hitler sought to avenge Germany's humiliating defeat. German aims in Europe linked with Japanese ambitions in Asia, resulting in the most destructive war in history.

THINK ABOUT IT •

What were the main causes and effects of World War II?

WORLD WAR II, 1939–1945

The rise of Fascist dictators in Italy, Germany, and elsewhere made the outbreak of war inevitable. These dictators glorified war and laid plans for national expansion through conquest.

THE ROAD TO WORLD WAR II

League of Nations Fails. The League relied on its members to help each other to prevent another war. Hitler, in violation of the Treaty of Versailles, rebuilt his armed forces. The League could do nothing to stop Hitler because its member states refused to take action. They feared any such steps might lead to war.

Appeasement. Hitler next claimed territories where Germans lived. He **annexed** (*took*) Austria early in 1938. Then Hitler claimed part of Czechoslovakia where a large number of Germans lived. British Prime Minister Chamberlain met with Hitler in Munich and tried **appeasement** (*granting concessions to an aggressor*). Hoping to avoid war, Chamberlain agreed to Hitler's demand for western Czechoslovakia.

Invasion of Poland. In 1939, Hitler made new demands for part of Poland. This time, Britain and France refused to give in. Hitler made a secret deal with Stalin to keep the Soviet Union out of the war. Germany then invaded Poland, starting World War II.

THE WAR IN EUROPE

Improvements in the automobile engine and other technologies again made new forms of warfare possible. The German army used planes, tanks, and motorized troop carriers to advance rapidly into enemy territory. This military tactic became known as the **blitzkrieg,** or "lightning warfare." By the end of 1940, Germany controlled most of Western Europe — only Britain held out.

German soldiers on the attack in World War II.

GERMANY INVADES THE SOVIET UNION

In 1941, Hitler betrayed Stalin by launching a surprise attack on the Soviet Union. The fierce winter of 1941–1942, however, froze German combat vehicles before their army could reach Moscow. One effect of Stalin's dictatorship was that he had increased Soviet industrial strength, making the Soviet Union a match for Hitler. By 1943, the Soviet army began to gradually push the Germans back. Over the next two years, Soviet soldiers and civilians bore the brunt of fighting Germany, with Soviet losses mounting to 21 million casualties.

THE HOLOCAUST

The **Holocaust** refers to the attempted **genocide** (*murder of an entire people*) of the Jews during World War II. Hitler called his plan the "Final Solution." Large concentration camps were built

at Auschwitz and other places where Jews from all over Nazi-controlled Europe were sent. Most were gassed and their bodies burned in large ovens. Some were spared to do the work of running the camp. These inmates were half-starved and subjected to inhuman conditions. It is estimated that six million Jews, two-thirds of all Jews then living in Europe, met their deaths in this tragedy. Six million gypsies, Slavs, political prisoners, elderly, and mentally disabled people also died in Nazi concentration camps.

This truckload of bodies was about to be disposed of when this concentration camp was captured by the U.S. Army.

THE WAR IN EUROPE ENDS

In December 1941, Japan attacked **Pearl Harbor,** Hawaii. Hitler supported his ally Japan by declaring war on the United States. Hitler was now opposed by the **Allied Powers** —Britain, the Soviet Union and the United States. Germany's supporters consisted of Italy and Japan, together known as the **Axis Powers.** Allied leaders decided to concentrate first on defeating Germany in Europe before turning against Japan. In July 1943, Allied forces landed in southern Italy and helped the Italians to overthrow Mussolini. Then, in June 1944, Allied troops invaded northern France on **D-Day**. Within months, the tide of war turned in favor of the Allies. By 1945, Soviet, British, American, and French troops occupied Germany, which surrendered in May.

NUREMBERG TRIALS

Hitler escaped prosecution by committing suicide, but several of the most important Nazi leaders were tried and convicted for "crimes against humanity" by an international tribunal at Nuremberg. The **Nuremberg Trials** revealed to the world the full extent of Nazi atrocities — the use of slave labor, medical experiments on humans, forced starvation, and mass genocide. The trial and conviction of Nazi leaders by this international court established the principle that there was something superior even to national law, and that a person could be guilty for "crimes against humanity." Germany itself

Major Nazi leaders on trial at Nuremberg.

was divided into four separate zones and occupied by the four victorious Allied Powers.

THE WAR IN ASIA

In the last chapter, you learned that Japan's late 19th century industrialization had been very successful. Japanese leaders soon realized that they needed more raw materials and markets for their growing industries. By the start of the 20th century, the Japanese began a series of imperialistic attacks on mainland Asia in order to become a world power.

◆ **Sino-Japanese War (1894–1895).** War broke out between China and Japan for control of Korea. Japan defeated China, alerting the world to Japan's new military strength.

◆ **Russo-Japanese War (1904–1905).** Japan went to war with Russia for control of Manchuria, a northern province of China. Japan's victory startled the world, since it was the first time a European great power was defeated by a non-European nation.

◆ **World War I (1914–1918).** Japan supported the Allies in World War I. Japan's reward for this support was to obtain several of Germany's colonial possessions in the Pacific.

◆ **Second Sino-Japanese War (1931–1939).** Japan invaded Manchuria in 1931. When world reaction was mild, Japan conquered more of China. Japanese leaders also concluded an alliance with Nazi Germany and Fascist Italy.

JAPAN IN WORLD WAR II (1941-1945)

When war broke out in Europe in 1939, Japan took advantage of the conflict. Japanese leaders set their sights on control of East Asia. However, they were opposed by the United States, which stopped the sale of iron and oil to Japan. In response, Japan launched a surprise attack on the U.S. fleet stationed at Pearl Harbor in late 1941.

Japanese pilots receive cheers as they depart for their surprise attack on Pearl Harbor, Hawaii.

At first, the Japanese achieved sweeping victories in Southeast Asia and the Pacific. The tide began to turn in 1943, when American forces began liberating Pacific islands from Japanese control. After Germany was defeated in 1945, the United States turned its full strength against Japan. In August 1945, the "Atomic Age" began when American atomic bombs were dropped on the Japanese cities of **Hiroshima** and **Nagasaki.** Each bomb devastated almost 2 square miles. Nearly 200,000 Japanese civilians were killed. Fearing additional attacks, Japan surrendered on August 14, 1945.

An atomic bomb explodes over Nagasaki

THE U.S. OCCUPATION OF JAPAN (1945–1952)

General MacArthur accepts Japan's surrender

By mid-1945, Japan was thoroughly defeated. Its military had been destroyed and its cities were in ruins. In September, 1945, American General **Douglas MacArthur,** who had led the Pacific campaign, accepted Japan's unconditional surrender on board the U.S. battleship *Missouri,* anchored in Tokyo Bay. With the war officially over, MacArthur was assigned the task of rebuilding and reforming post-war Japan. Under his leadership, important changes were introduced to make Japan less imperialistic and less aggressive.

War Leaders Punished. Japanese leaders responsible for wartime atrocities were put on trial and punished.

Territorial Losses. Japan's overseas empire was taken away, leaving Japan with just her home islands.

CHANGES IMPOSED ON POSTWAR JAPAN

Demilitarized. Japan's ability to wage war was virtually eliminated. Japan was forbidden to have any army or navy, except for a small "self-defense force." Japan also renounced the use of nuclear weapons.

A New Constitution. A new constitution made Japan one of the most democratic nations in the world. War was renounced, and the constitution removed power from the emperor. Control of government was placed in the hands of the Japanese people. The emperor was permitted to remain as a figurehead chief of state without real power.

THE GLOBAL IMPACT OF WORLD WAR II

World War II, the most destructive war in history, dramatically changed the world.

DEFEAT OF DICTATORSHIPS

Hitler's plans to conquer Europe and Japan's plans for dominating Asia were defeated. After the war, Germany, Italy, and Japan were occupied and turned into democratic, peaceful nations.

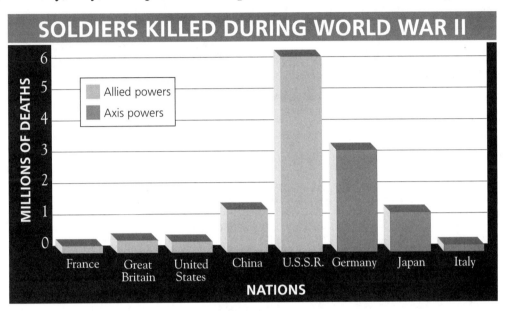

UNPARALLELED DESTRUCTION

World War II was a global conflict — fought in Europe, North Africa, East Asia, and on the Pacific and Atlantic Oceans. More than forty million people died, and much of Europe, North Africa and East Asia lay in ruins. Total war had destroyed cities, factories, railroads, homes — and lives.

By 1945, much of Europe was destroyed.

THE DECLINE OF THE COLONIAL POWERS

The war greatly stimulated the desire for national self-determination in Africa and Asia. European colonial powers like Britain, France, Holland, and Belgium had exhausted their resources in fighting the war and could no longer resist independence movements in their colonies.

THE RISE OF THE SUPERPOWERS AND THE COLD WAR

The collapse of Europe left two **Superpowers** in command of the world: the United States and the Soviet Union. Their differences in viewpoint and competing national interests rapidly led to the Cold War. You will learn more about this contest in the next chapter.

CREATION OF THE UNITED NATIONS

Despite the failure of the League of Nations, the victorious Allies launched a new international peace-keeping organization in 1945, known as the **United Nations.** The U.N. Charter stated that the purpose of this new organization was to maintain peace in the world, while encouraging friendship and cooperation among nations. Members agreed to give up the use of force in disputes, except in self-defense. Another goal of the U.N. was to eliminate world hunger, disease, and ignorance. The U.N.

Today, the U.N. counts most nations in the world among its members.

has sent forces to engage in "peacekeeping" operations in such places as Korea, Cyprus, Congo, Iraq, and Bosnia.

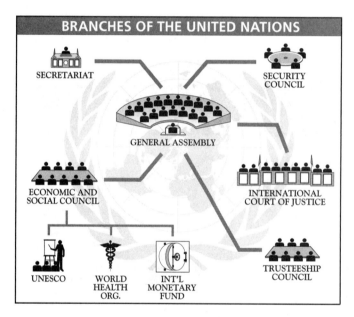

THE DECOLONIZATION OF ASIA AND AFRICA

One of the most significant results of World War II was the end of European imperialism in India, Indochina, Africa, and Indonesia. Historians refer to this development as **decolonization.** Several factors contributed this development. The aggressive ambitions of Nazi Germany and Imperial Japan had largely discredited imperialist beliefs. It was hard

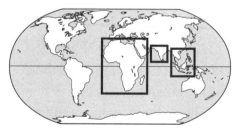

to fight for democracy in Europe and to deny it to others in Asia and Africa. Moreover, after World War II, the old colonial powers were simply exhausted. Most Europeans were not willing to endure further warfare overseas to maintain imperial rule against determined local resistance. Even so, the end of European colonialism in many parts of the world was not always bloodless.

INDIA'S ROAD TO INDEPENDENCE

The first major country to achieve independence in the post-war period was India. Under the leadership of **Mohandas Gandhi,** an Indian lawyer who had been educated in England, India had long been resisting British rule. Gandhi's genius was to appeal to ordinary Indians as well as the educated elite in the drive for independence. Gandhi used non-violent methods to show the British the futility of denying India its freedom. After World War II, British leaders recognized that they were too weak to resist Indian nationalist demands. In 1947, the British finally agreed to Indian independence.

Mohandas Gandhi

INDIA'S STRUGGLE FOR INDEPENDENCE

Non-Violence. Gandhi was a pacifist — a person opposed to using violence to settle disputes. He developed the policy of non-violent passive resistance in which Indians passively suffered British beatings and violence.

Civil Disobedience. Gandhi urged Indians to disobey unjust British laws. In 1930, he led a **Salt March** to protest a British salt tax. Gandhi's followers also conducted fasts and refused to work for the British. As a result, Indians were jailed in ever-increasing numbers.

Cottage Industries. Gandhi encouraged Indians to **boycott** (*refuse to buy*) British-made cotton goods, and to buy cotton goods that were homespun in India. Gandhi hoped to rebuild India's cottage industries to raise living standards.

The British delayed granting independence because of the threat of widespread violence between India's Hindu and Muslim populations. When independence was finally granted in 1947, India was partitioned into two separate nations: **India** became a Hindu nation, while **Pakistan** became a home for Muslims. Because there were large Muslim populations in both the east and west of British India, Pakistan became a divided nation — separated by over a thousand miles. Following independence, millions of Hindus and Muslims moved from their homes to new areas. Thousands were killed in riots during these migrations.

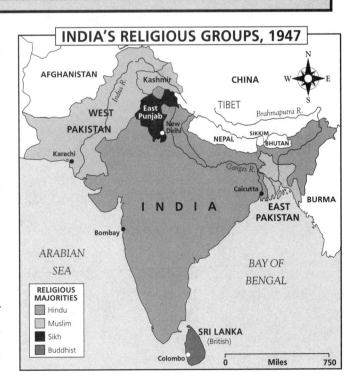

INDIA'S RELIGIOUS GROUPS, 1947

RELIGIOUS MAJORITIES
- Hindu
- Muslim
- Sikh
- Buddhist

SOUTHEAST ASIA'S ROAD TO INDEPENDENCE

Beginning in the 1500s, most of Southeast Asia had gradually fallen under European control. Europeans were especially attracted to spices like pepper and cinnamon found on the spice islands of Indonesia. During World War II, Japan occupied all of Southeast Asia, driving out the European powers. After the war, local nationalist leaders expected to achieve independence. In some places independence was granted peacefully; in others, it was only achieved through warfare.

The Philippines are a group of islands in the Pacific. The United States granted independence to the Philippines in 1946.

Myanmar and Malaysia. Great Britain granted both Burma (*Myanmar*) and Malaysia their indepence in 1948.

SOUTHEAST ASIA'S ROAD TO INDEPENDENCE

Indonesia. Indonesian leaders declared independence in 1945, but had to fight Dutch troops until 1949, when the Netherlands at last recognized Indonesian independence.

Vietnam. Guerillas, led by Ho Chi Minh, began a war against the French and won their independence in 1954. At an international conference, Vietnam was temporarily divided in two: (1) in the north, a Communist state was established, led by Ho Chi Minh; (2) in the south, a pro-Western state was recognized.

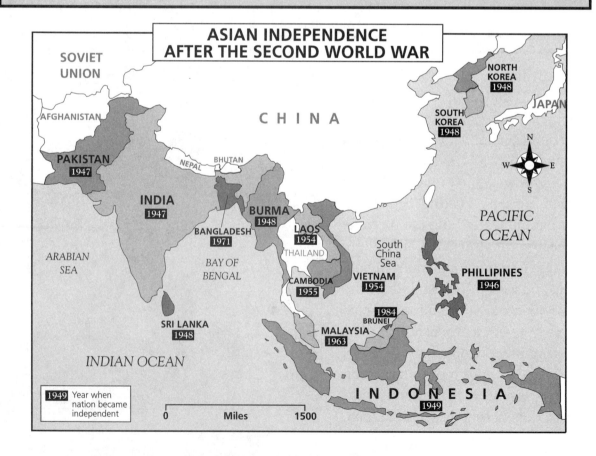

ASIAN INDEPENDENCE AFTER THE SECOND WORLD WAR

THE MIDDLE EAST AND NORTH AFRICA

The British had granted Egypt its independence back in 1922, but continued to treat Egypt as a British satellite state until Egypt's king was overthrown in the 1950s. Saudi Arabia also became independent in the inter-war period. After World War II, the French granted independence to Morocco, Tunisia, and Libya in North Africa and to Lebanon and Syria in the Middle East. But France was not willing to grant independence to Algeria, where many French settlers lived. In

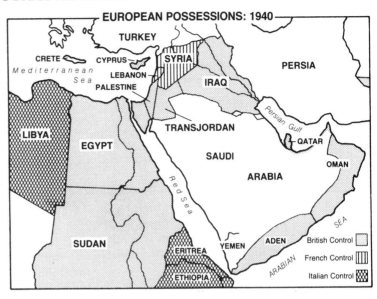

1954, Algerian nationalists launched a violent struggle for independence. After eight years of fighting, France finally recognized Algerian independence in 1962.

Another problem area was Palestine — once a part of the Ottoman empire. Starting in the 1880s, some European Jews began returning to Palestine as part of the **Zionist Movement.** After World War I, Palestine became a British mandate. In 1917, British leaders promised to create a Jewish homeland in Palestine. But the British limited Jewish emigration to Palestine during and after World War II to prevent Arab uprisings. Many Jewish survivors of the Holocaust nevertheless sought to emigrate there. British leaders came to fear that the end of colonial rule in Palestine would lead to a full-scale civil war between Jews and Arabs. Continued attacks by Jewish underground forces made the British realize their inability to continue governing Palestine. Finally, they decided to withdraw in 1947 and handed the problem over to the new United Nations. You will learn more about the birth of Israel in the next chapter.

Tens of thousands of European Jews emigrated to Palestine after the war.

SUB-SAHARAN AFRICA

The rising spirit of nationalism outside of Europe also led to the decolonization of Africa south of the Sahara in the post-war years. Before the war, the British and French had provided a European-style education to some native Africans. Members of this small, educated elite became leaders of new African nationalist movements.

Kwame Nkrumah, in the British colony known as the Gold Coast, followed Gandhi's example by demonstrating against British rule and boycotting British products. Nkrumah finally won independence for the Gold Coast in 1957. The country changed its name to **Ghana** (*after the ancient West African Kingdom*) and became the first black African colony to win its independence.

The former British colony of Somalia celebrates receiving its independence in 1960.

Other African leaders, like **Julius Nyerere** and **Jomo Kenyatta,** followed Nkrumah's example. In Tanzania, Nyerere sought to improve rural life, build a classless society, and create an independent economy. As Kenya's first Prime Minister, Kenyatta concentrated on building a market economy and expanding businesses in his nation. Over the next decade, almost all of sub-Saharan Africa achieved independence. In some cases, such as the former Belgian Congo and Kenya, independence was accompanied by bloodshed. For the most part, however, the former colonies became new nations without a major war.

Dr. Julius Nyerere, holding a ceremonial stick.

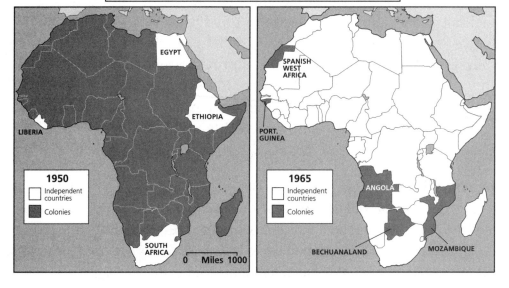

INDEPENDENCE MOVEMENTS IN AFRICA

EGYPT

ETHIOPIA

LIBERIA

1950
Independent countries
Colonies

SOUTH AFRICA

0   Miles 1000

SPANISH WEST AFRICA

PORT. GUINEA

ANGOLA

1965
Independent countries
Colonies

BECHUANALAND

MOZAMBIQUE

ANSWERING THE FOCUS QUESTION •

Writing

The main causes of World War II were _____

_____

Some of the most important effects of World War II were _____

_____

Directions: Complete each of the following vocabulary cards. Then answer the multiple-choice questions that follow.

UNITED NATIONS
What is the United Nations?
What is its purpose?

MOHANDAS GANDHI
What policies did Gandhi follow in resisting the British?
Why was British India partitioned in 1947?

1 The "Atomic Age" began with
   1 Japan's attack on Pearl Harbor
   2 The founding of the United Nations
   3 the bombing of Hiroshima and Nagasaki
   4 Nazi Germany's invasion of Poland

2 Which tactic did Mohandas Gandhi use to bring world attention to the injustices of British colonialism in India?
   1 Salt March   3 Sepoy Mutiny
   2 partition of India   4 formation of Indian Parliament

3 Which term best describes British Prime Minister Chamberlain's policy of giving western Czechoslovakia to Hitler?
   1 divine right   3 appeasement
   2 Mandate of Heaven   4 mercantilism

4 Which person is correctly paired with his country?
   1 Joseph Stalin — North Vietnam
   2 Mohandas Gandhi — Pakistan
   3 Kwame Nkrumah — Ghana
   4 Ho Chi Minh — Philippines

KEY TERMS, CONCEPTS, AND PEOPLE

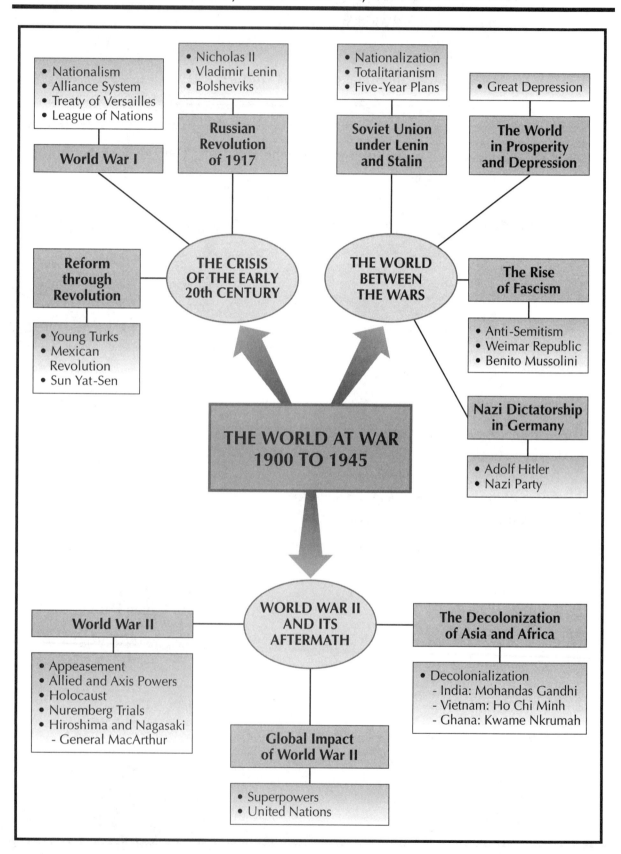

- Nationalism
- Alliance System
- Treaty of Versailles
- League of Nations

World War I

- Nicholas II
- Vladimir Lenin
- Bolsheviks

Russian Revolution of 1917

- Nationalization
- Totalitarianism
- Five-Year Plans

Soviet Union under Lenin and Stalin

- Great Depression

The World in Prosperity and Depression

Reform through Revolution

- Young Turks
- Mexican Revolution
- Sun Yat-Sen

THE CRISIS OF THE EARLY 20th CENTURY

THE WORLD BETWEEN THE WARS

The Rise of Fascism

- Anti-Semitism
- Weimar Republic
- Benito Mussolini

Nazi Dictatorship in Germany

- Adolf Hitler
- Nazi Party

THE WORLD AT WAR 1900 TO 1945

World War II

- Appeasement
- Allied and Axis Powers
- Holocaust
- Nuremberg Trials
- Hiroshima and Nagasaki
  - General MacArthur

WORLD WAR II AND ITS AFTERMATH

The Decolonization of Asia and Africa

- Decolonialization
  - India: Mohandas Gandhi
  - Vietnam: Ho Chi Minh
  - Ghana: Kwame Nkrumah

Global Impact of World War II

- Superpowers
- United Nations

SUMMARIZING YOUR UNDERSTANDING

COMPLETING AN OUTLINE

Directions: Use these headings to complete the outline below.

THE CRISIS OF THE EARLY 20TH CENTURY
The Rise of Fascism
The Global Impact of World War II
Reform through Revolution
THE WORLD BETWEEN THE WARS
THE WORLD AT WAR, 1900 TO 1945
The Russian Revolution of 1917
Prosperity and Depression
The Soviet Union under Lenin and Stalin
World War II
WORLD WAR II AND ITS AFTERMATH
The Decolonization of Asia and Africa
The Nazi Dictatorship in Germany
World War I

TITLE: _____

I. MAJOR DIVISION: _____
    A. Sub-topic: _____
    B. Sub-topic: _____
    C. Sub-topic: _____

II. MAJOR DIVISION: _____
    A. Sub-topic: _____
    B. Sub-topic: _____
    C. Sub-topic: _____
    D. Sub-topic: _____

III. MAJOR DIVISION: _____
    A. Sub-topic: _____
    B. Sub-topic: _____
    C. Sub-topic: _____

COMPLETING A GRAPHIC ORGANIZER

Complete the following graphic organizer by describing some of the major events of this time period.

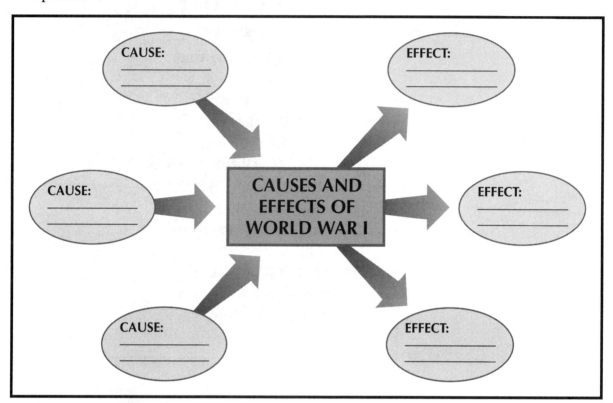

COMPLETING A TABLE

Use the table below to organize information on important individuals you have read about in this chapter.

Person	Country	Significance
Sun Yat-Sen		
Vladimir Lenin		
Joseph Stalin		
Adolf Hitler		
Mohandas Gandhi		
Kwame Nkrumah		

SHARPENING YOUR TEST-TAKING SKILLS

EXAMINING THE "ACTION" WORDS USED IN DOCUMENT-BASED ESSAY QUESTIONS

Document-based essay questions (which are discussed more fully in the next chapter) will often require you to understand certain key words. The most common "action words" are "*discuss*" and "*evaluate*." Let's examine each of these two "action" words to see what they require you to do.

DISCUSS

Discuss means to "to tell about it." The word "discuss" is used when you are asked for the "**who,**" "**what,**" "**when,**" and "**where**" of something. Not every discuss question requires all four of these elements, but your answer must go beyond just a word or sentence. Your answer must consist of an essay of several paragraphs.

The following is an example of a "discuss" question:

***Discuss* the religious differences between Hindus and Muslims.**

_____

_____

EVALUATE

Evaluate means "to examine and judge carefully." *Evaluate* questions ask you to make a judgment. Before writing your answer, you must consider the criteria upon which things are to be judged. Then you must weigh the facts by these criteria.

Let's look at a typical *evaluate* question:

***Evaluate* the general impact of imperialism on Africa.**

_____

_____

In order to answer this question, here is what you must do:

- Know some of the effects of imperialism on Africa
- Compare the good and bad effects of imperialism
- Make a judgement about the overall impact of imperialism on Africa

Let's look at a model answer to the sample "evaluate" question:

Model Answer:

Imperialism is the control of one country by another. By 1900, a few European nations controlled most of Africa. This control had both positive and negative effects on Africans. Among the positive effects, Europeans introduced modern medicine and improved nutrition, increasing the life-span of many Africans. They also brought new technologies, languages, and legal systems. Against this, we have to consider the negative effects. Existing African cultures and traditions were ignored by European imperialists. Tribes were often divided between different European colonies. Africans lost their independence and were treated as socially inferior to Europeans. Many were used as forced labor.

IF YOU THOUGHT IMPERIALISM WAS

MORE POSITIVE THAN NEGATIVE, YOU MIGHT CONTINUE AS FOLLOWS: *In considering the impact of imperialism as a whole, the most important thing to remember is that it brought Africa into contact with the rest of the world — a necessary step in African development. The benefits of imperialism therefore outweighed its disadvantages because it opened up new opportunities for later generations of Africans.*	**MORE NEGATIVE THAN POSITIVE, YOU MIGHT CONTINUE AS FOLLOWS:** *In considering the impact of imperialism as a whole, it is clear that the disadvantages outweighed the advantages. Under imperialism, Africa developed economically and culturally in ways that were less advantageous to native Africans and more beneficial to European imperial powers. Africans would have been better off if imperialism had never happened.*

Notice how the answer:

♦ first identifies the term imperialism,

♦ then lists the positive and negative effects of imperialism on Africans,

♦ finally reaches a general conclusion about the overall impact of imperialism on Africa.

Once you take a position in your answer, be sure that you have provided information to support it.

TESTING YOUR UNDERSTANDING

Test your understanding of this chapter by answering the following questions:

MULTIPLE-CHOICE QUESTIONS

1 Which statement best characterizes the governments of Stalin in the Soviet Union, Hitler in Germany, and Mussolini in Italy?
1 They were representative democracies.
2 They restricted the civil liberties of their people.
3 They allowed many political parties to exist.
4 They were constitutional monarchies.

Base your answer to question 2 on the map and your knowledge of global history.

2 The information on the map shows a part of Europe in which year?
1 1813   3 1913
2 1943   4 1993

3 The French Revolution of 1789, the Chinese Revolution of 1911 and the Russian Revolution of 1917 were similar in that all of these revolutions
1 were led by ruthless dictators
2 were motivated by a desire to overthrow a monarch
3 led directly to the establishment of Communism
4 established higher standards of living for the middle class

4 Stalin's Five-Year Plans and his decision to form collective farms are examples of
1 strategies to modernize the Soviet economy through forced Communism
2 a more friendly foreign policy toward China
3 methods of dealing with the United States during World War II
4 programs to Westernize, educate, and enlighten the population

5 Joseph Stalin's rule in the Soviet Union can best be characterized as a period of
1 democratic reform and nationalism   3 humanism and democracy
2 religious freedom and tolerance   4 censorship and terror

Base your answer to question 6 on the graph and your knowledge of global history.

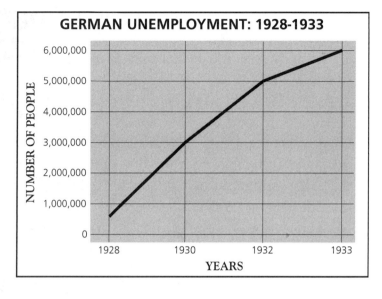

6 Which statement is most accurate?
1 German unemployment was highest in 1932.
2 Between 1928 and 1933, German unemployment remained unchanged.
3 By 1933, there were about about 6 million unemployed German workers.
4 The Nazi Party brought German unemployment under control in 1928.

Base your answer to question 7 on the graph and your knowledge of global history.

7 According to the graph, which statement is most accurate?
1 The costs of World War I were evenly spread among warring nations.
2 Russia spent more in World War I than all the other powers.
3 Germany spent more than Austria-Hungary, Italy and Russia combined.
4 War costs were greatest at the start of the World War I.

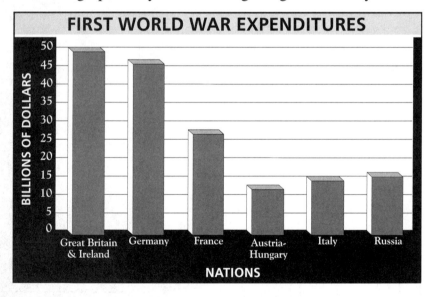

8 In 1947, the subcontinent of India became independent and was divided into India and Pakistan. This division recognized the
1 rivalries between religious groups
2 natural geographic boundaries
3 strength of Fascism in certain areas
4 colonial boundaries of British India

9 Which statement about India is a fact rather than an opinion?
1 Most Indians were happy with the Hindu practice of arranged marriages.
2 India is fortunate to be a country with great religious diversity.
3 The Mughals ruled India for more than 100 years.
4 The partition of British India in 1947 helped India prosper.

10 Four events important to the history of the world are listed below:

A. Start of the French Revolution	C. Start of the Meiji Restoration
B. Hitler comes to power in Germany	D. India achieves independence

Which is the correct chronological order of these events?

1 A → B → C → D   3 D → B → C → A
2 A → C → B → D   4 B → D → A → C

11 Europeans were able to dominate much of South and Southeast Asia in the 19th century primarily because
  1 Christianity appealed to the people of the region
  2 they had more advanced technology
  3 this region lacked political organization
  4 few natural resources were found in the region

12 Which is a secondary source of information about World War II?
  1 a college history textbook about World War II
  2 a photograph of U.S. soldiers landing in France in 1944
  3 U.S. battle maps from World War II
  4 General MacArthur's personal diary

INTERPRETING DOCUMENTS

I. INTERPRETING A TABLE

FIVE-YEAR PLANS IN THE SOVIET UNION (m = million)			
Item	1928: Before Five-Year Plans	1932: End of 1st Five-Year Plan	1937: End of 2nd Five-Year Plan
Industry	18.3 m. rubles	43.3 m. rubles	95.5 m. rubles
Electricity	5.05 m. kilowatts	13.4 m. kilowatts	36.6 m. kilowatts
Steel	4.00 m. tons	5.90 m. tons	17.7 m. tons
Grain Harvest	73.3 m. tons	69.9 m. tons	75.0 m. tons
Cattle	70.5 m. head	40.7 m. head	63.2 m. head

1 How much steel was produced in the Soviet Union in 1928? _____

2 According to the table, early Soviet Five-Year Plans emphasized:
  [circle one]:   consumer equipment   industrial goods   agriculture products

3 What was Stalin's goal in introducing Five-Year Plans to the Soviet Union?

_____

II. Interpreting a Bar Graph

1 Which nation on the graph had the most soldiers killed in World War I? _____

2 What factor might explain why the United States had the least number of casualties in World War I?

_____

_____

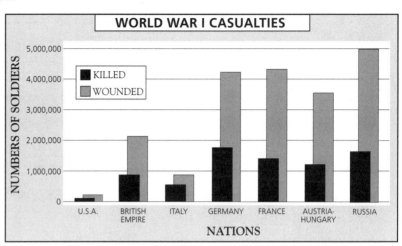

3 Explain how Russian casualties in World War I had far-ranging consequences for that country. _____

THEMATIC ESSAY QUESTION

Directions: Write a well-organized essay that includes an introduction, several paragraphs explaining your position, and a conclusion.

Theme: Change

> The ideas and actions of some individuals
> have had a significant impact on others.

Task:

> Choose *two* individuals from your study of global history and geography.
>
> For *each* individual:
> • Explain how that individual's ideas or actions changed his or her nation or another area of the world.
> • Describe one way in which the two individuals are similar or different.

You may use any example from your study of global history and geography. Some suggestions you may wish to consider include: Alexander the Great, Simon Bolivar, Martin Luther, Catherine the Great, Mohandas Ghandi, Adolf Hitler, Joseph Stalin, Mikhail Gorbachev, and Kwame Nkrumah.

You are *not* limited to these suggestions.

CHAPTER 11

FROM THE COLD WAR TO GLOBAL INTERDEPENDENCE, 1945 TO THE PRESENT

When Mao Zedong came to power in China, the Cold War extended to Asia.

SECTION 1:
THE COLD WAR, 1945–1970S
1. Superpower Rivalry and the Birth of the Cold War
2. The Cold War from the 1950s to the 1970s

Nations achieving independence in Africa, Asia and the Middle East faced new problems.

SECTION 2:
PROBLEMS OF THE DEVELOPING WORLD
1. Africa
2. The Middle East
3. South Asia
4. Latin America
5. New Democracies Emerge

SECTION 3:
THE POST-COLD WAR WORLD
1. Collapse of the Soviet Union
2. China's Economic Reform
3. Resolution of Old Disputes and Emergence of New Ones
4. New Economic Realities

Oil fires in Kuwait in the Gulf War showed how elusive world peace could be.

	1945	1959	1973	1987	2001
RUSSIA	STALIN	KHRUSHCHEV	BREZHNEV	GORBACHEV	C.I.S. / YELTSIN
W. EUROPE	MARSHALL PLAN	COMMON MARKET; NATO; RESISTANCE TO COMMUNISM			EUROPEAN UNION
E. EUROPE	SATELLITES OF THE SOVIET UNION				INDEPEN-DENCE
CHINA	MAO ZEDONG		DENG XIAOPING		JIANG ZEMIN
JAPAN	REBUILDING AFTER WORLD WAR II		ECONOMIC SUPERPOWER		
VIETNAM	FRENCH RULE	DIV. INTO N. & S. VIETNAM	VIETNAM WAR	COMMUNISTS RULE VIETNAM	
S. AFRICA	APARTHEID POLICY				APARTHEID ENDS
ISRAEL	WARS BETWEEN ISRAEL AND ARABS			UNEASY PEACE	
IRAN	RULE OF THE SHAH			ISLAMIC STATE	

1945	1959	1973	1987	2001

WHAT YOU SHOULD FOCUS ON

At the end of World War II, two Superpowers emerged. The Soviet Union had the world's largest army and occupied all of Eastern Europe. The United States possessed unparalleled economic strength and the atomic bomb. Their rivalry unleashed a "Cold War" that affected nearly every part of the globe. The collapse of Soviet Communism forty years later has led to equally monumental changes.

Against this background of Superpower rivalry, developing nations have struggled to improve their economies, Western Europe and Japan have gradually recovered from the destruction of World War II, and ethnic rivalries have turned some areas into global "hot spots."

In reviewing this chapter, keep in mind the following developments in the half-century since World War II:

Tomb of the Unknown Soldier (Moscow). Although suffering severe losses, Russia emerged from the war as a Superpower.

The Cold War. The Cold War started almost as soon as World War II ended. Eastern Europe, North Korea, and China became Communist. From the 1950s to the 1970s, the United States and Soviet Union avoided head-on confrontation but engaged in a world-wide competition for influence and in regional conflicts like the Vietnam War.

KEY DEVELOPMENTS AFTER WORLD WAR II

Problems of the Developing World. While the Superpowers engaged in the Cold War, the nations of Latin America, Africa, and Asia struggled to overcome poverty, illiteracy, ethnic conflicts, and political instability.

The Post-Cold War World. Between 1989 and 1991, Communism collapsed in the Soviet Union and Eastern Europe. In China, Communists introduced limited free-market measures. New economic realities emerged, as people depended more than ever on goods, services, and ideas from other countries.

In studying this era, you should focus on the following questions:
> ➤ What were the causes and consequences of the Cold War?
> ➤ What problems do developing nations continue to face?
> ➤ What factors led to the collapse of Communism?
> ➤ What challenges are faced by the post-Cold War world?

LOOKING AT THE PROBLEMS OF DEVELOPING NATIONS

WHAT IS A DEVELOPING NATION?

One way to view a country is to measure what its total economy produces (*G.D.P. or Gross Domestic Product*) and its **per capita income** (*income per person*). Countries that have high production and incomes are often known as **developed nations.** Nations that are trying to make more effective use of their resources are called **developing nations** — or **Third World** nations. These developing nations are located in Africa, Asia, and Latin America.

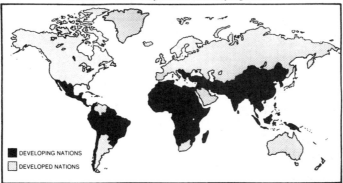

The World's Developed and Developing Nations

DEVELOPING NATIONS
DEVELOPED NATIONS

PROBLEMS FACED BY DEVELOPING NATIONS

The major problems faced by developing nations are often similar. Most of these countries must overcome similar obstacles:

Workforce. These countries often lack a skilled workforce. A majority of the population are peasant farmers who work without modern machinery and techniques. Many are unable to read and write.

Need for Capital Investment. Developing countries often lack roads, bridges, communications systems, urban centers, and manufacturing facilities. They need capital investment to develop a modern economy.

PROBLEMS FACING DEVELOPING NATIONS

Foreign Competition. It is difficult for developing countries to compete with developed countries on world markets. They cannot manufacture goods as cheaply because they lack the workforce, technology, and capital investment.

Population Growth. In developing nations, birth rates are often high, because families traditionally had a large number of children to help with farming and housework.

STRATEGIES TO OVERCOME THESE PROBLEMS

The leaders of developing countries have historically adopted various strategies to overcome the obstacles that face them.

◆ **Central Planning.** Many developing countries adopted single-party states and central planning to hasten economic development. The central government nationalized industries and built dams, roads, schools, and factories.

◆ **Green Revolution.** In the 1960s and 1970s, developing countries improved food production by applying modern science and technology to agriculture. New fertilizers, pesticides, and better methods of irrigation were introduced.

◆ **Population Control.** Many developing nations began programs to limit their birth rates. In China, for example, families were encouraged to have only one child.

Even as nations in Africa, the Middle East, and Asia move closer to developed status, remnants of underdevelopment die slowly.

◆ **Free-Market Approach.** In the late 1980s and 1990s, many nations turned to the free-market system to improve economic development. Foreign investors were attracted to invest their capital in developing countries because labor costs were low. At the present time, attracting foreign investment appears to be the best strategy for promoting economic development.

ANSWERING AN ESSAY QUESTION ON ECONOMIC DEVELOPMENT

Sometimes a global history examination question will ask you to discuss the problems faced by developing nations and to propose solutions. As you read this chapter you will learn more about the specific problems of the developing world. Pay particular attention to the methods used by the following areas to solve their economic problems:

Africa   Asia   Latin America   Middle East

MAJOR HISTORICAL DEVELOPMENTS

SECTION 1: THE COLD WAR, 1945–1985

During World War II, the United States and the Soviet Union were allies, even though their political, economic, and social systems were very different. In this section, you will read about how these differences led to a "Cold War" — first in Europe and then in Asia, Latin America, and Africa.

THINK ABOUT IT •

What were the causes and consequences of the Cold War?

SUPERPOWER RIVALRY
AND THE BIRTH OF THE COLD WAR

THE ROOTS OF THE COLD WAR

The **Cold War** was "cold" only in the sense that the two Superpowers never confronted one another directly in open warfare. But their global competition led to conflicts on every continent. The roots of the Cold War lay in the competing ideological systems of the Western democracies and Soviet Communism. While the United States and other Western nations hoped to spread democracy and capitalism, Soviet leaders promoted the spread of Communism.

	Western Democracies	**Soviet Communism**
Political System	Citizens elected representatives and national leaders. People had the right to form their own political parties.	The Soviet Union was a dictatorship controlled by Communist Party leaders. The Communist Party was the only political party permitted to operate.
Individual Rights	Citizens had basic rights, such as freedom of speech, freedom of the press, and freedom of religion.	Ordinary citizens had few rights. The government controlled radio, television, and newspapers. Secret police arrested all critics of the government. The practice of religion was discouraged.
Economic System	Under capitalism, people and corporations could own land and businesses. Businesses provided goods and services in order to make a profit.	Many forms of private property were abolished. With state ownership and central planning, the government controlled all production. Private farms became state-owned collective farms.

THE COLD WAR BEGINS IN EUROPE

Churchill, Roosevelt, and Stalin meet at Yalta on February 9, 1945.

Even before World War II ended, the chief Allied leaders — Roosevelt, Churchill, and Stalin — met to plan for the post-war world. They agreed to divide Germany into four zones of occupation, controlled by the United States, Britain, France, and the Soviet Union. Stalin also pledged to allow free elections in Eastern Europe.

When the war ended, however, Stalin failed to keep his promise. The Soviets were more interested in creating a safety zone around their country to protect it from future attack. Instead of holding elections, the Soviet army, which occupied Eastern Europe at the end of the war, placed local Communists in power. In 1946, an "**Iron Curtain**" fell on Eastern European nations, and they became Soviet **satellites** (*puppet states*). Trade and communication between Eastern and Western Europe was cut off. East European governments were forced to follow policies dictated by the Soviet Union.

GROWING AMERICAN INVOLVEMENT

With its strong economy and the atomic bomb, the United States was the only country powerful enough to resist the Soviet Union in the early post-war years. Many Americans, however, wanted to reduce American involvement in foreign affairs. President Truman eventually succeeded in persuading Americans to play a more active role on the world stage.

◆ **Military and Financial Aid.** In 1947, Communists threatened to take over both Greece and Turkey. Truman offered to support all free peoples resisting Communism. His plan, known as the **Truman Doctrine,** marked the beginning of America's policy to prevent Communism from spreading any further. This offer became known as the "**containment policy**" because it aimed to "contain" Communism.

President Harry Truman

The hunger and poverty faced by many Western European nations made them ripe for the spread of Communism. In an attempt to prevent the further spread of Communism in Europe, later in 1947 the United States also announced the **Marshall Plan.** Under the Marshall Plan, the United States gave Western European nations billions of dollars to help them rebuild their war-torn economies in order to resist Communism.

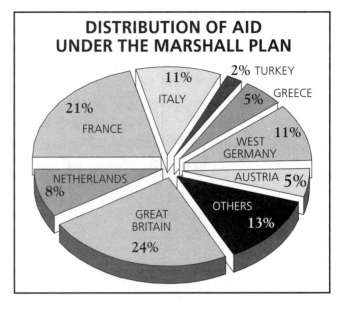

◆ **The Berlin Airlift and the Division of Germany.** In 1948, the Western allies took steps towards merging their zones of occupation in Germany. Although Berlin was within the Soviet zone, as the former capital of Germany it had been occupied by all four powers. The Soviets reacted to the steps taken by the Western allies by closing all highways and railroad links to Berlin. The Western allies began a massive airlift to feed and supply West Berlin. Within a year, the Soviets ended their blockade. In 1949, the three allied zones of occupation were merged into a new West German state. The Soviets responded by turning their zone into the independent country of East Germany. Thus, Germany was divided into two states.

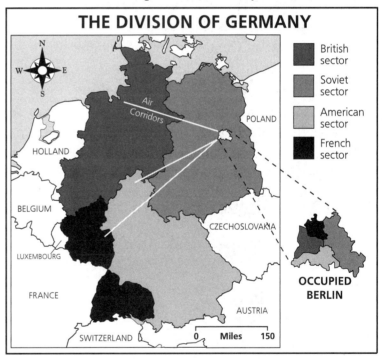

◆ **The Formation of NATO and the Warsaw Pact.** In 1949, the United States, Canada, and ten Western European countries formed the **N**orth **A**tlantic **T**reaty **O**rganization, or **NATO.** The main aim of this alliance was to protect Western Europe from Communist aggression. The Soviet Union responded to the creation of NATO by forming the **Warsaw Pact** with its Eastern European satellites in 1955.

THE COLD WAR REACHES ASIA

Just when the Western allies believed they had stopped the spread of Communism in Europe, it appeared in Asia.

THE COMMUNIST REVOLUTION IN CHINA, 1949

General Chiang Kai-Shek

Chiang Kai-Shek was the successor to Sun Yat-Sen as the Nationalist leader of China. Chiang finally defeated the warlords and united China. In 1928, Chiang became engaged in a struggle against Chinese Communists. **Mao Zedong,** the Communist leader, was forced to retreat with his forces in a **Long March** to northwestern China. In 1937, when Japan invaded China, a truce was called between the Chinese Nationalists (*the kuomintang*) and Communists, so that they could cooperate against the Japanese.

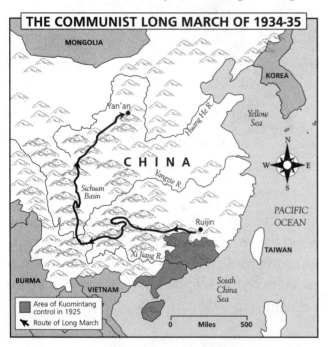

After Japan was defeated in 1945, fighting resumed between the Chinese Nationalists and Communists. The Communists were able to win the support of many peasants through their land-reform programs. In 1949, Mao Zedong and the Communists drove Chiang and his supporters out of mainland China. Chiang retreated to the island of **Taiwan** (*Formosa*). This created "**Two Chinas**" — Mao's Communist China and Chiang's Nationalist China on Taiwan.

Although a follower of Marx and Lenin, Mao and his comrades developed a new form of Communism that emphasized the role of the peasants over workers. Mao championed a form of revolutionary warfare that would first begin in the countryside and only later spread to industrial workers living in the cities. Once in power, Mao and his comrades faced the challenge of reconstructing China.

A victorious Mao Zedong in a government poster with workers and peasants.

MAO ZEDONG TRANSFORMS CHINA INTO A COMMUNIST STATE

As a first step, all aspects of life were brought under the control of the Communist Party. Mao dramatically changed traditional life in China:

Elimination of the "Capitalist Class". Landowners, factory-owners, village leaders, and better-off peasants were considered to be the "capitalist class". The Communists said these capitalists exploited others. At least one million of these so-called "capitalists" were killed.

CHANGES TO CHINA UNDER MAO

Re-education. Communist beliefs became required learning in all universities and schools. Newspapers and books were brought under the control of the government and had to promote Communism. Even art and music came under the direct supervision of the government.

The Family. Family authority was replaced by the authority of the Communist Party. Children were taught to obey the state, not their parents. Ancestor worship, which had once promoted family tradition, was forbidden. This prohibition further weakened the father's traditional role as family leader.

THE CULT OF MAO

Mao himself became a god-like figure, similar to the emperors of ancient China. His pictures and statues were prominently displayed throughout China. His sayings were published in *The Quotations of Chairman Mao*. Communist Party members and students were expected to memorize them. Students were taught to praise Mao, who could do no wrong.

Throughout China, statues of Chairman Mao abounded.

THE KOREAN WAR (1950–1953)

North Korea was occupied by the Soviet Union at the end of World War II, and became Communist at this time. In 1950, Communist North Korea invaded South Korea. The United States and other member countries of the U.N. intervened and drove the Communist Koreans back to North Korea. Led by General **Douglas MacArthur,** U.N. forces then invaded North Korea. MacArthur even hoped to invade China

American soldiers fighting in Korea.

to throw out the Communists, but President Truman refused to take this step. This disagreement led Truman to relieve MacArthur of his command. In 1953, a compromise ended the war, leaving North and South Korea divided along the same boundary line as before the war.

THE COLD WAR FROM THE 1950S TO THE 1970S

In 1949, the Soviet Union tested its first atomic bomb. Soon each Superpower developed hydrogen bombs and long-range missiles to deliver them. American and Soviet leaders quickly realized that these weapons could not easily be used because of their tremendous destructiveness. The Superpowers were thus forced to find other channels for competition rather than thermonuclear war. They soon became involved in a number of conflicts, some of which would eventually lead to warfare on a limited scale.

THE SOVIETS AND EASTERN EUROPE

Nikita Khrushchev

In 1953, Stalin died. **Nikita Khrushchev** emerged as the new Soviet leader. Khrushchev criticized Stalin's brutality for killing millions of Soviet citizens. This criticism marked the start of a policy in which the Soviets tried to rid themselves of Stalin's memory. Khrushchev also attempted to introduce several reforms. Despite his best efforts, he was unable to increase Soviet production of goods and services.

In Eastern Europe, some people saw Khrushchev's new policies as a chance to break away from Communist rule. Polish workers went on strike demanding greater freedom. When Hungarian leaders threatened to leave the Warsaw Pact in 1956, Soviet troops were sent into Hungary. Popular demonstrations were brutally repressed. In East Germany, large numbers of people were escaping through West Berlin to West Germany. Khrushchev finally ordered a wall built between East and West Berlin in 1961. For the next 28 years, the **Berlin Wall** served as a constant reminder of the Cold War.

COMMUNISM GETS A FOOTHOLD IN LATIN AMERICA

Fidel Castro (center)

In the Western Hemisphere, the spread of Communism also posed new challenges for the West. Widespread poverty made much of Latin America ripe for the spread of Communism. In 1959, **Fidel Castro** overthrew a dictatorship in Cuba and seized power. Once in power, Castro **nationalized** (*had the government take over*) many businesses. He also executed his opponents. The United States reacted by breaking off trade. Castro turned to the Soviet Union for support and transformed Cuba into a Communist state. Castro then threatened to export Communism to other Latin American nations. American leaders feared the United States would be encircled in a Communist ring.

◆ **Bay of Pigs Invasion.** In 1961, Cuban exiles, armed and trained by the United States, invaded Cuba at the Bay of Pigs. President Kennedy refused to supply the rebels with air support, and their invasion failed.

◆ **Cuban Missile Crisis.** In 1962, American leaders discovered that Cuba was secretly building bases to install Soviet missiles with nuclear warheads. If the plan succeeded, Soviet nuclear missiles would be within easy striking distance of major U.S. cities. President Kennedy blockaded Cuba and threatened to invade if the missiles were not withdrawn. Khrushchev finally agreed to withdraw the missiles for a pledge that the United States would not invade Cuba.

THE CUBAN MISSILE CRISIS: 1962

ATLANTIC OCEAN

New Orleans - 650 miles
Chicago - 1310 miles
Wash. D.C. - 1130 miles
New York - 1300 miles

Gulf of Mexico

Havana

BAHAMAS

CUBA

MEXICO

JAMAICA

HAITI

DOMINICAN REPUBLIC

PUERTO RICO

Missile Site
Zone of U.S. naval blockade
Range of targeted U.S. cities

0   Miles   500

COMMUNISM IN CHINA

Meanwhile, in China, Mao Zedong took further steps to implement Communism. In 1958, Mao introduced the "**Great Leap Forward,**" a five-year plan designed to increase China's industrial productivity and turn it into an industrial power. China's vast population was put to work building dams, bridges, roads, and factories. Because of poor planning, the Great Leap failed and China's total productivity actually dropped.

By 1962, Mao was concerned about the loss of enthusiasm among the people for Communism. Mao blamed the Chinese elite for this loss of enthusiasm and announced a "**Cultural Revolution.**" Mao closed China's schools and invited students to gather in Beijing as **Red Guards.** The Guards travelled throughout China attacking writers, scientists, doctors, and professors for abandoning Communist ideals. Scholars and professionals were sent to

Mao Zedong leads students into the countryside during the Cultural Revolution.

work as laborers in the fields. China became so disrupted that Mao called out the army to control the Red Guards. In 1969, Mao sent the Guards home, and brought the Cultural Revolution to a close.

THE WAR IN VIETNAM

Vietnam was divided into two when the French withdrew from Indochina in 1954. Nationalist leader **Ho Chi Minh** created a Communist state in North Vietnam, while South Vietnam established ties to the West. Southern leaders refused to hold promised elections to reunite the country, however, because they felt elections in the north would not be free. South Vietnamese Communists, known as **Viet Cong,** with North Vietnamese support, launched a guerrilla war against the South Vietnamese government.

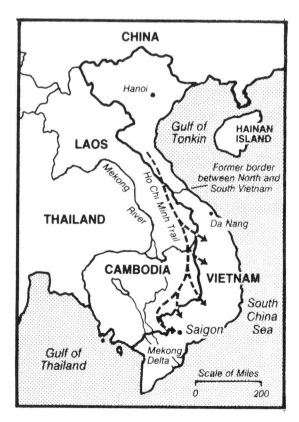

Once again, the United States stepped in to resist Communism. At first, Americans acted only as advisors to the South Vietnamese army. This advisory role changed in 1964 when American combat troops were sent in.

Although the United States eventually used extensive bombing, advanced technology, and sent over half a million troops to Vietnam, it was never able to turn the tide against the Viet Cong and North Vietnamese. In 1973, American troops withdrew from Vietnam in accordance with an agreement reached in Paris. In 1975, South Vietnam fell to North Vietnamese forces and the country was re-united under Communist rule.

President Johnson visits American soldiers in Vietnam.

CAMBODIA (KAMPUCHEA)

The withdrawal of American forces from Vietnam also led to the collapse of the government in neighboring Cambodia. In 1975, Cambodian Communists, known as the **Khmer Rouge,** seized control of Cambodia, changing the country's name to Kampuchea. **Pol Pot,** the Khmer Rouge leader, carried out a policy of **genocide** (*mass murder*) against city-dwellers and all people suspected of being unsympathetic to the Communist cause. City-dwellers were forced into the countryside, were they faced starvation and disease. It is estimated that the Khmer Rouge killed as many as four million Cambodians between 1975 and 1978. Pol Pot and his followers were finally overthrown by the Vietnamese army in 1978, when it intervened to end these atrocities.

ANSWERING THE FOCUS QUESTION •

Writing

The causes and consequences of the Cold War were:

_____ (Causes)

_____

_____ (Consequences)

_____

Directions: Complete each of the following vocabulary cards. Then answer the multiple-choice questions that follow.

COMMUNISM
What is Communism?
How did Soviet Communism differ from
Western democracy?

MAO ZEDONG
Who was Mao Zedong?
What changes did he introduce
to China?

1 In an outline, one of these is the main topic, and the others are sub-topics. Which is the main topic?

  1 Cold War   3 Marshall Plan

  2 Berlin Blockade   4 Vietnam War

2 One similarity between imperial China and China under Communist rule is that both societies stressed

  1 state-supported religion   3 loyalty to leaders

  2 the importance of women in society   4 limited population growth

3 Mao's Great Leap Forward in China and Stalin's Five-Year Plans in the Soviet Union were similar in that they both attempted to increase

  1 private capital investment   3 religious tolerance

  2 individual ownership of land   4 industrial productivity

4 Which statement would be most consistent with the views of Fidel Castro?

  1 The spread of Communism is the greatest danger facing Latin America.

  2 A strong U.S. military presence is key to the defense of Latin America.

  3 Latin American progress can only be achieved through Communism.

  4 The free market system will improve the economies of Latin America.

SECTION 2: PROBLEMS OF THE DEVELOPING WORLD

While the Superpowers were engaged in their deadly game of global rivalry, developing nations struggled with age-old problems of political instability and economic development. In this section, you will learn how they coped with these problems.

THINK ABOUT IT •

What problems do developing nations face?

AFRICA

Like most developing nations, countries in Africa generally followed a policy of **non-alignment** during the Cold War. This policy called for not taking sides with either Superpower so that they could receive economic aid from both.

EFFORTS AT POLITICAL DEVELOPMENT

Most African nations, despite achieving independence from colonial rule in the post-war years, lacked democratic traditions. Nationalist leaders often assumed dictatorial powers. A majority of Africans remained poor and lacked formal education. As in most of the developing world, Africans also struggled with problems of ethnic disunity and political instability. In fact, most African nations were based on former colonies that had been created without regard for tribal boundaries. Often there were rival tribes within the same country. In some cases, this arrangement led to violence between tribes.

Definition

Tribalism refers to the allegiance that many Africans had to their tribe rather than to their nation. Members of each tribe usually shared a common tradition, language, religion, and way of life.

ATTEMPTS AT ECONOMIC DEVELOPMENT

The need for rapid economic development was the most pressing problem facing new African states. Standards of living were among the lowest in the world. Most Africans were **subsistence** farmers, growing only enough food to meet the needs of their own family. After independence, many Africans migrated to cities in search of educational and employment opportunities. This rapid urban growth often outstripped job prospects and existing public facilities.

Many Africans were subsistence farmers — using methods little changed from those of their ancestors.

SOUTH AFRICA AND APARTHEID

One thing that united most African nations was their hostility to South Africa, which remained under the control of a white minority. In 1948, white South Africans began a policy of **apartheid** or racial "separateness." Blacks could not travel freely, use many public facilities, or marry whites. Many black South Africans resisted apartheid by violent means. When police killed demontrators in the **Sharpeville Massacre** in 1960, a general strike broke out among black Africans. In the **Soweto Uprising** in 1976, riots again spread throughout South Africa. The United States and other countries finally cut their economic ties with South Africa in order to promote social change.

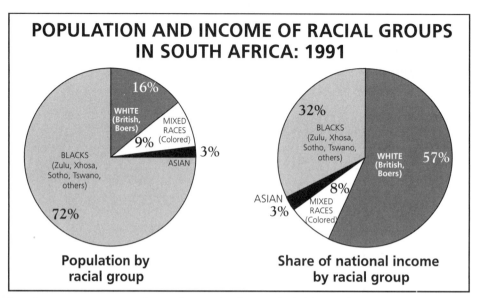

POPULATION AND INCOME OF RACIAL GROUPS IN SOUTH AFRICA: 1991

Population by racial group

Share of national income by racial group

Efforts by the government since the end of apartheid have been aimed at wider distribution of national wealth.

THE MIDDLE EAST

In the Middle East, most developing nations were united by the Islamic religion and the unique geographical features of their region.

SOCIAL CHANGES CHALLENGE TRADITIONAL LIFESTYLES

For centuries, most people in the Middle East had lived in villages. They were farmers or herded livestock. Families consisted of seven, eight, or more people, often living in a small, simply furnished home. By tradition, families were controlled by the eldest male. Women stayed at home doing housework, bearing children, and helping with farmwork. Sons followed their father's occupation. Marriages were arranged by parents. In the 1960s, however, these traditional lifestyles began to be challenged by new forces.

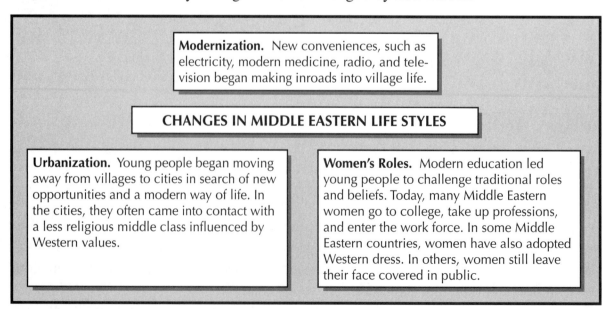

Modernization. New conveniences, such as electricity, modern medicine, radio, and television began making inroads into village life.

CHANGES IN MIDDLE EASTERN LIFE STYLES

Urbanization. Young people began moving away from villages to cities in search of new opportunities and a modern way of life. In the cities, they often came into contact with a less religious middle class influenced by Western values.

Women's Roles. Modern education led young people to challenge traditional roles and beliefs. Today, many Middle Eastern women go to college, take up professions, and enter the work force. In some Middle Eastern countries, women have also adopted Western dress. In others, women still leave their face covered in public.

ISRAEL STRUGGLES TO SURVIVE

The British promised they would create a homeland for Jews in Palestine in 1917. Jewish immigration to Palestine later swelled during the Nazi persecution of European Jews. Arabs, however, viewed this immigration as another form of Western imperialism. In 1947, the British handed the problem of Jewish-Arab relations to the United Nations. Partly in response to the Holocaust, U.N. members voted to partition Palestine and create **Israel** as a Jewish homeland. The emergence of Israel became a central issue in the Middle East.

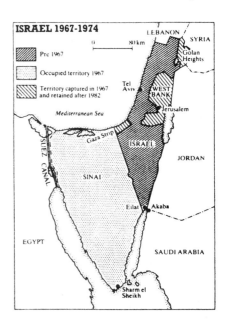

◆ **Israel's War For Independence.** Arab nations refused to recognize the new nation. They launched an attack on Israel, but were defeated. During the war, many Palestinian Arabs fled and became refugees in neighboring Arab lands.

◆ **Later Wars.** War erupted again in 1956, 1967, and 1973. In the 1967 war, Israel defeated its enemies and acquired the Gaza Strip and Sinai Peninsula from Egypt, the West Bank from Jordan, and the Golan Heights from Syria.

CAMP DAVID ACCORDS

In 1978, Egyptian President **Anwar el-Sadat** and Israel's Prime Minister **Menachim Begin** visited U.S. President Carter at Camp David. They agreed that Israel would return lands taken from Egypt in exchange for establishing peace between the two, ending thirty years of official hostility. Other Arab countries denounced the **Camp David Accords** and broke off diplomatic ties with Egypt.

In 1981, President Sadat was assassinated by extremists who saw the Camp David Accords as a surrender to Israel.

ISRAEL AND THE PALESTINIANS

Continuing hostility between Palestinian Arabs and Israeli Jews further complicated Israel's relations with its Arab neighbors.

◆ **The P.L.O.** In 1964, Palestinian Arabs formed the **Palestinian Liberation Organization.** They refused to recognize Israel and vowed to win back their homeland.

◆ **Use of Terrorism.** In the 1960s and 1970s, the PLO used terrorism as a political weapon. PLO leaders felt they had no other way to oppose Israel. In the 1970s and 1980s, Israel twice entered Lebanon to destroy PLO camps there.

◆ **Intifada ("Uprising").** In 1987, young Palestinians who had grown up under Israeli occupation began a series of violent demonstrations. Israel imposed harsh measures to stop the protests, but without much success.

You will learn about more recent Arab-Israeli developments in this chapter.

Israeli soldiers arrest an Arab student demonstrator.

OPEC AND THE LEAP IN OIL PRICES

The Middle East contains a large part of the world's oil reserves. In the early 1970s, oil-producing countries formed the **O**rganization of **P**etroleum **E**xporting **C**ountries, or **"OPEC."** Many OPEC members are located around the Persian Gulf: Saudi Arabia, Iran, Iraq,

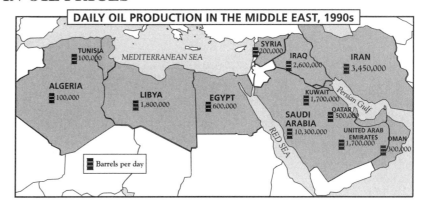

Kuwait, and the United Arab Emirates. In 1973, during a war with Israel, Arab OPEC members refused to sell oil to countries friendly to Israel. This reduction in the supply of oil set off a tremendous rise in the price of oil. After the war, OPEC nations continued to cooperate to keep up the price of oil. The West and non-oil-producing developing nations suffered high inflation and unemployment throughout the 1970s because of these high oil prices.

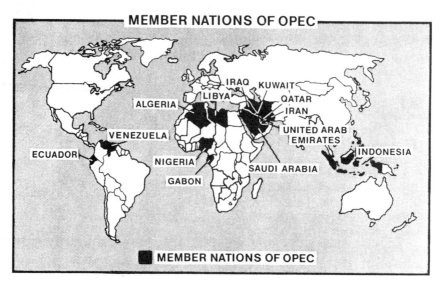

THE IRANIAN REVOLUTION AND ISLAMIC FUNDAMENTALISM

Unlike many other Middle Eastern countries, **Iran** (*known in earlier times as Persia*) was never part of Ottoman Turkey or colonized by European powers. The ruler of Iran in the post-war period, **Shah Pahlavi,** tried to adopt Western culture and technology. In 1979, public demonstrations overthrew the Shah in the **Iranian Revolution.** An Islamic Fundamentalist, **Ayatollah Khomeini,** became Iran's new ruler. Reacting against Western culture and values, Khomeini established a new constitution for Iran based on the Qu'ran. Civil law was replaced by Islamic law. Women were required to return to traditional dress. Khomeini also sponsored acts of terrorism, including the seizure of American hostages in the capital city of Tehran. Iran then became involved in an eight-year long war with Iraq over the control of oil fields near the Persian Gulf. Khomeini's successors have been less hostile to the West but generally maintain his policies.

Islamic Fundamentalists believe in returning to what they see as the basic values of Islam. Islamic Fundamentalism developed in large part as a reaction to the values and culture of the West.

SOUTH ASIA

Almost one-quarter of the world's population is found on the Indian Subcontinent. After independence, this region faced problems typical of developing areas. A local, educated elite helped the nations of this region create their own unique paths to development.

INDIA

With one billion people, India is the world's largest democracy. When India became independent, most Indians were farmers living in villages, who worked by hand or with farm animals. In the 1960s and 1970s, the government tried to improve agricultural production by applying modern science and technology. This effort became known as the **Green Revolution.** At first, most farmers were too poor to make use of the new seeds,

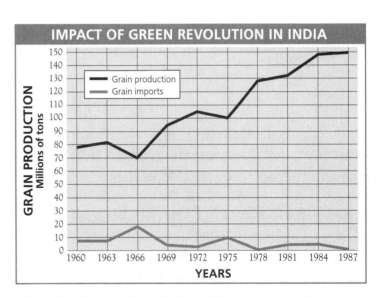

fertilizers, and equipment introduced by the Green Revolution. However, by the early 1980s, "miracle" seeds were producing one-third of India's total grain crop. At the same time, increases in population often used up the gains in food production and industrial productivity. To reduce population growth, the government provided benefits to families that limited themselves to having two children.

INDIA'S SOCIAL PROBLEMS

A steady stream of people flowing into India's cities has created overcrowding and slums. Indian cultural differences have added to existing social problems. For example, a large number of Muslims remain in largely Hindu India, even after the separation of India and Pakistan. The government has attempted to prohibit discrimination against "Untouchables" and lower castes, but has only been partially successful. Conflicts between Sikhs and Hindus in northern India have led to violence and the assassination of elected officials.

BANGLADESH

When Pakistan was formed in 1947, it consisted of two halves separated by nearly a thousand miles. In 1971, East Pakistan broke away from West Pakistan to became Bangladesh. Civil War erupted, ending only when India intervened. With a population of almost 120 million people, Bangladesh is one of the world's most densely populated nations. Bangladesh also continues to be one of the world's most economically troubled nations. Almost one-third of its children die before their fifth birthday. Most of its people cannot afford basic medical care. The country suffers from periodic floods. In bad years, three-quarters of the land is flooded, causing crop destruction, property loss, and death.

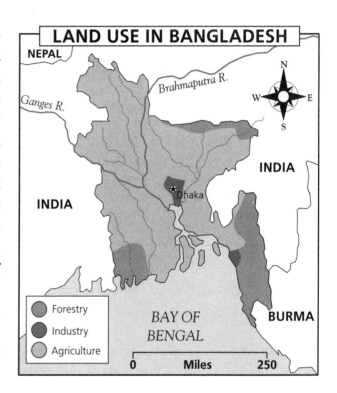

LATIN AMERICA

Although independent for over a century, many of the countries of Latin America still face problems similar to those of other developing countries: a continuing gulf between the rich and the poor, economic dependence on the West, and political instability.

LATIN AMERICAN POLITICS

Military governments continued to rule many Latin American countries from the 1930s to the 1980s. Latin American military leaders often justified their authority by their opposition to Communism. At the same time, these governments frequently violated their citizen's human rights.

Human rights **are the rights to life, liberty, and property enjoyed by citizens in democratic societies. The ability to criticize the government without fear of unjust punishment or death is a basic human right.**

Abuses of human rights occurred during the Cold War years in Argentina, Chile, Cuba, and El Salvador. In **Argentina,** thousands of people disappeared during the military rule that ended in 1984. In **Chile,** the military overthrew an elected government and tortured and killed opponents. In **Cuba,** Fidel Castro imprisoned and killed opponents of his rule. In **El Salvador,** "death squads" gunned down advocates of reform.

ECONOMIC DEVELOPMENT

The economic development of Latin America was hampered by a lack of capital for investment, an unskilled work force, and foreign competition. A great divide separated the rich elite from the poor majority. Population growth was so high that Latin America's population doubled every 25 to 30 years. This growth often used up any gains made in productivity, forcing many Latin American nations to spend money on importing food instead of making improvements. In the

Attempts to build their economies, like this fertilizer plant in Colombia, often depended on capital from foreign investments.

1970s and 1980s, some Latin American countries borrowed heavily from Western banks. Much of this money was spent unwisely and led to a financial crisis in the 1980s.

NEW DEMOCRACIES EMERGE IN ASIA, AFRICA, AND LATIN AMERICA

Suddenly in the late 1980s, remarkable changes started to take place in Asia, Africa, and Latin America. Many of these nations began moving in the direction of democracy.

THE PHILIPPINES

Once a United States colony, the Philippines became independent just after World War II. **Ferdinand Marcos** served as President from 1965 to 1986. Ruling the Philippines as a virtual dictator, Marcos grew increasingly corrupt. In 1986, Marcos was defeated in a re-election bid by **Corazon Aquino.** At first, Marcos refused to accept his election defeat, but mass demonstrations at home and pressure from the United States forced him to flee. His defeat was seen as a triumph for democracy.

LATIN AMERICA AND AFRICA

In the late 1980s and 1990s, dictators and military governments around the world suddenly began transferring power to democratically-elected leaders.

This remarkable change was closely connected to the collapse of Communism and the end of the Cold War. You will learn more about these events in the next section.

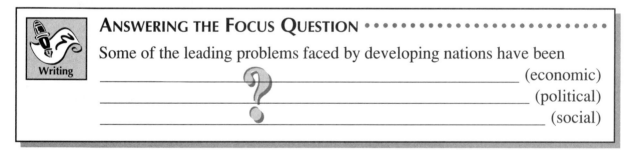

Argentina. The military government allowed a return to civilian rule, and the new government began investigating prior human rights violations.

Nicaragua. The Communist government of Nicaragua held elections in 1990 and peacefully handed power over to non-Communist leaders.

LATIN AMERICA MOVES TO DEMOCRACY

Panama. The United States intervened to overthrow military dictator General **Manuel Noriega**, who was accused of large-scale drug smuggling.

Haiti. Dictator **Jean-Claude Duvalier** was ousted from power. In 1990, **Jean-Bertrand Aristide** became Haiti's first democratically-elected president.

In Africa, dictators were driven from power in Somalia, Liberia, and Ethiopia. Several other African nations adopted multi-party systems. South Africa's leaders ended apartheid and gave citizens of all races the right to vote. You will read more about the end of apartheid in the next section.

ANSWERING THE FOCUS QUESTION •

Writing

Some of the leading problems faced by developing nations have been

_____ (economic)

_____ (political)

_____ (social)

Directions: Complete each of the following vocabulary cards. Then answer the multiple-choice questions that follow.

PLO
What is the PLO?
What are the aims of its members?

GREEN REVOLUTION
What was the Green Revolution?
How successful was it in solving food shortages?

1 In Africa, South Asia, and Latin America, people moved from rural villages to urban areas in order to
1 avoid the high cost of living in rural areas
2 escape the poor climates of rural areas
3 find new job opportunities
4 live among people of different ethnic backgrounds

2 The Sharpeville Massacre of 1960 and the Soweto Uprising in 1976 were reactions to
1 the creation of Bangladesh out of East Pakistan
2 the harsh policies of the Shah of Iran
3 the P.L.O. actions against Israel
4 South Africa's policy of apartheid

3 The first peace agreement between modern Egypt and Israel was known as the
1 P.L.O.   3 Intifada
2 Camp David Accords   4 Treaty of Versailles

4 One factor that has greatly contributed to continuing instability in the Middle East has been the
1 European demand for Middle Eastern oil
2 Palestinian and Israeli claims to the same land
3 presence of United Nations peace-keeping forces
4 attempt to unify all Arab-speaking peoples

SECTION 3: THE POST-COLD WAR PERIOD

In the Soviet Union, Eastern Europe, and elsewhere, Communism came to an abrupt end in the last decade of the 20th century. The Berlin Wall came tumbling down, and new democracies emerged in Eastern Europe. Although many problems of the Cold War period have been resolved, new problems have appeared on the horizon.

THINK ABOUT IT •

What challenges are faced by the post-Cold War world?

Thinking

THE COLLAPSE OF THE SOVIET UNION
AND THE LIBERATION OF EASTERN EUROPE

Some of the most dramatic events of this period occurred in the Soviet Union. The sudden and unexpected collapse of Soviet Communism led directly to the end of the Cold War.

THE BREZHNEV YEARS (1964–1982)

After the fall of Khrushchev in 1964, **Leonid Brezhnev** emerged as the next Soviet leader. Brezhnev's rule led to a period of Soviet stagnation (*failure to advance*). Farms failed to produce enough to feed the population. Consumer goods were of poor quality, living standards fell, and corruption became widespread. People had little incentive to work hard since under Communism a person's salary did not depend on how hard he or she worked. Communist party members, on the other hand, enjoyed special privileges. Brezhnev at first attempted an easing of the Cold War, known as **détente,** but sent Soviet troops into Czechoslovakia in 1968 and into Afghanistan in 1979 to maintain Soviet rule.

THE GORBACHEV YEARS (1985–1991)

A few years after Brezhnev's death, **Mikhail Gorbachev** became leader of the Soviet Communist Party. Gorbachev wanted to preserve Communism, but sought reform through a number of new policies:

Mikhail Gorbachev

◆ **Glasnost** introduced a greater "openness" to Soviet society. Restrictions on speech and the press were lifted. Dissidents were released from prison. Restrictions on Soviet Jews emigrating to Israel and the West were lifted. A **Congress of People's Deputies** was created, allowing Soviet citizens to elect their own representatives.

◆ **Perestroika** referred to economic reform, or "restructuring." Gorbachev hoped to move away from central planning to encourage more individual initiative in the Soviet economy. People were permitted to form small businesses, factory managers were given greater control over the production of their factories, and foreign companies were invited to invest in the Soviet Union.

◆ **New Directions in Foreign Policy.** Gorbachev withdrew troops from Afghanistan and entered into negotiations with the United States to reduce nuclear arms. He eventually allowed the countries of Eastern Europe to introduce democratic, non-Communist governments.

GORBACHEV'S PROBLEMS GROW

Gorbachev's policies failed to solve Soviet economic problems. The new openness of Glasnost unleashed ethnic nationalism and social discontent. The Soviet Union consisted of fifteen separate republics, made up of both Russian and non-Russian nationalities. Non-Russian nationalities, many of which had been joined to the Russian empire or Soviet Union by force, suddenly began demanding independence. The spirit of nationalism even spread to the Russian Republic, the very heartland of the Soviet Union. In 1991, **Boris Yeltsin** was elected President of the Russian Republic, and began to assert Russian authority over Gorbachev's Soviet government.

THE BREAK-UP OF THE SOVIET UNION (1991)

THE COMMONWEALTH OF INDEPENDENT STATES

In August 1991, Communist hard-liners overthrew Gorbachev in a military **coup** (*sudden takeover of the government by force*). Lacking popular support, the coup quickly collapsed. Because many Communists had supported the coup, the Communist Party was discredited. Gorbachev now recognized the independence of Lithuania and the other Baltic States. He attempted to negotiate a new arrangement within the Soviet Union, but in December 1991, Russia, Belarus, and Ukraine also declared their independence. These three states formed the basis of a new **Commonwealth of Independent States.** Each state was to be completely independent, with the Commonwealth serving limited functions.

Other former republics of the Soviet Union quickly joined the Commonwealth. The former Soviet Union was now dead, and Gorbachev resigned at the end of 1991.

RUSSIA UNDER YELTSIN AND PUTIN

President Boris Yeltsin

President **Boris Yeltsin** quickly took drastic steps to reform the Russian economy. He attempted to introduce the free market system by ending price controls on most goods, and by beginning to privatize state-owned industries. Despite these reforms, Russians continued to face rising unemployment, inflation, and crime.

By 1993, the Russian Parliament began to fear that Yeltsin was moving too fast. Legislators opposed to Yeltsin locked themselves inside the Parliament building. Using military force, Yeltsin disbanded the Parliament when it tried to remove him from office. Yeltsin's supporters won the next election, and Yeltsin continued to pursue his program of privatization.

Yeltsin resigned in 1999, naming **Vladimir Putin** as his successor. The Russian economy saw a return to moderate growth. One of Putin's greatest challenges has been dealing with separatists from Chechnya, a republic in the southwest. Chechen separatists have committed repeated acts of terrorism in Russia, while the Russian army has conducted a harsh campaign of retaliation in Chechnya.

EASTERN EUROPE AND THE UNIFICATION OF GERMANY

Even before the collapse of the Soviet Union, Gorbachev had allowed important changes in Eastern Europe. Poland led the way when **Lech Walesa** organized an independent trade union named **Solidarity.** Poles became the first East Europeans to elect a non-Communist government in the post-cold war world. These changes led to a lifting of the "Iron Curtain" between Western and Eastern Europe. The Berlin Wall, which had separated East and West Berlin, was taken down in 1989. Throughout most of Eastern Europe,

*Members of Solidarity met in Gdask.
Lech Walesha is at the podium.*

free elections suddenly brought non-Communist governments to power. These governments are now struggling with the transition to market economies, the re-emergence of ethnic conflicts, and a legacy of severe pollution of the environment.

One of the most important events of the post-cold war period was the reunification of Germany. West Germany's leader, **Helmut Kohl,** helped negotiate the reunification, which became official at the end of 1990. After a half a century of division, Germany is once again a unified nation.

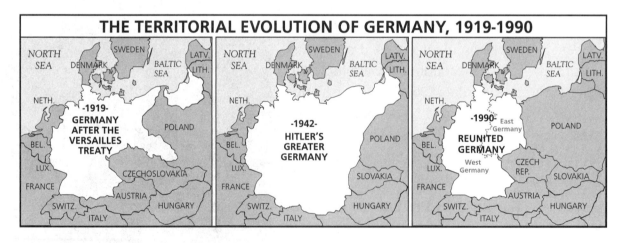

CHINA'S ECONOMIC REFORM

ECONOMIC REFORM UNDER DENG XIAOPING

While Eastern Europe and the former Soviet Union struggled with political and economic changes, China introduced a free market economy gradually without abandoning the Communist Party's monopoly of political power. After the death of Mao Zedong in 1976, **Deng Xiaoping** became China's principal leader. Deng had opposed Mao's Cultural Revolution and once in power he set out making practical reforms.

Deng's main goal was to "modernize" China by reforming its economy:

Land Reforms. Communes (*state-run farms*) were disbanded and peasants were allowed to rent former communal lands. This led to large increases in agricultural productivity, making China self-sufficient in food.

Consumer Goods. Under Mao, people had few consumer products. China began producing more consumer goods, such as radios and televisions.

ECONOMIC CHANGES UNDER DENG XIAOPING

New Factory Management. Central planners lost some degree of control to local factory managers. Managers and workers were allowed to sell some of their production to private buyers for a profit.

Limited Capitalism. Individuals were allowed to own small businesses. An owner was even allowed to hire a small number of workers. The private sector became responsible for a much of China's industrial output.

Foreign Investment. New laws encouraged foreign investment. Investors brought needed capital and high-technology to special enterprise zones in China. Foreign companies were allowed to form joint ventures with Chinese enterprises.

TIANANMEN SQUARE AND THE LIMITS OF REFORM

Although Chinese leaders encouraged economic reform, they refused to abandon the Communist system. In 1989, college students peacefully demonstrated in Beijing's **Tiananmen Square** for greater personal freedom and democracy. When the students refused to disperse, army tanks fired on the demonstrators, killing hundreds. In response, Western leaders reduced trade with China for a brief time.

Student demonstrators at Tiananmen Square are paraded in a truck before being executed.

Since then, trade has resumed and China now has one of the fastest growing economies in the world. Many foreign businesses now have manufacturing enterprises in China. In 1997 China attained control of Hong Kong. Although Deng Xiaoping died, his successors have generally followed his policies.

THE RESOLUTION OF OLD DISPUTES AND THE EMERGENCE OF NEW ONES

The end of the Cold War placed new pressures on some of the world's most stubborn problems. While some old problems showed signs of healing, new ones arose to take their place. Many of these problems were fueled as much by ancient hatreds as by conflicting economic interests.

OLD DISPUTES

ISRAEL AND THE MIDDLE EAST

The 1990s witnessed new hopes in Israel. Arab and Israeli leaders sat down at the **Middle East Peace Conference** in 1991. Israel's Prime Minister, **Yitzhak Rabin,** entered into negotiations with PLO leader **Yasir Arafat.** In 1993, they finally reached an agreement: Israel gave Palestinians self-government in the Gaza Strip and on the West Bank, establishing the Palestinian Authority. In exchange, the PLO ended its opposition to Israel's existence.

The conclusion of this agreement opened the way for Israeli negotiations with its neighboring Arab countries. However, in 1995, Rabin was assassinated by a Jewish student opposed to making further concessions to Palestinian Arabs. In 2000, Arafat met with Israelis at Camp David, but negotiations broke down over the future of Jerusalem. Violence then resumed in 2001. A new intifada arose against the Israeli occupation, Israel's new Prime Minister **Ariel Sharon**, attacked Arafat's compound in response to repeated suicide bombings. Arafat died in 2004, while Sharon began dismantling several Israeli West Bank settlements and building a security wall separating Israel from Palestinian areas.

SOUTH AFRICA AND THE END OF APARTHEID

Another surprising post-Cold War development was the sudden collapse of apartheid in South Africa. In 1989, white South Africans elected **F.W. De Klerk** as president. De Klerk ended apartheid and released **Nelson Mandela** and other political leaders from prison. He then negotiated with Mandela and other black leaders for a peaceful transition to a democratic multi-racial government. In 1994, South Africa held its first national

Nelson Mandela

election in which people of all races were permitted to vote. Nelson Mandela was elected as South Africa's first black president. Under Mandella and his successors, the majority government has been trying to correct past injustices while preserving stability and prosperity in South Africa.

IRELAND AND ITS RELIGIOUS CONFLICT

Back in the 16th century, when England became Protestant, the people of Ireland had remained Catholics. In an attempt to control Ireland, the English sent Protestant settlers to Ireland in the 1600s. These Protestants settled mainly in the north. The existence of a large Protestant community in Ireland later posed problems for Irish independence.

In 1922, most of Ireland became independent, but the Protestant majority in Northern Ireland chose to remain a part of Great Britain. Many Catholics objected to the division of Ireland. They formed the **Irish Republican Army (IRA)**. In 1969, open fighting erupted in Northern Ireland between the IRA and armed units of Northern Protestants. When the British sent in troops to preserve peace, open warfare was replaced by acts of terrorism. In 1993, British leaders negotiated a cease-fire with Irish leaders and the IRA. A broad framework for solving the Irish problem was agreed to in 1995.

NEW PROBLEMS EMERGE

THE BREAKUP OF YUGOSLAVIA

YUGOSLAVIA AND THE BOSNIAN WAR

The liberation of Eastern Europe saw a revival of age-old ethnic rivalries in Yugoslavia. With the collapse of Communism, Croatia and Slovenia declared their independence. Serb-dominated Yugoslavia responded by attacking Croatia. Fighting then erupted in Bosnia between Muslims and Serbs. Yugoslavia intervened on behalf of the Bosnian Serbs. Bosnian Serbs began murdering Muslim civilians in what they called **"ethnic cleansing."** Later, Serbs attacked Muslims in the province of Kosovo. After years of civil war, the United States and other NATO countries finally stopped the fighting and imposed a truce. Bosnia was divided into two republics — Muslim and Serb.

GENOCIDE IN AFRICA

Ethnic tensions also erupted in Africa in Rwanda and Burundi, while in Somalia people suffered from hunger and famine. In 1994, Rwanda's president, a member of the Hutu tribe, was assassinated. Government-sponsored Hutu troops began taking revenge against the Tutsi minority, who were blamed for the assassination. The United Nations estimates that half a million people, mostly Tutsi, were slain in this civil war. Fighting even spread to nearby Congo and Uganda.

Somalia, located on the northeastern "horn" of Africa, has suffered from recent droughts, the destruction of livestock, and famine. In the early 1990s, fighting among Somali warlords prevented other Somalis from receiving international aid, threatening millions with starvation. In 1992, the United States sent troops to Somalia to restore order and to protect food supplies.

IRAQ AND THE SECURITY OF THE PERSIAN GULF

Iraq occupies the lands of ancient Mesopotamia, where civilization first began. In 1979 **Saddam Hussein** seized power and imposed a brutal dictatorship on the people of Iraq. In 1980, he attacked Iran, leading to an 8-year war. In 1990, Hussein invaded neighboring Kuwait. Fearing an invasion of Saudi Arabia, the United States and a coalition of nations sent troops to expel the Iraqis from Kuwait. In the **Gulf War** that followed, Iraqi forces were quickly defeated. Allied leaders nevertheless allowed Hussein to remain in power in Iraq. Soon after, Hussein's army attacked the Kurdish minority in northern Iraq.

Hussein failed to honor his agreement to permit U.N. inspectors to monitor Iraq to ensure that he did not stockpile nuclear, biological, or chemical weapons of mass destruction (WMD). After the terrorist attack on **September 11, 2001,** America and other world powers insisted that Iraq show it was not hiding WMDs. Some members of the U.N. Security Council urged delay, but the U.S., Great Britain, and other allies invaded Iraq in March, 2003. Saddam Hussein's government quickly collapsed. Following the liberation of Iraq from Hussein's rule, allied forces have faced rising violence from insurgents and many other difficulties in trying to introduce democratic rule to Iraq.

AFGHANISTAN, THE TALIBAN AND AL QAEDA

Located in a mountainous region in the heart of Central Asia, Afghanistan achieved independence in the 1700s. In 1978, local Communists, with Soviet support, seized power. The countryside rebelled, and local guerilla fighters with U.S. and other foreign support overthrew Afghanistan's Communist government. Civil war among Afghanistan's various ethnic and religious groups followed.

The **Taliban,** a group of radical Muslim Fundamentalists, gradually gained control of the country. The Taliban imposed strict religious laws. Women were forbidden to appear in public without their bodies and faces being covered; they could not go to school or work. Men were not allowed to trim their beards. "Religious police" roamed the streets beating those who disobeyed. The Taliban also allowed the Islamic terrorist group **al Qaeda,** led by Osama bin Laden, to operate training camps in Afghanistan. On **September 11, 2001**, al Qaeda terrorists hijacked U.S. jetliners and crashed them into the Pentagon and the World Trade Center. President Bush responded by declaring a **War on Terrorism.** When the Taliban refused to turn over bin Laden, the U.S. and its allies invaded Afghanistan. They overthrew the regime, and helped the Afghans form a democratic government.

Iraqi military vehicles, destroyed by U.S. forces while trying to flee from Kuwait, litter the desert.

THE NEW ECONOMIC REALITIES

Twentieth-century advances in technology, from the airplane to the computer, have made the countries of the world more dependent upon each other than ever before. This mutual reliance is sometimes referred to as **global interdependence.** The end of the Cold War has placed a new emphasis on economics.

JAPAN'S ECONOMIC MIRACLE

Japan profited greatly from this new age of global interdependence. At the end of World War II, many of its industries and cities were destroyed. Yet by the 1970s, Japan was one of the world's leading economic powers, even though it lacks many natural resources.

Historical Factors. Throughout its history, Japan has borrowed and adopted from other cultures like China and the West.

Skilled Work Force. Japan's work force is well-educated and highly skilled. Workers place great emphasis on self-discipline and loyalty to their company.

REASONS FOR THE JAPANESE ECONOMIC MIRACLE

Government Support. The government coordinates national resources, provides money, loans, and tax breaks, and encourages research. Past governments also set high tariffs to keep foreign competition out of Japan.

Effective Management. Japanese companies borrowed U.S. management techniques and improved on them to produce the highest quality goods at the lowest price. Managers often work with employees to improve production.

Japan's economic miracle brought its people one of the world's highest standards of living. Japan prospered by exporting high-tech products to other developed nations. In the 1990s, Japan's economy began to face serious problems. The value of its currency fell, and Japanese manufactures faced increasing competition.

ASIA'S NEW ECONOMIC GIANT: CHINA

Since opening its economy to foreign investments and technology, China has undergone an economic revolution. After China joined the World Trade Organization, many restrictions on its exports were lifted. Its educated, low-wage workers have been a key factor in China's emergence as the world's fastest-growing economy.

With its huge population, China has emerged as an "economic powerhouse."

Counsulate of People's Republic of China

FROM COMMON MARKET TO EUROPEAN UNION

Just like Japan, Western Europe also emerged from the destruction of World War II to become an economic giant. In 1957, cooperation between Germany and France led to the formation of the European Economic Community (EEC) or **Common Market.**

In 1973, Great Britain, Ireland, and Denmark joined the **Common Market,** followed by Greece, Spain and Portugal in the 1980s. The purpose of the Common Market was to eliminate customs duties between its members. This created an immense free trade zone in which goods, money, and people could move freely. In 1991, EEC members agreed to replace the Common Market with the **European Union.** In a further move towards a united Europe, in 1999 E.U. members began using the **Euro** — a unified European currency. In 2004, a large number of countries from Eastern Europe joined the European Union.

THE NORTH AMERICAN FREE TRADE AGREEMENT

The economic success of the Common Market led the United States and Canada to sign a free trade agreement in 1989. **Free trade** means that neither country places tariffs (*import taxes*) on goods coming from the other country. In 1990, Mexico joined the United States and Canada, expanding the treaty into the **N**orth **A**merican **F**ree **T**rade **A**greement, or "**NAFTA.**" Under NAFTA, all three of these countries have pledged to gradually reduce tariffs on one another's goods.

ANSWERING THE FOCUS QUESTION •

Some of the challenges faced by the post-Cold War world are:

_____

_____

_____

Writing

Directions: Complete each of the following vocabulary cards. Then answer the multiple-choice questions that follow.

GLOBAL INTERDEPENDENCE
What is global interdependence?
What are some examples of global interdependence?

EUROPEAN UNION
What is the European Union?
What is the main purpose of European Union?

1 The policies of glasnost and perestroika were introduced during the government of which leader?
   1 Ayatollah Khomeini
   2 Mikhail Gorbachev
   3 Joseph Stalin
   4 Boris Yeltsin

2 One of the major goals introduced by Deng Xaoping in China was to
   1 modernize China by reforming its economy
   2 create large communes
   3 introduce political democracy
   4 re-unite the two Koreas

3 The end of the Cold War was best symbolized by the
   1 establishment of the Truman Doctrine and the Marshall Plan
   2 formation of NATO and the European Common Market
   3 withdrawal of U.N. forces from Somalia and Kuwait
   4 destruction of the Berlin Wall and the reunification of Germany

4 The civil war in Rwanda and Burundi, atrocities in the former Yugoslavia, and the fighting in Northern Ireland demonstrate the
   1 inability of a command economy to satisfy the needs of people
   2 fact that most conflicts are caused by economic interests
   3 isolation of these countries from international influences
   4 inability of some governments to resolve religious and ethnic differences

KEY TERMS, CONCEPTS, AND PEOPLE

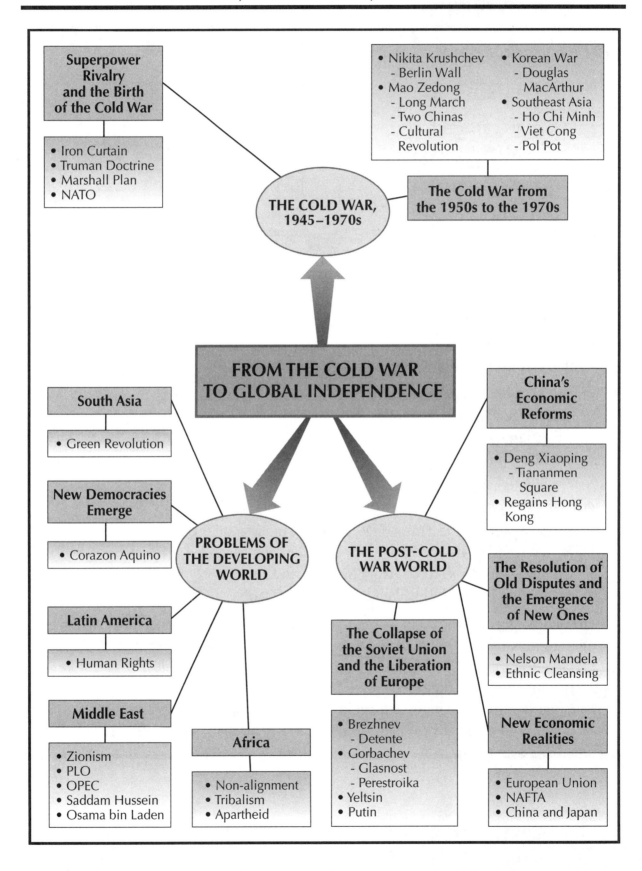

Superpower Rivalry and the Birth of the Cold War

- Iron Curtain
- Truman Doctrine
- Marshall Plan
- NATO

THE COLD WAR, 1945–1970s

The Cold War from the 1950s to the 1970s

- Nikita Krushchev
  - Berlin Wall
- Mao Zedong
  - Long March
  - Two Chinas
  - Cultural Revolution
- Korean War
  - Douglas MacArthur
- Southeast Asia
  - Ho Chi Minh
  - Viet Cong
  - Pol Pot

FROM THE COLD WAR TO GLOBAL INDEPENDENCE

South Asia

- Green Revolution

New Democracies Emerge

- Corazon Aquino

Latin America

- Human Rights

Middle East

- Zionism
- PLO
- OPEC
- Saddam Hussein
- Osama bin Laden

PROBLEMS OF THE DEVELOPING WORLD

Africa

- Non-alignment
- Tribalism
- Apartheid

THE POST-COLD WAR WORLD

China's Economic Reforms

- Deng Xiaoping
  - Tiananmen Square
- Regains Hong Kong

The Resolution of Old Disputes and the Emergence of New Ones

- Nelson Mandela
- Ethnic Cleansing

The Collapse of the Soviet Union and the Liberation of Europe

- Brezhnev
  - Detente
- Gorbachev
  - Glasnost
  - Perestroika
- Yeltsin
- Putin

New Economic Realities

- European Union
- NAFTA
- China and Japan

SUMMARIZING YOUR UNDERSTANDING

COMPLETING AN OUTLINE

Directions: Use these headings to complete the outline below.

Africa

China's Economic Reforms

Collapse of the Soviet Union and the Liberation of Eastern Europe

FROM THE COLD WAR TO GLOBAL INTERDEPENDENCE

Latin America

Middle East

New Democracies Emerge

New Economic Realities

PROBLEMS OF THE DEVELOPING WORLD

South Asia

Superpower Rivalry and the Birth of the Cold War

The Cold War from the 1950s to the 1970s

THE COLD WAR, 1945–1970s

THE POST-COLD WAR WORLD

The Resolution of Old Disputes and the Emergence of New Ones

TITLE: _____

I. MAJOR DIVISION: _____
   A. Sub-topic: _____
   B. Sub-topic: _____

II. MAJOR DIVISION: _____
   A. Sub-topic: _____
   B. Sub-topic: _____
   C. Sub-topic: _____
   D. Sub-topic: _____
   E. Sub-topic: _____

III. MAJOR DIVISION: _____
   A. Sub-topic: _____
   B. Sub-topic: _____
   C. Sub-topic: _____
   D. Sub-topic: _____

COMPLETING A GRAPHIC ORGANIZER

Complete the following cause-and-effect graphic organizer on the Cold War.

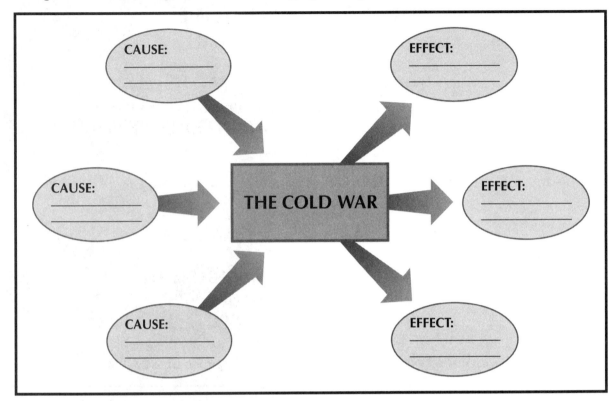

COMPLETING A TABLE

Use the table below to organize information you read about in this chapter.

Event	Year(s)	Main Cause(s)	Main Effect(s)
Division of Germany			
Chinese Revolution			
Arab-Israeli Conflict			
Cuban Revolution			
Iranian Revolution			
End of Soviet Union			

SHARPENING YOUR TEST-TAKING SKILLS

ANSWERING DOCUMENT-BASED ESSAY QUESTIONS

Some global history examinations may require you to answer a **document-based essay question,** sometimes referred to as a "D.B.Q." This type of question tests your ability to interpret historical documents and to write an essay based on the information they contain. It may focus on one historical era or ask you to draw comparisons between eras. Let's look at a sample document-based essay question:

This question is based on the accompanying documents (1–3). The question is designed to test your ability to work with historical documents. Some of the documents have been edited for the purpose of this question. As you analyze the documents, take into account both the source of each document and any point of view that may be presented in the document.

Historical Context:

During the late 1700s, a revolution occurred in France that greatly affected not only France but the rest of the world.

Task:

Using information from the documents and your knowledge of global history, answer the questions that follow each document in Part A. Your answers will help you write the Part B essay in which you will be asked to:

> Discuss the political and social changes brought about by the French Revolution.

NOTE: To simplify our explanation, this sample question contains only three documents. Most document-based questions will include 7–9 documents.

Part A
Short Answer

Directions: Analyze the documents and answer the questions that follow each document in the space provided.

DOCUMENT 1:

"1. Men are born and remain free and equal in rights; social distinctions can be established only for the common benefit.
2. The aim of every political association is the conservation of the natural rights of man; these rights are liberty, property, security, and resistance to oppression.
3. The source of all political power is found in the nation; no body, no individual can exercise authority which does not come from it expressly."
Declaration of the Rights of Man and of the Citizen, August 20–26, 1789

1. According to the document, what is the purpose of every government? _____

_____

DOCUMENT 2:

"The National Assembly decrees that hereditary nobility is forever abolished; ... the titles of prince, duke, count, marquis, viscount, vidame, baron, knight, ... and all other similar titles, shall neither be taken by anyone nor given to anyone."

Decree of the National Assembly, June 19, 1790

2. Based on this document, what was the effect of the French Revolution on the nobility of France? _____

DOCUMENT 3:

The beheading of Louis XVI, January 21, 1793

3. After studying this illustration, state the significance of the king's execution.

_____

Part B — Essay

Directions:
Write a well-organized essay that includes an introduction, several paragraphs, and a conclusion. Use evidence from at least three documents in your essay. Support your response with relevant facts, examples, and details. Include additional outside information.

Historical Context:
During the late 1700s, a revolution occurred in France that greatly affected not only France but the rest of the world.

Task:
Using information from the documents and your knowledge of global history, write an essay in which you:

> Discuss the political and social changes brought
> about by the French Revolution.

To answer this type of question, you must understand its basic structure. Notice that document-based essay questions have the following parts:

(1) directions on how to write the essay;
(2) a historical generalization that sets the stage for the essay question;
(3) a task you must perform;
(4) Part A, with documents for you to analyze and answer questions about; and
(5) Part B, where you write the final essay.

Parts (1), (2), and (3) above are instructions, while parts (4) and (5) are your actual tasks. To do well on this type of question, you should focus on three areas: (1) looking at the task; (2) analyzing the documents; and (3) writing the essay. An easy way to remember this approach is to think of the word "L•A•W."

L	ook at the task
A	nalyze the documents
W	rite the essay

"L" — LOOK AT THE TASK
Let's follow the "L•A•W" approach to see how it can be used to answer the essay. We'll start by "looking" at a typical task. Look at the **historical context** and **task** section.

EXAMPLE 1:

Historical Context:

During the late 1700s, a major revolution occurred in France that greatly affected not only France but the rest of the world.

Task:

Discuss the political and social changes brought about by the French Revolution.

Notice that the *Historical Context* sets the stage for the question. It provides the time and place. Notice also that the *Task* contains two important directions:

(1) an action word for you to follow: "Discuss

and

(2) the areas that you must cover: Political and Social changes

With this information, you now know the minimum number of paragraphs to write:

◆ **Paragraph 1** introduces your essay. It should include your thesis statement and a transition sentence. You may also include additional background information.

◆ **Paragraph 2** should deal with *political* changes brought about by the French Revolution. (*This could be more than one paragraph, based on how many examples and facts you can provide.*)

◆ **Paragraph 3** should deal with social changes brought about by the French Revolution. (*This could also be more than one paragraph.*)

◆ **Paragraph 4** should end the essay with your conclusion. How you close your essay will depend on the "action word" used in the question.

"A" — ANALYZE THE DOCUMENTS

The second part of the "L•A•W" approach deals with analyzing the documents. A document-based question often contains multiple documents. Read each document with care. Focus on the main idea. Look at the question that follows each document. Carefully reread the document in order to help you answer the question. The question following each document can also be used to help you answer the task. The question will directly relate the document to the task.

You may need a way to organize your analysis. One recommended method is to use an **Analysis Box.** The sample Analysis Box on the next page is based on the sample question.

SAMPLE ANALYSIS BOX

Document	Main Idea	Political	Social
Rights of Man	*This excerpt states that people are born free with equal rights, and that the purpose of government is to protect these rights. It also states the source of political power is found in the nation (the people).*	✓	✓
National Assembly Decree	*This decree abolished hereditary nobility in France.*		✓
Execution of Louis XVI	*Before the Revolution, France was ruled by absolute monarchs. In 1793, Louis XVI was beheaded. There was no turning back now.*	✓	✓

Related Outside Information:

- *All people called each other "citizen" and aristocratic clothing and wigs were replaced by simple dress.*
- *After Napoleon, the king and nobles returned but never achieved the same powers and privileges as before the Revolution.*

Let's look at the information in the Analysis Box:

◆ In the **Document** column, you should write a brief term or phrase to identify each document. For example, since the first document was a quotation from the Declaration of the Rights of Man, write "Rights of Man" in the first box.

◆ In the **Main Idea** column, briefly describe the main idea of each document. Use the answers you write to the questions after each document to help you identify what is important.

◆ The last columns will depend on what you have to cover in your essay. For example, since the first document deals with both **political** and **social** aspects of the French Revolution, check marks (✔) are placed in both columns.

◆ Note that the directions asked you to include **additional information** from your knowledge of world history. Use your outside knowledge to fill in the bottom of the box.

"W" — WRITING THE ESSAY

In the last part of the "L•A•W" approach, you organize and write your essay. You should follow the same general rules that you would in writing a thematic essay, except that you must now also include references to the documents in your answer. Following is a sample answer to this data-based question.

① The opening sentence gives the historical context.

During the late 1700s, a revolution occurred in France that affected not only France but the rest of the world. The French Revolution brought about both important political and social changes.

② The second sentence is the thesis statement.

③ Your second paragraph should discuss an example supporting the thesis statement.

One political change that occurred was that the French monarchy came to an end. Before the revolution, France had been ruled by absolute monarchs who claimed power through divine right. The French Revolution put an end to this. The new National Assembly, which pushed the revolution forward, issued **Document 1** — the Declaration of the Rights of Man. This stated that the source of political power was found in the nation (people), not divine right. Next, the French Revolutionaries overthrew their king and even beheaded him. (**see Document 3**).

④ Outside information related to the example is added here.

⑤ Write the information from the document in your own words.

⑥ Your third paragraph should discuss the second aspect of your thesis statement. Be sure to tie in other documents or outside information related to the example.

The French Revolution also brought about important social changes. For example, in **Document 2** we see that _____
_____
_____
_____

⑦ Again, be sure the information is not copied directly from the documents: it must be in your own words.

Thus, we can see that the French Revolution brought about many political and social changes. The elimination of the monarchy and nobility shows the degree of these changes.

⑧ Your closing paragraph should restate the thesis statement.

TESTING YOUR UNDERSTANDING

Test your understanding of this chapter by answering the following questions:

MULTIPLE-CHOICE QUESTIONS

1 Which concept is best illustrated by the formation of new nations from areas of the former Soviet Union?

1 self-determination
2 nonalignment
3 imperialism
4 utopianism

2 Which type of government was established by Ayatollah Khomeini as a result of the Iranian Revolution in 1979?

1 constitutional monarchy
2 democratic republic
3 Fundamentalist Islamic state
4 radical Marxist regime

Base your answer to question 3 on the table and your knowledge of global history.

NATIONS RECEIVING ECONOMIC AID UNDER THE MARSHALL PLAN
(in millions of dollars)

Country	Amount Received	Country	Amount Received
Great Britain	$2,826	Austria	$561
France	$2,445	Belgium	$547
Italy	$1,316	Denmark	$257
West Germany	$1,297	Norway	$237
Holland	$877	Turkey	$153

3 To which decade of European history does this chart refer?

1 1901-1910
2 1931-1940
3 1941-1950
4 1971-1980

4 The Cultural Revolution in China was Mao Zedong's attempt to

1 renew enthusiasm for Communism
2 increase the industrial output of China
3 promote artistic exchanges with the United States
4 encourage foreign investment in China

5 During the 1970s, the government of the Shah in Iran came under major criticism by religious leaders because of the

1 Shah's friendship with Israel
2 lack of political rights for women
3 increasing role of non-Islamic influences
4 Shah's return to traditional Islamic law

Base your answer to question 6 on the graph and your knowledge of global history.

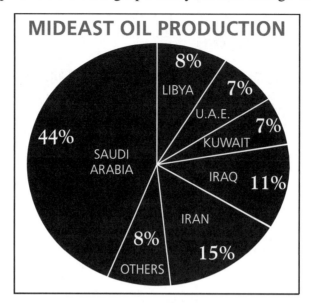

6 Based on the graph, which statement is most accurate?
1   OPEC controls most of the world's oil.
2   Algeria, Libya, and Kuwait produce most of the oil in the Middle East.
3   Saudi Arabia produces more oil than any other Middle Eastern nation.
4   Oil production in Saudi Arabia has been increasing.

7 In recent years, a major success of the European Union (EU) has been the
1   creation of a united military   3   adoption of single religion
2   elimination of trade barriers   4   acceptance of a single language

Base your answer to question 9 on the table and your knowledge of global history.

Formerly	Name Changed	Now Called
Burma	1948	Myanmar
East Pakistan	1971	Bangladesh
Ceylon	1972	Sri Lanka

8 A major factor explaining why these countries changed their names was
1   imperialism   3   socialism
2   capitalism   4   nationalism

9 One reason for the collapse of the Communist economic system in Eastern Europe in the early 1990s was that this system
1   lacked incentives for workers   3   used the principles of mercantilism
2   encouraged laissez-faire practices   4   relied on laws of supply and demand

10 Which headline concerning the Soviet Union refers to an event of the Cold War?

1 "Yeltsin Attacks Russian Parliament"

2 "Bolsheviks Overthrow Tsar"

3 "Germany invades U.S.S.R."

4 "Warsaw Pact Formed"

11 One similarity among the Meiji emperor of Japan, Peter the Great of Russia, and Shah Pahlavi of Iran was that they all supported

1 increasing the power of the aristocracy

2 introducing new religious beliefs

3 keeping their nations from industrial expansion

4 westernizing their nations

12 Four important events are listed below:

> A. The U.N. approves the creation of the State of Israel
> B. The Soviet Union dissolves
> C. Germany invades Poland
> D. The Treaty of Versailles is signed

Which is the correct chronological order of these events?

1 **A → C → D → B**   3 **D → C → B → A**

2 **D → C → A → B**   4 **B → D → A → C**

INTERPRETING DOCUMENTS

I. INTERPRETING A POLITICAL CARTOON

1 What is the main idea of the cartoon? _____

2 Circle the leader of China at the time referred to in the cartoon:

Manchu Emperor   Sun Yat-Sen

Mao Zedong   Deng Xiaoping

3 Citing historical evidence, explain why you chose that leader.

_____

_____

II. INTERPRETING A MAP

WORLD COMMUNISM

AT ITS HEIGHT

AT ITS LOW POINT

1 *Circle* the year the bottom map most likely refers to:

1925   1945   1975   1995

2 Give historical evidence to support your choice of year.

THEMATIC ESSAY QUESTION

Directions: Write a well-organized essay that includes an introduction, several paragraphs explaining your position, and a conclusion.

Theme: Justice and Human Rights

> Throughout human history, certain groups have faced injustice, discrimination, and brutality from those in power.

Task:

> Choose *two* groups from your study of global history and geography.
>
> For *each* group:
> • Show how that group faced injustice or brutality from those in power.
> • Explain how that group or the world community dealt with the injustice.

You may use any example from your study of global history and geography. Some suggestions you may wish to consider include: Protestants during the Reformation, Native Americans living under European rule, Jews in Nazi Germany, and black Africans under white South African rule.

You are *not* limited to these suggestions.

CHAPTER 12

GLOBAL CONCERNS

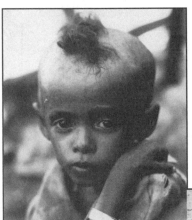

SECTION 1: PROBLEMS AND CONCERNS

1. Overpopulation
2. Hunger and Malnutrition
3. International Terrorism
4. Environmental Pollution
5. Deforestation and Desertification

Famine is a harsh reality to children in many nations.

SECTION 2: ISSUES

1. The North / South Dichotomy
2. The Status of Women
3. Global Migration
4. Urbanization and Modernization

SECTION 3: SCIENTIFIC AND TECHNOLOGICAL TRENDS

1. The Computer Revolution
2. Automation
3. Revolutions in Medicine
4. Transportation and Communication Advances
5. Space Exploration

In some developing nations, poverty forces children to work at hard labor.

KEY TECHNOLOGICAL BREAKTHROUGHS OF THE 20TH CENTURY

1903	First powered flight by the Wright Brothers
1928	Alexander Fleming discovers penicillin, the first antibiotic
1939	Pabst von Ohain builds the first jet engine for aircraft
1945	U.S. explodes the first atomic bomb
1953	First kidney transplant performed
1969	First humans land on the moon
1971	First pocket calculator introduced
1985	Surgical lasers first used to clean clogged arteries
1996	Computer chip does one billion calculations a second

WHAT YOU SHOULD FOCUS ON

Essay questions on global history examinations often ask about current global concerns, issues, or trends. This section provides an overview of what you need to know to answer this type of question.

The impact of deforestation on the rain forest in Western Brazil.

CONCERNS / PROBLEMS

Part of the challenge of the future will be to deal with some of the problems facing our world today. Test questions on global concerns frequently focus on such problems as:

Over-population

Deforestation

International Terrorism

Desertification

Pollution

Hunger

A GENERAL APPROACH

Although there are many aspects to these problems, most test questions will ask you to do the following:

1. Define the Problem. Define or describe the problem. A helpful hint might be to go through a mental checklist — *who, what, where,* and *when* — in defining or describing the problem.

2. Identify the Causes. Explain why or how something came about. Why, for example, is pollution increasing? Or why is the world's safety threatened by nuclear weapons?

3. Explain the Effects. Explain the effects or impact that the problem is having on the world. For example, what has been the impact of deforestation on the peoples of the Amazon?

4. Discuss Possible Solutions. Write about actions that have been taken by government agencies or private institutions to help solve the problem. You might also recommend other steps to provide a solution.

ISSUES

An **issue** is any public question that has two or more opposing viewpoints. Questions about issues will generally test your understanding of these different viewpoints. Some of the issues that might be tested are:

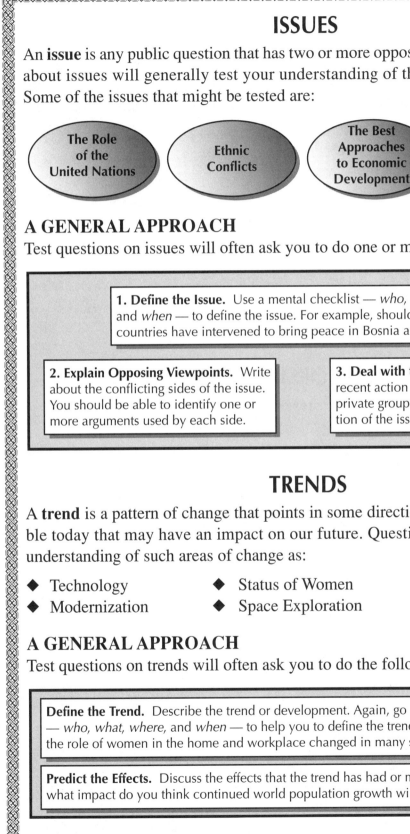

The Role of the United Nations

Ethnic Conflicts

The Best Approaches to Economic Development

Limits on Global Migration

A GENERAL APPROACH

Test questions on issues will often ask you to do one or more of the following:

1. Define the Issue. Use a mental checklist — *who, what, where,* and *when* — to define the issue. For example, should foreign countries have intervened to bring peace in Bosnia and Kuwait?

2. Explain Opposing Viewpoints. Write about the conflicting sides of the issue. You should be able to identify one or more arguments used by each side.

3. Deal with the Issue. Discuss some recent action taken by governments or private groups to bring about a resolution of the issue.

TRENDS

A **trend** is a pattern of change that points in some direction. Several trends are visible today that may have an impact on our future. Questions about trends test your understanding of such areas of change as:

- ◆ Technology
- ◆ Modernization
- ◆ Status of Women
- ◆ Space Exploration
- ◆ Urbanization
- ◆ Population Growth

A GENERAL APPROACH

Test questions on trends will often ask you to do the following:

Define the Trend. Describe the trend or development. Again, go through a mental checklist — *who, what, where,* and *when* — to help you to define the trend. For example, how has the role of women in the home and workplace changed in many societies?

Predict the Effects. Discuss the effects that the trend has had or may have. For example, what impact do you think continued world population growth will have on global resources?

LOOKING AT TECHNOLOGY

Technology refers to a people's tools and ways of doing things. Throughout history, people have made use of past technologies and attempted to improve on them. In more recent times, technological progress has accelerated, giving rise to new hopes but also to new problems. By the start of the 20th century, there was a conscious effort to promote scientific research and technology. The result has been a stream of inventions

Who would think that less than one hundred years ago the Wright brothers flew an aircraft for the first time?

throughout the century: the automobile, the airplane, radio, radar, television, antibiotics, nuclear energy, and the computer. Each of these has had a major impact on our social and cultural development.

FACTORS IN THE DEVELOPMENT OF TECHNOLOGY

Some of the main factors that sociologists believe affect the pace of technological development are the following:

> **The Role of Tradition.** Some societies pride themselves in following ancient ways. These traditional societies are not interested in technological progress. Instead, they attempt to preserve traditional ways of doing things. In these societies, technological progress is slow.

> **Exchange of Thought and Expression.** The free exchange of ideas is crucial to technological improvement. Societies with no free speech or free press often find progress to be slow. Progress is greatest when a society promotes the work of inventors and scientists by providing a system of rewards.

> **Cultural Diffusion.** During the Crusades, Muslims and Christians exchanged new products and ideas. Europeans and Native Americans also learned from each other. In Russia, Peter the Great borrowed Western European technologies. During the Meiji Restoration, the Japanese consciously adopted Western ideas.

THE CHALLENGE OF MODERN SCIENCE

Technological developments are not always put to good use. For example, improvements in technology have made weapons more destructive. Thus, technology can be compared to a hammer. We can use a hammer to build a house, or use the same hammer to damage our neighbor's house — the choice lies with us, not with the hammer. The challenge of modern science is to use technological advances beneficially.

MAJOR PROBLEMS, ISSUES, AND TRENDS

Today's rapid changes have made the world more **interdependent** than ever before, "shrinking" the world into a **global village.** As the world has grown "smaller," events in one area have a greater impact on other parts of the world. The effects of pollution or environmental destruction are not limited by natural borders. Even poverty in some regions affects others because of migration and the impact of poverty on the world economy.

THINK ABOUT IT •

What are the major problems, issues, and trends affecting the world today?

OVERPOPULATION, A CASE OF TOO MANY PEOPLE

In 1798, the English writer **Thomas Malthus** saw the effects of an exploding population — crowded slums, hungry families, and increasing poverty. He announced that growing populations would always outstrip food supplies. Poverty and misery, Malthus concluded, were unavoidable. Humans would be

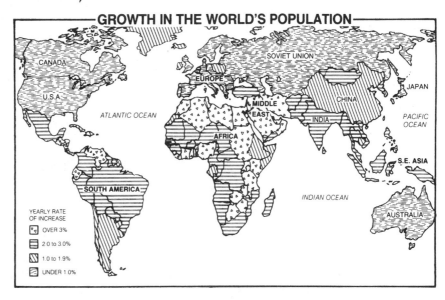

GROWTH IN THE WORLD'S POPULATION

YEARLY RATE
OF INCREASE
OVER 3%
2.0 to 3.0%
1.0 to 1.9%
UNDER 1.0%

condemned to an alternating cycle of population growth and decline through starvation. In 1800, there were 1 billion people in the world. Today, there are over 5 billion people, and the number almost doubles every 60 years. Such growth threatens to outrun the ability of nations to produce enough housing, fuel, and food. Many nations now promote family planning. However, people still have large families in areas where children are a source of labor and future support when parents grow old. Several religions oppose birth control, and many people have no knowledge of or access to modern family planning.

Possible Solutions. Many developing nations have adopted programs to limit their growth rates. The United Nations and other agencies are also expanding their efforts to educate people about family planning — teaching birth control methods, introducing new forms of birth control, and rewarding those who have smaller families. A few large countries hold the key to stabilizing world population growth: China, India, Pakistan, Bangladesh, Indonesia, Brazil and Nigeria.

HUNGER AND MALNUTRITION

The start of the twentieth century held out the promise of a new age of progress through science and technology. However, even at the end of the century, only a few nations are able to produce more food than their citizens need. For the rest of the world, hunger and malnutrition are common. In developing nations, about 150 million children under five years old go to bed hungry each night. Climatic changes and erosion have made the problem worse in some places, like Somalia. Moreover, as Malthus predicted, advances in producing more food are often met by an even faster increase in population.

Young victims of hunger..

In 1990, a United Nations agency estimated that one-third of the children in developing nations are malnourished. As many

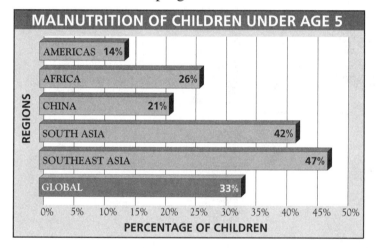

as 12 million children die each year before reaching the age of 5 from malnutrition. Malnutrition can be related as much to food customs as to a lack of food — which may lead to eating insufficient amounts of proteins or vitamins. The high death rate among malnourished children leads some parents to have more children, causing continuing malnutrition.

Possible Solutions. Technological advances are now providing more food in shorter periods of time. The **Green Revolution** brought new high-yield crops and better fertilizers. Environmentally safe insecticides are now being perfected. However, hunger cannot be avoided unless population growth is also brought under control.

INTERNATIONAL TERRORISM

Terrorism is the use of violence against civilians to achieve political goals. Terrorism is often used as a weapon to frighten governments into making concessions, or to draw attention to a group's grievances. The I.R.A., for example, used terrorism against the British in an attempt to unify Ireland. In the 1960s and 1970s, the PLO used terrorism against Israel. PLO leaders believed they were justified, arguing that Israelis had occupied their lands and they had no other way to resist. Terrorists organizations often make use of a variety of tactics:

Osama bin Laden

Taking Hostages. Israeli athletes were held hostage at the 1972 Munich Olympic Games. In 1979–1980, Iran held 52 American hostages for 15 months. Iraq took hostages at the start of the Gulf War, but then released them.

Explosions. In 1983, the U.S. Marines barracks in Beirut, Lebanon was bombed. The I.R.A. has also used such tactics against the British. Some terrorist groups place bombs on airplanes. Palestinian groups use "suicide bombers" against Israel. On September 11, 2001, members of al Qaeda hijacked U.S. airliners and crashed them into the World Trade Center and Pentagon, killing thousands of people.

Political Assassination. Egyptian extremists who opposed President Sadat's peace agreement with Israel assassinated him in 1981. In 1995, Israel's Prime Minister was assassinated by a Jewish student opposed to the Mideast peace process.

Possible Solutions. Many governments refuse to negotiate with terrorists. After September 11, 2001 attack, President George W. Bush declared a global **War on Terrorism**. U.S. actions included the invasion of Afghanistan and Iraq for ties with terrorists. The U.S. government has also attempted to seize the assets of terrorist organizations and has introduced tighter security measures at airports.

ENVIRONMENTAL POLLUTION

As countries become more economically developed and the earth's population increases, pollution of our air, water, and soil, becomes an ever greater threat to the world's environment.

◆ **Air Pollution.** Industrial growth often increases the amount of pollutants released into the air, creating such problems as **acid rain** and respiratory illness. Another threat to our environment is the destruction of the **ozone layer,** which protects the earth from the harmful effects of the sun's radiation. Increased carbon dioxide emissions and pollutants in the atmosphere appear to be making the earth

As nations industrialize, their factories contribute to the increasing amount of world pollution.

warmer. This worldwide warming, known as the **greenhouse effect,** may have harmful effects. If **global warming** causes excessive melting of the polar ice caps, there will be a considerable rise in the world's ocean levels. Countries with ocean coastlines could be permanently flooded.

◆ **Water Pollution.** Cities have become crowded, straining their ability to handle increased sewage and waste. Often this leads to dumping raw sewage into surrounding waters, contaminating drinking water and threatening health and safety.

◆ **Soil Pollution.** As farmers seek to make their lands more productive, more powerful fertilizers and toxic (*poisonous*) pesticides are often used. These often have harmful side effects.

◆ **Solid Waste.** Modern societies generate millions of tons of garbage. Much of it is placed in landfills, but these sites are now filling up. Burning the waste or dumping it into oceans or rivers also creates pollution.

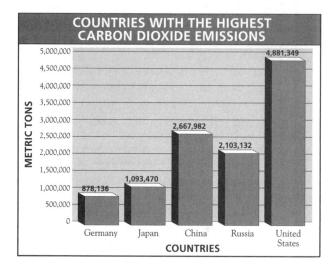

◆ **Nuclear Safety.** Nuclear weapons and power stations pose special dangers to the earth's environment. Nuclear waste can contaminate an area for millions of years. For example, in 1986, a meltdown at a Soviet nuclear power station in **Chernobyl** (*Ukraine*) caused radiation illness over a wide area, making some parts uninhabitable.

Possible Solutions. As the problem of pollution has grown more serious, a greater awareness of the need to preserve and protect the environment has developed. In 1992, most of the world's nations met in Brazil at the **Rio Conference**, in a special **Earth Summit.** The participants pledged themselves to the goal of industrial growth without pollution or environmental destruction. In 1997, an international conference on global warming was held in Kyoto, Japan. Since much pollution is caused by burning fossil fuels, there are efforts to harness energy from the sun and wind, and to develop safer nuclear reactors.

DEFORESTATION

The rain forests of Central and South America, Africa, and South and Southeast Asia provide much of the world's oxygen. Some countries in these areas have been clearing their rain forests. They sell the wood and grow food on the cleared land. However, heavy rains wash away the nutrients from these cleared lands. The remaining soil is of poor quality, produces few crops, and becomes barren. Loss of the rain forests also poses a threat to many **endangered species.**

Possible Solutions. An international campaign is encouraging governments and companies to stop cutting down rain forests.

WORLD HEALTH PROBLEMS

As ancient diseases are cured, new ones arise to take their place. More than 40 million people are now infected with the AIDS virus. The majority of these cases are in Africa, where few receive medical treatment. A new respiratory illness, SARS, only recently emerged in parts of Asia. Mosquito-borne West Nile Virus is now spreading to countries like the U.S. Millions also suffer or die each year from older, preventable diseases, like polio, malaria, or Guinea worm disease.

Possible Solutions. Using computers and new knowledge about viruses and DNA, scientists can determine the causes of new diseases and design effective treatments more rapidly than ever before. Nevertheless, the rising cost of new drugs often prevents effective treatment for poor people in many developing nations.

DESERTIFICATION

In some areas, especially eastern Africa, attempts were made to increase food production by clearing large tracts of land. This has been followed by several years of drought. In the **Sahel** region, just south of the Sahara, these events have led to **desertification** — an expansion of desert land. The United Nations has estimated that in Africa alone, an area half the size of New York State is turning into desert each year, risking malnutrition and starvation for millions of people.

Possible Solutions. Ways must be found to halt the erosion of the soil. **Reforestation** (*planting more trees*), restricting cattle grazing, and educating people about soil erosion are some approaches. Some inhabitants will also have to relocate.

This barrier is being built to contain water in the Sahel region of Africa.

ISSUES OF DEVELOPMENT

More than three-fourths of the world's population lives in the developing nations of the Third World. The gap between rich and poor nations continues to widen. This gap is sometimes referred to as the "North / South Dichotomy," or division.

The rich, industrialized nations are referred to as the "North," because most are in the Northern Hemisphere, while developing nations are known as the "South." Developing nations see the greater wealth and resources of developed nations and want to make the leap to full development.

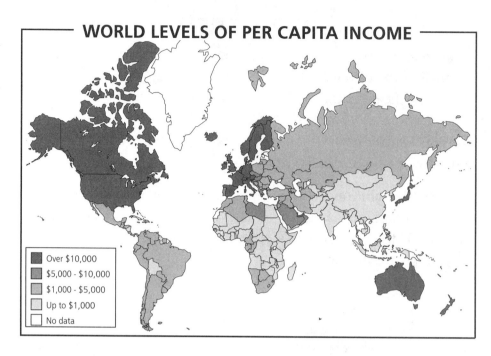

WORLD LEVELS OF PER CAPITA INCOME

- Over $10,000
- $5,000 - $10,000
- $1,000 - $5,000
- Up to $1,000
- No data

Alternative Viewpoints. Industrialized nations have sent aid and advisors to improve developing economies and raise living standards. One obstacle to achieving prosperity is Third World indebtedness: developing countries owe more than $1.2 trillion to industrialized nations. Some argue that the "North" should forgive these debts. Meanwhile, developing nations have made great progress in the last two decades by shifting to free markets, curbing inflation, and creating conditions for foreign investment. Institutions like the **World Bank** provide credit so long as developing nations take steps to build stronger economies.

THE STATUS OF WOMEN

Throughout much of history, men have held positions of authority, while women were considered inferior. In many societies, women could not hold property or participate in government, and had to obey their husbands. In the 19th and 20th centuries, the status of women began to change: many women entered the work force and achieved the right to vote. Nevertheless, women still suffer inferior status in many parts of the world today. In Africa and Asia, they suffer from forced mutilation of their bodies when they reach adolescence. In some Islamic countries, women must wear veils, refrain from public appearances, and are not permitted to drive automobiles. Even in Western countries, women are under-represented in politics and in top corporate jobs. On average, they earn less than men.

In some Islamic nations, women are not permitted in public unless much of their body is covered.

Alternative Viewpoints. In the 1960s, the **Women's Liberation Movement** emerged. Laws were passed in many countries guaranteeing women equal rights and prohibiting discrimination against women in education and employment. Some developing nations claim, however, that treating women equally violates their cultural traditions. Today, international organizations are trying to end the worst abuses against women in the developing world. In 1995, an international conference on women's rights worldwide was held in Beijing, China.

GLOBAL MIGRATION

Economic inequality and political conflict have led to migration on a global scale. After World War II, large numbers of foreign workers entered Western Europe to fill low-paying jobs. Turks and Italians migrated to Germany, North Africans to France, and Pakistanis to Great Britain. Many of these "guest workers" were Muslims and were not always accepted by Europeans as equals. Recently, Eastern European refugees have flooded into Western Europe. Latin Americans and Asians have similarly migrated to the United States.

Alternative Viewpoints. In times of high unemployment, foreign workers and refugees are often resented and attacked by local groups. In industrialized countries, many citizens have condemned such violence against immigrants and reaffirmed the principle of equal rights for all. Steps have also been taken to limit the number of refugees and immigrants to a manageable number, to avoid such resentment.

URBANIZATION AND MODERNIZATION

Urbanization refers to the movement of people into cities. Both poverty and improvements in farming have driven millions in developing countries to emigrate to cities in search of jobs and education. By 2000, a majority of the world's population will live in cities. Such rapidly rising urban

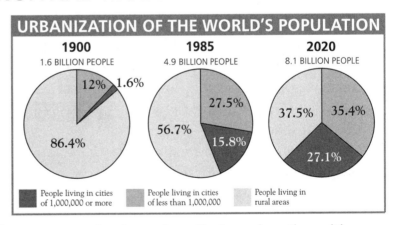

populations require more food, heat, water, schools, and medical services than cities can provide. Overcrowding leads to air and water pollution, huge traffic jams, and mountains of garbage and sewage. Rural newcomers also must struggle with new values. **Modernization** refers to the process of shedding traditional beliefs and adopting new methods, ideas, and technologies. Often cities are centers of change and modernization, creating social and psychological conflicts. Citizens in developing countries struggle to combine their traditional beliefs with modern ideas coming from developed nations.

Future Effects. Urbanization and modernization pose tremendous challenges for the developing world. Third World governments must try to improve conditions in the countryside to slow the tide of rural migration while also providing more services, housing, and education in the cities. Reducing population growth will also lessen urban congestion. Adjusting to these challenges often gives rise to social problems and cultural conflicts. In Iran, for example, Islamic Fundamentalist leaders opposed the effects that Western ideas and modernization were having on their local traditions, and have tried to suppress them.

SCIENTIFIC AND TECHNOLOGICAL CHANGE

Because of continuous progress in science and technology, we live in an age of constant change. The pace of change can make job skills obsolete before people have time to adjust or to learn new skills.

◆ **The Computer Revolution.** A central feature of recent decades has been the computer. Earlier computers required huge buildings to house their memory units. The invention of **silicon chips** has made it possible to build computers that perform billions of calculations in a few seconds but are small enough to fit on in one's palm. Many people use their computer to access the Internet, leading to a revolution in global communications. With computers, people can communicate and market goods all around the world. Some experts fear that the vast amounts of information now stored in computers might lead to invasions of individual privacy.

◆ **Automation.** Computer-controlled robots are now replacing many skilled workers. This provides cheaper products, but reduces the number of factory jobs. Some economists believe new jobs are being quickly created, but many workers find it hard to adjust.

◆ **Revolutions In Medicine.** Medical advances now seem to occur almost daily. Vaccines and antibiotics have wiped out many diseases. Only a few years ago, organ transplants made headlines; now they are commonplace. Lasers, powerful beams of light, allow doctors to perform surgery with minimal discomfort to patients. The next challenge in medicine lies in finding cures for diseases such as cancer, AIDS, and memory loss in the elderly. But medical costs are rising sharply. Most developing societies cannot afford the most modern health care — 40,000 children under five die every day from preventable illnesses.

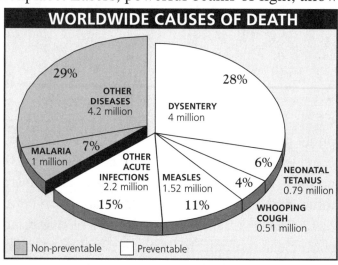

WORLDWIDE CAUSES OF DEATH

29% OTHER DISEASES 4.2 million

28% DYSENTERY 4 million

6% NEONATAL TETANUS 0.79 million

4%

WHOOPING COUGH 0.51 million

11% MEASLES 1.52 million

15% OTHER ACUTE INFECTIONS 2.2 million

7% MALARIA 1 million

Non-preventable　Preventable

◆ **Transportation.** When the internal combustion engine was developed to power automobiles, ships, and airplanes, the impact on people's daily lives was enormous. Cars gave people the freedom to travel quickly to any place they chose. However, increased traffic has brought smog, pollution, and gridlock to the world's cities.

◆ **Communications.** Inventions such as the telephone, radio, and television have permitted almost instant communications, turning our world into a "global village." Satellites now speed up communications by relaying television and telephone signals. The **Internet,** a global network allowing computer users to exchange information quickly and cheaply, is further increasing the knowledge available. People are better informed today, but often find it difficult to cope with this "information overload."

◆ **Space Exploration.** In 1957, the Soviets launched a satellite, **Sputnik I,** starting the "**space race**" between the Soviet Union and the United States. Both countries carried out complex space projects, sending astronauts and satellites into space in larger numbers. The first humans landed on the moon in 1969. Space exploration carries great national prestige, military advantages, and

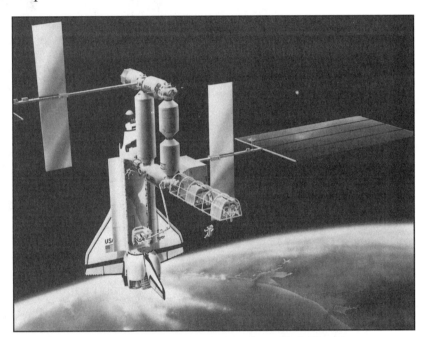

What future space stations may look like.

increased communication capabilities, but requires vast outlays of money.

Future Effects. No one can predict all the future effects of technological change. The key to dealing with new technologies will be to make them serve genuine human needs and to provide people with support in adjusting to rapid change.

ANSWERING THE FOCUS QUESTION •

Writing

Major problems, issues, and trends affecting the world today are:

_____ (Problems)

_____ (Issues)

_____ (Trends)

Directions: Complete each of the following vocabulary cards. Then answer the multiple-choice questions that follow.

THOMAS MALTHUS
What views did Malthus hold?
Do you agree that Malthus was correct?
Explain:

CHERNOBYL
What occurred at Chernobyl?
What impact did it have on the world's
environment?

1   In the 1980s, the governments of both Brazil and Malaysia supported the cutting of timber in their rain forests as a means of
    1   achieving economic prosperity
    2   increasing the national debt
    3   controlling the rebellions of native peoples
    4   preventing exploitation by imperialist nations

2   Many scientists believe that the "greenhouse effect" is the result of
    1   overgrazing on land in developing nations
    2   burning large amounts of gasoline, oil, and coal
    3   testing nuclear weapons in violation of the Nuclear Test Ban Treaty
    4   using natural fertilizers to increase crop production

3   Technological changes in developing countries have most often resulted in
    1   mass migrations from urban to rural areas
    2   fewer educational and employment opportunities
    3   a weakening of traditional values and family patterns
    4   the decreased use of natural resources

4   A study of the accident at the Chernobyl nuclear power plant in the former Soviet Union and the severe air pollution in Mexico City would lead to the conclusion that
    1   technology can cause problems throughout the world
    2   international trade is more profitable than domestic commerce
    3   modern science cannot solve most political problems
    4   the Green Revolution caused major world environmental problems

SUMMARIZING YOUR UNDERSTANDING

COMPLETING A GRAPHIC ORGANIZER

Complete the following graphic organizer on the impact of science and technology.

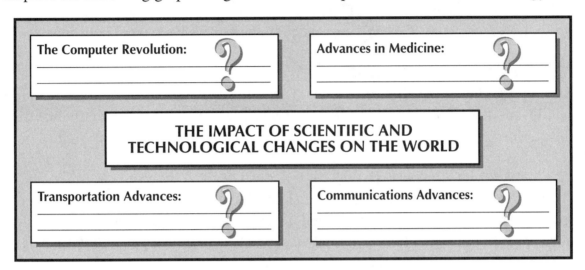

The Computer Revolution:

Advances in Medicine:

THE IMPACT OF SCIENTIFIC AND
TECHNOLOGICAL CHANGES ON THE WORLD

Transportation Advances:

Communications Advances:

COMPLETING A TABLE

Use the table below to organize the information you have read about in this chapter.

Concern	State the Problem	List a Possible Solution
Overpopulation		
International Terrorism		
Environmental Pollution		
Deforestation		
Desertification		
Status of Women		
Global Migration		
Urbanization		

SHARPENING YOUR TEST-TAKING SKILLS

A REVIEW OF THE "L•A•W" APPROACH

At the end of this chapter, you will answer a document-based question. Before you do so, let's review the "L•A•W" approach for answering this type of question.

"L"— LOOK AT THE TASK

Start by looking at the *Historical Context* and the *Task*. Focus on (1) the "action word," and (2) what you have to cover. This will determine how you will answer the question.

"A" — ANALYZE THE DATA

As you read each document, think about (1) who wrote it; (2) the time period when it was written; (3) the purpose for which it was written; and (4) what it says. Next, answer the key question following each document. Then create your **Analysis Box.**

> **NOTE:** Two important keys to writing a successful document-based essay are (1) to link the information in the documents to the topic, and (2) to use your own words instead of simply copying text from the document.

In the Analysis Box, be sure you show how information in each document supports a thesis statement you create out of the *Task*. Remember that you must also add other relevant information that is not contained in the documents.

"W" — WRITE THE ESSAY

In writing your essay answer, remember that you need the following:

◆ **Opening Paragraph.** Your first sentence should state the historical context and set the time and place. The next sentence is your thesis statement, which you can obtain from the question. Then write a transition sentence leading into the supporting paragraphs.

◆ **Supporting Paragraphs.** These paragraphs provide evidence that supports your topic statement. They must include references to the documents, in your own words, as well as additional related information from your knowledge of the topic.

◆ **Closing Paragraph.** The closing paragraph should restate the thesis statement. You may also want to summarize your most important evidence or ideas about the general topic.

TESTING YOUR UNDERSTANDING

Test your understanding of this chapter by answering the following questions:

MULTIPLE-CHOICE QUESTIONS

1 The global problems of uneven economic development, environmental pollution, and hunger reflect a need for
 1   a return to policies of economic mercantilism
 2   increased military spending
 3   a reduction in foreign aid provided by industrialized nations
 4   increased international cooperation

2 A valid statement about technology in the 20th century is that it has
 1   eliminated famine and disease
 2   delayed economic progress in developing countries
 3   discouraged the adoption of free trade policies
 4   accelerated the pace of cultural diffusion

Base your answers to questions 3 and 4 on the chart below and your knowledge of global history.

Nations	Birthrate (per 1,000 females)	Infant Mortality Rate (per 1,000 births)
Uganda	51	104.0
Somalia	50	122.0
Pakistan	40	109.0
Canada	14	6.8
France	13	6.7
Denmark	13	6.6
Germany	10	5.9
Japan	10	4.4

3 Which is a valid generalization based on the information in the chart?
 1   In developing nations, the infant mortality rate decreases as the birthrate increases.
 2   Industrialized nations have lower birthrates and infant mortality rates than developing nations do.
 3   Decreasing the infant mortality rate will limit population growth in developing nations.
 4   Industrialized nations have higher population densities than developing nations.

4 According to the chart, the lowest birth rates are found mostly in
1 Western Europe
2 North America
3 Southeast Asia
4 Africa

---

5 Acid rain damage, contamination from nuclear accidents, and deterioration of the earth's ozone layer indicate a need for
1 the elimination of fossil fuels
2 greater international cooperation
3 a favorable balance of trade
4 nationalization of major industries

6 A major cause of the high birth rates in many developing nations has been
1 the need for a large urban workforce
2 a desire to counteract an increasing death rate
3 a need to replace people killed during civil wars
4 traditional beliefs and the economic need to have large families

7 Russian grain purchases from the United States, sales of Japanese cars in Latin America, and European reliance on Middle Eastern oil are examples of
1 the creation of free-trade areas
2 economically self-sufficient nations
3 the rise of economic interdependence
4 a worldwide spirit of imperialism

8 "People are casting many wary glances at the sky and their surroundings — radioactivity needs no visa and has no respect for national frontiers."

Izvestia, May 9, 1986

The quotation most probably refers to
1 the nuclear accident that occurred at Chernobyl
2 the drought affecting Africa's Sahel region
3 deforestation that was caused by acid rain
4 monsoon floods in some areas of Southeast Asia

9 One of the main concerns about the destruction of the rain forests in Brazil and sub-Saharan Africa is that
1 cities will become seriously overcrowded
2 it will lead to a decrease in the amount of oxygen in the atmosphere
3 the per capita income in economically developing nations will increase
4 the availability of water in these areas will decrease

10 Which statement best describes the status of women today?
1 Women have achieved complete equality with men.
2 Women have more freedom in developing nations than in developed nations.
3 In the last 50 years, women's job opportunities have greatly increased in developed nations.
4 Women have made no progress in gaining social equality since 1945.

INTERPRETING DOCUMENTS

1   What is the major idea depicted in the cartoon?

_____

2   Select one concern. Explain why it is considered a problem. _____

_____

3   State one possible solution. _____

_____

> "The power of population is indefinitely greater than the power of the earth to produce (*food*) for man. Population, when unchecked, increases in a geometrical ratio (*multiplying*). Food only increases in an arithmetical ratio (*through addition*). By the law of nature, food is necessary to life: the effects of these two unequal powers must be kept equal."

1. What is the main idea of this statement by Thomas Malthus?

_____

2. What problem does this situation present? _____

THEMATIC ESSAY QUESTION

Directions: Write a well-organized essay that includes an introduction, several paragraphs explaining your position, and a conclusion.

Theme: Interdependence

> In today's world, global concerns pose challenges for both national and international efforts.

Task:

> Choose *two* global concerns from your study of global history.
> For *each* global concern:
> • Describe why it is considered to be a problem.
> • Show how the problem might be resolved.

You may use any example from your study of global history and geography. Some suggestions you may wish to consider include: environmental pollution, terrorism, over-population, hunger, and desertification.

You are *not* limited to these suggestions.

DOCUMENT-BASED ESSAY QUESTION

This task is based on the accompanying documents (1–7). Some of these documents have been edited for the purposes of this task. This task is designed to test your ability of work with historical documents. As you analyze the documents, take into account both the source of each document and the author's point of view.

Directions: Read the documents in Part A and answer the questions after each document. Then read the directions for Part B and write your essay.

Historical Context:
Throughout history, the introduction of new technologies has often been accompanied by significant social, economic, and political change.

Task:
Discuss the impact that technological change has had on history.

PART A — SHORT ANSWERS

Directions: Analyze the documents and answer the questions that follow each document.

DOCUMENT 1

"When food production became more efficient, there was time to develop the arts and sciences. Agriculture probably required a far greater discipline than did any form of food collecting. Seeds had to be planted at certain seasons, some protection had to be given to growing plants, harvests had to be reaped, stored, and divided. It has been suggested that writing may have come into existence because records were needed by agricultural administrators."

— Charles Heiser, *Seed To Civilization,* 1981

1   How did the introduction of agriculture bring about other changes? _____

DOCUMENT 2

"The most significant invention in the history of warfare prior to gunpowder was the stirrup. In conjunction with a saddle, stirrups welded horse and rider into a single organism. The long lance could now be held at rest under the right armpit. The increase in violence was immense."

— Lynn White Jr., *The Expansion of Technology*

2   How did the development of the stirrup transform warfare in the Middle Ages? _____

_____

DOCUMENT 3

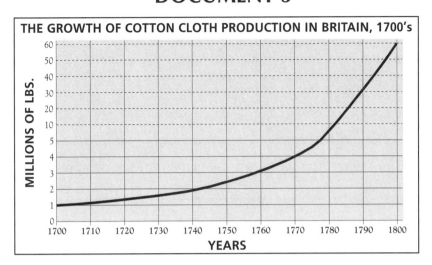

THE GROWTH OF COTTON CLOTH PRODUCTION IN BRITAIN, 1700's

MILLIONS OF LBS. / YEARS

3 How did the Industrial Revolution affect the production of cotton cloth in Britain?

DOCUMENT 4

"Labor in an industrial society… is overwhelming. Mechanized labor imposes a routine and monotony unlike pre-industrial work. Labor in the industrial age took place in the unprecedented environment of the big city. And what cities! It was not merely that smoke hung over them and filth impregnated them, that simple public services — water supply, sanitation, street-cleaning — couldn't keep pace with the mass migration. But more than this: the city destroyed society."

— Eric Hobsbawm, *Industry and Empire,* 1969

4 What is Hobsbawm's view of the effect of the Industrial Revolution on workers?

DOCUMENT 5

5 This photo shows the ruins of a Shinto shrine in Nagasaki, Japan, after an atomic bomb had been dropped on the city in August, 1945. What does this picture show about the impact of atomic weapons?

DOCUMENT 6

"The speed with which computers have spread is so well known. Costs have dropped so sharply and capacity has risen so spectacularly that, according to one authority, 'If the auto industry had done what the computer industry has done in the last 30 years, a Rolls-Royce would cost $2.50 and would get 2,000,000 miles to the gallon.'"

— Alvin Toffler, *The Third Wave*

6   What does Toffler see as an important achievement of the computer industry?

_____

DOCUMENT 7

7. Which two nations produce almost one-third of the world's air pollution?

_____

_____

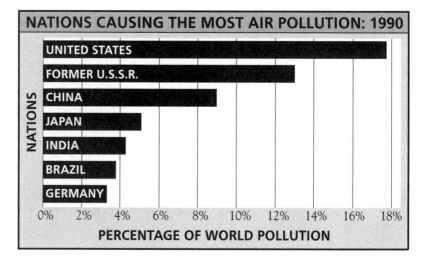

NATIONS CAUSING THE MOST AIR POLLUTION: 1990

Part B — Essay

Directions:
- Write a well-organized essay that includes an introduction, several paragraphs, and a conclusion
- Use evidence from the documents to support your response.
- Do not simply repeat the contents of the documents.
- Include specific related information.

Historical Context:

Throughout history, the introduction of new technologies has often been accompanied by significant social, economic, and political change.

Task:

Using information from the documents and your knowledge of global history and geography, write an essay in which you:

   Discuss the impact that technological change has had on history.

CHAPTER 13

A FINAL REVIEW

Congratulations. You have just reviewed more than 3,000 years of global history! At this point you may be wondering, how will you remember all of the events, people, and dates that you have read about?

In order to help you to remember, this chapter contains four sections that review the most important information you have learned. Let's look at what each section in this final review provides:

◆ **Section 1: Major Concepts.** This section provides a glossary of the most important concepts in global history.

Will you recall the importance of Gutenberg's printing press on events in Europe?

◆ **Section 2: Major Terms.** This section provides a checklist of major terms you need to review. Where each term on the list is discussed in the book can be found by looking in the Index. The names of key people are not included on this list but may be found on page 210.

◆ **Section 3: Study Organizers.** This section provides a group of study organizers for you to complete that bring together what you have learned by theme, such as major historical turning points, important revolutions, and major religions.

◆ **Section 4: Area Study Guides.** This last section presents a series of area study guides organized chronologically by region. These area study guides allow you to trace developments within a particular culture and to review what you have learned from a different perspective.

Reviewing global history also gives you an opportunity to pinpoint your weaknesses. If you have difficulty recalling any specific information referred to, consult the earlier chapters of this book.

SECTION 1: MAJOR CONCEPTS

Absolutism: A system of government in which a monarch exercises complete control over his subjects. Absolutism in Europe in the 16th and 17th centuries was closely associated with "divine right." Louis XIV of France was an absolute ruler.

Balance of Power: An international system in which no one nation is powerful enough to conquer other major nations in the system. Through diplomacy and war, the major nations participating in the system attempt to keep this "balance."

Capitalism: An economic system characterized by the private ownership of property and wealth. Under capitalism, capital (*wealth*) is invested in the hope of creating even more wealth for the entrepreneur — the individual investor. Consumers are free to buy or not to buy what is produced.

Civilization: An advanced form of human culture in which some people live in cities, have complex social institutions, use some form of writing, and are skilled in science and technology.

Communism: Communism developed in 19th-century Europe. In the early 20th century, Communism spread from the Soviet Union to China and other countries. Communists believe eliminating private property can end class struggle and lead to the ideal society. In practice, Communism has been characterized by government control of all aspects of production and distribution.

Culture: A people's way of life. It includes such things as language, clothes, houses, family organization, religion, and rituals.

Cultural Diffusion: The spread of ideas and products from one culture to another.

Decolonization. The process in which European colonies in Africa and Asia became independent states after World War II.

Democracy: A system in which citizens participate in government decisions either by voting directly on issues brought before them or by electing people to represent them. Democracy was first developed in Athens around the 5th century B.C.

Developing Countries: These are countries mainly in Africa, Asia, and Latin America that have lower productivity and income per capita than those of the developed countries. Developing countries are also sometimes referred to as the "Third World."

Dictatorship: A system in which citizens have few rights and the government is controlled by an individual or small group. For example, Nazi Germany under Adolf Hitler and the Soviet Union under Joseph Stalin were dictatorships.

Ethnic Group: A group of people united by a common culture. Ethnic groups may be based on race, religion, language, or a common history. Tribes are also ethnic groups.

Fascism: A European political movement that emerged in 1919–1939. Fascists believed that the state is supreme, that an absolute leader best expressed the needs of the state, and that citizens should make sacrifices for the state. Nazi Germany was an example of a Fascist state.

Genocide: An attempt to murder an entire race or ethnic group. The Nazi attempt to murder all European Jews during World War II, sometimes known as the Holocaust, was an example of genocide. Other examples of genocide are Saddam Hussein's attacks on the Kurds, and Turkish attacks against Armenians during World War I.

Golden Age: A peaceful period in the history of a culture in which its literature, the arts, and sciences flourish.

Global Interdependence: In an interdependent world, each nation depends on selling and buying goods and services from other nations.

Imperialism: Also known as colonialism. The political and economic control of one area or country by another. In the late 1800s, European imperialism led to European control of much of Africa and Asia.

Mercantilism: An economic theory held by Europeans in the 17th and 18th centuries. Mercantilists believed that a nation's wealth could be measured by the amount of its gold and silver. Mercantilists urged European rulers to acquire colonies and to export manufactured goods.

Modernization: The process of shedding traditional beliefs in favor of modern ideas, methods, and technologies.

Nationalism: The belief that each ethnic group or "nationality" is entitled to its own government and national homeland.

Revolutions: A sudden and basic change in the way in which people govern themselves, see the world, or make things. Political revolutions, like the French Revolution, often follow a common pattern: moderate reformers seize power when a government is under strain. Later, radicals take over and the revolution becomes more violent.

Scientific Method: A way of understanding nature and humankind through detailed observation, careful measurement, and the making and testing of hypotheses through experiments. The scientific method rejects reliance on authorities such as religions in favor of direct observation and experimentation.

Totalitarianism: A system in which a dictatorial government controls all aspects of life, even education, ideas, the economy, music, and art, and citizens have no individual rights. Stalin in the Soviet Union and Hitler in Nazi Germany imposed totalitarian governments.

Urbanization: The movement of peoples from rural areas to cities in search of jobs and new opportunities.

Westernization: The policy of some non-Western countries of imitating Western European customs and technology. Peter the Great "Westernized" Russia in the 18th century and Japan adopted similar policies in the 19th century during the Meiji Restoration.

SECTION 2: CHECKLIST OF MAJOR TERMS

❑ Anti-Semitism
❑ Apartheid
❑ Appeasement
❑ Aztecs
❑ Balance of Power
❑ Bolsheviks
❑ Boxer Rebellion
❑ Buddhism
❑ Byzantine Empire
❑ Caste System
❑ Chernobyl
❑ Civil Disobedience
❑ Code of Hammurabi
❑ Code of Justinian
❑ Cold War
❑ Commercial Revolution
❑ Communism
❑ Confucianism
❑ Congress of Vienna
❑ Counter Reformation
❑ Crusades
❑ Cuban Missile Crisis
❑ Cuban Revolution
❑ Cultural Revolution
❑ Deforestation
❑ Desertification
❑ Developing Nations
❑ Divine Right of Kings
❑ Encomienda System
❑ Enlightenment
❑ European Union
❑ Feudalism
❑ Final Solution
❑ French Revolution
❑ Genocide
❑ Glasnost
❑ Global Warming
❑ Great Leap Forward
❑ Green Revolution
❑ Gulf War

❑ Gupta Empire
❑ Hinduism
❑ Hiroshima
❑ Holocaust
❑ IRA
❑ Inca Empire
❑ Indus River Valley Civilization
❑ Industrial Revolution
❑ Intifada
❑ Iranian Revolution
❑ Islam
❑ Islamic Fundamentalism
❑ Judaism
❑ Kingdom of Ghana
❑ Kingdom of Mali
❑ Kingdom of Songhai
❑ Kush
❑ Laissez-faire
❑ League of Nations
❑ Manchu Dynasty
❑ Mandate of Heaven
❑ Marshall Plan
❑ Maurya Empire
❑ Maya
❑ Meiji Restoration
❑ Mesopotamia
❑ Mexican Revolution
❑ Middle Ages
❑ Ming Dynasty
❑ Mongols
❑ Monotheism
❑ Mughals
❑ NATO
❑ NAFTA
❑ Nazism
❑ Neolithic Revolution
❑ New Economic Policy
❑ Ninety-Five Theses
❑ Nuremberg Trials

❑ O.P.E.C.
❑ Open Door Policy
❑ Ottoman Empire
❑ P.L.O.
❑ Pan-Arabism
❑ Perestroika
❑ Pharoah
❑ Qin Dynasty
❑ Qing (Manchu) Dynasty
❑ Qu'ran
❑ Racism
❑ Reformation
❑ Renaissance
❑ Roman Empire
❑ Russian Revolution
❑ Russification
❑ Savanna
❑ Scientific Revolution
❑ Sepoy Mutiny
❑ Shogun
❑ Social Darwinism
❑ Spheres of Influence
❑ Steppes
❑ Sung Dynasty
❑ T'ang Dynasty
❑ Terrorism
❑ Third World Nations
❑ Tiananmen Square Protest
❑ Transatlantic Slave Trade
❑ Treaty of Versailles
❑ Tribalism
❑ Truman Doctrine
❑ United Nations
❑ Warsaw Pact
❑ World War I
❑ World War II
❑ Young Turks
❑ Zhou Dynasty

SECTION 3: STUDY ORGANIZERS

IMPORTANT CIVILIZATIONS

The rise and fall of different civilizations is a major theme in global history. Summarize your knowledge of what you have read by completing the following study organizer. The first item has been done for you as a model.

Civilization	Location	Major Characteristic	Reasons for its Rise or Fall
River Valley Civilizations	*Egypt, Mesopotamia, Indus River Valley, Huang He*	*They were the first civilizations in which people lived in cities and developed systems of writing.*	*The rivers deposited rich soils in annual floods, allowing farmers to grow surplus crops—making possible the rise of civilizations.*
Roman Empire			
Dynastic China			
Byzantine Empire			
Arab Islamic Empire			
Mesoamerican Civilizations			
West African Kingdoms			

MAJOR BELIEF SYSTEMS

Belief systems have had a major impact on the lives of people as well as on global history. Summarize your knowledge of belief systems by completing the following study organizer:

Belief System	Where It Was Found	Major Beliefs or Practices
Judaism		
Confucianism		
Christianity		
Buddhism		
Hinduism		
Islam		
Islamic Fundamentalism		

TURNING POINTS IN HISTORY

A number of significant milestones have had a profound impact on the history of the world. Summarize your knowledge of these by completing the following study organizer:

Turning Point	Describe the Turning Point	Its Impact on the World
Fall of Rome (476 A.D.)		
Birth of Islam (622–632)		
Mongol Conquests (1200s)		
European Encounter with Native Americans (1492)		
Fall of Constantinople (1453)		
French Revolution (1789)		
Perry's Arrival in Japan (1853)		
Russian Revolution (1917)		
Dropping the Atom Bomb on Japan (1945)		
Dissolution of the Soviet Union (1991)		

FORMS OF GOVERNMENT

Throughout history, different groups of people have had different types of governments. Many of these forms of government can be characterized by a particular guiding idea or belief. Summarize your knowledge of the different types of governments by completing the following study organizer:

Government	Its Major Idea or Feature	Examples
Democracy		
Feudalism		
Divine Right		
Absolutism		
Fascism		
Totalitarianism		

TYPES OF ECONOMIC SYSTEMS

An economic system describes the way a society meets it members' needs for goods and services. Throughout history, people have organized their economies to help meet their needs. These economic systems are often based on some major idea or goal. Summarize your knowledge of the various economic systems by completing the following study organizer:

Economic System	Major Features	Example
Traditional		
Feudal		
Mercantilist		
Capitalist		
Communist		

MAJOR REVOLUTIONS

Certain events in history have brought about great changes in government, ideas, or society with amazing speed. Summarize your knowledge of some of these major revolutions by completing the following study organizer:

Revolution	Where	When	Effects/Changes/Impacts
Neolithic Revolution			
Commercial Revolution			
Scientific Revolution			
French Revolution			
Industrial Revolution			
Russian Revolution			
Chinese Revolution			
Cuban Revolution			
Iranian Revolution			

MAJOR UPRISINGS

In addition to the revolutions listed on the previous page, a number of uprisings and protests have brought about important changes in the world. Summarize your knowledge of these events by completing the following study organizer:

Uprising or Protest	Major Causes	Major Effects
Protestant Reformation (1517)		
Sepoy Mutiny (1857)		
Boxer Rebellion (1899–1900)		
Viet Cong Uprising (1960–1974)		
Intifada (1987–1997)		
Tiananmen Square Protests (1989)		

THE MIDDLE EAST AND NORTH AFRICA

EARLY CIVILIZATION (10,000 B.C.–500 B.C.)	NEW CENTER OF CULTURE (330–1453)	ISLAMIC EXPANSION (570–1770)	OTTOMAN EMPIRE (1453–1918)	MIDDLE EAST IN THE 20TH CENTURY (1900–Present)
EARLY HUMAN SOCIETY • Neolithic Revolution **RIVER VALLEY CIVILIZATIONS** • Mesopotamia –*Fertile Crescent* –*Tigris & Euphrates* –*Code of Hammurabi* • Ancient Egypt –*pyramids* –*Pharoahs* –*hieroglyphics* • The Hebrews –*Judaism* –*monotheism* –*Ten Commandments* • Phoenicians –*first alphabet* **PERSIA** (550–100 B.C.) • Large empire uniting many peoples • Cyrus the Great • Zoroastrianism • Attempted conquest of Greek city-states	**BYZANTINE EMPIRE** • Continuation of East Roman Empire –*Emperor Constantine* –*Constantinople* • Legacy of Byzantium –*Code of Justinian* –*Eastern Orthodox Christianity* –*Hagia Sophia*	**RISE OF ISLAM** • Arose in Arabia • Mohammed –*Allah* –*Qu'ran (Koran)* • Five Pillars of Faith –*Confessions of Faith* –*Pray 5 times a day* –*Charity* –*Fasting during Ramadan* –*Pilgrimage to Mecca* • Golden Age of Islamic Rule **CRUSADES** (1096) • Seljuk Turks • Attempt to regain Holy Land • Cultural Diffusion	**OTTOMAN TURK EXPANSION** • Took Constantinople • Suleiman the Magnificent • Toleration of Jews and Christians **SAFAVID EMPIRE** • Persia –*Ruled by Shahs* –*Persian carpets* **DECLINE OF THE OTTOMAN EMPIRE** • Disunity • Warfare with Persia, Austria, Russia • Failure to modernize • Loss of territories (Balkans, Egypt)	**RISE OF NATIONALISM** • Br. and Fr. mandates • Independent states emerge **ARAB-ISRAEI CONFLICT** • Zionism • War of Independ. (1948) • Further Wars (1956, 1967, 1973) –*PLO/Intifada* –*Continued tensions* • Uneasy Peace –*Camp David Accords* –*Sadat and Begin* • Middle East Conference –*Rabin and Arafat* –*Palestinian Authority* **OTHER HOT SPOTS** • OPEC and Mid-East Oil • Iranian Revolution –*Islamic Fundamentalism* –*Ayatollah Khomeni* • Iran-Iraq War • First Gulf War, 1990 –*Saddam Hussein* • 9/11/01 terror attacks on U.S. • Overthrow of Taliban in Afghanistan • Second Gulf War, 2003

ASIA

EARLY CIVILIZATIONS (2500 B.C.–500 A.D.)	STABILITY AND CHANGE (500–1900)	TWENTIETH CENTURY (1900–Present)

CHINA
• Huang He Valley (2000–1027 B.C.)
• Shang Dynasty (1760–1027 B.C.)
• Zhou Dynasty (1027–221 B.C.)
  –Mandate of Heaven
  –Confucius
  –Lao Tzu & Daoism
• Qin Dynasty (221 B.C.–206 A.D.)
  –Shih-Huangti; was first emperor
  –Great Wall of China built
• Han Dynasty (206 B.C.–220 A.D.)
  –Silk Road
  –Examinations for imperial service
 	
INDIA
• Indus River Valley (2500–1500 B.C.)
  –Harappans
  –Aryan Invasions
  –Hinduism
  –Caste system
  –Buddhism
• Mauryan Empire (321 B.C.–232 A.D.)
  –Asoka the Great
• Gupta Empire (320–535)
  –Golden Age of Hindu Culture
  –Hun invasions
	CHINA
	• T'ang Dynasty (618–907)
	  –Golden Age: block printing
	• Sung Dynasty (960–1279)
	  –Golden Age: the compass
	• Yuan Dynasty (1279–1368)
	  –Mongol conquest
	  –Kublai Khan
	  –Marco Polo
	• Ming Dynasty (1368–1644)
	  –Middle Kingdom
	• Qing (Manchu) Dynasty (1644–1912)
	  –Boxer Rebellion (1899)
	  –Open Door Policy (1900)
	
	JAPAN
	• Chinese influence on Japan
	  –writing, Confucianism, Buddhism
	• Heian Period (794–1185)
	  –Golden Age: Tale of Genji
	• Shogunate (1200–1550)
	  –Japanese feudalism
	  –Shoguns and Daimyos, Samurai
	  –Bushido
	  –Tokugawa Shogunate
	• Meiji Restoration (1868–1912)
	  –Adoption of Western ways
	
	INDIA
	• Muslim Invasions
	• Mughal Empire (1526–1837)
	  –Akbar the Great
	  –Shah Jahan, Taj Mahal
	• British Rule (1800s–1947)
	  –British East India Company
		CHINA
		• Republican Period (1912–1949)
		  –Sun Yat-Sen & Three Principles
		  –Chiang Kai-Shek
		  –Japanese invasion (1937–1945)
		• Communist Period (1949–Present)
		  –Two Chinas: Mainland China and Taiwan
		  –Mao Zedong
		  –Red Guards and Cultural Revolution
		  –Deng Xiaoping
		  –Jiang Zemin
		
		JAPAN
		• Rise to power (1900–1930s)
		  –Russo-Japanese War
		  –Sino-Japanese War
		  –World War I
		• World War II (1935–1945)
		  –Pearl Harbor
		  –Hiroshima and Nagasaki
		  –U.S. Occupation of Japan
		  –Constitution of 1947
		• Rise of Japan as Economic Power (1970–present)
		  –Economic Superpower
		
		INDIA/SOUTHEAST ASIA
		• Independence Movements
		  –Mohandas Gandhi
		  –Ho Chi Minh
		• Partition of India (1947)
		  –Pakistan and India
		  –Bangladesh independence (1971)
		• Cold War in Asia
		  –Korean War (1950–1953)
		  –Vietnam War (1965–1974)

THE AMERICAS

PRE-COLUMBIAN CIVILIZATIONS (30,000 B.C.–1546 A.D.)

MIGRATIONS FROM ASIA (30,000 B.C.–10,000 B.C.)
- Settlers cross Bering Straits to the Americas

MAYA CIVILIZATION (1500 B.C.–1546 A.D.)
- In Guatemala, later moved to Yucatan
- Agricultural society
- Writing system
- Perfected calendar
- Made human sacrifices to their gods

AZTEC EMPIRE (1200–1521)
- Controlled Central Mexico
- Had a rigid social structure
- Human sacrifices to Sun God

INCA EMPIRE (1200–1535)
- Along Andes Mountains
- Rigid class structure
- Grew potatoes, root crops
- Built stone roads and stone buildings
- Developed a writing and number system
- Built cities with pyramids, palaces
  - *Machu Picchu*

EUROPEAN COLONIALISM (1500–1800)

EUROPEAN CONQUEST (1492–1542)
- Arrival of conquistadores
- Cortés defeats Aztecs (1521)
  - *Montezuma*
- Pizarro defeats Incas (1535)

EFFECTS OF CONQUEST
- New foods and products introduced to Europe
- Diseases devastated native populations
- Spread of Christian religion
- Spanish and Portuguese culture to Latin America

THE COLONIAL EXPERIENCE
- Rule of Spain and Portugal
- Colonial social classes
  - *Peninsulares*
  - *Creoles*
  - *Mestizos and mulattos*
  - *Native and Africans*
- Mercantilism

RECENT HISTORY (1800–Present)

INDEPENDENCE MOVEMENTS
- Causes
  - *Examples of French & American Revolutions*
  - *Weakening of Spain*
- Independence leaders
  - *Haiti: Toussaint L'Ouverture*
  - *Venezuela, Colombia: Simón Bolívar*
  - *Mexico: Miguel Hidalgo*

NINETEENTH CENTURY
- Monroe Doctrine (1823)
  - *stopped further colonization*
- Rule of the Caudillos

TWENTIETH CENTURY
- Mexican Revolution of 1910
  - *Portofio Diaz and Pancho Villa*
- *Mexican Constitution*
- Cuban Revolution (1959)
  - *Fidel Castro*
  - *Communism*
  - *Bay of Pigs invasion*
  - *Cuban Missile Crisis*
- Military dictatorships
- Debts to Western banks
- Problems of economic development

SUB-SAHARAN AFRICA

EARLY HISTORY (750 B.C.–1800 A.D.)

KINGDOM OF KUSH (750 B.C.–350 A.D.)
- Important iron producer
- Rich from ivory and ebony
- Egyptian cultural influence
- Developed its own writing

KINGDOM OF GHANA (750–1200)
- Rich from the gold-salt trade
- Captives used as slaves

KINGDOM OF MALI (1240–1400)
- Rich from gold and salt trade
- Kings adopted Islam
  - *Mansa Musa*
  - *Timbuktu: center of learning*

KINGDOM OF SONGHAI (1464–1600)
- Islamic kingdom
- Grew rich from trade

OTHER AFRICAN STATES
- Benin
- Great Zimbabwe
- Coastal Cities of East Africa
- Ethiopia

TRANSATLANTIC SLAVE TRADE
- Greatly expanded slave trade
- About 15 million Africans enslaved
- "Middle Passage": many died en route
- Disrupted African development

RECENT HISTORY (1800–Present)

CAUSES OF NEW IMPERIALISM (1870–1914)
- Expanded technology
- Economic motives
- National pride
- Balance of power
- Other motives
  - *Social Darwinism*

SCRAMBLE FOR AFRICA
- British take Egypt
- Berlin Conference (1884–1885)
- Boer War in South Africa

DECOLONIZATION
- Rise of nationalism
- W. W. II weakened European control
- Independence movements
  - *Kwame Nkrumah*
  - *Jomo Kenyatta*
- Single-party states
- Problems of economic development

MODERN DAY AFRICA
- South Africa
  - *Apartheid*
  - *Nelson Mandela*
  - *F. W. De Klerk*
- Tribalism
  - *Rwanda and Burundi*
- Hunger and famine
  - *Somalia*
- Shift to democratic governments

EUROPE

CLASSICAL CIVILIZATIONS (1000 B.C.–500 A.D.)	MIDDLE AGES & RENAISSANCE (500–1500)	BIRTH OF THE MODERN WORLD (1500–1770)	NEW CURRENTS (1700–1900)	THE WORLD AT WAR (1900–1945)	ATOMIC AGE (1945–Present)
GREEKS • City-states –Sparta –Athens • Golden Age –Pericles –Democracy –Parthenon • Achievements –philosophy –sculpture –drama • Hellenistic Period –Alexander the Great **ROMANS** • Roman Republic –12 Tables of Roman Law –Julius Caesar • Roman Empire –Augustus –Pax Romana –Rise of Christianity • Decline –slavery –economic problems –division into East and West Rome –barbarian invasions	**BYZANTINE EMPIRE** • East Roman Empire • Constantinople • Eastern Orthodox Christianity • Preservation of classical learning **CHAOS IN WEST** • Barbarian invasions • Rise of Franks • Charlemagne • Viking invasions **FEUDAL SOCIETY** • Lords/knights • Serfs/manors • Age of Faith –Crusades **DECLINE OF FEUDALISM** • Black Death • Rise of towns **AGE OF KINGS** • Rise of royal power • Divine right –Absolutism **RENAISSANCE** • Humanists • Key people –Leonardo Da Vinci –Michelangelo –Machiavelli	**REFORMATION** • Corruption in Church • Martin Luther –Ninety-five theses • Wars of religion • Catholic Counter-Reformation –Council of Trent **AGE OF DISCOVERY** • Columbus • Magellan • New foods to Europe **EUROPE'S CONQUEST OF AMERICAS** • Cortes/Aztec Civiliz. • Pizarro/Inca Civiliz. **COMMERCIAL REVOLUTION** • Mercantilism • Capitalism **AGE OF KINGS** • Rise of royal power • Divine right –Absolutism –Louis XIV **LIMITED MONARCHY** • Magna Carta (1215) • Rise of Parliament • Puritan Revolution (1642–1649) • Bill of Rights (1689)	**SCIENTIFIC REVOLUTION** • Scientific Method **ENLIGHTENMENT** • Belief in natural laws –Locke and Voltaire –Rousseau **FRENCH REVOLUTION** • Causes –Estates General –National Assembly • Reign of Terror • Rise of Napoleon • Congress of Vienna **INDUSTRIAL REVOLUTION** • Starts in Britain • Reform movements • Communism –Karl Marx **NATIONALISM** • Revolutions of 1848 • Italy unified –Count Cavour • Germany unified –Otto von Bismarck **IMPERIALISM** • India, Africa, China, Indochina	**WORLD WAR I** • Causes –Nationalism –Alliance system –Militarism • Major events –New weapons • Aftermath –Versailles Treaty –League of Nations **INTERWAR YEARS** • Prosperity • Great Depression • Rise of Fascism –Mussolini –Hitler & Nazis **WORLD WAR II** • Causes –Nazi aggression • Major events –Blitzkrieg –Holocaust –Atom bomb • Aftermath –Nuremberg Trials –U.N. created –Germany divided	**SUPERPOWER RIVALRY** • U.S. v. Soviet Union • Cold War –Truman Doctrine –Marshall Plan –Berlin Wall –NATO v. Warsaw Pact **END OF COLD WAR** • Policy of detente • Freedom for Eastern Europe –Lech Walesa –Solidarity • Reunification of Germany –Berlin Wall knocked down • Dissolution of the U.S.S.R. **EUROPE TODAY** • Common Market to European Union • Ethnic and religious conflicts –Bosnia –Northern Ireland • Immigration policies • Pollution • Economic problems of Eastern Europe

RUSSIA AND THE FORMER SOVIET UNION

EARLY HISTORY (800 A.D.–1917 A.D.)	A COMMUNIST STATE (1917–1991)	MOVE TO DEMOCRACY (1985–Present)

STATE OF KIEV (800s–1240)
• Vikings organized the Slavs into a kingdom
 	
MONGOL CONTROL (1240–1480)
 	
RISE OF MUSCOVY (1480–1598)
• Ivan the Great
 	
ROMANOV RULE (1613–1917)
• Peter the Great (1682–1725)
  –Westernization
  –Expansion
• Catherine the Great (1762–1796)
  –Continued Westernization
  –Serf conditions worsen
• Autocratic Russia
  –Autocratic rulers
  –Defeat of Napoleon
  –Tsar Alexander II
  –Emancipation of the Serfs
  –Russification
  –Pogroms against Jews
 	
RUSSIAN REVOLUTION (1905)
• Nicholas II grants limited reforms
	RUSSIAN REVOLUTION (1917)
	• Russia unprepared for World War I
	• Overthrow of Tsar Nicholas II
	• Bolsheviks take power
	• Russia withdraws from World War I
	
	RULE BY LENIN (1917–1924)
	• Introduces Communism
	  –Civil War: Reds vs. Whites
	  –New Economic Plan (N.E.P.)
	
	RULE BY STALIN (1924–1953)
	• Totalitarianism
	• Reign of Terror, purges, gulags
	• Economic changes
	  –Collectivization
	  –Five Year Plans: from agriculture to industry
	• World War II
	  –Hitler invades Russia (1941)
	  –Heavy Soviet Casualties
	  –Joins Allies against Germany
	
	COLD WAR (1945–1991)
	• Democracy vs. Communism
	• Occupation of Eastern Europe
	  –Soviet Satellites, Iron Curtain falls
	• U.S. Response
	  –Truman Doctrine & Marshall Plan
	• Division of Germany
	• NATO vs. Warsaw Pact
	• Khrushchev (1953–1964)
	  –Denounces Stalinism
	  –Cuban Missile Crisis (1962)
	• Brezhnev (1965–1982)
	  –Stagnation of Soviet economy
		GORBACHEV (1985–1991)
		• Reform policies
		  –Glasnost (greater openness)
		  –Perestroika (restructuring)
		  –New Foreign Policy
		  –Congress of People's Deputies
		• Gorbachev's reforms fail
		  –unfamiliar with free market system
		  –opposed by Communists
		  –political instability
		• Nationalities problem
		  –Baltic States
		  –Russia
		• Communist Coup of 1991
		• Dissolution of the Soviet Union (1991)
		
		COMMONWEALTH OF INDEPENDENT STATES (1991–present)
		• Association of independent states
		• Importance of Russian Republic
		• Yeltsin introduces changes
		  –Democracy
		  –Free Market System
		  –Conflict with Russian Parliament (1993)
		  –Yeltsin resigns (1999)
		• Putin
		  –Economic Recovery
		  –Conflict in Chechnya

CHAPTER 14

A PRACTICE TEST

Now that you have reviewed test-taking strategies and the chief content areas, you should measure your progress by taking the practice examination found in this chapter. First, let's take a look at some common-sense tips for test-taking:

◆ **Don't leave any questions unanswered.** Since there is no penalty for guessing, be sure to answer all the questions — even if you are only making an educated guess on some of them.

◆ **Use the process of elimination** in multiple-choice questions. Even if you do not know the right answer, it may be clear that certain choices are wrong. Choices will be wrong if they relate to a different time or place, have no connection with the question, or are simply inaccurate statements. After eliminating the wrong choices, choose the best answer from the choices that remain.

◆ **Underline any key words** in the question that you think are central to what it asks. If an unfamiliar word is used, try breaking it down into other words that are familiar to you. See if looking at the prefix (*start of the word*), root, or suffix (*word ending*) helps you to understand the meaning of the word.

Taking this examination will help you to identify areas that you might still need to study. We recommend that you take this practice test under test conditions in a quiet room without distraction. Good luck!

GLOBAL HISTORY PRACTICE EXAMINATION

This practice test has three parts:

◆ **Part I** has 50 multiple-choice questions
◆ **Part II** has one thematic essay
◆ **Part III** has one document-based essay

PART I:

1 Which geographic feature had the greatest influence on the development of ancient civilizations?
(1) dense forests
(2) mountain passes
(3) smooth coastlines
(4) river valleys

2 What is one characteristic of a society that practices subsistence agriculture?
(1) growth of surplus crops for export
(2) production of crops mainly for its own use
(3) establishment of large state-owned farms
(4) dependence on the use of slave labor for the production of crops

3 What was one cause of the development of many small independent city-states in ancient Greece?
(1) Greece and Rome were often at war.
(2) The mountainous terrain of Greece resulted in widely scattered settlements.
(3) Military leaders found small Greek settlements easy to control.
(4) The Greek people had many different languages and religions.

4 In India, Bangladesh, and much of Southeast Asia, agricultural productivity is most affected by the
(1) seasonal monsoons
(2) unnavigable rivers
(3) numerous deserts
(4) cold climate

5 Which belief is shared by Hindus and Buddhists?
(1) Everyone should have the same social status.
(2) People should pray five times a day.
(3) The soul can be reincarnated.
(4) Material wealth is a sign of the blessing of the gods.

Base your answer to question 6 on the passage below and on your knowledge of social studies.

> . . . *Muslims, Christians, and Jews lived together in peace. Because several Christian and Jewish prophets, including Adam, Abraham, and Moses, are named in the Qur'an and because the Jewish Torah and Christian gospels are recognized as revelations from Allah, the Muslim rulers called Christians and Jews "people of the Book" and permitted them much religious and personal freedom. Jews, especially, enjoyed many liberties, and many Jews distinguished themselves in science, the arts, and government. Convivencia, a Spanish word meaning "living together," helped make tenth-century al-Andalus the most civilized country in Europe. . . .*
> —Lawrence Houghteling, "Al-Andalus: Islamic Spain," Calliope, Nov.–Dec. 1995

6 What is the main idea of this passage?
(1) The Torah and the Bible were rejected in Muslim Spain.
(2) Arabs, Jews, and Christians shared places of worship in Muslim Spain.
(3) Religious tolerance in Muslim Spain encouraged the growth of a diverse culture.
(4) Spain was troubled by deep-rooted religious conflicts.

7 Some historians suggest that as a result of the Mongol invasions of Russia, the Russian people were
(1) united with the Ottomans
(2) converted to Christianity
(3) freed from serfdom
(4) cut off from most of western Europe

Base your answer to question 8 & 9 on the map below and on your knowledge of social studies.

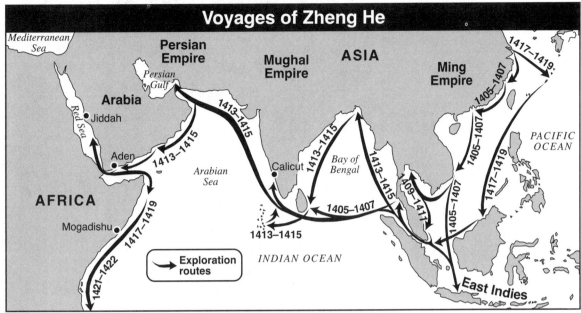

Voyages of Zheng He

Source: Elisabeth Gaynor Ellis and Anthony Esler, *World History, Connections to Today*, Prentice Hall (adapted)

8 The map shows that on his voyages, Zheng He explored
 (1) both the Pacific and the Atlantic Oceans
 (3) lands in the Western Hemisphere
 (3) at the same time as the Spanish explorers
 (4) Arabia and the east coast of Africa

9 One result of the voyages of Zheng He was that
 (1) Chinese merchants began trading with Africa
 (2) Christian missionaries arrived in China
 (3) Indian artisans showed the Chinese how to make Ming porcelain
 (4) China set up colonies in Europe

10 Many achievements of Islamic civilization reached European society by way of the
 (1) Crusades and eastern Mediterranean trading networks
 (2) merchant guilds and the Industrial Revolution
 (3) Middle Passage and the Columbian Exchange
 (4) conquests of the Germanic tribes and trade along the Silk Road

11 Prior to the Protestant Reformation, the medieval church in western Europe was criticized for
 (1) sponsoring explorations to the Middle East
 (2) allowing the Bible to be printed and distributed to the people
 (3) being too concerned with worldly power and riches
 (4) refusing to sell indulgences to peasants

12 Which statement about the geography of Africa is most accurate?
 (1) Much of the land in Africa is below sea level.
 (2) The variety of geographic barriers has served to promote cultural diversity.
 (3) Africa has an irregular coastline with many natural harbors.
 (4) Much of the land in Africa is tundra and forest.

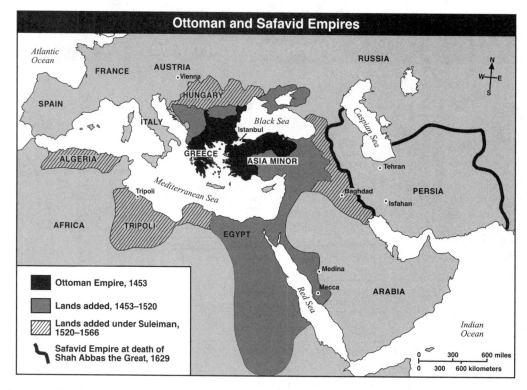

13 Which generalization is best supported by the information in this map?
(1) The Ottoman Empire controlled the largest amount of territory by 1453.
(2) The Safavid Empire controlled parts of western Europe by 1629.
(3) By the 1500s, the Ottoman Empire controlled parts of the Middle East, North Africa, and Europe.
(4) The Mediterranean Sea served as a cultural barrier between Asia Minor and North Africa.

14 "If from now on the King starts by rising early and going to bed late, and if the ministers take oaths to cut out the evils of parties and merriment, be diligent in cultivating frugality and virtue, do not allow private considerations from taking root in their minds, and do not use artifice as a method of operation in government affairs, then the officials and common people will all cleanse and purify their minds and be in great accord with his will."
— *Yi Hang-no, Korean Royal Adviser*

Which Confucian principle is reflected in this statement?
(1) The ruler must set an example for the people.
(2) Respect for elders is the foundation of civilization.
(3) Virtue increases with education.
(4) Compassion and sympathy for others is important.

15 Which statement best describes an impact of geography on the history of the Korean peninsula?
(1) Large deserts have led to isolation.
(2) Location has led to invasion and occupation by other nations.
(3) Lack of rivers has limited food production.
(4) Lack of natural resources has prevented development of manufacturing.

16 The expeditions of Hernán Cortés and Francisco Pizarro resulted in the
(1) destruction of the Aztec and Inca empires
(2) capture of Brazil by Portugal
(3) colonization of North America by Portugal
(4) exploration of the Philippines and East Indies

17 Which action would best complete this partial outline?

> I. Byzantine Heritage
>   A. Blended Christian beliefs with Greek art and philosophy
>   B. Extended Roman engineering achievements
>   C. Preserved literature and science textbooks
>   D. _____

(1) Adapted the Roman principles of justice
(2) Used a senate as the chief governing body
(3) Led crusades to capture Rome from the Huns
(4) Helped maintain Roman rule over western Europe

18 Which statement best describes a result of the Glorious Revolution in England (1688)?
(1) England formed an alliance with France.
(2) The power of the monarchy was increased.
(3) Principles of limited government were strengthened.
(4) England lost its colonial possessions.

19 One reason Italy and Germany were not major colonial powers in the 16th and 17th centuries was that they
(1) had self-sufficient economies
(2) lacked political unity
(3) rejected the practice of imperialism
(4) belonged to opposing alliances

20 The ideas of Rousseau, Voltaire, and Montesquieu most influenced
(1) the growing power of priests in the Roman Catholic Church
(2) improvements in the working conditions of factory workers
(3) the rise of industrial capitalism
(4) movements for political reform

21 During the late 19th century, which geographic factor helped attract European investors to southern Africa and southeast Asia?
(1) smooth coastlines
(2) navigable rivers
(3) natural resources
(4) temperate climates

22 One result of the Opium War was that China
(1) adopted democratic reforms
(2) gained control of Hong Kong
(3) regained control of Manchuria
(4) was divided into spheres of influence

23 "... The replacement of the bourgeois by the proletarian state is impossible without a violent revolution. The abolition of the proletarian state, i.e., of all states, is only possible through 'withering away.'..."

— V. I. Lenin, *State and Revolution*, 1917

This quotation is associated with the principles of
(1) imperialism
(2) capitalism
(3) communism
(4) militarism

24 In Europe during the 1920s and 1930s, severe inflation, high unemployment, and fear of communism all contributed to the
(1) overthrow of monarchies in Italy and Germany
(2) rise of Fascist governments in Italy, Germany, and Spain
(3) formation of the Common Market in Italy and Spain
(4) growth of democratic institutions

Base your answers to question 25 & 26 on the maps and on your knowledge of social studies.

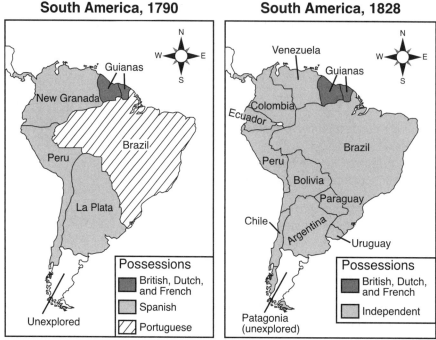

South America, 1790

South America, 1828

Source: Goldberg and DuPré, *Brief Review in Global History and Geography,*
Prentice Hall (adapted)

25 Based on a comparison of these maps of South America, which conclusion is accurate?
   (1) Many regions of South America gained their independence between 1790 and 1828.
   (2) All of South America was independent by 1828.
   (3) Spain continued to gain South American colonies in the 19th century.
   (4) Between 1790 and 1828, South American political boundaries remained unchanged except for Brazil.

26 Which individual is most closely associated with the changes indicated on these maps?
   (1) Emiliano Zapata
   (3) Porfirio Díaz
   (2) Simón Bolívar
   (4) Pancho Villa

Base your answers to question 27 on the cartoon below and on your knowledge of social studies.

27 This Thomas Nast cartoon shows the
   (1) competition between European nations for overseas territories after the Berlin Conference
   (2) aggressive action of the Triple Alliance before World War I
   (3) spread of communism throughout the world during the 19th century
   (4) concern of European nations for the welfare of developing nations at the end of the 19th century

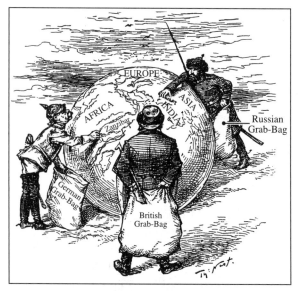

THE WORLD'S PLUNDERERS.
"It's English, you know."

28 "Gandhi Calls for Boycott of British Textiles"
  "Gandhi and Followers Complete March to the Sea"
  "Gandhi Begins Hunger Fast"

These headlines reflect Gandhi's belief in
(1) nonalignment
(2) isolationism
(3) appeasement
(4) nonviolence

Base your answers to question 29 & 30 on the passage and on your knowledge of social studies.

> . . . "From the beginning," says Marquis Ito, "we realized fully how necessary it was that the Japanese people should not only adopt Western methods, but should also speedily become competent to do without the aid of foreign instruction and supervision. In the early days we brought many foreigners to Japan to help to introduce modern methods, but we always did it in such a way as to enable the Japanese students to take their rightful place in the nation after they had been educated." . . .
>
> — Alfred Stead, *Great Japan*: A *Study of National Efficiency*, 1906

29 Which occurrence in Japanese history is described in the passage?
(1) Meiji Restoration
(2) Tokugawa shogunate
(3) assimilation of Buddhism
(4) adoption of Confucian practices

30 The author of the passage suggests that Japan
(1) remained isolated
(2) accepted new technologies in order to moderniz
(3) became dependent on foreign nations
(4) became militaristic

31 • Japan resigns from the League of Nations, 1933
  • Rome-Berlin-Tokyo Axis formed, 1936
  • Japan invades China, 1937
  • United States places embargo on scrap iron, steel, and oil exports to Japan, 1941

Which event occurred immediately after this series of developments?
(1) Manchuria became a Japanese protectorate.
(2) Pearl Harbor was attacked.
(3) The Japanese fleet was destroyed.
(4) The atomic bomb was dropped on Hiroshima.

32 A major result of the Nuremberg trials after World War II was that
(1) Germany was divided into four zones of occupation
(2) the United Nations was formed to prevent future acts of genocide
(3) the North Atlantic Treaty Organization (NATO) was established to stop the spread of communism
(4) Nazi political and military leaders were held accountable for their actions

33 The continued importance of the Middle East to the global economy is based on its
(1) research facilities
(2) exports of manufactured goods
(3) semiarid climate
(4) quantity of oil reserves

Base your answer to question 34 on the excerpt below and on your knowledge of social studies.

This excerpt is taken from a poem written about World War I.

"If I should die, think only this of me:
That there's some corner of a foreign field
That is for ever England. There shall be
In that rich earth a richer dust concealed;
A dust whom England bore, shaped, made aware,
Gave, once, her flowers to love, her ways to roam,
A body of England's, breathing English air,
Washed by the rivers, blest by suns of home. . . ."

— *Rupert Brooke, "The Soldier"*

34 Which idea is expressed in this excerpt from Brooke's poem?
(1) pacifism
(2) neutrality
(3) nationalism
(4) anarchy

Base your answer to question 35 on the excerpt below and on your knowledge of social studies.

Source: Henry Abraham and Irwin Pfeffer, *Enjoying World History*, AMSCO (adapted)

35 Which factor was the most significant force in causing the changes between 1914 and 1919 as shown on the two maps?
(1) worldwide depression
(2) treaties signed at the end of World War I
(3) rise of Mussolini
(4) dissatisfaction of the German people

36 ". . . The Nazi holocaust, which engulfed millions of Jews in Europe, proved anew the urgency of the re-establishment of the Jewish state, which would solve the problem of Jewish homelessness by opening the gates to all Jews and lifting the Jewish people to equality in the family of nations. . . ."

This statement is referring to the establishment of which nation?
(1) Jordan
(2) Poland
(3) Israel
(4) Ethiopia

37 Which statement related to the recent history of Pakistan is an opinion?
(1) Pakistan gained its independence from Britain in 1947.
(2) The majority of the people who live in Pakistan are Muslims.
(3) Pakistan would be better off if it was still part of India.
(4) Mohammed Ali Jinnah was a major leader in Pakistan's independence movement.

Base your answer to question 38 on the chart below and on your knowledge of social studies.

38 This chart shows the organization of the
(1) United Nations (UN)
(2) North Atlantic Treaty Organization (NATO)
(3) European Union (EU)
(4) Organization of American States (OAS)

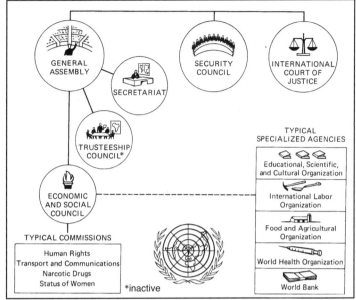

Source: Irving L. Gordon, *World History*, 2nd ed., AMSCO (adapted)

39 The caste system in India and the feudal system in Europe were similar in that both
(1) provided structure for society
(2) developed concepts of natural rights
(3) established totalitarian governments
(4) promoted peace and prosperity

Base your answer to question 40 on the cartoon below and on your knowledge of social studies.

40 What is the cartoonist's view about democracy in India since 1947?
(1) India has become a democratic nation after fifty years.
(2) India has led Asia in democratic reforms.
(3) India is not a democratic nation and has not been for the last five decades.
(4) India's progress in becoming a democratic nation has been slow.

Source: Cummings, *Winnipeg Free Press*, Cartoonists and Writers Syndicate

41 Which problem has faced both Cuba and North Korea under communist rule?
(1) Their monarchs have been ineffective rulers.
(2) Their governments have played a limited role in the economy.
(3) Their workers have called many strikes.
(4) Their command economies have been inefficient.

42 Which set of historical periods in European history is in correct chronological order?
A. Medieval Europe   B. Italian Renaissance   C. Golden Age of Greece   D. Enlightenment
(1) $C \rightarrow A \rightarrow B \rightarrow D$
(2) $A \rightarrow B \rightarrow D \rightarrow C$
(3) $C \rightarrow B \rightarrow D \rightarrow A$
(4) $B \rightarrow A \rightarrow C \rightarrow D$

43

> ". . . I have walked that long road to freedom. I have tried not to falter; I have made missteps along the way. But I have discovered the secret that after climbing a great hill, one only finds that there are many more hills to climb. I have taken a moment here to rest, to steal a view of the glorious vista that surrounds me, to look back on the distance I have come. But I can rest only for a moment, for with freedom comes responsibilities, and I dare not linger, for my long walk is not yet ended."
>
> — Nelson Mandela, *Long Walk to Freedom*

When Mandela referred to "climbing a great hill," he was referring to the struggle to
  (1) end apartheid in South Africa
  (2) modernize South Africa's economy
  (3) end economic sanctions against South Africa
  (4) stop majority rule in South Africa

44 Which statement best describes an impact of the computer on the global economy?
  (1) Countries can increase tariffs on imports.
  (2) Companies now market more products worldwide.
  (3 Wages have risen dramatically for most people in developing nations.
  (4) Prices of oil and other resources have declined worldwide.

45 Which belief is shared by an African who practices animism and a Japanese who practices Shinto?
  (1) Only one God rules the universe.
  (2) Periodic fasting is essential to spiritual purity.
  (3) Spirits exist in both living and nonliving things.
  (4) All suffering is caused by desire and selfishness.

46 Which headline would probably have appeared in a pamphlet during the Industrial Revolution?
  (1) "Michelangelo Completes Sistine Chapel"
  (2) "Karl Marx Attacks Capitalism"
  (3) "Martin Luther Speaks Out Against Sale of Indulgences"
  (4) "John Locke Calls for the People to Choose the King"

47 Which title would best complete this partial outline?

I. _____

  A. Formation of secret alliances
  B. Conflict over colonies in Africa
  C. Military buildup of European armies and navies
  D. Assassination of Archduke Ferdinand

  (1) Scramble for Africa   (3) Results of World War II
  (2) Causes of World War I   (4) Reasons for the United Nations

48 • Many of Africa's traditional musical instruments are made of gourds and shells.
  • Ancient Egyptians wrote on papyrus, a reed found growing near the Nile River.
  • A major feature of Japanese art is the relationship between humans and nature.

Which concept is illustrated in these statements?
  (1) role of education in the ancient world
  (2) development of traditional government
  (3) effect of artistic expression on religion
  (4) geography's effect on cultural development

Base your answer to question 49 on the cartoon below and on your knowledge of social studies.

49 What is the main idea of this 1995 cartoon?
(1) The United Nations supported the Serbians in Kosovo.
(2) The United Nations was ineffective in its attempt to end genocide in Kosovo.
(3) Killing in Kosovo stopped because of United Nations reprimands.
(4) The Serbians lost the battle for Kosovo.

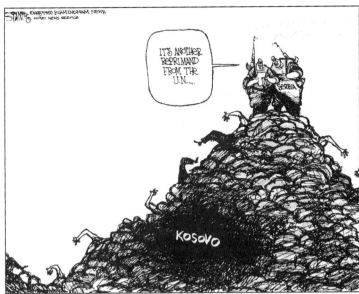

Source: Scott Stantis, *The Birmingham News*, Copley News Service

> Article 4: "No one shall be held in slavery or servitude;
> slavery and the slave trade shall be prohibited in all their forms."

— *Universal Declaration of Human Rights, United Nations, 1948*

> ". . . My best estimate of the number of slaves in the world today is 27 million. . . ."

— *Kevin Bales, Disposable People, University of California Press, 1999 Base*

50 Based on an analysis of these statements, which conclusion is accurate?
(1) All governments have taken active steps to end slavery.
(2) The United Nations has solved the problem of slavery.
(3) The number of enslaved persons has increased dramatically since 1948.
(4) Slavery remains a problem in the modern era.

PART II: THEMATIC ESSAY QUESTION

Directions: Write a well-organized essay that includes an introduction, several paragraphs addressing the task below, and a conclusion.

Theme: Economic Systems

> Societies have developed different economic systems for many reasons. Some of these economic systems include manorialism, capitalism, and communism.

Task:

> Identify one society and one economic system that has been used or is being used in that society and
> • Discuss the historical circumstances surrounding the development of that economic system
> • Describe two features of the economic system
> • Evaluate the impact the economic system had on this society during a specific period

You may use any society from your study of global history. Some suggestions you might wish to consider include western Europe during the Middle Ages, western Europe during the Industrial Revolution, the Soviet Union between 1917 and 1990, Japan after World War II, China since 1949, and Cuba since 1959.

You are not limited to these suggestions.

PART III: DOCUMENT-BASED QUESTION

This question is based on the accompanying documents (1–9). The question is designed to test your ability to work with historical documents. Some of the documents have been edited for the purpose of this question. As you analyze the documents, take into account both the source of each document and any point of view that may be presented in the document.

Historical Context:

Throughout global history, rapidly spreading diseases have had an impact on many societies. Epidemics such as the Black Death in the 14th century, smallpox in the 16th century, and AIDS in the 20th and 21st centuries have had significant effects on societies.

Task: Using information from the documents and your knowledge of global history, answer the questions that follow each document in Part A. Your answers to the questions will help you write the Part B essay, in which you will be asked to

---

Choose two epidemics and for each
- Explain why the epidemic spread
- Discuss the effects of the epidemic on a specific society or societies

---

You may not use the United States as one of the societies.

Document 1

The late-medieval depression began well before the coming of the Black Death (1348–1349). The fundamental trends of demographic and economic decline were not set off by the plague, but they were enormously aggravated by it. Carried by fleas that infested black rats, the bubonic plague entered Europe along trade routes from the East and spread with frightening speed. The death toll cannot be determined with any precision. The best estimate would probably be to of Europe's population. In many crowded towns the mortality rate may well have exceeded 50 percent, whereas isolated rural areas tended to be spared. Consequently, the most progressive, most enterprising, and best-trained Europeans were hit the hardest. Few urban families can have been spared altogether. Those who survived the terrible years 1348–1349 were subjected to periodic recurrences of the plague over the next three centuries. Fourteenth-century medical science was at a loss to explain the process of infection, and fourteenth-century urban sanitation was so primitive as to only encourage its spread. Some people fled their cities, some gave way to religious frenzy or stark lack of moderation, and some remained faithfully at their posts, hoping for divine protection against the disease. But none can have emerged from the ordeal unaffected.

Source: C. Warren Hollister, *Medieval Europe: A Short History,* Second Edition

---

1 Based on this document, identify two ways the Black Death spread throughout Europe. [2]

Document 2

... The plight of the lower and most of the middle classes was even more pitiful to behold. Most of them remained in their houses, either through poverty or in hopes of safety, and fell sick by thousands. Since they received no care and attention, almost all of them died. Many ended their lives in the streets at night and during the day; and many others who died in their houses were only known to be dead because neighbors smelled decaying bodies. Dead bodies filled every corner. Most were treated in the same manner by the survivors, who were more concerned to get rid of their rotting bodies than moved by charity towards the dead. With the aid of porters, they carried the bodies out of the houses and laid them at the doors, where every morning quantities of the dead might be seen. They then were laid on [coffin stands], or, as these were often lacking, on tables ... Not to pry any further into all the details of the miseries which afflicted [struck] our city, I shall add that the surrounding country was spared nothing of what befell Florence. The smaller villages were like the city; in the fields and isolated farms the poor wretched peasants and their families were without doctors and any assistance, and perished in the highways, in their fields and houses, night and day, more like beasts than men. Just as the townsmen became dissolute and indifferent to their work and property, so the peasants, when they saw that death was upon them, neglected the future fruits of their past labors both from the earth and from cattle, and thought only of enjoying what they had. Thus it happened that cows, asses, sheep, goats, pigs, fowls and even dogs, those faithful companions of man, left the farms and wandered at their will through the fields, where the wheat crops stood abandoned, unreaped and ungarnered [not gathered]. Many of these animals seemed endowed with reason, for, after they had pastured all day, they returned to the farms for the night of their own free will, without being driven. ... Oh, what great palaces, how many fair houses and noble dwellings, once filled with attendants and nobles and ladies, were emptied to the meanest servant! How many famous names and vast possessions and renowned estates were left without an heir! How many gallant men and fair ladies and handsome youths, whom Hippocrates would have said were in perfect health, at noon dined with their relatives and friends, and at night supped with their ancestors in the next world!

— Giovanni Boccaccio, *The Decameron*

2 According to this document, what was one impact of the Black Death on European society? [1]

Document 3

A 14th-century author writes about the effects of the Black Death in England between 1348–1350.

... Ox hides fell to a wretched price, namely 12d., and yet a pair of gloves would cost 10d., 12d., or 14d., and a pair of breeches 3s. or 4s. In the mean time the king sent word that mowers and other workmen should take no more than they had before [the outbreak of the plague], under the penalties laid down in the order, and thereupon made a statute. Nevertheless the workmen were so puffed up and contrary-minded that they did not heed the king's decree, and if anyone wanted to hire them he had to pay what they asked: either his fruit and crops rotted, or he had to give in to the workmen's arrogant and greedy demands. ... In the following winter there was such a want of hands, for every kind of work, that people believed that the like shortage had never been known at any time in the past, for cattle and such livestock as a man might have wandered about without a keeper, and there was no one to look after people's possessions. And thus the necessities of life became so dear, that what in previous times was worth 1d. now cost 4d. or 5d.

Source: G. H. Martin, ed., *Knighton's Chronicle 1337–1396*

3 Based on this document, state two effects of the Black Death on the economy of England. [2]

Document 4

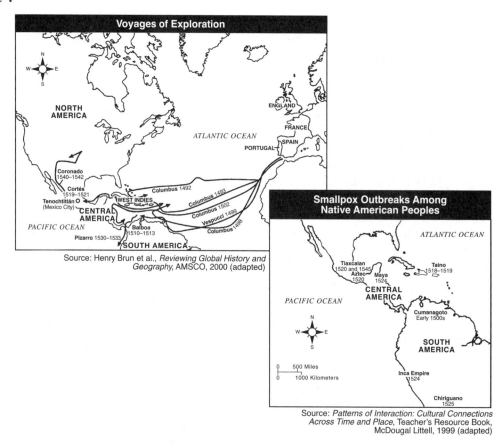

Source: Henry Brun et al., *Reviewing Global History and Geography*, AMSCO, 2000 (adapted)

Source: *Patterns of Interaction: Cultural Connections Across Time and Place*, Teacher's Resource Book, McDougal Littell, 1999 (adapted)

4 After studying these two maps, state one way smallpox was introduced to Central and South America. [1]

Document 5

. . . The first was a plague of smallpox, and it began in this manner. When Hernando Cortés was captain and governor, at the time that Captain Pánfilo de Narváez landed in this country, there was in one of his ships a negro stricken with smallpox, a disease which had never been seen here. At this time New Spain was extremely full of people, and when the smallpox began to attack the Indians it became so great a pestilence [disease] among them throughout the land that in most provinces more than half the population died; in others the proportion was little less. For as the Indians did not know the remedy for the disease and were very much in the habit of bathing frequently, whether well or ill, and continued to do so even when suffering from smallpox, they died in heaps, like bedbugs. Many others died of starvation, because, as they were all taken sick at once, they could not care for each other, nor was there anyone to give them bread or anything else. In any places it happened that everyone in a house died, and, as it was impossible to bury the great number of dead, they pulled down the houses over them in order to check the stench that rose from the dead bodies so that their homes became their tombs. This disease was called by the Indians 'the great leprosy' because the victims were so covered with pustules [pimples] that they looked like lepers. Even today one can see obvious evidences of it in some individuals who escaped death, for they were left covered with pockmarks. . . .

Source: Elizabeth A. Foster, ed., *Motolinía's History of the Indians of New Spain*

5 According to this document, what were two results of the smallpox epidemic in Latin America? [2]

Document 6

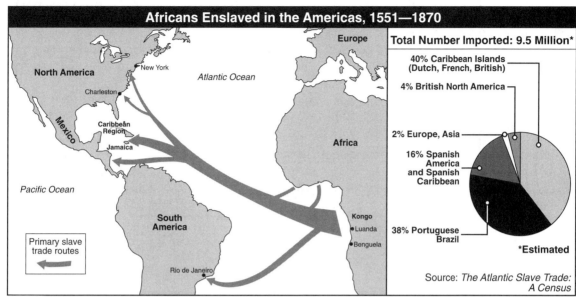

Source: Roger B. Beck et al., *World History: Patterns of Interaction*, McDougal Littell (adapted)

6 According to the information provided by this document, how did the decline in Latin America's native populations affect the population of Africa? [1]

Document 7

... In Donghu, residents estimate that more than 80 percent of adults carry H.I.V., and more than 60 percent are already suffering debilitating [disabling] symptoms. That would give this village, and the others like it, localized rates that are the highest in the world.

They add that local governments are in part responsible. Often encouraged by local officials, many farmers here in Henan contracted H.I.V. in the 1990s after selling blood at government owned collection stations, under a procedure that could return pooled and infected blood to donors. From that point, the virus has continued to spread through other routes because those officials have blocked research and education campaigns about H.I.V., which they consider an embarrassment. ...

"I do not know how many villages have a very grave problem, but I know that it's a lot more than just a handful," said a Chinese doctor who works in the province. "I've been a doctor for many decades, but I've never cried until I saw these villages. Even in villages where there was no blood selling, you now can find cases." Such transmission occurred through migration, marriage and sexual contact. ...

Source: Elisabeth Rosenthal, "Deadly Shadow Darkens Remote Chinese Village," *New York Times,* May, 2001

7 According to this document, what is one way HIV has spread in China? [1]

Document 8

> Like many countries before it, China has been slow in facing up to AIDS. Misconceptions, taboos and outright deceit have fostered denial among both officials and the broader population. This reluctance to be realistic is dangerous. In India, deeply rooted cultural norms and taboos hinder frank assessments and effective preventive measures, even though the U.N. estimates if the disease is not checked, 37 million people in India could be infected in the next 10 to 15 years. South Africa, where AIDS was barely acknowledged for years, today holds the dismal distinction of having the world's largest caseload of H.I.V. infection and AIDS, 4.5 million. And even in industrialized nations, like the United States, lingering social stigmas [disgrace] can still create substantial hurdles to combating the spread of H.I.V. . . .
>
> Source: Bates Gill and Sarah Palmer, "The Coming AIDS Crisis in China," *New York Times,* July 16, 2001

8 Based on this document, identify one factor that has contributed to the spread of AIDS. [1]

Document 9

> Across the [African] continent, AIDS has robbed schools of their teachers, hospitals of their doctors and nurses, and children of their parents. Until recently, orphanages have been relatively rare, because in Africa families take in the children of relatives. But AIDS has created some 12 million orphans. Orphanages have sprung up everywhere, and in rural villages, one can find huts where one big sister or one grandmother is trying to find food for 10 or more children. On a poor continent, the disease is overwhelming family love. At this stage of the epidemic, health authorities say preventing new cases—by distributing condoms, for example—is not enough. In order to spare the continent from complete collapse, something must be done for the millions already infected. But in a region where most people live on less than $2 a day, drugs that cost more than $10,000 a year are not an option. Of the 26 million HIV-infected Africans, only 10,000 have access to the drugs. . . .
>
> Source: Donald G. McNeil, Jr., "A Continent at Risk," *New York Times,* May 14, 2001

9 Based on this document, state two ways AIDS has affected Africa. [2]

DOCUMENT BASED-ESSAY

Directions: Write a well-organized essay that includes an introduction, several paragraphs, and a conclusion. Use evidence from at least *four* documents in your essay. Support your response with relevant facts, examples, and details. Include additional outside information.

Historical Context: Throughout global history, rapidly spreading diseases have had an impact on many societies. Epidemics such as the Black Death in the 14th century, smallpox in the 16th century, and AIDS in the 20th and 21st centuries have had significant effects on societies.

Task: Using information from the documents and your knowledge of global history, write an essay in which you

> Choose *two* epidemics and for *each*
> - Explain why the epidemic spread
> - Discuss the effects of the epidemic on a specific society or societies

You may *not* use the United States as one of the societies.

INDEX